Devavāṇīpra

An Introduction to the Sanskrit Language

Devavāṇīpraveśikā

An Introduction to the Sanskrit Language

ROBERT P. GOLDMAN
SALLY J. SUTHERLAND GOLDMAN

MOTILAL BANARSIDASS PUBLISHERS
PRIVATE LIMITED • DELHI

*Corrected Edition : Delhi, **2011***
First Indian Edition: Delhi, 2009
First published by University of California in 1980,
Third printing with corrections in 2004

ISBN: 978-81-208-3294-7 (Cloth)
ISBN: 978-81-208-3375-3 (Paper)

MOTILAL BANARSIDASS
41 U.A. Bungalow Road, Jawahar Nagar, Delhi 110 007
8 Mahalaxmi Chamber, 22 Bhulabhai Desai Road, Mumbai 400 026
203 Royapettah High Road, Mylapore, Chennai 600 004
236, 9th Main III Block, Jayanagar, Bangalore 560 011
Sanas Plaza, 1302 Baji Rao Road, Pune 411 002
8 Camac Street, Kolkata 700 017
Ashok Rajpath, Patna 800 004
Chowk, Varanasi 221 001

Phototypeset using Devanāgarī and Times Nāgarī Fonts.
Fonts designed by Richard Lasseigne

PRINTED IN INDIA
BY JAINENDRA PRAKASH JAIN AT SHRI JAINENDRA PRESS,
A-45 NARAINA, PHASE-I, NEW DELHI 110 028
AND PUBLISHED BY NARENDRA PRAKASH JAIN FOR
MOTILAL BANARSIDASS PUBLISHERS PRIVATE LIMITED,
BUNGALOW ROAD, DELHI 110 007

To our students and our teachers

नहि सुशिक्षितो ऽपि नटबटुः स्वस्कन्धमारोढुं पटुः

"No matter how well-trained the tumbler's boy,
he will never be able to stand on his own shoulders."

Preface to the Indian Edition 2011

This new printing of the *Devāvaṇīpraveśika, An Introduction to the Sanskrit Language*, is highly gratifying to us. When we first offered the primer for publication in an Indian edition, we had hoped that Sanskrit teachers and students in India would find the work to be an accessible, user-friendly, and affordable introductory textbook with which to study the basic grammar of the Sanskrit language. Apparently, this has proven to be the case, as demand for the primer is such that a second printing is needed.

The current reprinting has incorporated some corrections, additions, and modifications. Most of these are minor and have little impact on the content of the work. They will, however, we hope, serve to ease the efforts of students of Sanskrit if ever so slightly.

Robert P. Goldman
Sally J. Sutherland Goldman

January 2011
Berkeley, California, USA

Preface to the Indian Edition

The present edition is offered in response to numerous requests on the part of students, colleagues, and friends in India who have expressed interest in a modern, accessible, and user-friendly method to acquire or revive a fundamental knowledge of Sanskrit grammar. Many students at the college level have not had the opportunity of studying this fascinating language, while older friends, who may have studied it in their youth would now like to renew their acquaintance with it and so gain direct access to the seminal religious, philosophical, and literary texts of pre-modern India. It is to them that this edition is dedicated in the hopes that it may spark renewed interest in one of India's and the world's greatest cultural legacies.

पठत संस्कृतं वदत संस्कृतं लसतु संस्कृतं गृहे गृहे च पुनरपि ॥

Robert P. Goldman
Sally J. Sutherland Goldman
Maharṣi Vālmīki's Jayantī 2006

Preface to the Third Edition

With the need for a new printing of the *Devavāṇīpraveśikā*, we decided that it would be desirable to produce a new edition, further refining and modifying various grammatical explanations and exercises in the text. Many of the resultant changes arose out of suggestions made by students and colleagues who were using our Sanskrit primer. We are most grateful for their suggestions. Two of the most important changes in this edition are the addition of an English to Sanskrit Glossary as well as an Index. The lack of these has been felt by our students over the years, and we are glad that we have finally been able to address it in this new edition.

We would like to express our very special thanks to Chandan Narayan, graduate student in the Department of South and Southeast Asian Studies, without whose energy and tireless efforts this project never would have been completed. We would also like to thank Richard Lasseigne of the Space Sciences Laboratory at the University of California at Berkeley for letting us use his fonts, "Devanāgarī" and "Times Nāgarī," to typeset this edition and for his good-natured help in solving our many technical problems its use entailed. We would also like to thank Deven Patel, a graduate student in the Department of South and Southeast Asian Studies, for helping us enter the text into the computer. We would also like to express our gratitude to the staff at the Center for South Asia Studies, especially Raba Gunasekara, Choo Hawj Yaj, and Ann Higgins, for their help and support in this project. Finally we would also like to extend a special word of thanks to the students in the 1998-99 first year Sanskrit class, who suffered through the rough draft of the revised text. Their thoughtful and insightful comments and suggestions have been invaluable in the revision of this work. Special thanks go to Simone Barretta, Karen Beal, Prudence Farrow Bruns, Ami Buch, Mukhesh Darke, Hung Van Ho, Eun-Sun Jang, Hudaya Kandahjaya, Manali Kasbekar, Michael Gressett, Layne Little, Hollis Meyer-deLancey, V. Sundararajan, and Kristin Johnston Sutton.

Robert P. Goldman and Sally J. Sutherland Goldman
Berkeley 1999

Preface to the First Edition

No American Sanskritist, or for that matter no student of Sanskrit in America who has suffered through the "traditional," quasi-inductive Whitney-Perry-Lanman method, would question the desirability of new Sanskrit teaching materials. Indeed, the interest in and enthusiasm for such materials that I[1] have seen on the part of numerous Sanskrit teachers and students is undoubtedly the result of a growing frustration with the limits of the existing materials.

I do not mean to denigrate the work of the above named authors. On the contrary I shall continue to use Lanman as my first reader; while it is clear that, aside from the dated nature of his terminology and the archaism of his style, Whitney has stood the test of time admirably, remaining a valuable reference grammar for Sanskrit and Vedic.

The problem in the teaching of Sanskrit in this country has been simply that books like Whitney's Grammar and Lanman's Reader have, for want of acceptable alternatives, been used for a task to which they are poorly suited. Most students find it at best frustrating and painful to try to learn any language, not to mention a language like Sanskrit, from a reference grammar and from the depressingly small portions of a reader that one can cover in such a first-year course. That some students do manage to continue and ultimately gain some measure of control over the language speaks largely for an enthusiasm and dedication on the part of teacher and student which are able to keep them going *in spite* of the first-year materials. Even those relatively few students who persevere and do well in comparison with their classmates seldom have any usable knowledge of Sanskrit as they enter the second year.

The origins of this problem are, I think, to be found, in part, in the history of Sanskrit in American universities. With a few distinguished exceptions, most American (and European) Sanskritists have come to the study of Sanskrit in a roundabout way. Many have been linguists,

---

[1] The "I" in the preface refers to Robert P. Goldman, who put together the original draft for *Devavāṇīpraveśikā*. In 1980, Sally J. Sutherland [Goldman] was given co-author status.

philologists or classicists for whom Sanskrit has been a secondary interest and who, because of their profound knowledge of the classical languages, were able to teach themselves and their students, after a fashion, on the basis of such materials as described above. Others, like some comparative religionists, have come to regard Sanskrit as a "tool" whereby they would be able to get at the "meat" of some circumscribed type of text. For their purposes the "traditional" method was adequate.

Yet, as professional Indologists know, a mere "working knowledge" of Sanskrit will not do for those who are truly interested in the almost overwhelming richness of India's traditional culture; literary, intellectual, scientific, and spiritual. For the Sanskrit language is not merely an abstruse code to be cracked laboriously to read a given message. Neither is it solely of interest insofar as it represents a well-preserved example of an old Indo-European language. Rather, it has served as the very medium of much of the finest in India's long and illustrious history of art, science, philosophy, and religion. In its timelessness, in its subtlety, in its delight in the profusion of its own forms, the Sanskrit language is a kind of mirror for the whole of traditional Indian culture. It is no wonder that for classical India the study of grammar was regarded as men's highest intellectual endeavor.

But my intention here is not to write a polemic on the value of Sanskrit education. Rather, I shall introduce materials which, my experience has shown, can make that education a more efficient and more rewarding experience.

Since I began teaching Sanskrit I have been approached by literally hundreds of students interested in India—in Indian literature, religions, and philosophies. Many of these students, though bright and motivated, had no Greek or Latin, no training in linguistics, and often only a nodding acquaintance with languages other than English. Students like these have been turning up in fair numbers for first year Sanskrit for years, to go on, thanks to the typical 80-90% attrition rate, only in a trickle to more advanced courses. This problem has become more noticeable in the past few years as more and more students have expressed interest in things Indian.

Potentially good students were dropping out of Sanskrit simply for the want of a clear, self-contained progressive Sanskrit textbook which did not presuppose advanced linguistic or philological training on their part. My aim here has been to provide such a text. My own experience with it, over three years of use, has been most encouraging. I am satisfied that most of my students know, by the end of their first year, as much Sanskrit as I and my contemporaries knew at the end of our second. But the real test of these materials is in the hands of teachers other than the author. It is for them and their students to say how far I have succeeded in my aim.

My purpose, then, in writing this primer, was to provide a self-contained primer, workbook and reader for teaching first-year Sanskrit to students with no previous linguistic training. The work is not intended to serve as a comprehensive reference grammar of the classical language. There are already a fair number of these, some of which, like Gonda's useful work, are specially aimed at the student of linguistics. Rather, I have tried throughout the work to introduce, explain and illustrate the most significant features of the language and through verses, quotations, and readings encourage the growing interest in Sanskrit as a means of expression and a medium of a rich culture.

To these ends the grammar has been, in several areas, simplified to prevent the beginner from being more hampered than is absolutely necessary by relatively insignificant paradigms, rules, and exceptions. This does not mean that the course is by any means an easy one. There is all the material that the best students can handle in their first year and much to which the more advanced will wish to return repeatedly. The study of Sanskrit is by its nature demanding and I have accordingly geared this approach to the student with some natural aptitude for the language.

Upon completion of this course, students should have a real working knowledge of the major outlines of Sanskrit grammar. They should be able to read and compose sophisticated Sanskrit sentences with some facility and read, with dictionary, approximately five to ten verses of the *Vālmīki Rāmāyaṇa* or a similar text in an hour.

Method:

The grammar of classical Sanskrit is, for many reasons, an unusually complex system for students to master. For this reason I have throughout this work excluded many rules, exceptions, forms, and grammatical subtleties that I regard as unnecessary for an elementary course. Many of these items occur but rarely and, as such, seem to me to place a strain on the already overburdened memory of the first-year student without repaying the effort required to learn them. This notion has led me to what might be described as a sort of "statistical" method whereby I have stressed forms, rules and even lexical items which are statistically quite common in texts and in the usage of the *paṇḍits* and enable the student to express general ideas simply. I have adhered to this practice even when more common and useful forms are themselves exceptions to general rules. Thus, for example, I cite and stress the important, though irregular, root *jñā* to illustrate the ninth *gaṇa*. As examples of simplification I have throughout cited verbal roots as being either *parasmaipada* or *ātmanepada* even in cases in which optional conjugation is permitted by the grammarians. The arrangement of the material in the text was intended to enable the student to increase his repertoire of usable grammatical material steadily. Thus, verbal and nominal paradigms are introduced together, the more common or useful appearing in the earlier chapters. In addition to this rough functional ordering of the material, the amount of time spent on explanation of the various grammatical features of Sanskrit has been weighted in accordance with the degree to which a given formation normally presents conceptual difficulties to the English speaker. Thus, much of the material, even when it is complex, like the *gaṇa*-s of the present system and the problems of the perfect system, requires a good deal of simple memorization but no special explanation as to usage. On the other hand, it has been my experience that certain issues, especially the nature of the *karmaṇi prayoga*, the uses of participles and, of course, the formation and application of *bahuvrīhi* compounds are almost always perplexing to my students. I have accordingly spent a proportionately greater amount of time and effort on these forms. This will be clear from an examination of Lessons 13 and 15 where I have preferred the risk of seeming repetitive to the certainty that, without such repetition, the use of the *bahuvrīhi*-s and the present participles will remain mysterious to most students.

Pronunciation, Script, Sandhi:

Three issues which deserve special mention here, and form the subjects of the first three lessons, are pronunciation, script, and *sandhi*. Teaching the proper pronunciation of Sanskrit is, I think, important. Sanskrit has the distinction of being perhaps the only language in the world which is neither "dead" nor "living." It is a special, timeless language whose recitation, chanting, and even speaking are still much practiced and prized in certain contexts in India. I found in my own case and in the case of my students, the ability to speak and understand spoken Sanskrit has had the twin advantages of increasing the morale and motivation of the students and, partly because of this, noticeably increasing their ability to grasp and internalize the common forms and regular syntactic patterns of the language. Moreover, ability to properly pronounce Sanskrit and to correctly recite a few well-known verses and proverbs makes a good impression upon Indian Sanskritists and facilitates what should be a very valuable communication with them.

Pronunciation of Sanskrit is not really very difficult. Only a few points cause serious difficulty for English speakers. On the other hand, it is clearly not possible to master the pronunciation of any language without a proper model. For this purpose, I have been fortunate to have available to me a series of traditionally trained *paṇḍits* fluent in spoken Sanskrit. This is, alas, not possible at most places where Sanskrit is taught. For this reason I am preparing, with some *paṇḍits*, a series of tapes[2] for use with the primer. These will serve as a basis for emulation. Until these tapes are obtained, careful study of the material in Lesson 1 will have to serve, however poorly, to provide the basics of Sanskrit phonology.

---

2 "Many users have called and written over the years in order to secure copies of the tapes for assistance with pronunciation. These tapes, including a supplement with all the new verses, may be ordered directly from the Language Laboratory, University of California at Berkeley, 94720." Taken from the Preface to the Second Edition, 1986, p. xvii [SJG 1998].

The issue of the use of the *devanāgarī* script is to my mind a simple one. This text is aimed primarily at students who plan to make some serious use of Sanskrit literature. I have found that failure to introduce the *devanāgarī* script at a very early stage leads to an excessive reliance on transliteration, which, in many cases has led to a lasting inability to read comfortably what is after all not a very difficult script. In order to avoid this I have introduced the *devanāgarī* script in the second lesson. From that point on until the tenth lesson, forms and examples are given both in *nāgarī* and transliteration. This enables students to become increasingly familiar with the script while they are not dependent upon it for an understanding of grammar. From the tenth lesson onwards the use of transliteration is abandoned and the student is compelled to rely upon his knowledge of the script. The readings are given only in *nāgarī* throughout. As a result of this method, I have rarely had a student for whom the script presents any serious problem by the middle of the course.

In the case of *sandhi*, as with the grammar in general, I have found it useful to minimize or eliminate rules of rare or trivial application. My general purpose in the *sandhi* lesson (Lesson 3) is to provide the minimum number of rules for the generation and interpretation of syntactic units. Accordingly, I have stressed the basic rules of external *sandhi*. It has been my experience that it is very difficult for beginning students to master what, in the absence of any knowledge of the grammar and vocabulary, is an almost wholly abstract system of sound changes. Therefore, except for some important exceptions, I have left many of the individual important issues of internal *sandhi* to be presented in conjunction with morphological processes in which they figure prominently.

Thus the treatment of *sandhi* in this primer, while more than sufficient for the first-year student, is not intended to be exhaustive or systematic. Such a treatment, however, is to be found in the elegant and useful *Sanskrit Sandhi and Exercises* of M. B. Emeneau and B. A. van Nooten published by the University of California Press. I recommend that students work through these exercises after completing those of Lesson 3 and while working through the materials of the following lessons.

Use of Sanskrit Grammatical Terminology:

One additional point which requires some comment is the usage of Sanskrit grammatical terminology. I have used this terminology throughout the primer for various reasons. Apart from the interests of classicists and comparative philologists, there seems to me to be no reason whatever to abandon the precise and sophisticated terminology of the Indian grammarians for the poorly adapted and often simply misleading terminology of classical grammars. For one thing it is something of a disservice to the most incisive and accurate tradition of linguistics that the world has known. Indeed, many modern linguists are turning to Sanskrit for its subtle terminology. Moreover, learning the proper terms, like learning proper pronunciation, contributes to the enthusiasm and sense of progress in a new study which is important to student motivation.

In any case the Sanskrit terminology is designed for Sanskrit grammar. Many of the terms (e.g., *tatpuruṣa, bhūte kṛdanta,* etc.) are themselves examples of the forms they designate. On the other hand, Western terminology is frequently confusing. Thus, we have been taught to contrast active and passive voice as well as active and middle when the term "active" represents two completely different concepts. The term "past passive participle" is used to indicate a form which is by no means always "passive." Indeed, with regard to something like the issue of "passive" to "active" transformation, the whole idea of subject and object which we learn in school is rather different from that expounded by the Sanskrit grammarians. To avoid confusion on the part of those who have had some Sanskrit previously, I have always given the Western term alongside the Sanskrit term. I suggest, however, that the latter be used. A glossary of Sanskrit grammatical terms has been provided.

For similar reasons I have given paradigms to be learned in the traditional Indian fashion rather than in the usual Western way. One additional reason for this is that it seems, especially in the case of nominal declension, simpler to learn groups of three (one case at a time) than to try to get sets of seven (one number at a time) by heart.

A Note on Vocabulary:

The vocabulary of Sanskrit presents a serious problem to the learner. First of all he is deprived of the help of the many cognates so easily recognizable in European languages. Moreover, the lexicon of Sanskrit is extremely large. There is a great deal of true synonymity while homonyms abound. Indeed, the whole problem is made more complex by the fact that each different type of text has, to a large extent, its own specialized vocabulary. For the second-year student these problems become dominant; however, as I think that the first duty of the beginner is to master the grammar, I do not place any great emphasis in the first year on vocabulary acquisition. I have found that students will manage to learn a fair working vocabulary from the readings in this text and are able to summarize the story as they go along with little difficulty. Nonetheless, the grammar is ample material for the beginner and accordingly, I usually provide a small glossary for all words that I feel the students do not know readily, on all quizzes and examinations.

Use of the Primer:

This primer is intended to provide material for approximately the first twenty weeks of an elementary Sanskrit course. The actual rate at which a class is able to move through the lessons will vary somewhat with the circumstances, number of hours per week, etc. The course has been designed to cover the first two of three ten-week quarters of First Year Sanskrit at the University of California at Berkeley. This class meets for 41/2 hours per week. I have also used the same material for a special ten-week intensive course which met for 15 hours per week. In general a rate of one lesson per week should be about right but time should be allowed for frequent review and, in any case, there is no point in rushing a class through the material. Each class will find its own rate. Each lesson from Lesson Four to Lesson Twenty-one consists of rules and forms illustrated with Sanskrit examples and explained so that the student may follow the rationale behind the rules. Each lesson is followed by a series of exercises consisting of practice in translation from Sanskrit to English and English to Sanskrit and various types of grammatical drill. A special feature of the primer is that each of these lessons is followed by a graded reading passage which specially illustrates the forms introduced in that particular chapter while providing increasingly sophisticated use of previously acquired material. These readings are also of cultural value as they form, together, a concise retelling of the main story of the *Vālmīki Rāmāyaṇa* from the curse of Daśaratha to the abduction of Sītā. The readings of the later lessons incorporate more and more verses from the epic text itself, while Lesson Twenty-two consists wholly of a selection of verses which complete the epic tale.

Exercises and reading should be assigned daily and may be broken up into whatever units are deemed advisable. I have found it advisable to have students read a little ahead of the material being covered in class and in the homework.

In the later chapters I have provided some verses from various works of Sanskrit literature. These generally illustrate some of the grammar of the lessons in which they appear. They are to be memorized for classroom recitation and this, along with reading from the Rāma story, should be drilled regularly in class.

I have also found it useful to have students keep current their own short version of the main elements of the Rāma story to be read and discussed in class.

Quizzes should be frequent, not less than every two or three lessons. When the primer is completed, the rest of the first year should be used to build vocabulary and grammatical skills by reading and practicing composition. Lanman's reader is very useful for this purpose, especially his selections from the *Hitopadeśa* and the *Kathāsaritsāgara*. I have found it entertaining and very helpful to ask the students to write their own brief *Hitopadeśa* stories based on the characters and situations of the selections chosen from Lanman. If the students are quick and desire some variety, they may be given some *Rāmāyaṇa* or *Mahābhārata* (especially *Gītā*) towards the end of the year.

R. P. Goldman

Acknowledgments

A work of this kind owes much to many people; my teachers, my colleagues, and my students. Many teachers have inspired and guided me in my Sanskrit studies. Among these my debt is greatest to Dr. W. Norman Brown who set, by his scholarship and kindness, an example easy to admire, impossible to emulate. Paṇḍit Śrīnivāsa Śāstrī of the Deccan College, with his profound learning and flawless Sanskrit, has been a constant inspiration. Professors Ernest Bender and Ludo Rocher of the University of Pennsylvania through teaching and guidance prepared me in many ways to undertake this work. Special mention must be made of Professor Royal Weiler who first introduced me to the intricacies and frustrations of *sandhi* and the other terrors of Sanskrit which I have inflicted, in turn, on a new generation of Sanskritists.

My colleagues at the University of California have always been ready to examine and discuss this work as it took shape and it has benefited greatly from the suggestions of them all. Professor Murray Emeneau was kind enough to read through the first draft and made a number of helpful suggestions. My associate Vidvān Vinayaka Parameshwara Bhatta worked through these materials in class with me three times and has on innumerable occasions given me the benefit of his advice in matters of grammar and style. The present work owes much to his careful reading. Finally, I find it difficult to express fully my gratitude to my teacher, friend and colleague, Professor V. W. Paranjpe of Poona University. While teaching at the University of California at Berkeley during the academic year 1973-1974, Dr. Paranjpe read through the manuscript several times. His never-failing counsel, based on his masterful knowledge of Sanskrit grammar, style, metrics, indeed virtually every aspect of Sanskrit language and literature, enabled me time and again to clarify, for myself as well as my students, a number of difficulties in the following chapters and, especially, in the reading selections.

If this work has been inspired by my teacher and encouraged by my colleagues, still it is to my student that it owes its existence and to whom it is dedicated. It was through working with many students at the Universities of Rochester and California that I realized the pressing nature of the need for new Sanskrit teaching materials. All my students have encouraged me in my desire to provide such materials and borne with me patiently while serving as guinea pigs in this experiment. They have suffered cheerfully through missing glossary entries, misnumberings, and opacities of presentation in the working draft. That they have maintained their enthusiasm through all this and still managed to learn Sanskrit in an efficient fashion is, I think, a tribute to their dedication. My thanks to all of them. A number of my students have taken on the special burden of helping with the actual preparation of the text. They have worked efficiently and creatively in the most difficult circumstances, presses by deadlines, working with difficult materials and still carrying on their own school work with distinction. Reed Slatkin took on the task of editing and typing the first draft from my minimally legible handwritten copy and carried it out with his typical enthusiasm and energy. Matthew Kapstein corrected the copy and wrote out, in a clear and elegant hand, all the *devanāgarī* for the first working text. Both these men offered many valuable suggestions and corrections. Their job was particularly hard as I was teaching from the text all the time forcing them to meet copy-service and classroom deadlines week after week. The *devanāgarī* for the corrected copy was written by Denis Lahey who also assisted with the revision and expansion of the exercises. Cynthia Dzendzel had perhaps the hardest job of all. Knowing no Sanskrit she managed to type the final copy from a seemingly incoherent mass of corrections, and revisions full of Sanskrit transliteration, with a speed and accuracy that were truly remarkable.

Finally, I should like express my gratitude to the South and Southeast Asia Center of the University of California, and to its most recent directors—Professors Warren Ilchman, Eugene Irschick, and Bruce Pray—for providing support without which this work would simply not have been possible.

Berkeley 1980

Acknowledgments to the Second Edition: We would like to express our gratitude to Ms. Kathy Glass and Ms. Sali Peterson for their assistance in the preparation of this edition.

R. P. Goldman and S. J. Sutherland
Berkeley 1986.

TABLE OF CONTENTS

LESSON 1

Phonology

1.0 The Sanskrit language, like any other natural language, has for its irreducible units a series of articulable sounds. These can be represented by a series of abstract graphic symbols. There are various systems of such symbols (scripts), but the one with which we will be chiefly concerned is known as the *devanāgarī* (or *nāgarī*) *lipi* (script), the vehicle of the overwhelming majority of printed Sanskrit texts.

1.1 There are two interesting features of this script and the phonetic system of Sanskrit that make them in some ways easier to learn and memorize than English and its use of the roman script. The first of these features is that in the *devanāgarī* script, there is a one to one correspondence between each distinct graphic symbol and a unique phonetic symbol. Thus, each "letter" of the script corresponds to one and only one sound. Compare English and its roman script where, for example, the symbol "a" may indicate many sounds, and where the symbols "c" and "s" may indicate the same sound.

1.2 The second and more significant of the features of the Sanskrit phonetic (and graphic) system is the fact that it is unique among all the world's languages (with the exception of those languages whose systems are derived from Sanskrit) in having its sounds (and by 1.1 necessarily its script) systematically arranged on a scientific basis.

1.3 The Sanskrit phonetic system, then, consists of some forty-nine discrete sounds, represented by an equal number of discrete symbols.

1.4 The sounds are divided into two basic types: *svara*, or "sounded," corresponding to "vowels," or syllabic sounds, and *vyañjana*, or "manifesting," corresponding to "consonants," which cannot, without a sound of the *svara* group, form an articulable syllable.

1.5 The *svara* sounds are twelve in number arranged in six pairs, each of which is distinguished by a short-long alternation, which is one of the chief characteristics of the sound pattern of classical Sanskrit.

1.6 The *svara* sounds (vowels) are:

a	ā
i	ī
u	ū
ṛ	ṝ
ḷ	
e	ai
o	au

Each pair is produced at the same point of articulation in the vocal apparatus, but the occlusion, or closing of the stream of breath at each point is minimal. The first four pairs of vowels are called simple (*śuddha*) vowels, while the remaining two pairs (e, ai; o, au) are said to be complex (*saṃyukta*). (See 1.18.a for pronunciation.)

1.7 The *vyañjana* sounds likewise are of a number of types. The greatest number of the consonants fall into a series of five sets each consisting of five sounds. The sets, or *varga*-s, are arranged by point of contact (*sparśa*) in the vocal apparatus and consist of four ordered sounds, each characterized by a high degree of occlusion at a given point, and one corresponding nasal. Such occlusive sounds are sometimes called "stops."

1.8 The groups are defined by their points of articulation (*sthāna*). These points range from the back to the front of the vocal apparatus. The points of contact are: the velum (*kaṇṭha*), soft palate (*tālu*), hard palate (*mūrdhan*), teeth (*danta*), and lips (*oṣṭha*). The series is then, in order: *kaṇṭhya* (velar) or "ka" *varga*, *tālavya* (palatal) or "ca" *varga*, *mūrdhanya* (retroflex) or "ṭa" *varga*, *dantya* (dental) or "ta" *varga*, and *oṣṭhya* (labial) or "pa" *varga*, named either for the point of articulation or the initial sound in each series.

1.9 Except for the nasal that belongs to each *varga*, the sounds within each *varga* are differentiated in accordance with the presence or absence of two phenomena: voicing (or the use of the vocal chords) and aspiration (or a concomitant strong explosion of breath in their articulation). The order of the occurrence of these phenomena is the same in all the *varga*-s. If V stands for voicing and A for aspiration and (+) and (-) indicate respectively presence and absence of the phenomena, the order in the *varga*-s is as follows:

[-V-A] [-V+A] [+V-A] [+V+A]

1.10 The varga-s then are: (with vowel "a" to permit articulation)

	-V-A	-V+A	+V-A	+V+A	NASAL
1. *kaṇṭhya*	ka	kha	ga	gha	ṅa
2. *tālavya*	ca	cha	ja	jha	ña
3. *mūrdhanya*	ṭa	ṭha	ḍa	ḍha	ṇa
4. *dantya*	ta	tha	da	dha	na
5. *oṣṭhya*	pa	pha	ba	bha	ma

1.11 Most of these sounds occur in some environments in the various dialects of English. Thus, for example, most English speakers habitually use a somewhat retroflex "ṭ" and "ḍ." Others use a more dental "t" and "d," but since no one English dialect is apt to use both (i.e., make a distinction), some care is required in learning to distinguish, both in hearing and speaking, the two different series. (See 1.18b.1.c-d for pronunciation.)

1.12 The other major problem that English speakers are likely to encounter with the *sparśa*-sounds arises from the juxtaposition of the phenomena of voicing and aspiration. English speakers maintain distinctions of aspiration and non-aspiration, but these distinctions are intimately related to the question of voicing and position. Thus, for example, non-voiced stops (*sparśa*-s) in English are generally aspirated when in word-initial position, and non-aspirated when in other positions; (e.g., pot vs. spot). This makes initial voiceless non-aspirated stops and non-initial aspirated voiceless stops (both of which occur in Sanskrit) tricky for English speakers. Similarly, aspirated voiced stops, which never occur in English, are a little difficult at first for English speakers. These sounds "gha," "jha," "ḍha," "dha," and "bha" must be realized (despite their roman representation) each as one simple sound: a voiced stop accompanied by a discharge of air. They are *not* to be pronounced as two separate sounds, stop plus voiced "h." (See 1.18.b.1 for pronunciation.)

1.13 The remaining *vyañjana*-s fall into two small groups.

1.14 The first is known as *antaḥstha*, or "in between," that is, between the vowels and consonants (semivowels). These are "ya," "ra," "la," and "va" and are associated with the *tālavya*, *mūrdhanya*, *dantya*, and *oṣṭhya varga*-s, respectively. (See 1.18.b.2 for pronunciation.)

1.15 The final group of consonants is called *ūṣman*, "heated," or subjected to friction (sibilants). These are (back to front) "śa" (*tālavya*), "ṣa" (*mūrdhanya*), "sa" (*dantya*) and "ha." ("ha," a member of the *kaṇṭhya varga*, is not in the usual order of back to front.) (See 1.18.b.3 for pronunciation.)

1.16 It is important to distinguish, in reading and writing, the palatal sibilant (ś) from the retroflex sibilant (ṣ) although, in fact, they are not often clearly distinguished in speech.

1.17 The other sounds of Sanskrit are a nasalization of vowels called *anusvāra* (ṃ), and a slightly velarized aspiration called *visarga* (ḥ). (See 1.18c for pronunciation.)

1.18 **Note on pronunciation**

The pronunciation of Sanskrit is usually not very difficult for English speakers. The few exceptions to this rule simply require a little practice. It is, of course, impossible to learn proper pronunciation from a printed page alone. This must be learned either from a teacher whose pronunciation is good or from taped materials designed for this purpose. However, a few guidelines here will serve to clarify the basic pronunciation of the sounds of Sanskrit as used by fluent speakers of Sanskrit in most parts of India. English examples are based on hypothetical "dictionary" pronunciation.

a. ***svara*** **sounds**

The *svara* sounds, with the exception of the "long" *saṃyukta* sounds (ai and au), are always pronounced with a single clear effort like the vowels of standard Italian and are not, like many English vowel sounds, allowed to glide into diphthongal sequences. Long vowels are generally held about twice as long as their corresponding short vowels.

a	pronounced like the u in "but"
ā	pronounced like the o in "mom"
i	pronounced like the i in "bit"
ī	pronounced like the ee in "beet"
u	pronounced like the first u in "suture"
ū	pronounced like the oo in "pool"
ṛ	pronounced like the ri in "rig"
ṝ	is rare in Sanskrit and has no English equivalent. It is pronounced like ṛ but the sound is held approximately twice as long.
ḷ	pronounced somewhat like the "lur" in "slurp."
e	pronounced like the a in "gate"
ai	pronounced somewhat like the i in "high." This sound is diphthongized to glide slightly into an "i" vowel.
o	pronounced like the o in "rote"
au	pronounced somewhat like the ou of "loud" with a similar lip-rounding glide.

b. ***vyañjana*** **sounds**

Pronunciation of the *sparśa* sounds is problematic for English speakers chiefly because of the first and fourth item in each *varga*. The second item is tricky only in some environments. The first (non-voiced, non-aspirated) occurs commonly enough in English, but never in word initial position. Such sounds occur, however, in all positions in Sanskrit. Thus some difficulty arises when they occur in initial position. Try to resist the natural (English) tendency to aspirate these sounds. When they are properly distinguished from their aspirated equivalents, they will at first sound almost like their corresponding *voiced* non-aspirates. Practice will clarify this issue. The second sound in each *varga* (non-voiced, aspirated) is the same sort of sound given to initial non-voiced stops in English. Be sure, however, not to lose the aspiration in non-initial occurrences (e.g., *sthūla*). The third sound in each *varga* (voiced, non-aspirated) should present no special difficulty to English speakers. The fourth sound in each varga (voiced, aspirated) is of a type that does not really occur in English in any position, hence no English equivalents have been given. Try to repeat these sounds as you hear them from your teacher or from tapes. Remember to give the sounds both voicing and the same strong aspiration that you normally give to the non-voiced stops in initial position.

1. *sparśa* sounds

   a. *kaṇṭhya varga*:

k	like the k in "skate"
kh	like the k in "Kate"
g	like the g in "gate"
ṅ	like the n in "sing"

   b. *tālavya varga*:

c	like the ch in "eschew"
ch	like the ch in "chew"
j	like the j in "Jew"
ñ	like the n in "cinch"

   c. *mūrdhanya varga*: These sounds are similar to the "t" and "d" sounds of most English dialects but the tip of the tongue should be curled back further to the roof of the mouth for the proper Sanskrit pronunciation.

ṭ	like the first t in "start"
ṭh	like the first t in "tart"
ḍ	like the d in "dart"
ṇ	like the n in "tint"

d. *dantya varga*: These sounds, which occur in place of the preceding in the speech of many New Yorkers, are realized with the tip of the tongue protruding slightly between the teeth. The sounds thus produced are characteristically "flatter" and less resonant than those of the preceding varga. The same English examples may be used, since no English dialect has both series of sounds.

e. *oṣṭhya varga*:

p	like the p in "spin"
ph	like the p in "pin"
b	like the b in "bin"
m	like the m's in "mumps"

2. *antaḥstha* sounds:

y	like the y in "yellow"
r	a fronted, *mūrdhanya* sound, rather like the r in "drama"
l	like the l in "lug"
v	produced generally with just the slightest contact between the upper teeth and the lower lip; slightly greater than that used for English w (as in "wile") but less than that used for English v (as in "vile")

3. *ūṣman* sounds

ś	like the sh in "shove"
ṣ	produced with the tongue-tip further back (in the *mūrdhanya* position) than for the śṣ, but giving a very similar sound.
s	like the s in "so"
h	like the h in "hope." Make sure that the sound is fully voiced.

c. **additional sounds**

The following two sounds, although they frequently are the forms taken by certain consonants in certain environments, are not, themselves, consonants. Rather they generally are to be regarded as "colorations" of a preceding vowel.

1. ṃ *anusvāra*: This sound is realized by permitting the air used in the articulation of a preceding vowel to escape through the nose. If, however, the *anusvāra* is immediately followed by a *sparśa* consonant, it will be realized as the nasal belonging to the same *varga* as that consonant: e.g., *vanaṃ gacchati* would be pronounced "*vanañ gacchati.*"

2. ḥ *visarga*: The *visarga* is an aspiration of a preceding vowel and is pronounced, almost like an echo, as an "h" followed by the short form of the preceding vowel. The *saṃyukta* vowels e and o will echo as themselves, respectively. After long *saṃyukta* vowels, the "echo" vowel will be the short form of the simple vowel corresponding in point of articulation to the *saṃyukta* vowel. Thus, for ai the "echo" will be i, while for au, the echo will be u. The following are some examples. Echo sounds are put in brackets.

devaḥ	pronounced as deva(ha)
devāḥ	pronounced devā(ha)
muniḥ	pronounced muni(hi)
dhīḥ	pronounced dhī(hi)
viṣṇuḥ	pronounced viṣṇu(hu)
muneḥ	pronounced mune(he)
devaiḥ	pronounced devai(hi)

Note: These "echo" or "ghost syllables" are not truly syllabic in a word or line. Often, when *visarga* occurs within a word, the "echo" is not clearly articulated. In this case it is audible just as a slight "hiss" of air at the velum.

1.19 Stress

Stress accent, while perhaps not as important in Sanskrit as in English, is usual in proper pronunciation. The general rule is that the penultimate syllable (next to last) receives mild stress if it is as heavy (*guru*—see 17.6.c.i). If the penultimate is light (*laghu*—see 17.6.c.i), the stress falls on the syllable that precedes it (antepenultimate) regardless of its weight. Secondary stress is not usual; all the remaining syllables receive equal stress.

Example:

vikramorvaśī́ya	(penultimate heavy)
rāmā́yaṇa	(penultimate light)

EXERCISES

A. Repeat the following and memorize.

1. a, ā, i, ī, u, ū, ṛ, e, ai, o, au, (a)ṃ, (a)ḥ

2.

ka	kha	ga	gha	n̄a
ca	cha	ja	jha	ña
ṭa	ṭha	ḍa	ḍha	ṇa
ta	tha	da	dha	na
pạ	pha	ba	bha	ma
ya	ra	la	va	
śa	ṣa	sa	ha	

B. Repeat A.2 with each of the following *svara*, *anusvāra*, and *visarga* sounds

a, ā, i, ī, u, ū, ṛ, e, ai, o, au, aṃ, aḥ

C. Repeat the following.

1. ko 'yam? (see 2.26)
   Who is this?

kāko 'yam.
This is a crow.

api sthūlaḥ?
Is he fat?

atha kiṃ! kākaḥ sthūlaḥ.
Yes, indeed! The crow is fat.

kutra tiṣṭhati sthūlakākaḥ?
Where is the fat crow located?

vaṭavṛkṣe tiṣṭhati kākaḥ.
The crow is in the fig tree.

api dharmaṃ jānāti kākaḥ?
Does the crow know *dharma*?

atha kiṃ! dharmaṃ jānāti dvijatvāt.
Yes! He knows *dharma* because he is twice-born.
(*dvija*—brahman/bird)

kiṃ tu tasya dharmapravṛttir nāsti.
But he does not practice *dharma*.

bhavatu! vayaṃ sarve dharmācaraṇaṃ ca dharmaṃ ca jānīmaḥ.
Let it be! We all know proper conduct and *dharma*!

kiṃ tu, yathā sthūlakākā dharmarakṣaṇaṃ vayaṃ ghoraṃ bhayam iva paśyāmaḥ.
But, like the fat crows, we look upon the protection of *dharma* as a dreadful danger.

2. kaṣyaitat phalam?
Whose fruit is this?

phalaṃ mama.
[It is] my fruit.

mahyam anyat phalam ānaya.
Bring me another fruit.

astu, ahaṃ phalārthaṃ jhaṭiti gacchāmi.
Certainly, I go at once for fruit.

LESSON 2

The Devanāgarī Script

2.0 Learning the *nāgarī* script is made somewhat simpler by the fact noted above (1.1) of each letter's representing one, and only one, phonetic entity.

2.1 The script with its correct transliteration is as follows:

स्वर (*svara*):

अ = a	आ = ā
इ = i	ई = ī
उ = u	ऊ = ū
ऋ = ṛ	ॠ = ṝ
ऌ = ḷ*	
ए = e	ऐ = ai
ओ= o	औ = au

*This sound, vocalic ḷ, is articulated as an l preceding the vowel ṛ. It is almost non-existent in Sanskrit and you need not be too concerned with it.

व्यञ्जन (*vyañjana*):

वर्ग *varga*	स्पर्श *sparśa*				अनुनासिक *anunāsika*	अन्तःस्थ *antaḥstha*	ऊष्मन् *ūṣman*
	-V-A[1]	-V+A	+V-A	+V+A	+V	+V	-V
कण्ठ्य *ka ṇṭhya*	क ka	ख kha	ग ga	घ gha	ङ n̄a		[ह] [ha]
तालव्य *tālavya*	च ca	छ cha	ज ja	झ jha	ञ ña	य ya	श śa
मूर्धन्य *mūrdhanya*	ट ṭa	ठ ṭha	ड ḍa	ढ ḍha	ण ṇa	र ra	ष ṣa
दन्त्य *dantya*	त ta	थ tha	द da	ध dha	न na	ल la	स sa
ओष्ठ्य *oṣṭhya*	प pa	फ pha	ब ba	भ bha	म ma	व va	

[1] -V non-voiced; -A non-aspirate; +V voiced; +A aspirate

ह voiced, not considered a marker of sibilant *varga*, although it is an ऊष्मन् (*ūṣman*)

variants: for अ (a)— अ

for झ (jha)— झ

for ण (ṇa)— ण

additional signs: ं—ṃ (*anusvāra*) e.g., अं-aṃ

ः—ḥ (*visarga*) e.g., अः-aḥ

(see 1.18.c)

2.2 Notice that the script typically frames the distinctive portion of a given letter with a vertical and a horizontal line (ा). In writing, the distinctive portion is written first, then the vertical line, and only last is the top line added; e.g., to write "ja" (ज). In general, write left to right and top to bottom;

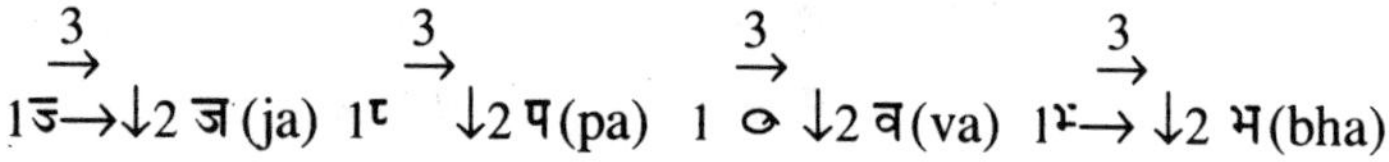

Note that in the list of *nāgarī* symbols, each consonant has been transliterated with the vowel "a" (अ) although this is not indicated in the script.

2.3 Herein lies the basis and the central peculiarity of the *devanāgarī* writing system; i.e., that the vowel "a" (अ), by far the most frequently recurring vowel in Sanskrit, is considered, without any graphic representation, to follow every consonant symbol **unless** it is otherwise indicated. This fact explains in whole or in part, the use of the three most striking and initially confusing features of the script: (1) the use of vowel signs, (2) the non-vowel sign or *virāma*, and (3) conjunct consonants.

2.4 Vowels and vowel signs. The symbols for the *svara,* or vowel sounds, are given in order at 2.1 above.

2.5 A major peculiarity of the system is that these signs are used only in those cases in which a vowel begins a syllable (regardless of word boundary) and does not form a part of a syllable begun by a preceding consonant. (See below 2.23.)

2.6 In cases in which a vowel does not begin a syllable, and these form the greatest majority of instances, the vowels are each represented by a special post-consonantal ligature or symbol.

2.7 Sanskrit's most commonly occurring vowel, "अ (a)," has no post-consonantal symbol and is assumed after every consonantal sign **if not otherwise indicated** (2.3).

2.8 Thus the simple sign for any consonant is to be read as that consonant followed by *a*.

So क = ka, च = ca, य = ya, घ = gha, etc.

The word कवच is to be read as *kavaca*.

The word गगन is to be read as *gagana*.

2.9 The post-consonantal forms for the other vowels replace "a." They are as follows: (All are shown with the consonant "क्" to indicate proper placement.)

अ → Ø ; क—ka	आ → ा ; का—kā
इ → ि ; कि—ki	ई → ी ; की—kī
उ → ु ; कु—ku	ऊ → ू ; कू—kū
ऋ → ृ ; कृ—kṛ	ॠ → ॄ ; कॄ—kṝ
ऌ → -ऌ; कॢ—kḷ*	
ए → े ; के—ke	ऐ → ै ; कै—kai
ओ → ो ; को—ko	औ → ौ ; कौ—kau

*See note to 2.1

2.10 Note that in the case of the vowel symbols themselves, there is a general typological similarity between long and short vowel signs of the same point of articulation. Keeping this in mind will aid memorization.

2.11 One or two points concerning the post-consonantal vowel signs require special attention.

a. By far the greatest source of confusion, especially in the writing of the script, is the fact that the post-consonantal sign for इ, ि ("i") is written "before," i.e., to the left of the consonant it follows, despite the fact that the vowel sound follows the consonant.

b. The subscribed signs (ु), (ू) and (ृ) are written in special form or placed in special juxtaposition with a few consonants.

   i. Thus, the "u" signs (ु) and (ू) are attached at the right middle of the consonant र् (r), while the short sign is inverted. Thus रु—ru, रू—rū.

   ii. The vowel "ṛ" sign is very closely combined with the consonant द—d; thus दृ—dṛ.

   iii. It is also placed peculiarly in juxtaposition with ह्—h; thus हृ—hṛ.

2.12 Thus far, the issue of writing post-consonantal vowels is clear. A consonant is written and read as being followed by a vowel "a" **unless** it is marked by the sign for another vowel.

2.13 The simplest way of indicating a consonant not followed by a vowel is to append to the consonant a short stroke, called *virāma*, which signals the elision of the inherent vowel "a." Thus त्—t; पद्—pad; ऋच्—ṛc; etc.

This sign is sometimes used in printed texts to separate words when a word boundary falls within a conjunct, but is generally restricted in use to the elucidation of particularly complex conjuncts (e.g., पङ्क्त्या or पङ्क्त्या [paṅktyā]) and to marking consonants that occur in absolute final position. (See below 3.25.)

2.14 **Consonant sequences. (Conjunct consonants)**

The zero form of the non-syllable-initial "a" vowel, which lends a certain elegance to the *nāgarī* system of writing, creates, at the same time, a problem in the script-realization of sequences of consonants with no intervening vowel.

2.15 This problem is handled by the script in an ingenious but slightly clumsy manner. Only the final consonant of a sequence appears in its full form while only the distinctive portions of the earlier members of the sequence are prefixed to it.

2.16 Thus, if we wish to properly write the sequence "tva," we cannot write तव as this would yield "tava." The proper method then is to take the distinctive portion of त, that is त्, and prefix it to the व. Thus, the proper result is त्व "tva."

2.17 Most conjunct clusters are transparent and are evidently the lateral or vertical sequences of distinctive portions of consonants prefixed to the final member of the cluster.

2.18 Consonants, like भ्, न्, त्, etc., which have their distinctive portion well to the left of the vertical line, tend to form horizontal (i.e., left to right) conjuncts with similar following consonants. For example,

त्म—tma, क्व—kva, भ्य—bhya, स्थ—stha,
स्य—sya, स्व—sva, त्य—tya, ह्य—hya, etc.

2.19 When final members of a cluster have a chiefly vertical axis (distinctive portion on, on both sides of, or in place of the vertical line) or have a horizontal axis, but occupy only a small vertical space compared to the height of the full vertical line (e.g., प्, द्, ट्, ष्, etc.), the cluster may be written vertically. For example,

प्ति—pti, द्धो—ddho, ष्ट—ṣṭa, ट्ट—ṭṭa.

2.20 In general, read the clusters as they are written, i.e., left to right and top to bottom.

2.21 A few consonants have special reduced or altered forms when they occur in conjunction with other consonants. These require special note.

a. श—ś, when followed by a consonant with which it combines vertically (see 2.19) (and, irregularly, by a subscribed vowel sign), is generally changed to श्.

For example,

श्च—śca, श्व—śva, (and शु—śu, शृ—śṛ)

but श्य—śya, श्म—śma.

b. र—ra has two peculiar forms when in conjunction depending upon whether it is first or non-first in a conjunct.

i. When first, it appears as a superscribed hook, *which is always written as far to the right as possible over the last member of the conjunct or the last member's vowel sign*, whichever is farthest right. If, however, the syllable of which the "r" is the initial, ends in *anusvāra*, the sign for this will appear *within* the hook. So arthaḥ—अर्थः ; arthī—अर्थी; dharme—धर्मे; svargaṃ—स्वर्गं.

ii. When other than first, it appears as a straight line below and to the left of the letter it follows, rising about 45° from the horizontal. So pra—प्र; kri—क्रि.
Note: under a few letters, like ट and ठ, this appears as ट्र—ṭra, ठ्र—ṭhra.

c. त्—t, when preceding another त्, is reduced to a simple line त्त—tta. It is similarly reduced when followed by र. Thus त्र—tra.

2.22 There are two common conjuncts that provide no apparent clue to their composition. These are ज्ञ—jña, and क्ष—kṣa. These must simply be learned as special forms.

2.23 Note that Sanskrit is written syllabically as well as by words, and so it is the common practice not to separate words written in a sentence or unit of verse unless the word boundary coincides with a syllable boundary. A syllable (अक्षर—akṣara) is generally considered to be either a single vowel, or a consonant (or consonant cluster) followed by a vowel. The vowel in either case may be nasalized (अनुस्वार—*anusvāra*) or aspirated (विसर्ग—*visarga*). Thus, for example, the famous utterance of the *Chāndogya Upaniṣad*, *tat tvam asi*, "you are that," would be syllabified as ta-, ttva-, ma-, -si. Since no word boundary corresponds to a syllabic boundary, it then would be written in नागरी (*nāgarī*) as तत्त्वमसि. In the same way, if a word final consonant precedes a word initial vowel, the two will form a single syllable and the vowel will take its post-consonantal sign, if any.

Examples:
agnir asmy aham अग्निरस्म्यहम् । (I am fire.)
syllabically a-gni-ra-smya-ham
gām ānaya गामानय । (Bring a cow.)
syllabically gā-mā-na-ya
However, in the very common case in which a word ending in a vowel (with or without विसर्ग—*visarga* [ḥ] or अनुस्वार—*anusvāra* [ṃ]) precedes a word beginning with a consonant or in certain cases (see 3.21) a vowel, word boundary is indicated, since it coincides with a syllable boundary. Thus, *matsyā iva janā nityaṃ bhakṣayanti parasparam* would be written: मत्स्या इव जना नित्यं भक्षयन्ति परस्परम् । (Like fish, men always are devouring one another.) Here all the word boundaries happen to coincide with syllable boundaries.

2.24 Words are separated in roman transliteration. Except where (for reasons discussed at 3.3-4) a single roman letter obscures the point of word boundary. For example, गामानय and अग्निरहम् would be transliterated as *gām ānaya* and *agnir aham.* But रामागच्छ (राम + आगच्छ) must be transliterated as *rāmāgaccha* since we cannot break up the roman symbol ā (see 3.3).

2.25 The देवनागरी (*devanāgarī*) numerals, which are, in fact, the source of our "arabic" numerals, are:

१	२	३	४	५	६	७	८	९	०
1	2	3	4	5	6	7	8	9	0

They are used in exactly the same way as our numbers. Thus २४०६८ 24,068.

2.26 A sign (ऽ), called अवग्रह (*avagraha*) or separation, is often used to separate words whose initial "a" or "ā" vowel has been lost or has combined with another vowel from words that precede them. It is represented in transliteration as apostrophe (') in place of the missing letter. For example, काकः + अयम् → काको ऽयम् (3.35), is transliterated as, "kāko 'yam." (This is a crow.)

EXERCISES

A. Transliterate Exercise 1C (pp. 9-10) into देवनागरी (*devanāgarī*).

B. Transliterate the following into roman transcription. (Do not worry about proper word division.)

१. इक्ष्वाकूणामिहाद्यैव कश्चिद्राजा विधीयताम् ।
अराजकं हि नो राष्ट्रं विनाशं समवाप्नुयात् ॥१॥
नाराजके जनपदे बीजमुष्टिः प्रकीर्यते ।
नाराजके पितुः पुत्रो भार्या वा वर्तते वशे ॥२॥

Let a king of the Ikṣvāku line be consecrated immediately;
For without a king, our land would be destroyed;
In a land without a king, not a handful of grain is sown;
In a land without a king, sons do not obey their fathers nor wives their husbands.

२. कुलीनान्रूपसंपन्नान्गजान्परगजारुजान् ।
शिक्षितान्गजशिक्षायामैरावतसमान्युधि ॥

(Hanumān saw) elephants of noble lineage, of beautiful form, murderous to the elephants of the enemy; well-instructed in elephant training, and the equal of Airāvata in battle.

३. योगो योगविदां नेता प्रधानपुरुषेश्वरः ।
नरसिंहवपुः श्रीमान्केशवः पुरुषोत्तमः ॥

He is yoga incarnate, foremost among those who know yoga, lord among great men, he takes on the form of a man-lion, he is the majestic Keśava, the supreme spirit.

C. Transliterate the following words.

दृष्ट्वा	शब्देन	आच्छादिताः
मार्गेण	कामरूपिणः	लक्ष्मणेन
गौरवम्	राक्षसः	अश्वः
बुद्धः	सख्यम्	षष्ठ्याम्
प्रसन्नात्	काञ्चनः	धार्मिकाय
रक्तस्य	हेमपिङ्गले	वाल्मीकिः

D. Write the following words in देवनागरी (*devanāgarī*).

tattvasya	parvāṇi	bhayaṅkareṇa
ārtāya	trāhi	nīlakaṇṭhaḥ
daṃṣṭrābhyām	svāhā	patrarathaḥ
jyāḥ	dṛśyamānāḥ	dūrgāt
khaḍgāni	labdhvā	dāridryam
gacchanti	manasvinaḥ	ṛṣabhaḥ

LESSON 3

सन्धि (Sandhi)

3.0 Perhaps the most peculiar, and initially dismaying, feature of Sanskrit is its complex system of conditional phonological change known as सन्धि (*sandhi*), or combination. Various kinds of environmentally conditioned change occur in all languages, but no other has so formalized and systematized them as has Sanskrit.

3.1 There are two basic applications of the सन्धि (*sandhi*) rules, depending on the circumstances under which the sound changes occur. Many of the same rules hold for both applications. The first historically and morphologically more significant application applies to the junctures of the morphemes, or meaningful parts of words. This is called internal सन्धि (*sandhi*). Less, perhaps, in historical significance, but of greater importance for the beginner, is the external सन्धि (*sandhi*), which occurs at word boundaries and between members of compounds. Without familiarity with the rules of external सन्धि (*sandhi*), it is impossible to read or understand a Sanskrit sentence.

Therefore, while all सन्धि (*sandhi*) changes are of interest, it is essential, at the outset, to learn the rules for external सन्धि (*sandhi*) and a few internal सन्धि (*sandhi*) rules of common application. Let's examine the rules as they apply first to vowels and then to consonants.

3.2 **External Vowel सन्धि** (*sandhi*)

In general, the basic rule governing vowel सन्धि (*sandhi*), in internal as well as external combination, is that two vowels should not come into direct contact. That is to say, except in a few cases (see 3.21), vowel hiatus is avoided. It is avoided by the collapse of the two juxtaposed vocalic syllables into one. This in turn may be accomplished in three ways: the coalescence of the two vowels into one, the change of the prior vowel to a consonant, which then forms a single syllable with the remaining vowel, or by the loss of one of the vowels.

3.3 Coalescence

The simplest kind of coalescence, or at any rate the easiest to remember, involves like vowels. Any two concurrent simple vowels of the same pair of long-short alternates (a, i, u, ṛ), regardless of the length of either one, coalesce to form the long vowel of the set. Vowel length is not an issue, as any such sequence yields a long vowel.

Examples:

अ + अ → आ; रामेण + सह + अगच्छत् + सीता → रामेण सहागच्छत्सीता ।
a + a → ā; rāmeṇa saha agacchat sītā → rāmeṇa sahāgacchat sītā.

अ + आ → आ; रामेण + सह + आगच्छति + सीता → रामेण सहागच्छति सीता ।
a + ā → ā; rāmeṇa saha āgacchati sītā → rāmeṇa sahāgacchati sītā.

आ + अ → आ; सीतया + अगच्छत् + सुमित्रा → सीतयागच्छत्सुमित्रा ।
ā + a → ā; sītayā agacchat sumitrā → sītayāgacchat sumitrā.

आ + आ → आ; सीतया + आगच्छति + रामः → सीतयागच्छति रामः ।
ā + ā → ā; sītayā āgacchati rāmaḥ → sītayāgacchati rāmaḥ.

In the same way, any two concurrent "i" vowels, long or short, yield "ī," and any two concurrent "u" vowels, long or short, yield "ū."

Examples:

गच्छामि + इति + वदति → गच्छामीति वदति ।
gacchāmi + iti + vadati → gacchāmīti vadati. ("I'm going," he says.)

कुरु + उत्तम → कुरूत्तम (supreme Kuru)
kuru + uttama → kurūttama (supreme Kuru)

3.4 Coalescence may also occur as a result of the contact of two dissimilar vowels but *only* if the prior vowel is an "a" vowel (a or ā). Here again, the length of the two vowels is immaterial to the result.

Examples:

आ + ई → ए; महा + ईश → महेश

ā + ī → e; mahā + īśa → maheśa (great lord)

अ + उ → ओ; लम्ब + उदर → लम्बोदर

a + u –. o; lamba + udara → lambodara (pot belly)

आ + ऋ → अर् ; महा + ऋषि → महर्षि

ā + ṛ → ar; mahā + ṛṣi → maharṣi (great sage)

अ + ए → ऐ; अत्र + एव → अत्रैव

a + e → ai; atra + eva → atraiva (right here)

अ + ऐ → ऐ; गच्छ + ऐश्वर्यम् → गच्छैश्वर्यम् ।

a + ai → ai; gaccha + aiśvaryam → gacchaiśvaryam.
(Become a sovereign.)

आ + ओ → औ; सा + ओदनं पचति → सौदनं पचति ।

ā + o → au; sā + odanaṃ pacati → saudanaṃ pacati.
(She cooks rice.)

अ + औ → औ; यच्छ + औदुम्बरम् → यच्छौदुम्बरम् ।

a + au → au; yaccha + audumbaram → yacchaudumbaram.
(Give the *udumbara* fruit.)

Note that the complex vowels ऐ (ai) and औ (au) may be regarded as the "long" form of the complex vowels ए (e) and ओ (o), respectively. Since length is the maximal grade, the coalescence of अ (a) with either the short or long form yields the long form.

3.5 **Vowel Strength**

Closely related to the results of the previous series of coalescences, although not identical, is a system of vowel grade or strength which is pervasive in Sanskrit and must be learned.

3.6 The two grades of vowel strength are called गुण (*guṇa*) and वृद्धि (*vṛddhi*). These grades are similar to the coalescence in

3.4, except that they distinguish vowel length of the strengthened "a" vowel. गुण (*guṇa*) increases the अ (a) vowel, as it were, by short अ (a), and वृद्धि (*vṛddhi*) by आ (ā).

3.7 गुण (*guṇa*) and वृद्धि (*vṛddhi*) apply only to the simple vowels and are as follows:

स्वर	अ,आ	इ,ई	उ,ऊ	ऋ
svara	a, ā	i, ī	u, ū	ṛ
गुण	अ,आ	ए	ओ	अर्
guṇa	a, ā	e	o	ar
वृद्धि	आ	ऐ	औ	आर्
vṛddhi	ā	ai	au	ār

Note that the extremely common vowel अ (a) (short) is unchanged in गुण (*guṇa*). This is sometimes expressed by the statement: अ (a) is its own गुण (*guṇa*).

This series of changes is **extremely important**, especially in internal सन्धि (*sandhi*) processes of word derivation, and must be learned immediately and thoroughly.

3.8 When two dissimilar vowels are juxtaposed and the first is not an "a" vowel (long or short), the syllabic coalescence is effected by changing the first vowel into its corresponding homorganic nonsyllabic semivowel.

3.9 The correspondences are:

इ/ई → य् (i/ī → y); उ/ऊ → व् (u/ū → v); ऋ/ॠ → र् (ṛ/ṝ → r)

Examples:

आगच्छामि + अहम् → आगच्छाम्यहम् ।

āgacchāmi + aham → āgacchāmy aham. (I am coming.)

जयतु + आर्यपुत्रः → जयत्वार्यपुत्रः ।

jayatu + āryaputraḥ → jayatv āryaputraḥ. (May my lord be victorious.)

पितृ + ईप्सितम् → पित्रीप्सितम्

pitṛ + īpsitam → pitr īpsitam (. . . desired by the father)

3.10 **Complex Vowels**

The complex vowels, which are, as we can now see, vocalic sounds that may be analyzed into other vowel sounds, betray their complex form when juxtaposed with a vocalic sound (simple or complex).

3.11 To understand this process, it is essential to have a clear idea of the structure of the complex vowels. Keep in mind that:

ए (e) is the गुण (*guṇa*) of इ/ई (i/ī) and represents अ + इ/ई (a + i/ī)
ऐ (ai) is the वृद्धि (*vṛddhi*) of इ/ई (i/ī) and represents आ + इ/ई (ā + i/ī)
ओ (o) is the गुण (*guṇa*) of उ/ऊ (u/ū) and represents अ + उ/ऊ (a + u/ū)
औ (au) is the वृद्धि (*vṛddhi*) of उ/ऊ (u/ū) and represents आ + उ/ऊ (ā+u/ū)

3.12 Now, when one of these four complex vowels occurs immediately before a vowel sound and is juxtaposed with it, two processes, as it were, take place:

a) the complex vowel is analyzed into its components, and
b) the final "i" or "u" element of that analysis is changed into its corresponding semivowel.

3.13 Clear examples from internal सन्धि (*sandhi*):

a. The analysis of the word जयतु (*jayatu*—May he be victorious; 3.9, ex. 2) is as follows: The vowel of the verbal root जि (*ji*—conquer, be victorious) is, for reasons to be learned later (see 7.14), subjected to गुण (*guṇa*) in the formation of the stem required here. Thus जि →जे (ji → je). When the ए (e) is juxtaposed with the अ (a) of the class marker, the following steps occur (although only the final result is evident):

ए + अ → (अ + इ) + अ; (अ + इ) + अ → अ + य् + अ
e + a → (a + i) + a; (a +i) + a → a + y +a
so: जे + अ + तु → जय् + अ + तु → जयतु
je + a + tu → jay + a + tu → jayatu (see 7.14)

b. In the same way, the root भू (*bhū*—to be) in forming भवतु (*bhavatu*—let it be), undergoes a parallel series of सन्धि (*sandhi*) changes:
√भू + गुण → भो; भो + अ → भ् (अ + उ) + अ;
bhū + *guṇa* → bho; bho + a → bh (a + u) + a;
√भव् + अ + तु → भवतु
bhav + a + tu → bhavatu

3.14 This process, with regard to the complex vowels ओ (o) and औ (au) is similar to that in external सन्धि (*sandhi*).

3.15 Thus, the sequence उभौ + एव (*ubhau* + *eva*—both of them):
उभा + उ + एव → उभा + व् + एव → उभावेव
ubhā + u + eva → ubhā + v + eva → ubhāv eva

3.16 Final ओ (o), except as the result of another सन्धि (*sandhi*) operation (3.35), is not common in word-final position.

3.17 This process is obscured in external सन्धि (*sandhi*) by the important additional rule that: the य् (y) element of the complex vowel ए (e) is lost before a word-initial vowel **other than short अ (a)** (3.20), and, in the case of ऐ (ai), before **any vowel**.

3.18 So, in the sequence स्वर्गे + इन्द्रः (*svarge* + *indraḥ*—Indra is in heaven), the result would be:
स्वर्ग इन्द्रः (svarga indraḥ). The process might be depicted as follows:
स्वर्गे + इन्द्रः → (१) (स्वर्ग + इ) + इन्द्रः →
svarge + indraḥ → (1) (svarga +i) + indraḥ →
(२) स्वर्ग + य् + इन्द्रः → (३) य् → Ø (४) स्वर्ग इन्द्रः
(2) svarga + y + indraḥ → (3) y → Ø (4) svarga indraḥ

Also, in the sequence तस्मै + अददात् (*tasmai* + *adadāt*—He gave to him), the process could be seen as:
तस्मै + अददात् → (१) तस्मा + इ + अददात्
tasmai + adadāt → (1) tasmā + i + adadāt →
(२) तस्मा + य् + अददात् → (३) य् → Ø (४) तस्मा अददात्
(2) tasmā + y + adadāt → (3) y → Ø (4) tasmā adadāt

3.19 Note that when vowel hiatus (the sequence of two vowels) occurs as a **result of a सन्धि** (*sandhi*) **rule** or series of सन्धि (*sandhi*) rules, it is permitted to remain. In other words, in the case of vowels, only one pass through the सन्धि (*sandhi*) rules is valid. One must not subject the resultant hiatus to further सन्धि (*sandhi*).

3.20 In the case where a final ए (e) immediately precedes a short अ (a), the ए (e) remains unchanged while the अ (a), frequently unstable in initial position (3.35), is lost.

Thus:

ते + अब्रुवन् → ते ऽब्रुवन्

te + abruvan → te 'bruvan (They said.)

भारतदेशे + अवसत् → भारतदेशे ऽवसत्

bhāratadeśe + avasat → bhāratadeśe 'vasat. (He lived in India.)

3.21 **प्रगृह्य** (*Pragṛhya*) **Vowels**

Certain vowels in certain restricted environments are not subject to the above rules. They are called प्रगृह्य (*pragṛhya*) vowels and are as follows:

a. vowels इ, ई (i, ī), उ, ऊ (u, ū), and ए (e), when they serve as dual endings (4.12, 27)

b. the इ, ई (i, ī) of the pronoun अमी (*amī*) (See 19.1.b)

c. the vowels of particles or interjections

Examples:

द्वे + कन्ये + आगच्छतः → द्वे कन्ये आगच्छतः

dve + kanye + āgacchataḥ → dve kanye āgacchataḥ. (Two girls come.)

हे + आर्यपुत्र → हे आर्यपुत्र

he + āryaputra → he āryaputra (O my lord)

3.22 **Initial and Final Positions**

Since **external** सन्धि (*sandhi*) applies, by definition, at the junctures of words, it is useful to have a set of terms that describe sounds that occur at these junctures, namely at the beginning and end of words.

a. The terminology for sounds occurring at the beginning of words is quite simple. Such sounds are called **initial** sounds or are said to be in **initial position**.

b. The situation for sounds that occur at the end of words is, however, a little more complicated. This is so because sounds in this **final position** are liable to various kinds of change depending upon whether another sound (i.e., an initial sound of a following word) follows them, and, if one does, upon the nature of that sound.

   i. Therefore, when we refer to a sound that occurs at the end of a word, regardless of what may or may not follow it, we say that the sound is a **word final** or in **word final position**.

   ii. When we refer to a word final sound that has no other sound following it in a sentence, as at the end of a sentence, or a single word cited by itself, we say that the sound is in **absolute final position.**

   iii. In addition, we will also have occasion to refer to certain sounds that almost always change when they occur in word final position. Obviously such sounds will usually be represented in final position by other sounds. We will call the original sounds (which are important despite the fact that they rarely occur in final position) **original finals**.

3.23 **Possible Absolute Finals**

Despite the large number of sounds in Sanskrit, only a surprisingly small number can occur in **absolute final position**. This is important because, especially with regard to consonants, external सन्धि (*sandhi*) operations are performed on word-finals with the **absolute final** as the point of origin.

3.24 **Vowels in Absolute Final Position**

Any of the vowels, long or short, simple or complex, may occur in absolute final position.

3.25 **Consonants in Absolute Final Position**

a. **Non-palatal stops**

Of the stops (स्पर्श-s (*sparśa*-s) of the वर्ग-s (*varga*-s) other than the palatal (तालव्य—*tālavya*), only the first (non-voiced, non-aspirated) of each वर्ग (*varga*) is possible in absolute final position, i.e., क् (k), ट् (ṭ), त् (t), and प् (p). If others of the series (with either or both of the features of voicing and aspiration) occur as **original finals**, they are replaced by the first of the series.

Examples:

अनुष्टुभ् → अनुष्टुप्; सुहृद् → सुहृत्

anuṣṭubh → anuṣṭup; suhṛd → suhṛt

b. **Palatal stops**

Palatals cannot appear in absolute final position; original final च् → क् (c → k), ज् → ट् or क् (j → ṭ or k).

Examples:

वाच् → वाक्; भिषज् → भिषक्; विराज् → विराट्

vāc → vāk; bhiṣaj → bhiṣak; virāj → virāṭ

c. **Original Final "-स्"** (-s)

The most common of the consonantal original finals, "-स्" (-s), becomes विसर्ग (visarga) ":" (-ḥ) in absolute final position (see 3.26).

d. **Nasals**

"-म्" (-m) and "-न्" (-n) are extremely common in absolute final position but are subject to a number of important changes (see 3.46).

e. **Original Final "-र्" (-r)**

Original final "-र्" (-r) becomes ":" (-ḥ) and behaves **in some environments** like final "-स्" (-s) (see 3.40).

f. **Original Final Consonant Clusters**

Original final consonant clusters are reduced to the first consonant of the cluster.

Example:

गच्छन्त् → गच्छन्

gacchant → gacchan

3.26 सन्धि (*Sandhi*) **of Original Final** "-स्" (-s)

By far the most confusing aspect of nonvocalic सन्धि (*sandhi*) and the one most essential to grasp quickly and thoroughly concerns the phonological permutations of original final "-स्" (-s), which may be replaced with the postvocalic aspiration called विसर्ग (*visarga*) ":" (ḥ) or with the semivowel "र्" (r). The treatment of this sound in the various final positions is a little complex. However, it is especially important to learn, as "-स्" (-s) is among the most common original final sounds in the language.

3.27 Treatment of final विसर्ग (*visarga*) is, like almost everything in Sanskrit grammar, systematic and elegant and should cause little difficulty if learned as such.

3.28 Treatment of original final "-स्" (-s) varies broadly according to whether or not the "-स्" (-s) follows an "अ" (a) vowel or a non-"अ" (a) vowel. The treatment of the final "-स्" (-s) in each of these cases then further depends upon the consonant or vowel that follows; whether or not that sound is voiced or voiceless, and in the case of a voiceless consonant, the वर्ग (*varga*) to which it belongs.

3.29 "-स्" (-s) **Following Any Vowel but** अ (a) **or** आ (ā)

a. Original final "-स्" (-s) becomes विसर्ग (*visarga*) in **absolute final position**.

Example:

अग्निस् → अग्निः agnis → agniḥ (fire)

b. Final "-स्" (-s) before any voiced initial (i.e., any vowel or any **voiced** consonant) becomes "र्" (r).

Examples:

अग्निस् + इव → अग्निरिव

agnis + iva → agnir iva (like fire)

विष्णोस् + आयुधम् → विष्णोरायुधम्

viṣṇos + āyudham → viṣṇor āyudham (Viṣṇu's weapon.)

गतिस् + नास्ति (न + अस्ति) → गतिर्नास्ति

gatis + nāsti (na + asti) → gatir nāsti (no way)

हरेस् + गौस् → हरेर्गौः

hares + gaus → harer gauḥ (Hari's cow)

There is no exception to this rule, but if the following initial voiced sound happens to be an "र्" (r), then to avoid the sequence "rr," there is a further change whereby the first "र्" (r), the result of the change "स्" (s) → "र्" (r), is lost, and in compensation the preceding vowel, if short, is lengthened.

Example:

अग्निस् + रोचते → अग्निर् + रोचते → अग्नि (ø) + रोचते →

agnis + rocate → agnir + rocate → agni (ø) + rocate →

अग्नी रोचते ।

agnī rocate (Fire shines.)

c. Original final "स्" (-s) before non-voiced initials again varies according to two categories of following initial. The categories are:

i. Stops (स्पर्श-s—*sparśa*-s) of the three वर्ग-s (*varga*-s) homorganic with the three non-voiced sibilants

(ऊष्मन्-s—*ūṣman*-s). The sibilants are "श्" (ś), "ष्" (ṣ), and "स्" (s), and they correspond to the palatal (तालव्य—*tālavya*), retroflex (मूर्धन्य—*mūrdhanya*), and dental (दन्त्य—*dantya*) classes. Non-voiced stops (स्पर्श-s—*sparśa*-s) of these वर्ग-s (*varga*-s), then, are the following six:

"च्" (c); "छ्" (ch);

"ट्" (ṭ); "ठ्" (ṭh);

"त्" (t); "थ्" (th).

ii. All other non-voiced consonants (including the sibilants themselves).

3.30 In the first case, original final "-स्" (-s) becomes the sibilant corresponding to the वर्ग (*varga*) of the following initial.

Examples:

हरिस् + चलति → हरिश्चलति ।

haris + calati → hariś calati. (Hari goes.)

विष्णोस् + छाया → विष्णोश्छाया

viṣṇos + chāyā → viṣṇoś chāyā (Viṣṇu's shadow)

हरिस् + टीकां करोति → हरिष्टीकां करोति ।

haris + ṭīkāṃ karoti → hariṣ ṭīkāṃ karoti. (Hari writes a commentary.)

अग्निस् + तीक्ष्णः → अग्निस्तीक्ष्णः ।

agnis + tīkṣṇaḥ → agnis tīkṣṇaḥ (no change) (Fire is fierce.)

a. Of these six stops (स्पर्श-s—*sparśa*-s) only "च" (ca), "छ" (cha), and "त" (ta) are really common in word-initial position. Therefore, the most frequently encountered changes are "स्" → "श्" (s → ś) and "स्" → "स्" (s → s) (no change). Still, if one is aware of the correspondences here, the changes are easy to master.

3.31 Original final "-स्" (-s) before all other non-voiced word-initial phonemes is changed to विसर्ग (*visarga*).

Examples:

हरिस् + पश्यति → हरिः पश्यति ।

haris + paśyati → hariḥ paśyati. (Hari sees.)

हरिस् + खनति → हरिः खनति ।

haris + khanati → hariḥ khanati. (Hari digs.)

3.32 **Original Final "स्" (s) after "अ" (a) Vowels**

The changes of final "स्" (s) after "अ" (a) and "आ" (ā) are peculiar in several ways, and, since the morphological endings "-अस्" (-as) and "-आस्" (-ās) are of extremely common occurrence, it is important to learn the forms these endings take before the various kinds of word-initial phonemes.

3.33 Original final "स्" (s) after "अ" (a) and "आ" (ā) behaves in the same way as original final "स्" (s) after other vowels in **absolute final position** and before **non-voiced initials**.

Examples:

रामस् + पश्यति → रामः पश्यति ।

rāmas + paśyati → rāmaḥ paśyati. (Rāma sees.)

रामस् + सीतां + पश्यति → रामः सीतां पश्यति ।

rāmas + sītāṃ paśyati → rāmaḥ sītāṃ paśyati. (Rāma sees Sītā.)

रामस् + चलति → रामश्चलति ।

rāmas + calati → rāmaś calati. (Rāma goes.)

3.34 Original final "-अस्" (-as) before voiced initials undergoes one of two transformations depending upon whether the initial is

a. any voiced consonant or the vowel (short) "अ" (a), or
b. any vowel other than (short) "अ" (a).

3.35 Before voiced consonants or a short "अ" (a), original final "-अस्" (-as) changes to "-ओ" (-o), while a following initial short "अ" (a) is, additionally, lost.

Examples:

रामस् + गच्छति → रामो गच्छति ।

rāmas + gacchati → rāmo gacchati. (Rāma goes.)

पश्यतस् + राज्ञः → पश्यतो राज्ञः
paśyatas + rājñaḥ → paśyato rājñaḥ
(While the king watches . . .)

रामस् + अयम् → रामो ऽयम् ।
rāmas + ayam → rāmo 'yam. (He is Rāma.)

पश्यतस् + अर्जुनस्य → पश्यतो ऽर्जुनस्य
paśyatas + arjunasya → paśyato 'rjunasya
(While Arjuna watches . . .)

3.36 Before any vowel but short "अ" (a), original final "-अस्" (-as) becomes "अ" (a), and the vowel hiatus remains unchanged.
Examples:
रामस् + उवाच → राम उवाच
rāmas + uvāca → rāma uvāca (Rāma said.)

बुद्धस् + इव विद्यया → बुद्ध इव विद्यया
buddhas + iva vidyayā → buddha iva vidyayā (like the Buddha in wisdom)

3.37 One further restriction on the conditioning of original final "-अस्" (-as) needs to be memorized. This is a restriction not only with regard to phonological environment but a restriction to two specific lexical items.

3.38 Original final "-अस्" (-as), when it ends either of the common nominative singular masculine pronouns "सः" (saḥ) or "एषः" (eṣaḥ) (see 5.5), becomes "अ" (a) before **any consonant**, voiced or unvoiced.
Examples:
सस् + कृष्णस् → स कृष्णः ।
sas + kṛṣṇas → sa kṛṣṇaḥ. (He is Kṛṣṇa.)

एषस् + शुकस् + अस्ति → एष शुको ऽस्ति ।
eṣas + śukas + asti → eṣa śuko 'sti. (That is a parrot.)

3.39 The treatment of original final "आस्" (-ās) is quite simple: "आस्" (-ās) becomes "आ" (-ā) before *any* voiced word-initial (vowel or consonant) without exception.

Examples:

हतास् वीरास् गच्छन्ति स्वर्गलोकम् →

hatās vīrās gacchanti svargalokam →

हता वीरा गच्छन्ति स्वर्गलोकम् ।

hatā vīrā gacchanti svargalokam. (Slain heroes go to heaven.)

3.40 **Original Final** "-अर्" (-ar)

In addition to the very common original final "-अस्" (-as), there occur, in only a very few words, instances of original final "-अर्" (-ar). Original final "-अर्" (-ar) before non-voiced consonants and in absolute final position behaves like final "-अस्"(-as) (see 3.29.c). Before voiced sounds, except "-र्" (-r), it remains. Don't forget, Sanskrit does not allow the consonantal sequence र्र् (rr) (3.29.b).

a. There are a few instances in the language where final "-र्" (-r) is preceded by a vowel other than "अ" (a). The rules for these are the same as those for "-अर्" (-ar).

b. Final "-अर्" (-ar) should not be confused with "-अस्" (-as) despite the fact that 1) original final "स्" (s) (only after a **non "अ" (a) vowel**) becomes "र्" (r) before an initial voiced sound and 2) original final "-अर्" (-ar) becomes "-अः" (-aḥ), "-अश्" (-aś), "-अष्" (-aṣ), or "-अस्" (-as), in the same environments as does original final "-अस्" (-as).

REMEMBER: Before voiced initials, original finals "-अस्" (-as) and "आस्" (-ās) **never** become "-अर्" (-ar) and "-आर्" (-ār), while original final "-अर्" (-ar) **never** becomes "-ओ"(-o). Original final "-अर्" (-ar) is virtually restricted to the two adverbs पुनर् (*punar*—again), and प्रातर् (*prātar*—in the morning).

Learn these words with the original final "-र्" (-r) so as to avoid confusion.

Examples:

पुनर् + पुनर् → पुनः पुनः

punar + punar → punaḥ punaḥ (again and again),

but पुनर् + पुनर् + दानवान् + हन्ति → पुनः पुनर्दानवान्हन्ति

punar +punar +dānavān +hanti → punaḥ punar dānavān hanti

(Again and again he kills the demons.)

प्रातर् + आगमिष्यति → प्रातरागमिष्यति

prātar + āgamiṣyati → prātar āgamiṣyati

(He will come in the morning.)

3.41 **General Principles of Consonant सन्धि** (*Sandhi*)

Just as the avoidance of vowel hiatus serves as a general principle of vowel सन्धि (*sandhi*), so an overriding principle of much consonantal सन्धि (*sandhi*) is the avoidance, to a great extent, of the contact of markedly dissimilar consonants. Such contact, where it occurs, is often mitigated by the alteration of at least one feature of one or sometimes both of the juxtaposed sounds.

3.42 **Assimilation in External सन्धि** (*Sandhi*) **of Final स्पर्श** (*Sparśa*) **Sounds**

The alteration of one or more features of a sound to make it more like another sound is known as **assimilation**. When a sound assimilates to a following sound, the assimilation is said to be **regressive**. When a sound assimilates to a preceding sound, the assimilation is said to be **progressive**. External consonant सन्धि (*sandhi*) generally involves assimilation with respect to the feature of voicing. The assimilation is generally **regressive**.

3.43 In general, a non-voiced final स्पर्श (*sparśa*) of any वर्ग (*varga*) becomes the voiced (non-aspirate) of the same वर्ग (*varga*) before a voiced initial (स्वर—*svara* or व्यञ्जन—*vyañjana*). In general, such finals are unchanged before non-voiced initials.

Examples:

क्रोधात् + भवति + संमोहः → क्रोधाद्भवति संमोहः ।

krodhāt + bhavati + saṃmohaḥ → krodhād bhavati saṃmohaḥ.
(Confusion comes from anger.)

आसीत् + असुरः → आसीदसुरः ।

āsīt + asuraḥ → āsīd asuraḥ. (There was a demon.)

संमोहात् + स्मृतिविभ्रमः → संमोहात्स्मृतिविभ्रमः ।

saṃmohāt + smṛtivibhramaḥ → saṃmohāt smṛtivibhramaḥ.
(Loss of memory arises from confusion.)

3.44 A very important exception is that final "त्" (-t), when it precedes an initial स्पर्श (*sparśa*) of the palatal class (तालव्य—*tālavya* or "च"—ca वर्ग—*varga*) or retroflex class (मूर्धन्य—*mūrdhanya* or "ट"— ṭa वर्ग—*varga*) becomes a de-aspirated स्पर्श (*sparśa*) of the same class as the initial and is voiced or non-voiced just as in 3.43.

Examples:

तत् + चिकीर्षति → तच्चिकीर्षति।

tat + cikīrṣati → tac cikīrṣati. (He wants to do that.)

तत् + जहाति → तज्जहाति ।

tat + jahāti → taj jahāti. (He abandons that.)

3.45 An important corollary of this requires special attention. Final "त्" (-t), when it precedes initial "-श्" (-ś), (the palatal sibilant), becomes "च्" (c) and the following "श्" (ś) becomes "छ्" (ch).

Examples:

तत् + श्रुत्वा + कुपितस् + अभवत् + शिवः →

tat + śrutvā + kupitas + abhavat + śivaḥ →

तच्छ्रुत्वा कुपितो ऽभवच्छिवः ।

tac chrutvā kupito 'bhavac chivaḥ
(Upon hearing that, Śiva became enraged.)

3.46 **External सन्धि (*Sandhi*) of Nasals**

Nasals, whether the first or second of a pair of juxtaposed consonants, constitute exceptions to the above rule in that such consonant contacts generally entail more thorough assimilation than in the case of non-nasal contacts. In external consonant contact involving a nasal, assimilation may affect not only the voicing of a स्पर्श (*sparśa*) but also its mode and even the point of articulation (oral/nasal and वर्ग—*varga*).

3.47 Thus, any word-final stop before a word-initial nasal becomes the nasal of its proper वर्ग (*varga*).

Examples:

एतत् + मा + कुरु → एतन्मा कुरु ।

etat + mā + kuru → etan mā kuru. (Don't do that!)

वाक् + मयः → वाङ्मयः

vāk + mayaḥ → vāñmayaḥ (consisting of speech)

3.48 **सन्धि (*Sandhi*) of Absolute Final Nasals**

Absolute final nasals are subject to a number of rules of varying importance for the beginner.

3.49 By far the most important and most commonly invoked rule concerns absolute final "-म्" (-m), one of the most frequent finals in the language. Final "-म्" (-m) becomes अनुस्वार (*anusvāra*) " ं " (-ṃ) before **any** following initial consonant (voiced or unvoiced).

Examples:

रामस् + वनम् + गच्छति → रामो वनं गच्छति ।

rāmas + vanam + gacchati → rāmo vanaṃ gacchati.
(Rāma goes to the forest.)

ऋषीणाम् + पुस्तकम् + पठति → ऋषीणां पुस्तकं पठति ।

ṛṣīṇām + pustakam + paṭhati → ṛṣīṇāṃ pustakaṃ paṭhati.
(He reads the sages' book.)

There are no exceptions to this rule.

3.50 **Treatment of Absolute Final "-न्" (-n)**

"-न्" (-n), also a common final, is the subject of the following changes.

3.51 Final "-न्" (-n) before a non-voiced stop (स्पर्श—*sparśa*) of the three "sibilant" वर्ग-s (*vargas* -s) (see 3.29.c) becomes अनुस्वार (*anusvāra*) "ं" (ṃ). In addition, the sibilant homorganic with the following initial is inserted between the new final (ṃ) and the initial.

Examples:

कस्मिन् + चित् + नगरे + अवसत् + राजा →

kasmin + cit + nagare + avasat + rājā →

कस्मिंश्चिन्नगरे ऽवसद्राजा ।

kasmiṃś cin nagare 'vasad rājā. (The king lived in a city.)

मूर्खान् + त्यजति + पण्डितः → मूर्खांस्त्यजति पण्डितः ।

mūrkhān + tyajati + paṇḍitaḥ → mūrkhāṃs tyajati paṇḍitaḥ.

(A wise man leaves fools alone.)

3.52 Final "-न्" (-n) before a voiced initial of the तालव्य (*tālavya*) or मूर्धन्य (*mūrdhanya*) वर्ग-s (*varga*-s) becomes the nasal of the वर्ग (*varga*) in question.

Example:

दानवान् + जयति + इन्द्रः → दानवाञ्जयतीन्द्रः ।

dānavān + jayati + indraḥ → dānavāñ jayatīndraḥ.

(Indra conquers the demons.)

3.53 Final "-न्" (-n) before initial "श्" (ś) becomes "ञ्" (ñ), and the "श्" (ś) becomes "छ्" (ch) (cf. 3.45).

Example:

मधुरान् + शब्दान् + शृणोति → मधुराञ्छब्दाञ्छृणोति ।

madhurān + śabdān + śṛṇoti → madhurāñ chabdāñ chṛṇoti.

(He hears sweet sounds.)

3.54 Final "-न्" (-n) before initial "ल्" (l) becomes "ं" (ṃ) (अनुस्वार—*anusvāra*), and an additional "ल्" (l) is inserted before the original one.

Example:

उत्तमान् + लोकान् + लभते + धर्मज्ञः →

uttamān + lokān + labhate + dharmajñaḥ →

उत्तमाँल्लोकाँल्लभते धर्मज्ञः ।

uttamāṃl lokāṃl labhate dharmajñaḥ.

(A knower of *dharma* attains to excellent worlds.)

3.55 Final "ङ्" (-ṅ), "ण्" (-ṇ), and "न्" (-n) are written as doubled when they occur after a short vowel and precede any initial vowel.

Examples:

स्तुवन् + आगच्छति → स्तुवन्नागच्छति ।

stuvan + āgacchati → stuvann āgacchati (He comes praising.)

हसन् + इव → हसन्निव ।

hasan + iva → hasann iva (as though laughing)

3.56 Initial "ह्" (h) after a final स्पर्श (*sparśa*) becomes the voiced aspirated स्पर्श (*sparśa*) of the वर्ग (*varga*) of the preceding final.

Example:

एतत् + हरति + चौरः → एतद्धरति चौरः ।

etat + harati + cauraḥ → etad (3.43) dharati cauraḥ.

(The thief carries that away.)

वाक् + हि + देवता → वाग्घि देवता ।

vāk + hi + devatā → vāgghi devatā. (For speech is a divinity.)

3.57 **Internal सन्धि (*Sandhi*)**

Most of the above rules apply to external सन्धि (*sandhi*) situations. Some, especially those concerning vowel सन्धि (*sandhi*) are applicable to internal सन्धि (*sandhi*) as well. In the case of consonantal सन्धि (*sandhi*), however, the rules for external and internal सन्धि (*sandhi*) often differ considerably. Internal सन्धि (*sandhi*) rules are complex and, moreover, in order to be properly understood, depend upon knowledge of a great variety of different morphological units and processes. Therefore, it is better to leave discussion of most particular internal सन्धि (*sandhi*) rules for consonants to be dealt with as they arise in our survey of the various grammatical categories and forms of Sanskrit. Before proceeding to that survey, however, we may consider two simple but important and very common internal सन्धि (*sandhi*) changes. These are the changes of the दन्त्य ऊष्मन् (*dantya ūṣman*) "स्" (s) and nasal "न्" (n) to the मूर्धन्य ऊष्मन् (*mūrdhanya ūṣman*) "ष्" (ṣ) and nasal "ण्" (ṇ), respectively.

3.58 The dental ऊष्मन् (*ūṣman*) "स्" (s)—if not in *word final* position or followed by the अन्तःस्थ (*antaḥstha*) "र्" (r)—is changed to "ष्" (ṣ) if immediately preceded in a word by any vowel other than the "अ" (a) vowels or by the consonants "क्" (k) or "र्" (r). Examples:

सीदति (*sīdati*—he sits), *but* विषीदति (*viṣīdati*—he sinks down)

-सु (-su—locative plural ending): कन्यासु (*kanyāsu*—among maidens), *but* देवेषु (*deveṣu*—among gods)

-सि (-si—second person singular ending): अत्सि (*atsi*—you eat), *but* भुनक्षि (*bhunakṣi*—you eat)

-स्य (-sya—future tense marker): दास्यति (*dāsyati*—he will give), *but* भविष्यति (*bhaviṣyati*—he will be)

3.59 If the दन्त्य (*dantya*) nasal "न्" (n) is preceded in a word by the मूर्धन्य ऊष्मन् (*mūrdhanya ūṣman*) "ष्" (ṣ), the अन्तःस्थ (*antaḥstha*) "र्" (r), or the vowels "ऋ" (ṛ) or "ॠ" (ṝ), and if no तालव्य (*tālavya*), मूर्धन्य (*mūrdhanya*), or दन्त्य (*dantya*) consonant (except the तालव्य अन्तःस्थ [*tālavya antaḥstha*] "य्" [y]) intervenes between the two, then the "न्" (n) is changed to "ण्" (ṇ) if it is immediately followed by a vowel, semivowel, or nasal.

3.60 This alarmingly conditional rule may seem to be a bit complex for such a seemingly minor change, and perhaps it is. Still, since the change is quite common, it is necessary to know the rule in order to spell many words correctly. For the moment, it will suffice to remember that "न्" (n) when preceded by "र्" (r), "ष्" (ṣ), or "ऋ" (ṛ) is retroflexed in many environments and that the change, therefore, is a common one.

Examples:

राम (*rāma*) + एन (ena—instrumental singular ending) → रामेण (*rāmeṇa*—by Rāma)

ब्रह्मन् (*brahman*—the Absolute) + आ (ā—instrumental singular ending) → ब्रह्मणा (*brahmaṇā*—by the Absolute)

3.61 The operation of these two rules (3.59 and 3.60), in fact, accounts for the great majority of the occurrences of the sounds "ष्" (ṣ) and "ण्" (ṇ) in Sanskrit.

EXERCISES

A. Write out in Roman the following sequences supplying the proper सन्धि (*sandhi*) where necessary. Transliterate into देवनागरी (*devanāgarī*). The words in the section are cited in absolute final form, except for those that have original final र् (r). These sections are graded, you need only perform सन्धि (*sandhi*) relevant to the section numbers.

1. Exercises for 3.1-3.9

   paśyāmi indram
   atra āsīt
   yadā abhavat
   sītā icchati
   parama īśvaraḥ
   yathā īpsitam
   mahā ṛṣiḥ
   sā eva

iti āha
sītā ūrmilā

2. Exercises for 3.10-3.20
vane asti iti uktam
tasmai adadāt pustakam
bhojanaṃ tau ubhau icchataḥ
tasmai eva ahaṃ pustakaṃ dadāmi
kau api gṛhe āsāte

3. Exercises for 3.26-3.40
aśvaḥ āgacchati eva iti uktam
dhanuḥ udaharat
punar punar mānuṣaḥ avadat
devāḥ ūcuḥ
raghuḥ roditi
devāḥ jalpanti evam
muneḥ āgacchati
viśvāmitraḥ atiṣṭhat
rāmaḥ lakṣmaṇaḥ tathā vane avasatām
gataḥ asmi aham
gatā asmi aham
saḥ kṛṣṇaḥ

4. Exercises for entire lesson:
ekasmin ca
sāgaraḥ iva
asti uttarasyām diśi
tataḥ tu
etasmin gate eva sati
ṣaṭ mukhaḥ
mahā uraga
nāga indra
etat eva
bhavān śārdūla
tau ubhau

tau antarikṣagau
asmin granthe
saḥ avasat vane
eṣaḥ puruṣaḥ vanam gacchati
kāmān labhate indravat
śāntapuruṣāt bhayam na asti loke
maitreyyai adadāḥ tvam yājñavalkya
devāḥ ca asurāḥ ca yuddham kurvanti iti uktam

B. Read the following passages aloud and memorize them. They will serve as valuable mnemonic devices for recurrent सन्धि (*sandhi*) problems. Write out the sentences in नागरी (*nāgarī*).

1. sarvaṃ khalv idaṃ brahma (u + i → vi). (All this is indeed Brahman.)
2. mana eva manuṣyāṇāṃ kāraṇaṃ bandhamokṣayoḥ (as + non-"a" vowel). (The mind alone is the cause of men's bondage or liberation.)
3. prāsādaśikhare 'pi san na kāko garuḍāyate (e + a; -as + voiced consonant). (Even on the pinnacle of a palace a crow does not become an eagle.)
4. te hi no divasā gatāḥ ("āḥ" + voiced consonant). (Those days are gone.)
5. so 'ham (as + a). (I am he!)
6. dharmakṣetra ity ārabhyate bhagavad-gītā (e + non-"a" vowel; i + a; t + g). ("On the field of the dharma," so begins the *Bhagavadgītā*.)

LESSON 4

Parts of Speech and the Sanskrit Sentence

4.0 **Conjugation of Verbs; Declension of Nouns and Pronouns**

Despite the fact that Sanskrit preserves many formal distinctions no longer maintained in English, it expresses ideas in sentences that are in many ways quite close to English sentences. A grammatical sentence in either language normally requires that certain categories be filled, either explicitly or implicitly.

4.1 All the words of the Sanskrit language may be divided roughly into three basic types. These may, for the moment, be crudely designated as nominal (nouns and adjectives), verbal, and adverbial.

4.2 It is important at the outset to understand that the only unambiguous basis for this classification is formal rather than functional. In other words, despite grade school training, one should avoid regarding nouns as "things" and verbs as "actions."

4.3 The distinctions that will concern us are as follows:

a. A finite verb, तिङन्त (*tiñanta*), is a word that varies in accordance with **person, number, tense, mode,** and **voice.**

b. A nominal item, सुबन्त (*subanta*), is a word that varies in accordance with **case, number,** and **gender**.

c. An adverbial item अव्ययपद (*avyayapada*) is a word that never varies, (except, of course, when affected by सन्धि [*sandhi*] rules).

4.4 **The Sanskrit Verb**

The Sanskrit verbal system comprises several conjugations. These permutations of several hundred, mostly monosyllabic, verbal roots (धातु-s—*dhātu*-s) constitute perhaps the single most intimidating aspect of the language to the beginner. It must be kept in mind, however, that many of the possible forms are of very rare occurrence and are retained only because of the conservative and artificial nature of the language. In this course we shall be concerned chiefly with a relatively small number of forms which will not absolutely defy your command. Remember, the first rule of learning Sanskrit is **Don't Panic**; everybody in the class is going through the same thing.

4.5 **Finite Verbs**

A finite verb is a verbal root, modified in accordance with the categories of **person, number, tense, mode,** and **voice.** Such modifications comprise the conjugation of a verb. A finite verb is the heart of a Sanskrit sentence. Without a finite verb, either expressed or implied, there can be no complete grammatical sentence or independent clause. On the other hand, a finite verb by itself may (with an implied or expressed subject) constitute a minimal sentence.

Examples:

पश्यामः । हन्यते ।
paśyāmaḥ (we see); hanyate (he, she, it is killed);

त्यजेत् । छिन्दन्ति ।
tyajet (he, she, it should abandon); chindanti (they cut);

करिष्यति । भवतु ।
kariṣyati (he, she, it will do); bhavatu (let it be);

जगाम । अस्मि ।
jagāma (he, she, it went); asmi (I am)

4.6 Thus, the finite verb is the key word of any Sanskrit sentence or independent clause and must be discerned and understood in order to construe the sentence. This fact is basic to the understanding of any sentence, and we shall refer to it repeatedly when discussing the technique of reading a Sanskrit sentence.

4.7 You will have noticed that in the above examples a single word seems to specify the act, the person, the number of actor(s), the time of action, the way or mode in which the speaker intends the action (i.e., as a description, or prescription, or command, or wish, etc.), and even the distinction of passive/active. All these categories are, in fact, specified in a given Sanskrit finite verb and are encoded in a given verbal form by the presence or absence of several series of subverbal units.

4.8 These units are interrelated and may vary according to the other determinants in the same word.

4.9 **Person**

"Person" specifies the relationship among the actor(s) or subject(s) of a finite verb, the user(s) or speaker(s) of the clause or sentence of which the verb forms a part, and the audience, person, thing, or group to whom the sentence is addressed. The possible relationships are:

a. First Person: The actor and the speaker are the same.
   Example:
   आगच्छामि ।
   āgacchāmi (I'm coming.)

b. Second Person: The actor and audience are the same.
   Example:
   तत्त्वमसि ।
   tat tvam asi.(You are that.)

c. Third Person: The actor is neither the speaker nor the audience.
   Examples:
   रामो वदति ।
   rāmo vadati. (Rāma speaks.)

   देवा नन्दन्ति ।
   devā nandanti. (The gods rejoice.)

4.10 Person, then, is used just as in English. First person means that "I" or "we" is the subject of the verb. Second person means that "you" (any number) is the subject of the verb. Third person means that "he, she, it, *or* they" is the subject of the verb.

4.11 Since we shall be using traditional Sanskrit grammatical terminology, it is important to note here that, since verbs tend to be cited in their "third person" form (as opposed to the English practice of citing "infinitives"), the third person is called in Sanskrit प्रथमपुरुष (*prathamapuruṣa*), which means literally "first person." Second person is called मध्यमपुरुष (*madhyama puruṣa*), literally "middle person," and first person is called उत्तमपुरुष (*uttama puruṣa*), literally "last person." Thus, Sanskrit students in India learn their verbal paradigms "upside down" with respect to the way in which paradigms are learned in European languages, insofar as the issue of person is concerned.

4.12 **Number**

This category specifies the number of subjects (or in some cases—see Lesson 9—objects) of a finite verb. Thus, we have in Sanskrit, as in English, a singular and a plural. In addition, Sanskrit has retained a third category, the **dual**, which is used with verbs having two subjects. The numbers with their Sanskrit names and function, are:

Singular—एकवचन (*ekavacana*), speech for one, one subject.
Dual—द्विवचन (*dvivacana*), speech for two, two subjects.
Plural—बहुवचन (*bahuvacana*), speech for many, three or more subjects.

Examples:

एकवचन (*ekavacana*)—शुको वदति
śuko vadati. (The parrot speaks.)

द्विवचन (*dvivacana*)—शुकौ वदतः (*śukau vadataḥ*)
śukau vadataḥ. (The two parrots speak.)

बहुवचन (*bahuvacana*)—शुका वदन्ति
śukā vadanti. (The parrots speak.)

4.13 **Tense**

Generally, the "tense" of a Sanskrit verb indicates the time of the action or state expressed by the verb, relative to the time at which the verb is used. Basically, there are three such times, past (भूतकाल—*bhūtakāla*), present (वर्तमानकाल—*vartamānakāla*), and future (भविष्यत्काल—*bhaviṣyatkāla*), although these do not actually correspond to the tense systems of Sanskrit. These systems will be studied individually.

Examples:

रामो वनं गच्छति ।

rāmo vanaṃ gacchati. (Rāma goes to the forest.)

रामो वनमगच्छत् ।

rāmo vanam agacchat. (Rāma went to the forest.)

रामो वनं गमिष्यति ।

rāmo vanaṃ gamiṣyati. (Rāma will go to the forest.)

वनं जगामेति वक्ष्यति ।

vanaṃ jagāmeti vakṣyati. (He will say, "I went to the forest.")

4.14 **Mode**

Distinctions of mode specify how a finite verb is to be used or how the actor or the subject is related to the action. Important examples are the indicative (description or narration), imperative (injunction, command), and optative (exhoration, prescription).

Examples:

रामो वनं गच्छति ।

rāmo vanaṃ gacchati. (Indicative: Rāma goes to the forest.)

हे राम, वनं गच्छ ।

he rāma, vanaṃ gaccha! (Imperative: Rāma! Go to the forest.)

रामो वनं गच्छेत् ।

rāmo vanaṃ gacchet. (Optative: Rāma should go to the forest.)
(The modes will be learned individually as we proceed.)

4.15 **Voice**

The distinction of voice is one of the most pervasive and initially puzzling aspects of the Sanskrit verbal system. Essentially, it is a binary distinction, encoded along with person and number in the verbal paradigm. What is puzzling about it is not that it presents any special difficulties in memorization. In fact, such difficulty is minimal, as the binary voice-pairs are usually closely similar. The problem is that, for the most part, voice has lost its semantic significance in Sanskrit, persisting in the main as a purely formal, but nonetheless significant, distinction.

4.16 In accordance with the distinction of voice, then a verb is classified as either परस्मैपद (*parasmaipada*—word for another) or आत्मनेपद (*ātmanepada*—word for one's self). These forms are frequently referred to in Western grammars as active and middle voice. However, the Sanskrit terms should be memorized immediately to avoid confusion with the binary pair active/passive, a wholly different issue.

4.17 उभयपद (*Ubhayapada*) **Verbs**

Many verbal roots (धातु-s—*dhātu*-s) of classical Sanskrit are conjugated either in the आत्मनेपद (*ātmanepada*) or the परस्मैपद (*parasmaipada*). However, a large number may be conjugated, sometimes under certain conditions, in either पद (*pada*). Such roots are sometimes called उभयपद (*ubhayapada*—word for both). Still, to facilitate your mastery of the verbal paradigms, and to avoid confusion, in general verbal roots have been cited only in the पद (*pada*) in which they most commonly appear and in which it is, therefore, most convenient to learn them. Thus, in the glossaries, verbal roots will be followed by the signs (Ā) or (P) to indicate either आत्मनेपद (*ātmanepada*) or परस्मैपद (*parasmaipada*).

4.18 These, then, are the major categories involved in the conjugation of Sanskrit verbs. As will be clear from the fact that there are three persons, three numbers, some five modes, four tense systems, and, throughout, two voices, a Sanskrit verb may potentially have a very large number of forms. Of these, however, in the case of a given verb, many never occur or are only theoretical. Of those that do occur, many are rare and even deliberately obscure. Of the remainder, only a small portion are very common and need be mastered in the first year.

4.19 वर्तमाने लट् (*Vartamāne Laṭ*): **The Present Indicative**

The Sanskrit grammarians have, for the sake of precision and concision, designated each of the tenses of the language with its own little code word. All of these words consist of the letter "ल्" (l) followed by a vowel and a consonant. These little code words are often used in conjunction with other words which signify relative time, past (भूत—*bhūta*), present (वर्तमान—*vartamāna*), or future (भविष्य—*bhaviṣya*). One of the most common and useful of the tenses is the present indicative, a tense used for simple description or narration of actions, states, or events occurring in the (relative) present or even the immediate past and future. The grammarians call this tense वर्तमाने लट् (*vartamāne laṭ*).

4.20 The endings for the वर्तमाने लट् (*vartamāne laṭ*) are as follows:

परस्मैपद (*parasmaipada*) active

वचन *vacana* (number) → पुरुष ↓ *puruṣa* (person)	एकवचन *ekavacana*	द्विवचन *dvivacana*	बहुवचन *bahuvacana*
प्रथमपुरुष *prathamapuruṣa*	ति -ti	तः -taḥ	अन्ति -anti
मध्यमपुरुष *madhyamapuruṣa*	सि -si	थः -thaḥ	थ -tha
उत्तमपुरुष *uttamapuruṣa*	मि -mi	वः -vaḥ	मः -maḥ

आत्मनेपद (*ātmanepada*) middle

वचन *vacana* (number) →	एकवचन *ekavacana*	द्विवचन *dvivacana*	बहुवचन *bahuvacana*
पुरुष ↓ *puruṣa* (person)			
प्रथमपुरुष *prathamapuruṣa*	ते -te	आते -āte	अन्ते -ante
मध्यमपुरुष *madhyamapuruṣa*	से -se	आथे -āthe	ध्वे -dhve
उत्तमपुरुष *uttamapuruṣa*	ए -e	वहे -vahe	महे -mahe

Examples:

रामो वनं गच्छति ।
rāmo vanaṃ gaccha*ti*. (Rāma goes to the forest.)

सीतालक्ष्मणावपि वनं गच्छतः ।
sītālakṣmaṇāv api vanaṃ gaccha*taḥ*.
(Sītā and Lakṣmaṇa also go to the forest.)

सीते किं भाषसे ।
sīte! kiṃ bhāṣa*se*? (Sītā, what are you saying?)

यत्र गच्छन्ति वीरास्तत्रापि गच्छाम्यहम् ।
yatra gacch*anti* vīrās tatrāpi gacchā*my* aham.
(Wherever the heroes go, I also go.)

साधु वयमपि गच्छामः ।
sādhu! vayam api gacchā*maḥ*. (Very well. We too are going.)

Note that there are some characteristic clues to person, number, and voice.

a. "–इ" (-i) is typical of the singular active (एकवचन—*ekavacana,* परस्मैपद—*parasmaipada*) and the third person plural (प्रथमपुरुष—*prathamapuruṣa,* बहुवचन—*bahuvacana* परस्मैपद—*parasmaipada*).

b. "-ए" (-e) is characteristic of all the आत्मनेपद (*ātmanepada*) endings.

c. "त्-" (t-) is characteristic of (प्रथमपुरुष—*prathamapuruṣa*, एकवचन—*ekavacana*), the third person singular in both the आत्मनेपद (*ātmanepada*) and परस्मैपद (*parasmaipada*).

Note that the उत्तमपुरुष एकवचन (*uttamapuruṣa ekavacana*—first person singular) आत्मनेपद (*ātmanepada*—middle) ending is simply "ए" (e), with no characteristic consonant. The very important singular voice contrast, then, is:

प्	P	आ	Ā
ति	-ti	ते	-te
सि	-si	से	-se
मि	-mi	ए	-e

4.21 The paradigms for the verbs वद् (√*vad*—speak) परस्मैपद (*parasmaipada*), and भाष् (√*bhāṣ*—speak) आत्मनेपद (*ātmanepada*) are as follows:

वद् (प्) vad (P)	एक° eka	द्वि° dvi	बहु° bahu
प्रथम° prathama°	वदति vadati	वदतः vadataḥ	वदन्ति vadanti
मध्यम° madhyama°	वदसि vadasi	वदथः vadathaḥ	वदथ vadatha
उत्तम° uttama°	वदामि vadāmi	वदावः vadāvaḥ	वदामः vadāmaḥ

भाष् (आ) bhāṣ (Ā)	एक° eka	द्वि° dvi	बहु° bahu
प्रथम° prathama°	भाषते bhāṣate	भाषेते bhāṣete	भाषन्ते bhāṣante
मध्यम° madhyama°	भाषसे bhāṣase	भाषेथे bhāṣethe	भाषध्वे bhāṣadhve
उत्तम° uttama°	भाषे bhāṣe	भाषावहे bhāṣāvahe	भाषामहे bhāṣāmahe

4.22 It is important that the following rules be learned now.

a. When the vowel "-अ-" (-a-) precedes any of the above endings which begin with either "म्" (m) or "व्" (v), it is lengthened.

Examples:

वदति

vadati (He speaks.)

but वदामि

vaḍāmi (I speak.)

गच्छति

gacchati (He goes.)

but गच्छावः

gacchāvaḥ (We two go.)

b. When the vowel "-अ-" (-a-) (short) precedes either of the third person plural endings (प्रथमपुरुष बहुवचन—*prathamapuruṣa bahuvacana*), it is lost.

गच्छ + अन्ति → गच्छन्ति

gaccha + anti → gacchanti (They go.)

भाष + अन्ते → भाषन्ते

bhāṣa + ante → bhāṣante (They speak.)

c. When "-अ-" (-a-) precedes the first person singular middle ending (उत्तमपुरुष एकवचन—*uttamapuruṣa ekavacana*), it is lost.

Example:

मन्य + ते → मन्यते

manya + te → manyate (He thinks.)

but मन्य + ए → मन्ये

manya + e → manye (I think.)

d. After "-अ-" (-a-) the initial "आ" (ā) of the प्रथमपुरुष (*prathamapuruṣa*) and मध्यमपुरुष द्विवचन (*madhymapuruṣa dvivacana*—second and third person dual) आत्मनेपद (*ātmanepada*—middle) ending becomes "ए" (e) and as in the previous rule (c) the "-अ-" (-a-) is lost.

Example:

मन्य + आते → मन्येते

manya + āte → manyete (Two people think.)

e. After any letter *but* "-अ-" (-a-) the nasal "-न्-" (-n-) of the प्रथमपुरुष, बहुवचन, आत्मनेपद (*prathamapuruṣa, bahuvacana, ātmanepada*) is lost.

Example:

युञ्ज् + अन्ते → युञ्जते

yuñj + ante → yuñjate

but युञ्ज् + अन्ति → युञ्जन्ति

yuñj + anti → yuñjanti

4.23 **The verbal root अस् (√*as*—to be)**

One of the most common and useful of the Sanskrit verbal roots is अस् (*as*—to be). It is regularly used in the sense of "there is" or "there are" and is especially common as a copula to establish predication of the sort "A is (are) B," where A and B are any two nouns or a noun and an adjective. One peculiarity of this verb is that, when it is used as a copula, it need not actually appear in the sentence and may be "understood."

Examples:

अस्त्यस्मिन्देशे नृपः ।

asty asmin deśe nṛpaḥ. (There is a king in this country.)

स्वर्गे सन्ति देवाः ।

svarge *santi* devāḥ. (The gods are in heaven.)

रामो नृपः ।

rāmo nṛpaḥ. (*asti* understood) (Rāma is king.)

काकाः कृष्णाः ।

kākāḥ kṛṣṇāḥ. (*santi* understood) (Crows are black.)

वानरो ऽस्मि ।
vānaro *'smi*. (I am a monkey.)
वानरो ऽहम् ।
vānaro 'ham. (*asmi* understood) (I am a monkey.)

One slight problem that arises out of this frequent omission of the copula is that there may be some difficulty, on occasion, in distinguishing between a descriptive and a predicate adjective or between nouns that are in a predicate relationship and those that are in apposition. Thus, the phrase कृष्णः काकः (*kṛṣṇaḥ kākaḥ*) might mean "The crow is black," or "The black crow. . ." By the same token, the phrase दशरथो नृपः (*daśaratho nṛpaḥ*) could mean "Daśaratha is king," or "King Daśaratha . . ." In these and similar examples only the context can serve as a sure guide. It is clear, for example, in sentences like कृष्णः काको वृक्षे वसति । (*kṛṣṇaḥ kākaḥ vṛkṣe vasati*) "The black crow lives in the tree," and दशरथो नृपः सुखं जीवति । (*daśaratho nṛpaḥ sukhaṃ jīvati*) "King Daśaratha lives happily," that the copula is not involved.

4.24 Memorize immediately the वर्तमाने लट् (*vartamāne laṭ*) paradigm of this important verb. अस् (*as*) प् (P)

	एक° eka	द्वि° dvi	बहु° bahu
प्रथम° prathama°	अस्ति asti	स्तः staḥ	सन्ति santi
मध्यम° madhyama°	असि asi	स्थः sthaḥ	स्थ stha
उत्तम° uttama°	अस्मि asmi	स्वः svaḥ	स्मः smaḥ

The irregularities of this paradigm will be discussed in a later chapter.

4.25 Declension: The Sanskrit Noun

Nominal forms together with the finite verbs make up the skeletal structure of the Sanskrit sentence. Just as verbs are conjugated, i.e., vary in accordance with person, number, tense, mode, and voice, so nominal items are "declined," i.e., vary in accordance with gender, number, and case.

4.26 लिङ्ग (*Liñga*) Gender

Gender is a thoroughgoing distinction throughout the declensional system of Sanskrit. Sanskrit, like German, has three genders, masculine (पुंलिङ्ग—*puṃliñga*), feminine (स्त्रीलिङ्ग—*strīliñga*), and neuter (नपुंसकलिङ्ग—*napuṃsakaliñga*). The genders are "natural" insofar as animals and people are usually masculine or feminine according to their sex, but for the most part words simply belong to a given gender on a rather arbitrary basis and must simply be learned with their proper gender.

Examples:

पुरुषः	(*puruṣaḥ*)	(m)	man
देवी	(*devī*)	(f)	goddess
भार्या	(*bhāryā*)	(f)	wife
कन्या	(*kanyā*)	(f)	girl
मित्रम्	(*mitram*)	(n)	friend
ग्रन्थः	(*granthaḥ*)	(m)	book
पुस्तकम्	(*pustakam*)	(n)	book

Adjectives have no inherent gender and take on the gender of the nouns they modify.

4.27 वचन (*Vacana*) Number

As with verbs (4.12), nouns are singular, dual, or plural, depending upon whether one, two, or more than two of the persons, places, things, actions, etc., represented by the noun are indicated.

अजः (*ajaḥ*)—goat; अजौ (*ajau*)—2 goats; अजाः (*ajāḥ*)—goats

Note: The category of number is the only one which is applicable to both nouns and verbs. Because of this, verbs and their subjects (or objects [see Lesson 9]) must always be in number agreement.

Examples:

पुरुषो गच्छति ।

puruṣ*o* gacch*ati* (The man goes.)

पुरुषौ गच्छतः ।

puruṣ*au* gaccha*taḥ* (The two men go.)

पुरुषा गच्छन्ति ।

puruṣ*ā* gacch*anti* (The men go.)

4.28 विभक्ति (*Vibhakti*) **Case**

Cases are a series of formal modifications, marked by special terminations, that define precisely the function of a noun in a sentence, that is, the relation of that noun to a verb or to another noun. The case endings thus serve much the same function that is served in English by word order and prepositions.

4.29 There are seven differentiated case functions in Sanskrit. This fact, although appalling at first, makes for a system that is much more lucid in its fine distinctions than are the declensions of many other Indo-European languages, which must define the same relations with a smaller number of cases. The seven cases विभक्ति-s (*vibhakti*-s) are usually distinguished by the first seven ordinal numbers in Sanskrit and are, with their Sanskrit names, Western names, some principal functions, and corresponding English prepositions:

1. प्रथमा (*prathamā*—first) Nominative, naming, subject, or direct object case.
2. द्वितीया (*dvitīyā*—second) Accusative, direct object case.
3. तृतीया (*tṛtīyā*—third) Instrumental, agentive, or subject case. (with, by)
4. चतुर्थी (*caturthī*—fourth) Dative, indirect object case. (to, for)
5. पञ्चमी (*pañcamī*—fifth) Ablative, source case. (from)

6. षष्ठी (*ṣaṣṭhī*—sixth) Genitive, possessive (partitive) case. (of)

7. सप्तमी (*saptamī*—seventh) Locative, location case. (in, on)

Examples: (numbers following words indicate case)

दशरथस्य वचनं श्रुत्वा नगरान्निःसृत्य

daśarathasya (6) vacanaṃ (2) śrutvā, nagarān (5) niḥsṛtya,

लक्ष्मणेन सहेहागत्य धर्माय वने वसति रामः ।

lakṣmaṇena (3) sahehāgatya, dharmāya (4) vane (7) vasati rāmaḥ (1).

Having heard *Daśaratha's* (6) *speech* (2), having come out *from the city* (5), and having come here *with Lakṣmaṇa* (3), *Rāma* (1) lives *in the forest* (7) for *the sake of righteousness* (4).

4.30 To this list is often added an eighth item which is not a true case. This is the vocative, or संबोधन (*saṃbodhana*), the form of direct address.

Example:

हरे कृष्ण हरे कृष्ण कृष्ण कृष्ण हरे हरे ।

hare kṛṣṇa, hare kṛṣṇa, kṛṣṇa kṛṣṇa, hare hare

O Hari! O Kṛṣṇa, etc.

4.31 Sanskrit nouns fall into several declensions depending upon their phonological structure (predeclension stem final) and inherent gender.

4.32 **The Citation of Nouns**

Although it is common practice in the West to cite Sanskrit nouns in their stem forms (i.e., predeclensional forms), we shall depart from this practice to a certain extent. For "-अ-" (-a-) stems particularly, it is advisable to learn the nouns in their nominative singular form. In this way, the gender of each item can be learned along with the word itself. These nominative forms should then be cited in absolute final position. For example, cite पुरुष (*puruṣa*) as पुरुषः (*puruṣaḥ*) (nom. sing. masc.)

"man"; and cite पुस्तक (*pustaka*) as पुस्तकम् (*pustakam*) (nom. sing. neut.) "book." Nouns ending in other vowels, particularly "ऋ" (ṛ) and in consonants should be learned **both** in stem-form and nominative singular.

Examples:

stem	*nom.*	
पितृ (*pitṛ*) (m)	पिता (*pitā*)	father
राजन् (*rājan*) (m)	राजा (*rājā*)	king
ब्रह्मन् (*brahman*) (n,m)	ब्रह्म (*brahma*) (n)	brahman
	ब्रह्मा (*brahmā*) (m)	Brahmā

4.33 Declension of the "-अ-" (-a-) stems.

Example: पुरुषः (*puruṣaḥ*) पुंलिङ्ग (*puṃliñga*) (masculine) man

वचन vacana →	एक° eka°	द्वि° dvi°	बहु° bahu°
विभक्ति ↓ vibhakti			
प्रथमा prathamā	पुरुषः puruṣaḥ	पुरुषौ puruṣau	पुरुषाः puruṣāḥ
द्वितीया dvitīyā	पुरुषम् puruṣam	पुरुषौ puruṣau	पुरुषान् puruṣān
तृतीया tṛtīyā	पुरुषेण puruṣeṇa	पुरुषाभ्याम् puruṣābhyām	पुरुषैः puruṣaiḥ
चतुर्थी caturthī	पुरुषाय puruṣāya	पुरुषाभ्याम् puruṣābhyām	पुरुषेभ्यः puruṣebhyaḥ
पञ्चमी pañcamī	पुरुषात् puruṣāt	पुरुषाभ्याम् puruṣābhyām	पुरुषेभ्यः puruṣebhyaḥ
षष्ठी ṣaṣṭhī	पुरुषस्य puruṣasya	पुरुषयोः puruṣayoḥ	पुरुषाणाम् puruṣāṇām
सप्तमी saptamī	पुरुषे puruṣe	पुरुषयोः puruṣayoḥ	पुरुषेषु puruṣeṣu
सम्बोधन sambodhana (vocative)	पुरुष puruṣa	पुरुषौ puruṣau	पुरुषाः puruṣāḥ

Example: पुस्तकम् (*pustakam*) नपुंसकलिङ्ग (*napuṃsakaliṅga*) (neuter) book

वचन vacana →	एक° eka°	द्वि° dvi°	बहु° bahu°
विभक्ति ↓ vibhakti			
प्रथमा prathamā	पुस्तकम् pustakam	पुस्तके pustake	पुस्तकानि pustakāni
द्वितीया dvitīyā	पुस्तकम् pustakam	पुस्तके pustake	पुस्तकानि pustakāni
तृतीया tṛtīyā.	पुस्तकेन pustakena	पुस्तकाभ्याम् pustakābhyām	पुस्तकैः pustakaiḥ
चतुर्थी caturthī	पुस्तकाय pustakāya	पुस्तकाभ्याम् pustakābhyām	पुस्तकेभ्यः pustakebhyaḥ
पञ्चमी pañcamī	पुस्तकात् pustakāt	पुस्तकाभ्याम् pustakābhyām	पुस्तकेभ्यः pustakebhyaḥ
षष्ठी ṣaṣṭhī	पुस्तकस्य pustakasya	पुस्तकयोः pustakayoḥ	पुस्तकानाम् pustakānām
सप्तमी saptamī	पुस्तके pustake	पुस्तकयोः pustakayoḥ	पुस्तकेषु pustakeṣu
सम्बोधन sambodhana	पुस्तक pustaka	पुस्तके pustake	पुस्तकानि pustakāni

4.34 The declensions of the masculine and neuter stems differ *only* in the first and second cases. This is true of almost all sets of masculine and neuter nouns with the same stem final.

4.35 The संबोधन (*saṃbodhana*), or vocative, form differs from the nominative **only** in the singular. This is true of all nouns regardless of stem final or gender.

4.36 **Memorization of paradigms**

This is perhaps the least stimulating aspect of language learning. Unfortunately, however, it is necessary to memorize at least the major paradigms in order to avoid constant reference to grammar books. Paradigms should be learned in the traditional

Indian fashion (i.e., case by case "across" the number). Thus, the declension of पुरुषः (*puruṣaḥ*) should be recited as पुरुषः (*puruṣaḥ*) / पुरुषौ (*puruṣau*) / पुरुषाः (*puruṣāḥ*); पुरुषम् (*puruṣam*) / पुरुषौ (*puruṣau*) / पुरुषान् (*puruṣān*); etc. In the same way, the conjugation of verbs is learned person by person "across" the number. Thus, the conjugation of वदति (*vadati*) should be recited as: वदति (*vadati*) / वदतः (*vadataḥ*) / वदन्ति (*vadanti*); वदसि (*vadasi*) / वदथः (*vadathaḥ*) / वदथ (*vadatha*); etc.

4.37 **Parts of Speech, the** क्रियापद (*kriyāpada*) **and the** कर्तृ (*kartṛ*)

a. As mentioned above (4.6) a finite verbal form may be considered to be the heart of and indeed, the minimal requirement for a grammatical Sanskrit sentence. Considered as an element of a sentence, such a verbal form may be called the क्रियापद (*kriyāpada*—action word) in that it is expressive of the action or state that is indicated by a given verbal धातु (*dhātu*) or root. There is normally only one finite verb in a clause.

b. The next most important word, or group of words in a sentence is the कर्तृ (*kartṛ*), the agent or **subject**. The कर्तृ (*kartṛ*) denotes the person, thing, place, or even abstract concept that carries out the action or experiences the state or condition expressed by the धातु (*dhātu*). All grammatical sentences must have a finite verb (or some equivalent form) and a nominal subject whether or not the words for those items actually appear in the sentence. Thus, in the sentence रामः पश्यति (*rāmaḥ paśyati*—Rāma sees), the word पश्यति (*paśyati*—sees), which is the प्रथमपुरुष (*prathamapuruṣa*) एकवचन (*ekavacana*) परस्मैपद (*parasmaipada*) वर्तमाने लट् (*vartamāne laṭ*) of the root पश् (*paś*), is clearly the क्रियापद (*kriyāpada*). The ending "-ति" (-ti) here specifies the number of the subject. If we ask now "Who sees?" we must answer "Rāma." "Rāma" then is the कर्तृ (*kartṛ*) or the subject; the one who does the seeing. It is important to note here, for later reference, that the subject कर्तृ (*kartṛ*) of a Sanskrit sentence is **always** the agent of the action, regardless of whether the sentence is "active" or "passive." Thus, although we might say that "dog" is the subject of the English sentence, "The dog bites the man," but that "man" is the subject of the sentence, "The man is bitten by the dog," Sanskrit grammarians would not hesitate for a moment in saying that "dog," the biter, is the कर्तृ (*kartṛ*) of both.

4.38 **Parts of Speech Continued: सकर्मक** (*sakarmaka*) **and अकर्मक** (*akarmaka*) **धातु-s** (*dhātu*-s) **and the कर्मन्** (*karman*).

The verbal **धातु-s** (*dhātu*-s) must be distinguished according to whether or not they express an action that may have, in addition to the necessary कर्तृ (*kartṛ*) an immediate and direct recipient of its force. This distinction corresponds to the one we know that separates **transitive** from **intransitive** verbs. The immediate recipient of the force of an action is called the कर्मन् (*karman*) or **direct object**. Transitive roots are said to be सकर्मकधातु-s (*sakarmakadhātu*-s—roots with a direct object) while intransitive roots are called अकर्मकधातु-s (*akarmakadhātu*-s—roots without a direct object). In general, it is correct to say that a Sanskrit root is सकर्मक (*sakarmaka*) when its English equivalent is transitive. The equivalence holds for अकर्मक (*akarmaka*) or intransitive roots. One should note here, however, a peculiarity concerning the treatment in Sanskrit of verbs of motion (see 4.41). Despite the fact that such verbs are regarded, like their English equivalents, as intransitive, it is the usual practice in Sanskrit to place the *goals* of motion in the cases appropriate to the genuine direct objects. Thus, in the sentence रामो नृपं पश्यति । (*rāmo nṛpaṃ paśyati*—Rāma sees the king), नृपः (*nṛpaḥ*), the one who is seen, is thereby the कर्मन् (*karman*) or the direct object of the verbal धातु (*dhātu*) पश् (*paś*). This too, would be so whether the sentence were active or passive. In addition, in the sentence रामो वनं गच्छति । (*rāmo vanaṃ gacchati*—Rāma goes to the forest), वनम् (*vanam*), the goal of Rāma's going, is treated like a direct object.

4.39 **The Cases and Their Functions**

It is by no means accurate to say that each case has one and only one function. Some of the cases may have several functions in different contexts while one function may be served by more than one case. Moreover, even so cultivated a language as Sanskrit shows numerous examples of what may be called "loose construction," whereby a case may be forced to serve a function other than its own. This is especially true in the language of the epics. On the other hand, it is true that each case generally does have, if not one, then a fairly restricted range of uses. It is these significant uses that must be learned now.

4.40 **प्रथमा विभक्ति** (*Prathamā Vibhakti*): **The Nominative Case**

The प्रथमा विभक्ति (*prathamā vibhakti*) has a variety of functions, all of which may be subsumed under the heading of "naming." It is unique among the cases in that it is used to name or specify parts of speech whose form has already been determined by the form of a finite verb. Thus when a nominal item in a sentence appears in the प्रथमा विभक्ति (*prathamā vibhakti*), it must be in number agreement with a finite verb whether that verb actually occurs in the sentence or is "understood." The full application of this mysterious statement will not be clear until you have studied the contents of Lesson 9. Until then, however, it will suffice to say that, in general, the प्रथमा विभक्ति (*prathamā vibhakti*), is used to denote the subject of a finite verb in a clause or sentence. It may also be used as the citation case for a noun.

Examples:

नृपो वदति ।

nṛpo vadati. (*The king* speaks.)

ब्राह्मणौ नृपं पश्यतः ।

brāhmaṇau nṛpaṃ paśyataḥ. (*The two brāhmans* see the king.)

तत्र पुस्तकानि न सन्ति ।

tatra *pustakāni* na santi. (There are no *books* there.)

4.41 द्वितीया विभक्ति (*Dvitīyā Vibhakti*): **The Accusative Case**

The द्वितीया विभक्ति (*dvitīyā vibhakti*) or accusative case is predominantly the case that marks the direct object of a transitive verb or the goal of a verb of motion.

Examples:

पुरुषो मृगं हन्ति ।

puruṣo *mṛgaṃ* hanti. (The man kills *the deer.*)

ब्राह्मणाः पुस्तकानि पश्यन्ति ।

brāhmaṇāḥ *pustakāni* paśyanti. (The brāhmans see *the books.*)

रामो वनं गच्छति ।

rāmo *vanaṃ* gacchati. (Rāma goes to the forest.) (See 4.38.)

It may also be used with words meaning units of time to indicate duration.

Example:

रामः संवत्सरं वने वसति ।

rāmaḥ saṃvatsaraṃ vane vasati. (Rāma lives in the forest *for a year.*)

The accusative singular of many nouns may be used adverbially. The resulting forms are, of course, अव्ययपद-s (*avyayapada*-s—indeclinables).

Examples:

अस्ति नृपो दशरथो नाम ।

asti nṛpo daśaratho *nāma*. (There is a king *by name* Daśaratha.)

दशरथः सुखं जीवति ।

daśarathaḥ *sukhaṃ* jīvati. (Daśaratha lives *happily.*)

4.42 तृतीया विभक्ति (*Tṛtīyā Vibhakti*): **The Instrumental Case**

The तृतीया विभक्ति (*tṛtīyā vibhakti*) or instrumental case, serves several functions.

a. It is the case of agency or accompaniment.
   Example:
   शरेण हन्ति बालकम् ।
   śareṇa hanti bālakam. (He kills the boy *with an arrow.*)
   When accompaniment is meant, the instrumental is frequently followed by one of three अव्यय (*avyaya*) words: सह (*saha*), समम् (*samam*), or साकम् (*sākam*).
   Example:
   दशरथेन सह संवदति ब्राह्मणः ।
   daśarathena saha saṃvadati brāhmaṇaḥ.
   (The brāhman converses *with Daśaratha.*)

b. The तृतीया विभक्ति is the agent or subject case in so-called "passive," or कर्मणि प्रयोग (*karmaṇi prayoga*) constructions, (Lesson 9)

c. The तृतीया विभक्ति (*tṛtīyā vibhakti*) has a number of important idiomatic usages, among which you should learn the following:

   1. With the अव्यय (*avyaya*) word विना (*vinā*) the तृतीया विभक्ति (*tṛtīyā vibhakti*) (like the accusative and sometimes the ablative) is used to indicate the absence of something in the sense of "without," or "excluding."
      Example:
      बालकेन विना वनं गच्छति ब्राह्मणः ।
      bālakena *vinā* vanaṃ gacchati brāhmaṇaḥ.
      (The brāhman goes to the forest *without* the boy.)

   2. With the invariable word अलम् (*alam*—enough, sufficient), the instrumental is used in the sense of "enough of . . !"

Example:
अलमनेन वचनेन ।
alam anena vacanena! (Enough of this talk!)

3. With the interrogative pronoun किम् (*kim*), the तृतीया विभक्ति is used in the sense of "what of (it)," signifying lack of interest or belief in the relevance or use of something.
   Example:
   किमनेन पुस्तकेन ।
   kim anena pustakena? (What's the use of this book?)

4.43 षष्ठी विभक्ति (*Ṣaṣṭhī Vibhakti*): **The Genitive Case**

The षष्ठी विभक्ति (*ṣaṣṭhī vibhakti*) or genitive, is the possessive case, and unlike the other cases, it generally relates one noun to another.

Examples:
ब्राह्मणस्य पुत्रः ।
brāhmaṇasya putraḥ (the son *of the brāhman*)

ब्राह्मणस्य पुत्रस्य मित्रम् ।
brāhmaṇasya putrasya mitram
(the friend *of the son of the brāhman*)

It is very commonly used with a verb "to be" to indicate possession, as Sanskrit has no verb really equivalent to English "to have." In this important construction the possessor is put in the genitive while the thing possessed in the nominative is the subject of the copula.

Examples:
ब्राह्मणस्य पुत्रो नास्ति ।
brāhmaṇasya putro nāsti. (*The brāhman* has no son.)

दशरथस्य द्वे पुस्तके (स्तः) ।
daśarathasya dve pustake (staḥ). (*Daśaratha has two books.*)

4.44 **Word Order**

Since the case endings of Sanskrit so precisely specify the relationships of all the parts of speech, there is no need for the rigidly restricted word order associated with English. For example the sentence रामो मृगं पश्यति । (*rāmo mṛgaṃ paśyati*— Rāma sees the deer) will be perfectly clear, regardless of the sequence of the words. Thus, मृगं पश्यति रामः । पश्यति रामो मृगं । (*mṛgaṃ paśyati rāmaḥ; paśyati rāmo mṛgaṃ*); both mean exactly the same thing. This is clearly not the case with the English translation. Because of this, word order is relatively free in Sanskrit, and in some cases, because of the requirements of metrical composition, words of a complex sentence may occur in fairly jumbled order with, for example, a noun and its modifier at opposite ends of the sentence. However, there is a general order of words in Sanskrit prose to which we should closely adhere when composing sentences, unless there is an overriding reason to ignore it. The order is basically subject-object-verb. Other parts of speech are inserted within this framework, and all modifiers of a given noun should be contiguous.

For example:

राक्षसानां नृपो दशरथस्य पुत्रं रामं सरोषं पश्यति ।

rākṣasānāṃ *nṛpo (*subj.) daśarathasya *putraṃ rāmaṃ (*obj.) *saroṣaṃ paśyati (*adverb-verb).

(The king of the rākṣasas views Daśaratha's son Rāma with anger.)

One regular departure from this order is that narratives, or stories, often begin with a form of the verb अस् (*as*—to be).

Example:

अस्ति नृपो दशरथो नाम ।

asti nṛpo daśaratho nāma.

(There is a king named Daśaratha.)

4.45 Personal Pronouns

Sanskrit has a large and varied system of personal and demonstrative pronouns (सर्वनामन्-s—*sarvanāman*-s), and it is convenient to learn this system as quickly as possible. The pronouns of the first two persons उत्तमपुरुष (*uttamapuruṣa*) and मध्यमपुरुष (*madhyamapuruṣa*) are closely analogous and are alike in not distinguishing gender.

4.46 a. अहम् (*aham*—I): The उत्तमपुरुष (*uttamapuruṣa*) or first person pronoun.

वचन vacana →	एक° eka°	द्वि° dvi°	बहु° bahu°
विभक्ति ↓ vibhakti			
1.	अहम् aham	आवाम् āvām	वयम् vayam
2.	माम् (मा) mām (mā)	आवाम् āvām	अस्मान् (नः) asmān (naḥ)
3.	मया mayā	आवाभ्याम् āvābhyām	अस्माभिः asmābhiḥ
4.	मह्यम् (मे) mahyam (me)	आवाभ्याम् āvābhyām	अस्मभ्यम् (नः) asmabhyam (naḥ)
5.	मत् mat	आवाभ्याम् āvābhyām	अस्मत् asmat
6.	मम (मे) mama (me)	आवयोः āvayoḥ	अस्माकम् (नः) asmākam (naḥ)
7.	मयि mayi	आवयोः āvayoḥ	अस्मासु asmāsu

b. त्वम् (*tvam*): Just as the pronoun of the first person is derived from various stems मत् (*mat*), अस्मत् (*asmat*), etc., so that of the second person त्वम् (*tvam*) is similarly derived from त्वत् (*tvat*), युष्मत् (*yuṣmat*), etc.

वचन vacana →	एक° eka°	द्वि° dvi°	बहु° bahu°
विभक्ति ↓ vibhakti			
1.	त्वम् tvam	युवाम् yuvām	यूयम् yūyam
2.	त्वाम् (त्वा) tvām (tvā)	युवाम् yuvām	युष्मान् (वः) yuṣmān (vaḥ)
3.	त्वया tvayā	युवाभ्याम् yuvābhyām	युष्माभिः yuṣmābhiḥ
4.	तुभ्यम् (ते) tubhyam (te)	युवाभ्याम् yuvābhyām	युष्मभ्यम् (वः) yuṣmabhyam (vaḥ)
5.	त्वत् tvat	युवाभ्याम् yuvābhyām	युष्मत् yuṣmat
6.	तव (ते) tava (te)	युवयोः yuvayoḥ	युष्माकम् (वः) yuṣmākam (vaḥ)
7.	त्वयि tvayi	युवयोः yuvayoḥ	युष्मासु yuṣmāsu

The shorter forms in parentheses which follow some of the forms above are equivalent but are generally subordinate in that they can never occur at the beginning of a sentence or in position of great emphasis.

Examples:

तव दासो ऽहम् ।

tava dāso 'ham. (I am your servant.)

वयं न जानीमः ।

vayaṃ na jānīmaḥ. (We don't know.)

पुस्तकं नः पठति ।

pustakaṃ naḥ paṭhati. (He reads our book.)

मम भार्या ग्रामं गच्छति ।
mama bhāryā grāmaṃ gacchati. (My wife is going to the village.)

Note: These forms are declined pronouns and not adjectives. Therefore, there is no issue of agreement between them and the things they appear to modify. Keep this in mind especially with regard to the षष्ठी (*ṣaṣṭhī*) or the genitive case.
Examples:
मम पुत्रः । (*mama putraḥ*) (m) my son
मम भार्या । (*mama bhāryā*) (f) my wife
मम पुस्तकम् । (*mama pustakam*) (n) my book

4.47 निपात (*Nipāta*): **Particles**

a. The particle स्म (*sma*), when it appears after a लट् (*laṭ*—present indicative) form, makes of the form a simple past tense.
Examples:
गच्छति । gacchati. (He goes.)
गच्छति स्म । gacchati sma.(He went.)

b. The particle इति (*iti*) is one of the most important and useful of the Sanskrit particles. It functions frequently as a quotation mark immediately after the speech, thought, or idea quoted. Since Sanskrit rarely uses indirect quotation, the use of इति (*iti*) is extremely common. Thus, नृपो ऽहमिति वदति । (*nṛpo 'ham iti vadati*), "He says he is the king" or literally, "He says, 'I am the king'." इति (*iti*), then, has the function of setting off independent sentences within sentences. Thus, in the above example there are two sentences; नृपो ऽहम् (*nṛpo 'ham*—I am the king); and वदति (*vadati*—he says). Unless the इति (*iti*) is understood, the two will be confused and difficult to separate. If you find an इति (*iti*) in a sentence, then, use it as a convenient point to break the sentence down into smaller, more manageable units.

EXERCISES

A. Translate the reading selection into English.

B. Translate the following sentences into Sanskrit.

1. The brāhman's son sees the angry king.
2. The people say that our king is a fool. (Use *iti.*)
3. The king and the brāhman see our son. (Use dual.)
4. The king kills the beautiful deer with your arrow.
5. The brāhman says again that the king does an evil act. (Use *iti.*)
6. Rāma, the son of king Daśaratha, dwells there without sorrow.
7. King Daśaratha, afflicted with sorrow, thinks, "How will I live without a son?"
8. The angry brāhman sees and curses the righteous king.
9. The king, though a young man, experiences grief.
10. "Oh! Rāma is afraid," thinks the fool. (Use *iti.*)
11. The fool sees the two slain deer and again becomes very angry.
12. The beautiful boy and the righteous king live in the forest.
13. I have a sharp arrow. You have (two) sharp arrows. (Use द्विवचन.) We have (many) sharp arrows. (Use बहुवचन.) (See 4.43.)
14. We both think that the king is angry.
15. How do you (all) afflicted with misery speak to righteous people (use द्वितीया विभक्ति)?

READING

॥ श्रीरामस्य चरितम् ॥

अस्ति नृपो दशरथो नाम । सो ऽतीव धार्मिको भूमिपः सुखं जीवति । नृपस्य दुःखं नास्तीति भाषन्ते जनाः । एकदा दशरथो वनं गच्छति । तस्मिन्वने* ब्राह्मणस्य पुत्रो वसति । अहो सुन्दरं मृगं पश्याम्यहमिति चिन्तयति नृपः । बालकं च तीक्ष्णेन शरेण हन्ति । ब्राह्मण आगच्छति हतं पुत्रं पश्यति च । सो ऽतीव कुपितो भवति । नृपं च शपति । हे मूर्ख । त्वं किमिति मम पुत्रं हंसि । तव दुष्कृतेनाहं दुःखमनुभवामि । पुत्रेण विना न जीवामि । त्वमप्यहमिव पुत्राच्छोकमनुभवसीति । नृपो वदति । हा हा नश्यामीति । शोकेन पीडितो गृहं गच्छति ॥

---

* See 5.5

GLOSSARY

ABBREVIATIONS

m—masculine

f—feminine

n—neuter

adj—adjective

ind—indeclinable

prop—proper name

pr—pronoun

Ā—ātmanepada (numbers are *gaṇa*-s) (See Lesson 7)

P—parasmaipada (numbers are *gaṇa*-s)

अतीव

atīva (ind)—exceedingly, very

अनु + भू (अनुभवति)

anu + √bhū (1P) (anubhavati)—experience, feel

अपि

api (ind)—also, too, even; question marker indefinitiser (with interrogative pronouns) (see 6.19)

अस् (अस्ति)

√as (2P) (asti)—be

अहम्

aham (pr)—I (See 4.46.a)

अहो

aho (ind)—"Aha!" "Oh!"

आ + गम् (आगच्छति)

ā + √gam (1P) (āgacchati)—come

इति

iti (ind)—quotation mark (see 4.47.b)

इव

iva (ind)—like, as (follows word to which it refers)

एकदा

ekadā (ind)—once, one time

एवम्

evam (ind)—thus, in this way

कथम्

katham (ind)—how? How is it . . . ?

किमिति

kimiti (idiom)—What's this?, why?

कुपित

kupita (adj)—enraged, angry

कृ (करोति)

√kṛ (8P) (karoti)—do, make (See glossary lesson 5)

गम् (गच्छति)

√gam (1P) (gacchati)—go

गृहम्

gṛham (n)—house, home

च
ca (ind)—and (placed after a series or between each pair of a series, e.g., रामश्च लक्ष्मणश्च or रामो लक्ष्मणश्च)

चरितम्
caritam (n)—adventures, life story

चिन्त् (चिन्तयति)
√cint (10P) (cintayati)—think, consider

जनः
janaḥ (m)—person; as collective noun—people; plural—folk

जीव् (जीवति)
√jīv (1P) (jīvati)—live, survive

तत्र
tatra (ind)—there, with regard to that

तीक्ष्ण
tīkṣṇa (adj)—sharp

त्वम्
tvam (pr)—you (See 4.46.b)

दशरथः
daśarathaḥ (m) (prop)—famous king, Rāma's father

दुःखम्
duḥkham (n)—sorrow, misery

दुष्कृतम्
duṣkṛtam (n)—evil act

धार्मिक
dhārmika (adj)—righteous

न
na (ind)—negative particle

नश् (नश्यति)
√naś (4P) (naśyati)—perish, be destroyed

नाम
nāma (ind)—"by name," namely

नृपः
nṛpaḥ (m)—king

पश् (पश्यति)
√paś (4P) (paśyati)—see

पीडित
pīḍita (adj)—afflicted, oppressed

पुत्रः
putraḥ (m)—son

पुनः (पुनर्)
punaḥ (punar) (ind)—again; पुनःपुनः again and again, (for सन्धि see 3.40)

बालकः
bālakaḥ (m)—boy, young man

ब्राह्मणः
brāhmaṇaḥ (m)—a brāhman

भाष् (भाषते)
√bhāṣ (1Ā) bhāṣate—speak, say, address

भीत

bhīta (adj)—afraid

भू (भवति)

√bhū (1P) (bhavati)—be, become

भूमिपः

bhūmipaḥ (m)—king

मन् (मन्यते)

√man (4Ā) (manyate)—think

मूर्खः

mūrkhaḥ (m)—fool

मृगः

mṛgaḥ (m)—deer

वद् (वदति)

√vad (1P) (vadati)—speak

वनम्

vanam (n)—forest

वस् (वसति)

√vas (1P) (vasati)—dwell

विना

vinā (ind)—without (use after द्वितीया, तृतीया or पञ्चमी विभक्ति)

शप् (शपति)

√śap (1P) (śapati)—curse

शरः

śaraḥ (m)—arrow

शोकः

śokaḥ (m)—grief, sorrow

सः

saḥ (pr)—he (See 5.5, and 3.38)

श्रीरामः

śrīrāmaḥ (m) (prop)—"glorious Rāma"

सुखम्

sukham (ind)—happily

सुन्दर

sundara (adj)—beautiful, handsome

स्म

sma (ind—see 4.47) (used after लट् to form simple past tense)

स्वयम्

svayam (ind)—by one's self, to one's self

हत

hata (adj)—killed

हन् (हन्ति)

√han (2P) (hanti)—kill, strike

हा

hā (ind)—vocative particle ("Ah") expressing grief

हे

he (ind)—vocative particle ("O") precedes vocative

LESSON 5

स्त्रीलिङ्ग (*strīliñga*—Feminine) Nouns in आ (ā); चतुर्थी, पञ्चमी and सप्तमी विभक्ति-s (Caturthī, Pañcamī and Saptamī Vibhakti-s); Demonstrative Pronouns

5.0 In addition to the पुंलिङ्ग (*puṃliñga*—masculine) and नपुंसकलिङ्ग (*napuṃsakaliñga*—neuter) nouns in -अ (-a), there is an important class of स्त्रीलिङ्ग (*strīliñga*—feminine) nouns in -आ (-ā). Some of these nouns are related in meaning to some of the पुंलिङ्ग (*puṃliñga*—masculine) nouns in -अ (-a).

Examples:

बालः (*bālaḥ*) boy   बाला (*bālā*) girl

सुतः (*sutaḥ*) son   सुता (*sutā*) daughter

5.1 The paradigm is as follows: कन्या (*kanyā*) girl, daughter

वचन vacana →	एक° eka°	द्वि° dvi°	बहु° bahu°
विभक्ति ↓ vibhakti			
1.	कन्या kanyā	कन्ये kanye	कन्याः kanyāḥ
2.	कन्याम् kanyām	कन्ये kanye	कन्याः kanyāḥ
3.	कन्यया kanyayā	कन्याभ्याम् kanyābhyām	कन्याभिः kanyābhiḥ
4.	कन्यायै kanyāyai	कन्याभ्याम् kanyābhyām	कन्याभ्यः kanyābhyaḥ
5.	कन्यायाः kanyāyāḥ	कन्याभ्याम् kanyābhyām	कन्याभ्यः kanyābhyaḥ
6.	कन्यायाः kanyāyāḥ	कन्ययोः kanyayoḥ	कन्यानाम् kanyānām
7.	कन्यायाम् kanyāyām	कन्ययोः kanyayoḥ	कन्यासु kanyāsu
sam.	कन्ये kanye	कन्ये kanye	कन्याः kanyāḥ

Note that although the paradigm differs considerably from the ones already learned, particularly in the singular, several endings remain the same. Note especially the चतुर्थी (*caturthī*) and षष्ठी (*ṣaṣṭhī*) बहु° (*bahu*°), the षष्ठी (*ṣaṣṭhī*) and सप्तमी (*saptamī*) द्वि° (*dvi*°), and the तृतीया (*tṛtīyā*), चतुर्थी (*caturthī*) and पञ्चमी (*pañcamī*) द्वि° (*dvi*°). These endings— -आम् (-ām), -ओः (-oḥ), -भ्यः (-bhyaḥ), -भ्याम् (-bhyām)—are the same for all stems of all genders in the language.

5.2 चतुर्थी विभक्ति (*Caturthī Vibhakti*): **The Dative Case**

a. The fourth, or so-called dative case, is the case of the indirect object. It expresses the relations covered in English by the prepositions "to" and "for." It is also regularly used in the sense of "for the purpose of."
Examples:
द्विजो भार्यायै सर्वं ददाति, वनं च गच्छति ।
dvijo *bhāryāyai* sarvaṃ dadāti, vanaṃ ca gacchati.
(The brāhman gives everything *to his wife* and goes to the forest.)

युद्धायागच्छामीति भणति वीरः ।
*yuddhāyā*gacchāmīti bhaṇati vīraḥ.
(The hero says, "I come *for battle*.")

b. It is regularly used with objects of "reverence" नमस् (*namas*).
Example:
॥ ॐ रामाय नमः ॥
oṃ *rāmāya* namaḥ ("OṂ" Reverence *to Rāma*)

5.3 पञ्चमी विभक्ति (*Pañcamī Vibhakti*): **The Ablative Case**

a. The fifth case, or ablative, is the case of origin, or source.
Example:
सङ्गात्संजायते कामः कामात्क्रोधो ऽभिजायते ।
saṅgāt saṃjāyate kāmaḥ *kāmāt* krodho 'bhijāyate.
(Desire arises *from attachment*, and anger springs *from desire*.)

नगराद्वनं गच्छति कुमारः ।
nagarād vanaṃ gacchati kumāraḥ.
(The boy goes to the forest *from the city*.)

b. The पञ्चमी is used for objects of fear.
Example:
राक्षसान्न बिभेति रामः ।
rākṣasān na bibheti rāmaḥ.
(Rāma does not fear the *demon*.)

c. This case may, like the द्वितीया (*dvitīyā*) and तृतीया (*tṛtīyā*), be used before the invariable word विना (*vinā*) in the sense of "without."
Example:
रामाद्विना क्वायोध्या ।
rāmād vinā kvāyodhyā?
(Where is Ayodhyā *without Rāma*?)

5.4 सप्तमी विभक्ति (*Saptamī Vibhakti*): **The Locative Case**

a. The seventh, or locative case, expresses location (in, on, etc.).
Examples:
वृक्षे वसति द्विजः ।
vṛkṣe vasati dvijaḥ. (The bird lives *in the tree*.)

अयोध्यायां वसति दशरथः ।
ayodhyāyāṃ vasati daśarathaḥ.
(Daśaratha lives *in Ayodhyā*.)

देवेष्वपि रामस्य तुल्यो नास्ति ।
deveṣv api rāmasya tulyo nāsti.
(Rāma has no equal, even *among the gods*.)

b. The locative is also used to indicate reference to something.
Example:
ब्राह्मणस्य हनने प्रायश्चित्तं नास्ति ।
brāhmaṇasya *hanane* prāyaścittaṃ nāsti. (*With respect to the murder* of a brāhman, there is no expiation.)

c. It is also used idiomatically for the object of love, attachment, or devotion.
Examples:
राधायां स्निह्यति श्रीकृष्णः ।
rādhāyāṃ snihyati śrīkṛṣṇaḥ. (Kṛṣṇa loves *Rādhā*.)

धर्मे रतो नृपः ।
dharme rato nṛpaḥ. (The king is devoted *to dharma*.)

कामेषु सङ्गात्क्रोध उपजायते ।
kāmeṣu saṅgāt krodha upajāyate.
(Anger arises out of attachment *to objects of desire*.)

5.5 सर्वनामन् (*Sarvanāman*): **Demonstrative Pronouns**

Sanskrit has several pronouns that may correspond as third person प्रथम पुरुष (*prathama puruṣa*) to the two personal pronouns given in Lesson 4. These pronouns, however, distinguish gender and frequently serve as demonstrative pronouns or even as definite articles.

Examples:
तं बालकं पश्यति स नृपः ।
taṃ bālakaṃ paśyati sa nṛpaḥ.
(*The* [*that*] king sees *that* [*the*] boy.)

तस्मिन्वने वसति सः ।
tasmin vane vasati *saḥ*. (*He* lives *in that* forest.)

One of the most common of these pronouns is "that," cited in its neuter nominative singular form as तत् (*tat*). The paradigm is as follows:

पुंलिङ्ग (*puṃliṅga*)

वचन vacana →	एक॰ eka॰	द्वि॰ dvi॰	बहु॰ bahu॰
विभक्ति ↓ vibhakti			
1.	सः saḥ	तौ tau	ते te
2.	तम् tam	तौ tau	तान् tān
3.	तेन tena	ताभ्याम् tābhyām	तैः taiḥ
4.	तस्मै tasmai	ताभ्याम् tābhyām	तेभ्यः tebhyaḥ
5.	तस्मात् tasmāt	ताभ्याम् tābhyām	तेभ्यः tebhyaḥ
6.	तस्य tasya	तयोः tayoḥ	तेषाम् teṣām
7.	तस्मिन् tasmin	तयोः tayoḥ	तेषु teṣu

नपुंसकलिङ्ग (*napuṃsakaliṅga*)

वचन vacana →	एक॰ ekə॰	द्वि॰ dvi॰	बहु॰ bahu॰
विभक्ति ↓ vibhakti			
1.	तत् tat	ते te	तानि tāni
2.	तत् tat	ते te	तानि tāni
3.	तेन tena	ताभ्याम् tābhyām	तैः taiḥ
4.	तस्मै tasmai	ताभ्याम् tābhyām	तेभ्यः tebhyaḥ

5.	तस्मात् tasmāt	ताभ्याम् tābhyām	तेभ्यः tebhyaḥ
6.	तस्य tasya	तयोः tayoḥ	तेषाम् teṣām
7.	तस्मिन् tasmin	तयोः tayoḥ	तेषु teṣu

स्त्रीलिङ्ग (*strīliṅga*)

वचन vacana →	एक° eka°	द्वि° dvi°	बहु° bahu°
विभक्ति ↓ vibhakti			
1.	सा sā	ते te	ताः tāḥ
2.	ताम् tām	ते te	ताः tāḥ
3.	तया tayā	ताभ्याम् tābhyām	ताभिः tābhiḥ
4.	तस्यै tasyai	ताभ्याम् tābhyām	ताभ्यः tābhyaḥ
5.	तस्याः tasyāḥ	ताभ्याम् tābhyām	ताभ्यः tābhyaḥ
6.	तस्याः tasyāḥ	तयोः tayoḥ	तासाम् tāsām
7.	तस्याम् tasyām	तयोः tayoḥ	तासु tāsu

Note that in several cases, these forms correspond closely to the equivalent forms of -अ (-a) and -आ (-ā) stem nouns. This is especially so in the singular of the तृतीया (*tṛtīyā*) and षष्ठी (*ṣaṣṭhī*) विभक्ति-s (*vibhakti*-s) and for the पुंलिङ्ग (*puṃliṅga*), नपुंसकलिङ्ग (*napuṃsakaliṅga*) तृतीया बहुवचन (*tṛtīyā bahuvacana*). These forms are typical of the pronominal declension, and their correspondence indicates that the -अ (-a) and आ (-ā) declensions, although statistically overwhelming, are, in fact, irregular among the nouns in that they show, in the cases cited, the typically pronominal endings (e.g., -एन [*-ena*], -अस्य [*-asya*], -ऐः [*-aiḥ*], etc.). The neuter तत् (*tat*) is of particular importance as an abstract impersonal pronoun, used much as we use "that" or "it" in English.

Examples:

तत्समीचीनं भवति ।

tat samīcīnaṃ bhavati. (*That's* okay.)

नृपो तस्य ब्राह्मणस्य पुत्रं हन्ति ।

nṛpo *tasya* brāhmaṇasya putraṃ hanti.

(The king kills the brāhman's son.)

तेन ब्राह्मणो दुःखमनुभवति ।

tena brāhmaṇo duḥkham anubhavati. (*Because of that* [literally, "by that"], the brāhman experiences grief.)

Memorize: It is a good idea to memorize the instrumental तेन (*tena*) and especially the ablative तस्मात् (*tasmāt)*, which are commonly used in the sense of "therefore."

Example:

रामो नगरं त्यजति । तस्माज्जना दुःखिता भवन्ति ।

rāmo nagaraṃ tyajati. *tasmāj* janā duḥkhitā bhavanti.

(Rāma leaves the city. *Therefore*, the people become sorrowful.)

5.6 A closely related pronominal stem एतत् (*etat*) has, with the prefix ए (e), the same paradigm as तत् (*tat*). Thus its प्रथमा एक° (*prathamā eka*°) forms are: एषः (*eṣaḥ*—m, see 3.58), एतत् (*etat*—n), and एषा (*eṣā*—f). For other important pronominal, stems see 19.0-2.

5.7 **Adjectives of Pronominal Declension**

Quite aside from the partial similarity between the -अ (-a) stem nominal items (nouns and adjectives) and that of the demonstrative pronoun, there is a small but fairly important group of

-अ (-a) stem adjectives whose declension is virtually identical with that of this pronoun. Five of the more common of these adjectives are:

अन्य	(*anya*)	other
एक	(*eka*)	one (in बहुवचन—several)
पर	(*para*)	other, next, higher
पूर्व	(*pūrva*)	previous, former
सर्व	(*sarva*)	each, every, all

Examples:

एकस्मिन्देश एको नृपः ।
ekasmin deśa *eko* nṛpaḥ.
(*In one* country there is [only] *one* king.)

ब्राह्मणस्य सर्वे पुत्रा हताः ।
brāhmaṇasya *sarve* putrā hatāḥ.
(*All* the sons of the brāhman are killed.)

पूर्वस्मिन्संवत्सरे वीरा वनं गच्छन्ति स्म ।
pūrvasmin saṃvatsare vīrā vanaṃ gacchanti sma.
(*Last* year the heroes went to the forest.)

सर्वेषां पुरुषाणां राम उत्तमः ।
sarveṣāṃ puruṣāṇāṃ rāma uttamaḥ.
(Rāma is the best of *all* men.)

अन्यत्पुस्तकं तव नाहं पश्यामि ।
anyat pustakaṃ tava nāhaṃ paśyāmi.
(I don't see your *other* book.)

5.8 The paradigms of these adjectives are exactly like that of demonstrative pronouns in all three genders except that of all of them only अन्य (*anya*) shows the ending -त् (-t) in the प्रथमा (*prathamā*) and द्वितीया (*dvitīyā*), एक° (*eka*°), of the नपुंसक° (*napuṃsaka*°).

Example:

नृपः सर्वं ब्राह्मणेभ्यो ददाति स्म । तेन तस्यान्यत्किमपि न भवति ।

nṛpaḥ *sarvaṃ* brāhmaṇebhyo dadāti sma. tena tasy*ānyat* kim api na bhavati.

(The king gave *everything* to the brāhmans. Therefore he has nothing *else*.)

EXERCISES

A. Translate the reading into English.

B. Write out and learn the paradigms in all three genders for पूर्व (*pūrva*), and in नपुंसक° (*napuṃsaka°*) for अन्य (*anya*).

C. Translate the following sentences.

1. Therefore, the king loves all his sons. (See 5.4)
2. In Ayodhyā, all sons of the king are handsome.
3. The angry brāhman does not hear the words of the king's wife.
4. All righteous kings rule for the sake of their subjects.
5. Kings do not perform sacrifices without brāhmans. (See 4.42.b.)
6. Because of those (two) sacrifices, the kingdom is peaceful.
7. King Daśaratha loved especially his eldest offspring. (Use स्म—sma.)
8. But, in the course of time, the two wives forget the sacrifice.
9. With those wives, the heroes dwell in Ayodhyā.
10. Rāma goes to the forest for the sake of righteous people.
11. The hero hears the words of his wife and becomes angry.
12. Joyfully the girl thinks, "I am listening to the adventures of Rāma."

D. Memorize the following verse

रामो राजमणिः सदा विजयते रामं रमेशं भजे
रामेणाभिहता निशाचरचमू रामाय तस्मै नमः ।
रामान्नास्ति परायणं परतरं रामस्य दासो ऽस्म्यहं
रामे चित्तलयः सदा भवतु मे भो राम मामुद्धर ॥

Rāma, jewel among kings, is always victorious.
I worship Rāma, Ramā's (Sītā's) lord.
By Rāma the hosts of night-stalkers are destroyed.
Homage to Rāma.
There is no higher recourse than Rāma.
I am a servant of Rāma.
Let the focus of my thoughts always be on Rāma.
O Rāma, save me!

READING

दशरथस्तस्य कुपितस्य ब्राह्मणस्य वचनं शृणोति । किंतु कालेन तं शापं विस्मरति । अयोध्यायां भार्याभिः सह सुखं वसति राज्यं करोति च । सुखितस्य नृपस्यैकं दुःखम् । तस्य पुत्रो नास्तीति । ततो ब्राह्मणैः सह स प्रजायै यज्ञं करोति । अथ कालेन पुत्राणां चतुष्टयमुद्भवति । रामश्च लक्ष्मणश्च भरतश्च शत्रुघ्नश्चेति पुत्राणां नामधेयानि । पार्थिवस्य पुत्राः सुन्दराः शान्ता वीराश्च । तेषु ज्येष्ठो रामो गुणैः श्रेष्ठो भवति । तस्मान्नृपो रामे स्निह्यति विशेषतः ॥

GLOSSARY

अथ
atha (ind)—now, then

अन्य
anya (adj)—other (declined pronominally; see 5.7)

अयोध्या
ayodhyā (f prop)—Daśaratha's capital city

उद् + भू (उद्भवति)
ud + √bhū (1P) (udbhavati)—come into being, be born

एक
eka (adj)—one (declined pronominally; see 5.7)

कालः
kālaḥ (m)—time

कालेन
kālena (ind)—in the course of time

किंतु
kiṃtu (ind)—but, however

कृ (करोति) (कुर्वन्ति—प्रथमपुरुष बहु°)
√kṛ (8P) (karoti) (kurvanti—prathamapuruṣa, bahu°)—do, make, conduct, etc.

गुणः
guṇaḥ (m)—excellence, quality, virtue

चतुष्टयम्
catuṣṭayam (n)—a foursome, set of four

ज्येष्ठ
jyeṣṭha (adj)—eldest

ततः
tataḥ (ind)—hence, then

नामधेयम्
nāmadheyam (n)—name

पर
para (adj)—distant, next (declined pronominally; see 5.7)

पार्थिवः
pārthivaḥ (m)—king

पूर्व
pūrva (adj)—previous, former (declined pronominally; see 5.7)

प्रजा
prajā (f)—offspring, children, people of a kingdom or realm

भरतः
bharataḥ (m prop)—one of Rāma's brothers

भार्या
bhāryā (f)—wife

यज्ञः
yajñaḥ (m)—ritual offering to the gods (a Vedic sacrifice)

राज्यम्

rājyam (n)—kingly rule, kingdom (with √कृ—to rule, reign)

लक्ष्मणः

lakṣmaṇaḥ (m prop)—one of Rāma's brothers

वचनम्

vacanam (n)—speech, words

विशेषतः

viśeṣataḥ (ind)—especially

वि + स्मृ (विस्मरति)

vi + √smṛ (1P) (vismarati)—forget

वीरः

vīraḥ (m)—hero; (adj)—heroic

वृत् (वर्तते)

√vṛt (1Ā) (vartate)—be, exist, occur

शत्रुघ्नः

śatrughnaḥ (m prop)—one of Rāma's brothers

शान्त

śānta (adj)—calm, peaceful

शापः

śāpaḥ (m)—curse

श्रु (शृणोति)

√śru (5P) (śṛṇoti)—hear, hear about

श्रेष्ठ

śreṣṭha (adj)—best

सर्व

sarva (adj)—each, all, every (declined pronominally; see 5.7)

सह

saha (ind)—with (used after तृतीया as marker of accompaniment)

सानन्दम्

sānandam (ind)—joyfully

सुखित

sukhita (adj)—happy

स्निह् (स्निह्यति)

√snih (4P) (snihyati)—love (with object of love in सप्तमी)

LESSON 6

Nominal Stems in -इ (-i) and -उ (-u); Interrogative, Relative, and Correlative Clauses: The क्-य्-त् (k-y-t) Series of Indeclinables and Pronouns

6.0 Sanskrit has a large number of nominal stems in short -इ (-i) and short -उ (-u) whose declensions are closely analogous. The nouns are of all genders, although पुंलिङ्ग (*puṃliṅga*) and स्त्रीलिङ्ग (*strīliṅga*) nouns in -इ (-i) are the most important class. नपुंसकलिङ्ग (*napuṃsakaliṅga*) -इ (-i) stems and स्त्रीलिङ्ग (*strīliṅga*) -उ (-u) stems are relatively rare and, therefore, their paradigms are omitted here. (See 6.2.c below.)

6.1 The paradigms are:

a. पुंलिङ्ग (*puṃliṅga*) -इ (-i) मुनिः (*muniḥ*) sage, holy man

वचन vacana →	एक° eka°	द्वि° dvi°	बहु° bahu°
विभक्ति ↓ vibhakti			
1.	मुनिः muniḥ	मुनी munī	मुनयः munayaḥ
2.	मुनिम् munim	मुनी munī	मुनीन् munīn
3.	मुनिना muninā	मुनिभ्याम् munibhyām	मुनिभिः munibhiḥ
4.	मुनये munaye	मुनिभ्याम् munibhyām	मुनिभ्यः munibhyaḥ
5.	मुनेः muneḥ	मुनिभ्याम् munibhyām	मुनिभ्यः munibhyaḥ
6.	मुनेः muneḥ	मुन्योः munyoḥ	मुनीनाम् munīnām
7.	मुनौ munau	मुन्योः munyoḥ	मुनिषु muniṣu
सम्° sam.	मुने mune	मुनी munī	मुनयः munayaḥ

b. स्त्रीलिङ्ग (*strīliṅga*) -इ (-i) गतिः (*gatiḥ*) way or path

वचन vacana →	एक° eka°	द्वि° dvi°	बहु° bahu°
विभक्ति ↓ vibhakti			
1.	गतिः gatiḥ	गती gatī	गतयः gatayaḥ
2.	गतिम् gatim	गती gatī	गतीः gatīḥ
3.	गत्या gatyā	गतिभ्याम् gatibhyām	गतिभिः gatibhiḥ
4.	गत्यै (गतये) gatyai (gataye)	गतिभ्याम् gatibhyām	गतिभ्यः gatibhyaḥ
5.	गत्याः (गतेः) gatyāḥ (gateḥ)	गतिभ्याम् gatibhyām	गतिभ्यः gatibhyaḥ
6.	गत्याः (गतेः) gatyāḥ (gateḥ)	गत्योः gatyoḥ	गतीनाम् gatīnām
7.	गत्याम् (गतौ) gatyām (gatau)	गत्योः gatyoḥ	गतिषु gatiṣu
सम्° sam.	गते gate	गती gatī	गतयः gatayaḥ

Note: The पुंलिङ्ग (*puṃliṅga*) and स्त्रीलिङ्ग (*strīliṅga*) paradigms differ of necessity only in the instrumental singular and the accusative plural, while the feminine has alternate endings for cases 4, 5, 6, and 7, one of which is the same as the masculine -इ (-i) stem and the other of which is the same as the feminine -ई (-ī) stem (see 7.1). Since the stem forms and the nominative singular forms are the same for both the पुंलिङ्ग (*puṃliṅga*) and स्त्रीलिङ्ग (*strīliṅga*) forms, it is important to memorize the correct genders of such words as they are learned. There is a general, but by no means invariable, rule that words that end in -ति (-ti), -धि (-dhi) and -टि (-ṭi) are usually स्त्रीलिङ्ग (*strīliṅga*).

c. पुंलिङ्ग (*puṃliṅga*) -उ (-u) शत्रुः (*śatruḥ*) enemy

वचन vacana →	एक° eka°	द्वि° dvi°	बहु° bahu°
विभक्ति ↓ vibhakti			
1.	शत्रुः śatruḥ	शत्रू śatrū	शत्रवः śatravaḥ
2.	शत्रुम् śatrum	शत्रू śatrū	शत्रून् śatrūn
3.	शत्रुणा śatruṇā	शत्रुभ्याम् śatrubhyām	शत्रुभिः śatrubhiḥ
4.	शत्रवे śatrave	शत्रुभ्याम् śatrubhyām	शत्रुभ्यः śatrubhyaḥ
5.	शत्रोः śatroḥ	शत्रुभ्याम् śatrubhyām	शत्रुभ्यः śatrubhyaḥ
6.	शत्रोः śatroḥ	शत्र्वोः śatrvoḥ	शत्रूणाम् śatrūṇām
7.	शत्रौ śatrau	शत्र्वोः śatrvoḥ	शत्रुषु śatruṣu
सम्° sam.	शत्रो śatro	शत्रू śatrū	शत्रवः śatravaḥ

d. नपुंसकलिङ्ग (*napuṃsakaliṅga*) -उ (-u) मधु (*madhu*) honey

वचन vacana →	एक° eka°	द्वि° dvi°	बहु° bahu°
विभक्ति ↓ vibhakti			
1.	मधु madhu	मधुनी madhunī	मधूनि madhūni
2.	मधु madhu	मधुनी madhunī	मधूनि madhūni
3.	मधुना madhunā	मधुभ्याम् madhubhyām	मधुभिः madhubhiḥ
4.	मधुने madhune	मधुभ्याम् madhubhyām	मधुभ्यः madhubhyaḥ

5.	मधुनः madhunaḥ	मधुभ्याम् madhubhyām	मधुभ्यः madhubhyaḥ
6.	मधुनः madhunaḥ	मधुनोः madhunoḥ	मधूनाम् madhūnām
7.	मधुनि madhuni	मधुनोः madhunoḥ	मधुषु madhuṣu
सम्° sam.	मधो (मधु) madho (madhu)	मधुनी madhunī	मधूनि madhūni

6.2 a. The -इ (-i) and the -उ (-u) stems are exceptions to the general rule that पुंलिङ्ग(*puṃliṅga*) and नपुंसकलिङ्ग (*napuṃsaka*) nouns in the same stem final are identical except in the प्रथमा (*prathamā*) and द्वितीया (*dvitīyā*) विभक्ति-s (*vibhakti*-s).

b. Note that in these declensions -इ (-i) and the -उ (-u) are treated analogously, each remaining unchanged, being "guṇated" (see 3.6-7), lengthened, or changed to the corresponding semivowel in the same cases.

c. नपुंसक (*napuṃsaka*) -इ (-i) stems and स्त्रीलिङ्ग (*strīliṅga*) -उ (-u) stems (not illustrated here) are similarly analogous to नपुंसक (*napuṃsaka*) -उ (-u) and स्त्रीलिङ्ग (*strīliṅga*) -इ (-i) stems, respectively. Thus the स्त्रीलिङ्ग (*strīliṅga*) noun धेनु (dhenu), "cow," declines similarly to गतिः (gatiḥ): धेनुः (dhenuḥ), धेनू (dhenū), धेनवः (dhenavaḥ), etc. The नपुंसकलिङ्ग (*napuṃsakaliṅga*) noun वारि (vāri), "water," declines similarly to मधु (madhu): वारि (vāri), वारिणी (vāriṇī), वारीणि (vārīṇi), etc.

d. Keep in mind that the सप्तमी एक° (*saptamī eka*°) of the पुंलिङ्ग (*puṃliṅga*) (optionally स्त्रीलिङ्ग [*strīliṅga*]) stems in **both** -इ (-i) and -उ (-u) is -औ (-au). This often causes further confusion among already confused Sanskrit students, especially since this ending is the one which marks the प्रथमा (*prathamā*) and द्वितीया द्विवचन (*dvitīyā dvivacana*) of many stems.

Examples:

-इ (-i);

अग्नौ प्रक्षिपति घृतम् ।

agnau prakṣipati ghṛtam. (He throws the ghee in the fire.)

-उ (-u);

शत्रावपि स्निह्यति साधुः ।

śatrāv api snihyati sādhuḥ.

(A good man loves even his enemy.)

e. In addition to the nouns that end in इ (i) and उ (u), there are a number of adjectives that have their stems in इ (i) and उ (u). These of course must agree in gender, number and case with the noun they modify.

Example:

बहवः शिष्याः पुस्तकं पठन्ति ।

bahavaḥ śiṣyāḥ pustakam paṭhanti. (Many students read the book.)

6.3 Interrogative, relative, and correlative: The क्-य्-त् (k-y-t) series

As in English, a Sanskrit sentence may be either **declarative** or **interrogative**, while a clause of a sentence may be **subordinate** or **independent**.

a. **Interrogative sentences**

A sentence may be marked as interrogative in a number of ways.

i. One way is by giving a declarative sentence a rising inflection at its end similar to the inflection used for this purpose in English. This, however, cannot be represented in the written language. Another simple way to turn a declarative sentence into an interrogative is to make the अव्ययपद (*avyayapada*—indeclinable) अपि (*api*) the first word of the sentence. Here again a rising inflection is usually employed in speech. These two techniques serve to form general questions with regard to an entire statement. Such questions can be answered either "yes" or "no."

Examples:

declarative:

रामः सीतया सह वनं गच्छति ।

rāmaḥ sītayā saha vanaṃ gacchati.

(Rāma goes to the forest with Sītā.)

interrogative:

अपि रामः सीतया सह वनं गच्छति ।

api rāmaḥ sītayā saha vanaṃ gacchati?

(Does Rāma go to the forest with Sītā?)

ii. Another very important kind of interrogative sentence is that in which a particular part of speech is replaced by an appropriate interrogative element. This kind of question calls for a specific answer.

Examples:

declarative:

रामः सीतया सह वनं गच्छति ।

rāmaḥ sītayā saha vanaṃ gacchati.

(Rāma goes to the forest with Sītā.)

interrogatives:

कः सीतया सह वनं गच्छति ।

kaḥ sītayā saha vanaṃ gacchati?

(*Who* goes to the forest with Sītā?)

रामः किं करोति ।

rāmaḥ *kiṃ* karoti? (*What* does Rāma do?)

रामः कया सह वनं गच्छति ।

rāmaḥ *kayā* saha vanaṃ gacchati?

(*With whom* does Rāma go to the forest?)

रामः कुत्र वसति ।

rāmaḥ *kutra* vasati? (*Where* does Rāma live?)

कस्त्वं कस्मादागच्छसि ।

kas tvaṃ? *kasmād* āgacchasi.

(*Who* are you? *Where* do you come *from*?)

All of these "question words," whether pronouns, adjectives, or adverbs, begin with the sound क् (k).

b. **Subordinate Clauses**

As in English, a Sanskrit clause may be either independent, i.e., able to stand alone as a sentence, or subordinate, i.e., unable to stand alone. Subordinate clauses may be participial or relative. The former will be considered in connection with the various participles. The latter correspond to English relative clauses such as:

"all **who** wish to leave . . ."

"**where** the sun never shines . . ."

"the girl **with whom** you were speaking . . ."

Clauses of this kind in Sanskrit always include a relative marker. These are pronouns, adjectives, or adverbs corresponding closely to the interrogative markers. These words, however, always begin with the sound य् (y). This distinction is in contrast to English where the same words are generally used both in interrogative and relative senses. Examples:

यः सीतया सह वनं गच्छति

yaḥ sītayā saha vanaṃ gacchati . . .

([the man] *who* goes to the forest with Sītā . . .)

यया सह रामो वनं गच्छति

yayā saha rāmo vanaṃ gacchati . . .

([the woman] *with whom* Rāma goes to the forest . . .)

यत्र वसति रामः

yatra vasati rāmaḥ . . . (*where* Rāma lives . . .)

c. **Correlative Clauses**

Correlative clauses are independent clauses that "complete" relative clauses to form complex sentences. They are like the English clauses: "*All* who wish to leave *may go*," "*I couldn't live* where the sun never shines," "*The girl* with whom you were speaking *is my sister*." Notice that in the English examples only the relative clause contains a marker (in these cases a pronoun). Sanskrit usage differs from that of English in that it generally requires that the correlative clause, too, contain a corresponding marker. Thus it is as though we were to say, "All who wish to leave *they* may go," "Where the sun never shines I couldn't live *there*," or "The girl with whom you were speaking *she* is my sister." Such correlatives are marked by a series of pronouns, adjectives, and adverbs corresponding to the interrogative and relative markers. The pronouns in this case are none other than those you have already learned as demonstrative pronouns (5.5). With the exception of the प्रथमा एक° (*prathamā eka°*) of the पुंलिङ्ग (*puṃliñga*) and स्त्रीलिङ्ग (*strīliñga*), सः (*saḥ*) and सा (*sā*), all these forms begin with the sound त् (t).

Examples:

यः सीतया सह वनं गच्छति स रामः ।
yaḥ sītayā saha vanaṃ gacchati *sa rāmaḥ*.
(*Rāma is the one* who goes to the forest with Sītā.)

यया सह रामो वनं गच्छति सा सीता ।
yayā saha rāmo vanaṃ gacchati *sā sītā*.
(*Sītā is the one* with whom Rāma goes to the forest.)

यत्र वसति रामस्तत्र वसति सीता
yatra vasati rāmas *tatra vasati sītā*.
(*Sītā lives* where Rāma lives.)

6.4 Knowledge of this य्-त् (y-t) set of markers is essential in that it enables one quickly to break up seemingly imposing sentences into simple, easily manageable units.

Example:

यया [कन्यया] सह वनं गच्छति दशरथस्य पुत्रस्तामहं पश्यामि ।

yayā [kanyayā] saha vanaṃ gacchati daśarathasya putras tām ahaṃ paśyāmi. (I see her [the girl] with whom the son of Daśaratha is going to the forest.)

In this sentence the य्-त् (y-t) (relative/correlative) correspondence यया (*yayā*) / ताम् (*tām*) shows us that we have two clauses with a common referent. (For convenience we will use the most common prose word order for such clauses according to which the relative and the correlative marker each appear at the beginning of their respective clauses.) Each clause may now be read as a separate entity, each with its own syntax. Thus the independent clause is the simple sentence: तामहं पश्यामि । (*tām ahaṃ paśyāmi*—I see her), while the relative clause is the simple sentence: कन्यया सह वनं गच्छति रामः (*yayā saha vanaṃ gacchati rāmaḥ*—Rāma goes to the forest with a girl), made relative by the substitution of the appropriate relative pronoun.

6.5 अव्ययपद-s (*Avyayapada*-s—**Indeclinables**) **of the** क्-य्-त् (k-y-t) **series.**

The अव्ययपद-s (*avyayapada*-s—indeclinables) belonging to this series are adverbs with a variety of meanings, which are more or less closely related to the basic case system and each of which is represented by a particular ending or letter.

6.6 The meanings, corresponding case (if any), and distinctive endings are shown in the following chart.

Ending	**General meaning**	**Corresponding case**
°थम् / था (*-tham* or *-thā*)	manner	तृतीया (*tṛtīyā*)
°तः (*-taḥ*)	source-origin (time, place, etc.)	पञ्चमी (*pañcamī*)
°दा (*-dā*)	time	सप्तमी (*saptamī*)
°त्र (*-tra*)	place	सप्तमी (*saptamī*)

6.7 These endings are affixed to a syllable consisting of क् (k), य् (y), or त् (t) (depending on whether an interrogative, relative, or correlative is intended) and a short vowel (which is always अ [a], except in the case of two interrogatives which have उ [u]).

6.8 The adverbs of the series, then, are:

Interrogative	**Relative**	**Correlative**
कथम् (*katham*) how? in what way?	यथा (*yathā*) just as, in the manner in which	तथा (*tathā*) thus, in that way
कुतः (*kutaḥ*) whence? why? since when?	यतः (*yataḥ*) since, from the point that	ततः (*tataḥ*) from that, therefore, after that
कदा (*kadā*) when?	यदा (*yadā*) when, whenever	तदा (*tadā*) then
कुत्र (क्व) (*kutra* or *kva*) where?	यत्र (*yatra*) where, wherever, concerning which	तत्र (*tatra*) there, concerning that

6.9 With this list one should also learn the relative-correlative correspondences for:

यदि (*yadi*) if	तर्हि (*tarhi*) then
यावत् (*yāvat*) as long as, to the extent that	तावत् (*tāvat*) so long, to the extent that

6.10 These series must be committed to memory as quickly as possible. In addition, the general meanings of the endings listed in 6.6 should be memorized, as this will make their other applications quite simple to grasp.

Examples:

कथं धर्मं जानासि त्वम् ।

(Q) *katham* dharmaṃ jānāsi tvam.
(*How* do you know what is right?)

यथा त्वं जानासि तथाहं जानामि ।

(A) *yathā* tvaṃ jānāsi, tathāhaṃ jānāmi.
(I know *in the same way* as you.)

कुतः प्रणश्यति पुरुषः ।

(Q) *kutaḥ* praṇaśyati puruṣaḥ.
(*From what* does a man perish?)

यतो बुद्धिर्नश्यति तत एव प्रणश्यति पुरुषः ।

(A) *yato* buddhir naśyati, *tata* eva praṇaśyati puruṣaḥ.
(*Whence* the intellect is destroyed, *from that very thing* a man perishes.)

कदा वनं गच्छन्ति मुनयः ।

(Q) *kadā* vanaṃ gacchanti munayaḥ.
(*When* do sages go to the forest?)

यदा पुत्राणां पुत्रान्पश्यन्ति तदा गृहं त्यजन्ति वनं च गच्छन्ति ।

(A) *yadā* putrāṇāṃ putrān paśyanti, *tadā* gṛhaṃ tyajanti vanaṃ ca gacchanti. (*When* they see their sons' sons, they abandon home and go to the forest.)

तदा कुत्र वसन्ति ।

(Q) tadā *kutra* vasanti. (Then *where* do they live?)

यत्र रमणीयाः शान्ता आश्रमा वर्तन्ते तत्रैव तेषां निवासः ।

(A) *yatra* ramaṇīyāḥ śāntā āśramā vartante *tatra*iva teṣāṃ nivāsaḥ. (They have their dwelling *where* there are charming and tranquil āśrams.)

यावद्रामो वनं न गच्छति तावद्राक्षसास्तत्र नन्दन्ते ।

yāvad rāmo vanaṃ na gacchati *tāvad* rākṣasās tatra nandante. (*As long as* Rāma does not go to the forest, [*so long do*] the demons rejoice there.)

6.11 The adverbs in -दा (-dā) and -त्र (-tra) can be repeated to indicate a distributive sense of various times or places. Thus:
यत्र यत्र रामो गच्छति तत्र तत्र सीतानुगच्छति ।
yatra yatra rāmo gacchati *tatra tatra* sītānugacchati.
(*To whichever places* Rāma goes, *there* Sītā follows.)

यदा यदा हि धर्मस्य ग्लानिर्भवति भारत ।
अभ्युत्थानमधर्मस्य तदात्मानं सृजाम्यहम् ॥ भगवद्गीता ४।७

yadā yadā hi dharmasya glānir bhavati bhārata,
abhyutthānam adharmasya tadātmānaṃ sṛjāmy aham.
(Whenever, o Bhārata, there is a waning of righteousness and an increase of unrighteousness, then I create myself.)
(*Bhagavadgītā* 4.7)
(Memorize this verse.)

6.12 The adverbial endings given at 6.6 are not restricted to the क्-य्-त् (k-y-t) stems. They may also be added to a variety of other pronominal (and in a few cases nominal) stems to form adverbs with the same general meanings. This is especially so in the case of the pronominally declined adjectives listed at 5.7. Some of the more common and useful of these forms are:

-था (*-thā*):	अन्यथा	(*anyathā*)	otherwise
	सर्वथा	(*sarvathā*)	every which way
-तः (*-taḥ*):	अन्यतः	(*anyataḥ*)	from another source
	एकतः	(*ekataḥ*)	from one side, on the one hand
	सर्वतः	(*sarvataḥ*)	from all sides
-दा (*-dā*):	अन्यदा	(*anyadā*)	another time
	एकदा	(*ekadā*)	once, one time
	सर्वदा	(*sarvadā*)	always, all the time
-त्र (*-tra*):	अन्यत्र	(*anyatra*)	elsewhere
	एकत्र	(*ekatra*)	in one place
	सर्वत्र	(*sarvatra*)	everywhere
	परत्र	(*paratra*)	in another place, in the next world

6.13 **सर्वनामन्** (*Sarvanāman*—**Pronouns) of the क्-य्-त्** (k-y-t) **series**. The same क्-य्-त् (k-y-t) correspondence exists throughout the regular pronominal system.

6.14 If the third person demonstrative pronouns given in 5.5 are taken as the correlatives, then the relatives are formed simply by substituting य् (y) for the initial consonant स् (s) or त् (t) of the desired form. The interrogatives are likewise formed by the substitution of क् (k) for the initial, except in the case of the प्रथमा (*prathamā*) and द्वितीया एक° नपुंसक (*dvitīyā eka° napuṃsaka*), where the very common interrogative किम् (*kim*—what) is substituted for तत् (*tat*)—यत् (*yat*).

6.15 **Usage of क्-य्-त्** (k-y-t) **Series Pronouns**

In order for there to be true correlation between two pronominal items, one relative and one correlative, they must, of course, agree in **gender** and in **number**. The **gender** of the person, place, thing, action, etc., is inherent. The **number** is dependent upon the context. One feature of this type of compound sentence, however, is often confusing to the beginner and should be made clear at the outset. This is the fact that the **case** of the relative need not be the same as that of its correlative. For, unlike gender and number, case is strictly a function of a given syntactical sequence, i.e., of the relation of words in a clause. As we saw at 6.4, each clause in such a sentence is itself a syntactical unit.

Consider the following sentence:

येषां राक्षसानां रावणो नृपस्तान्हन्ति रामः ।
yeṣāṃ rākṣasānāṃ rāvaṇo nṛpas *tān* hanti rāmaḥ.
(Rāma kills the demons *whose* king is Rāvaṇa.)

Here the noun राक्षस (*rākṣasa*) plays a role in both clauses. The gender is, of course, पुंलिङ्ग (*puṃliṅga*). Since the context requires many राक्षस-s (*rākṣasa*-s), the number must be बहु° (*bahu*°). Regarding the cases, however, each clause must be treated individually. In the independent clause, the राक्षस-s (*rākṣasa*-s) represented by the correlative pronoun are the कर्मन्

(*karman*—direct object) of the verbal root √हन् (*han*). Therefore, the word must be in the द्वितीया (*dvitīyā*). In the relative clause, however, the कर्तृ (*kartṛ*—subject) of the verbal root √अस् (*as*) (understood), the king *of* the demons, is in the प्रथमा (*prathamā*) while the relativised demons must be put in the appropriate षष्ठी (*ṣaṣṭhī*).

Examples:

येन पुरुषेण सह भाषते नृपः स मुनिः ।
yena puruṣeṇa saha bhāṣate nṛpaḥ *sa* muniḥ.
(The man *with whom* the king is speaking, [*he*] is a sage.)

यस्मिन्वने वसति रामस्तस्मिन्वने न विद्यन्ते राक्षसाः ।
yasmin vane vasati rāmas, *tasmin* vane na vidyante rākṣasāḥ.
(*In the forest where* Rāma lives, [*in that forest*] there are no demons.)

याभ्यां सह गच्छति सीता तौ रामश्च लक्ष्मणश्च ।
yābhyāṃ saha gacchati sītā, *tau* rāmaś ca lakṣmaṇaś ca.
(The *two with whom* Sitā is going are Rāma and Lakṣmaṇa.)

यस्यान्या गतिर्नास्ति स संस्कृतं पठति ।
yasyānyā gatir nāsti, *sa* saṃskṛtaṃ paṭhati.
(*Who* has nothing else to do, *he* studies Sanskrit.)

यस्मान्नोद्विजते लोको लोकान्नोद्विजते च यः स मे प्रिय इति वदति श्रीकृष्णः ।
yasmān nodvijate loko lokān nodvijate ca *yaḥ*, *sa* me priya iti vadati śrīkṛṣṇaḥ. (*On account of whom* the world does not tremble, *and who* does not tremble on account of the world, *he* is dear to me, so says Śrīkṛṣṇa.)

6.16 It should be clear that learning the above indeclinables and pronouns will provide you with powerful tools for generating complex sentences, especially in response to a specific question. Such questions and answers, with respect to a specific story or reading, form a major part of the traditional method of Sanskrit instruction.

6.17 **Indefinite and Absolute Negative Constructions**

These same forms of the interrogative and relative adverbs and pronouns may be used in conjuction with a few simple particles to generate phrases indicating indefiniteness and absolute negativity.

6.18 A very simple technique to indicate indefiniteness is to use the corresponding relative and interrogative in succession, often following the pair by the particle अपि (*api*).

Examples:

यत्र कुत्रापि (*yatra kutrāpi*) somewhere or other

येन केनाप्युपायेन (*yena kenāpy upāyena*) by some means or other, by hook or by crook

6.19 The interrogative alone followed by the particles अपि (*api*), चन (*cana*), or चित् (*cit*) serves to indicate something not really specified. This construction often has a force similar to that of the indefinite article in English. It is especially common where the name of a person or place is not specified or not important.

Examples:

मह्यं किंचिद्वदति ।

mahyaṃ *kiṃcid* vadati. (He tells me *something*.)

तत्र कश्चन ब्राह्मणो वसति ।

tatra *kaścana* brāhmaṇo vasati. (*A* [*Some*] brāhman lives there.)

कस्मिंश्चिन्नगरे वसति स्म नृपः ।

kasmiṃś cin nagare vasati sma nṛpaḥ.
(The king lived *in a* [*some*] city.)

6.20 The addition of the negative particle न (*na*) to one of the above phrases indicates absolute exclusion or negativity.

Examples:

न कश्चन शृणोति माम् ।

na kaścana śṛṇoti mām. (*Nobody* listens to me.)

न कयापि कन्यया सह संवदति ।

na kayāpi kanyayā saha saṃvadati.

(He is not speaking *with any* girl.)

न मे नश्यति किंचन ।

na me naśyati *kiṃcana*. (*Nothing* of mine is destroyed.)

6.21 **Negation**

Negation in Sanskrit is basically of two kinds. These may be called propositional negation, whereby a verbal phrase is negated, and term negation, whereby a nominal item alone is negated. In propositional negation the negative particle न (*na*) (or मा [*mā*]; see 11.18) is inserted into the clause, normally before the finite verb if it is expressed.

Examples:

रामो वनं न गच्छति ।

rāmo vanaṃ na gacchati. (Rāma doesn't go to the forest.)

नाहं ब्राह्मणः ।

nāhaṃ brāhmaṇaḥ. (I am not a brāhman.)

In term negation, a nominal item alone may be negated by the prefixation of the syllable अ (a), similar in meaning to English un-, in-, non-, im-, etc. If the item begins with a vowel, the prefix is अन् (an).

Examples:

तदसमीचीनं भवति ।

tad asamīcīnaṃ bhavati.

(That is not good.)

अनार्याः कुत्र वसन्ति ।

anāryāḥ kutra vasanti?

(Where do non-āryans live?)

EXERCISES

A. Translate the reading into English and be prepared to answer simple questions about it in Sanskrit.

B. Translate into Sanskrit:

1. The woman with whom Rāma is speaking is Sītā.
2. A certain brāhman told me that Viṣṇu is the supreme god.
3. When Rāma goes to the sage's āśrama, the demons tremble.
4. Who is there? Who is there? Nobody at all.
5. Whoever knows the highest bliss, he does not tremble.
6. The sage of whom he is afraid is very clever.
7. Whenever the gods speak, no one understands.
8. When the rākṣasa comes, all the women (नारी, see 7.1) say "hā hā."
9. Rāma saw the demon on account of whom Sītā was distressed.
10. Since the sage is a protector of demons, what is the alternative?
11. A twice-born who is skilled (clever) in archery will not experience worry.
12. Who is that woman who goes quickly to the hermitage?

C. Memorize the क्-य्-त् (k-y-t) adverb series.

D. 1. Write out the paradigms of interrogative and relative pronouns based on 5.5.
2. Write out the paradigms for the adjectives शुचि (*śuci*), "white, pure," and लघु (*laghu*), "light *or* small," in all three genders. (See 6.2.)

E. Memorize the following verse.

भो दारिद्र्य नमस्तुभ्यं सिद्धो ऽहं त्वत्प्रसादतः ।
पश्याम्यहं जगत्सर्वं न मां पश्यति कश्चन ॥

Homage, O Poverty, to you.
Through your grace, I have acquired magic powers.
I can see the whole world, but not a soul sees me.

READING

यदा यदा दशरथो ज्येष्ठं पुत्रं रामं पश्यति तदा तदा परममानन्दमनुभवति । रामो ऽपि मत्या युतः । स सर्वान्वेदानवगच्छति धनुर्वेदस्यापि पारं गच्छति । यदा स बाणमुद्धरति तदा देवा अपि कम्पन्ते स्वर्गे । एकदा कश्चन मुनिरयोध्यां प्रत्यागच्छति । दशरथं प्रति वदति च । भो नृप । वयं मुनयो राक्षसैरत्यन्तं पीडिता भवामः । त्वमेव प्रजानां रक्षको ऽसि । यदि त्वं न कंचन वीरं प्रेषयसि तर्हि वयं सर्वे नष्टाः स्म इति । दशरथो वदति । भो मुने । येभ्यो राक्षसेभ्य ऋषयो ऽप्युद्विजन्ते तेषां हनने कः समर्थ इति । मुनिर्वदति । कौचन समर्थौ वीरौ वर्तेते अयोध्यायामिति । कौ ताविति पृच्छति दशरथः । तव पुत्रौ रामो लक्ष्मणश्चेति भाषते द्विजः । यदा नृपो मुनेर्वचनं शृणोति तदा सो ऽतीव दुःखितो भवति । यतो ब्राह्मणो मनुष्येषु देवो भवति ततो नृपो ऽपि ब्राह्मणस्य वचनं करोति । ततः प्रियौ च पुत्रौ वनं प्रेषयति ब्राह्मणेन सह ॥

GLOSSARY

अत्यन्तम्
atyantam (ind)—exceedingly

अथ
atha (ind)—now, then

अपि
api (see 6.19)

अव + गम् → अवगच्छति
ava + √gam (1P) → avagacchati—understand

आनन्दः
ānandaḥ (m)—joy, bliss

आश्रमः
āśramaḥ (m)—hermitage

उद् + विज् → उद्विजते
ud + √vij (6Ā) → udvijate—tremble

उद् + हृ → उद्धरति
ud + √hṛ (1P) → uddharati—lift up

ऋषिः
ṛṣiḥ (m)—sage

एव
eva (ind)—emphatic particle, emphasizes preceding word

कथम्
katham (ind)—how

कदा
kadā (ind)—when

कम्प् → कम्पते
√kamp (1Ā) → kampate—tremble

कुतः
kutaḥ (ind)—whence

कुत्र
kutra (ind)—where

क्व
kva (ind)—where

गतिः
gatiḥ (f)—way, "alternative" state of existence

गुरु
guru (adj)—heavy

चन
cana (see 6.19)

चित्
cit (see 6.19)

चिन्ता
cintā (f)—care, worry, anxiety

ज्ञा → जानाति
√jñā (9P) → jānāti—know

तत्
tat (n)—that, this

ततः
tataḥ (ind)—thence

तत्र
tatra (ind)—there

तथा
tathā (ind)—thus

तदा
tadā (ind)—then

तर्हि
tarhi (ind)—then

तावत्
tāvat (ind)—so long, to that extent

दुःखित
duḥkhita (adj)—unhappy

देवः
devaḥ (m)—god

द्विजः
dvijaḥ (m)—brāhman, "twice-born"

धनुर्वेदः
dhanurvedaḥ (m)—science of archery

नष्ट
naṣṭa (adj)—ruined, destroyed

नारी
nārī (f)—woman (for declension see 7.1)

निपुण
nipuṇa (adj)—clever

परम
parama (adj)—supreme

पारः
pāraḥ (m)—lit., "far shore;" with गम् (√gam) excel at, fully

पुरुषः
puruṣaḥ (m)—man, person

प्रच्छ् → पृच्छति
√prach (6P) → pṛcchati—ask

प्र + इष् → प्रेषयति
pra + √iṣ → preṣayati (causative, conjugated as 10P)—send, dispatch

प्रति
prati (ind) (with preceding acc.)—to, until, towards

प्रिय
priya (adj)—dear, beloved

बाणः
bāṇaḥ (m)—arrow

बाधित
bādhita (adj)—afflicted, distressed, oppressed

भोः
bhoḥ (ind)—hail or greeting "hey, hail, oh" *note on sandhi*: before initial voiced sound "bhoḥ" loses "ḥ."

मतिः
matiḥ (f)—mind, intelligence

मनुष्यः
manuṣyaḥ (m)—mortal, human

मुनिः
muniḥ (m)—sage

यः
yaḥ (m) (pr)—who (relative)

यत्
yat (n)—what (relative)

यतः
yataḥ (ind)—whence, since

यत्र
yatra (ind)—where

यथा
yathā (ind)—as, like (relative)

यदा
yadā (ind)—when

यदि
yadi (ind)—if

या
yā (f pr)—who (relative)

यावत्
yāvat (ind)—so long as, to the extent that

युत
yuta (adj)—endowed with

रक्षकः
rakṣakaḥ (m)—protector

राक्षसः
rākṣasaḥ (m)—demon

लघु
laghu (adj)—light, small

वेदः
vedaḥ (m)—Veda

शीघ्रम्
śīghram (adv)—quickly

शुचि
śuci (adj)—pure, white

समर्थ
samartha (adj)—capable, competent

सीता
sītā (f prop)—Sītā

स्वर्गः
svargaḥ (m)—heaven

हननम्
hananam (n)—killing

LESSON 7

स्त्रीलिङ्ग (*strīliñga*—Feminine) Stems in ई (-ī); The गण-s (Gaṇa-s) of the Present System

7.0 Aside from स्त्रीलिङ्ग (*strīliñga*—feminine) stems in -आ (-ā), the most common स्त्रीलिङ्ग (*strīliñga*—feminine) stem ending is -ई (-ī). The paradigm is as follows:

7.1 स्त्रीलिङ्ग (*strīliñga*) -ई (-ī) देवी (*devī*) lady, goddess

वचन vacana →	एक° eka°	द्वि° dvi°	बहु° bahu°
विभक्ति ↓ vibhakti			
1.	देवी devī	देव्यौ devyau	देव्यः devyaḥ
2.	देवीम् devīm	देव्यौ devyau	देवीः devīḥ
3.	देव्या devyā	देवीभ्याम् devībhyām	देवीभिः devībhiḥ
4.	देव्यै devyai	देवीभ्याम् devībhyām	देवीभ्यः devībhyaḥ
5.	देव्याः devyāḥ	देवीभ्याम् devībhyām	देवीभ्यः devībhyaḥ
6.	देव्याः devyāḥ	देव्योः devyoḥ	देवीनाम् devīnām
7.	देव्याम् devyām	देव्योः devyoḥ	देवीषु devīṣu
सम्° sam.	देवि devi	देव्यौ devyau	देव्यः devyaḥ

7.2 **The Present System**

The present system comprises an extensive complex of tenses, modes, and participles, which together make up the most significant coherent portion of the Sanskrit verbal system. The "present" system is the basis for the लट् (*laṭ*—present indicative), the लङ् (*laṅ*—imperfect), the लोट् (*loṭ*—imperative), the विधि लिङ् (*vidhi liṅ*—optative) and the वर्तमाने कृदन्त (*vartamāne kṛdanta*—present participle). These together make up a great portion of verbal forms actually in use.

7.3 All these different forms are said to belong to a single system because of the fact that regardless of which personal endings, modal signs, or verbal prefixes they may involve, they all share a common feature. All are formed from a special verbal base derived from the verbal roots, धातु -s (*dhātu-s*), by several processes. This base is called the present stem.

7.4 **The गण-s (*Gaṇa*-s) of the Present System**

A few verbal roots, धातु -s (*dhātu-s*), have no forms belonging to the present system. The great majority of roots, धातु -s (*dhātu-s*), however, do have such forms. These roots, धातु -s (*dhātu-s*), are divided into ten separate conjugations classes, called गण-s (*gaṇa*-s) according to the way in which their present stem, the base for conjugation, is formed.

7.5 To form their present stems, the roots belonging to the different गण-s (*gaṇa*-s) may be augmented in one or both of two ways:

1. By the addition of a characteristic गण (*gaṇa*) sign.
   a) It may be (and is in eight of the ten गण-s [*gaṇa*-s]) suffixed to the root.
   b) It may be (as in the third गण [*gaṇa*]) prefixed into the root.
   c) It may be (as in the seventh गण [*gaṇa*]) infixed to the root itself.
2. By गुण (*guṇa*) (see 3.7) of the root vowel in some or all of the forms of the paradigm.

7.6 The गण-s (*gaṇa*-s) are ten in number and are so numbered by traditional grammarians. They are also given names based on a typical root for each गण (*gaṇa*). Thus, the first class is named for the root भू (√*bhū*—to be) and is called भ्वादिगण (*bhvādigaṇa*) or the गण (*gaṇa*) consisting of भू (√*bhū*), etc. We can call this the भू गण (*bhū gaṇa*).

7.7 **"a" गण-s** (*gaṇa*-s) **and "non-a" गण-s** (*gaṇa*-s)

Although the fact is not indicated by any grouping in the traditional ordering, the ten गण-s (*gaṇa*-s) fall typologically into two basic groups:

1. Those whose गण (*gaṇa*) sign either is or ends in the vowel अ (a) and is suffixed to the root, and
2. All other गण-s (*gaṇa*-s).

7.8 The major difference that should be grasped between the two groups is that roots of the first group (the "a" group) form a present stem that, once formed, is invariable throughout the conjugation(s) regardless of changes of number and voice, while roots of the second group ("non-a") form stems that are liable to variation, by a change either in the root or in the gaṇa sign.

7.9 **Strong and Weak Forms**

Roots of the "non-a" गण-s (*gaṇa*-s) have, in sharp contrast to those of the "a" गण-s (*gaṇa*-s), stronger and weaker stem forms.

7.10 The basis for the strong/weak distinction in the "non-a" गण-s (*gaṇa*-s) is quite simple and regular and must be memorized at once. The only strong forms are:

1. The three एकवचन परस्मैपद (*ekavacana parasmaipada*) persons of the लट् (*laṭ*) and लङ् (*laṅ*—imperfect [Lesson 8]).
2. The प्रथमपुरुष एकवचन परस्मैपद (*prathamapuruṣa ekavacana parasmaipada*) and *all* उत्तमपुरुष (*uttamapuruṣa*) forms (परस्मैपद [*parasmaipada*] and आत्मनेपद [*ātmanepada*] regardless of number) of the लोट् (*loṭ*—imperative [Lesson 11]).

In other words, with regard to the लट् (*laṭ*), the only conjugation that you need concern yourself with at the moment, only the three एकवचन परस्मैपद (*ekavacana parasmaipada*) forms are strong. All others (i.e., एकवचन आत्मनेपद [*ekavacana ātmanepada*] and all द्वि° [*dvivacana*] and बहु° [*bahuvacana*]) are weak.

7.11 The traditional list of the गण-s (*gaṇa*-s) is given below. Each is listed with its traditional number and name, the गण (*gaṇa*) sign, the stem strength, if any, and the प्रथमपुरुष एकवचन लट् (*prathmapuruṣa ekavacana laṭ*) of the root which names the गण (*gaṇa*). The problems of the individual गण-s (*gaṇa*-s) will be discussed separately below.

7.12 **The गण-s (*gaṇa*-s) of the Present System**

number	name root	gaṇa sign	placement of sign	stem strength	लट्	meaning
1.	भू √bhū	अ a	suffix to root	गुण of root vowel in *all* forms where possible (see 7.16)	भवति bhavati	he is, becomes
2.	अद् √ad	(Ø)	–	गुण of root vowel in strong forms	अत्ति atti	he eats
3.	हु √hu	अभ्यास (abhy-āsa)	prefix to root	गुण of root vowel in strong forms	जुहोति juhoti	he offers
4.	दिव् √div	य ya	suffix to root	none	दीव्यति dīvyati (note long ī)	he plays
5.	सु √su	नु nu	suffix to root	गुण of गण sign vowel in strong forms	सुनोति sunoti	he presses

number	name root	gaṇa sign	placement of sign	stem strength	लट्	meaning
6.	तुद् √tud	अ a	suffix to root	none	तुदति tudati	he pushes
7.	रुध् √rudh	न/न् na/n	infixed in root	infix is न (-na-) in strong forms, न् (-n-) in weak	रुणद्धि ruṇaddhi	he blocks
8.	तन् √tan	उ u	suffix to root	गुण of गण sign vowel in strong forms	तनोति tanoti	he stretches
9.	क्री √krī	ना/नी nā/nī	suffix to root	suffix is ना (-nā-) in strong forms, नी (-nī-) in weak	क्रीणाति krīṇāti	he buys
10.	चुर् √cur	-अय -aya	suffix to root	गुण of root vowel where possible (see 7.16)	चोरयति corayati	he steals

7.13 The remainder of this lesson deals in greater detail with the individual गण-s (*gaṇa*-s), their irregularities, and the most common and useful roots of each class. Where indicated, particular roots, with their present stem, should be learned immediately.

7.14 The first, or भू गण (√*bhū gaṇa*)

This is perhaps the most important of all the गण-s (*gaṇa*-s). Most of the verbs that we have already encountered belong to this class. To form their present stems, अ (a) is suffixed to the root, whose vowel takes गुण (*guṇa*) (3.7) if possible (see 7.16). The personal endings are added to this stem.

Examples:

त्यज् + अ → त्यज + ति → त्यजति

√*tyaj* + a → tyaja + ti → tyajati (he, she, it abandons)

भू + अ → भो + अ → भव् + अ + ति → भवति

√*bhū* + a → bho + a → bhav + a + ti → bhavati

(he, she, it is) (see 3.13.b)

वृत् + अ → वर्त् + अ + ते → वर्तते

√*vṛt* + a → vart + a + te → vartate (he, she, it is/exists)

जि + अ → जे + अ → जय् + अ + ति → जयति

√*ji* + a → je + a → jay + a + ti → jayati

(he, she, it conquers) (3.13.a)

वद् + अ → वद + मि → वदामि

√*vad* + a → vada + mi → vadāmi (see 4.22) (I say)

7.15 Irregular Roots of the भू गण (√*bhū gaṇa*)

a. A few roots with nasalized vowels lose the nasalization in the formation of the present stem.

Example:

दंश् → दशति

√daṃś → daśati (he, she, it bites)

सर्पस्तं दशति ।

sarpas taṃ daśati. (The snake bites him.)

b. Two very important roots of the भू गण (√*bhū gaṇa*) lose their final consonants and replace them with the conjunct च्छ् (-cch-).

Examples:

गम् रामो गच्छति ।

√gam rāmo gacchati. (Rāma goes.)

यम् सीता यच्छति ।

√yam sītā yacchati. (Sītā gives.)

Learn these roots.

c. The root सद् (√*sad*—to sit) has an irregular present stem, सीद (*sīda*).

Example:

अर्जुनो विषीदति ।

arjuno viṣīdati. (Arjuna sinks down in despair.)

d. The two important roots स्था (√*sthā*—stand, be located) and पा (√*pā*—drink) are conjugated on the basis of the irregular stems तिष्ठ (*tiṣṭha*), and पिब (*piba*), respectively.

Examples:

देवाः सोमं पिबन्ति ।

devāḥ somaṃ pibanti. (The gods drink soma.)

रामश्च सीता च कुत्र तिष्ठतः ।

rāmaś ca sītā ca kutra tiṣṭhataḥ?

(Where are Rāma and Sītā standing?)

7.16 Exceptions to regular गुण (*guṇa*) strength

There are two instances in which a root vowel, even though it should be subjected to गुण (*guṇa*), is exempt from this strengthening.

1. A long root vowel followed by a final consonant.
2. Any root vowel followed by a final consonant cluster.

Examples:

जीव् (1 P) → जीवति

√jīv (1P) (lives) jīvati (he lives). The root vowel ई (ī) is by rule 1 above not subject to गुण (*guṇa*) even though first गण (*gaṇa*) roots normally take it.

चिन्त् (10P) → चिन्तयति

√cint (10P) (thinks) → cintayati (he thinks). Here इ (*i*) is exempt from गुण (*guṇa*) by rule 2 even though tenth गण (*gaṇa*) roots normally take it.

7.17 **The second, or अद् गण** (*√ad gaṇa*)

This गण (*gaṇa*) is sometimes referred to as "root class" because of the fact that its present stem is the same as the root. This results from the fact that this गण (*gaṇa*) has no characteristic गण (*gaṇa*) sign. The root vowel takes गुण (*guṇa*) in the strong forms (7.10).

7.18 **Internal Consonant सन्धि** (*Sandhi*)

In this and several of the other non-a गण-s (*gaṇa*-s), the present stem may often end in a consonant, which must then be frequently placed in juxtaposition with an initial consonant of an ending. This brings into play a number of internal सन्धि (*sandhi*) rules. Some of the more important of these rules will be mentioned here and at other appropriate points.

a. A voiced non-aspirated स्पर्श (*sparśa*) before any non-voiced व्यञ्जन (*vyañjana*) (as in absolute final position) is changed to its corresponding non-voiced स्पर्श (*sparśa*).

   Example:

   विद् + ति → वेत्ति

   √vid (2P) (know) + ti → vetti (he knows)

b. A स्पर्श (sparśa) or a nasal of the दन्त्य वर्ग (*dantya varga*) following any sound of the मूर्धन्य वर्ग (*mūrdhanya varga*) except र् (r) is normally changed to its corresponding मूर्धन्य (*mūrdhanya*) sound. (Compare 3.58–3.59.)

Example:

   द्विष् + ति → द्वेष्टि

   √dviṣ (2P) (hate) + ti → dveṣṭi (he hates)

c. The sound ष् (ṣ), when it precedes the sound स् (s), is generally changed to क् (k). The following स् (s) is then (by rule 3.58) changed itself into ष् (ṣ).
Example:
द्विष् + सि → द्वेक्षि
√dviṣ (2P) (hate) + si → dvekṣi (you hate)

d. A nasal before स् (s) is changed to अनुस्वार (*anusvāra*).
Example:
हन् + सि → हंसि
√han (2P) (kill) + si → haṃsi (you kill)

e. Root final च् when it precedes any व्यञ्जन (*vyañjana*) other than a nasal or the अन्तःस्थ व् (*antaḥstha* "v"), is treated as though it were the sound क् (k) in the same position.
Example:
वच् + ति → वक्ति
√vac (2P) (speak) + ti → vakti (he speaks)

वच् + सि → वक्षि
√vac (2P) (speak) + si → vakṣi (you speak)
(See c. above)

7.19 **Some Examples of Second गण (*gaṇa*) Forms**

Examples:
इ + ति → एति
√i (go) + ti (strong) → eti (he goes)

इ + मः → इमः
√i (go) + maḥ (weak) → imaḥ (we go)

इ + अन्ति → यन्ति
√i (go) + anti (weak) → yanti (they go)

द्विष् + सि → द्वेक्षि
√dviṣ (hate) + si (strong) → dvekṣi (you hate)

द्विष् + अन्ति → द्विषन्ति
√dviṣ (hate) + anti (weak) → dviṣanti (they hate)

विद् + मि → वेद्मि
√vid (know) + mi (strong) → vedmi (I know)
विद् + वः → विद्वः
√vid (know) + vaḥ (weak) → vidvaḥ (we two know)

7.20 **Irregular Roots of the अद् गण** (*√ad gaṇa*)

a. By far the most important root of the गण (*gaṇa*) is अस् (*√as*—be). It is irregular in that it loses its initial vowel in weak forms of all parts of the present system except the लङ् (imperfect) and loses its स् (s) before the स् (s) of the मध्यम° एक° परस्मैपद (*madhyama° eka° parasmaipada*) ending. This paradigm, given at 4.24, should by now have been memorized.

b. The very common root ब्रू (*√brū*—speak, say) takes the additional vowel ई (ī) between its strong stem and an initial consonant of an ending.
Examples:
ब्रवीमि
bravīmi (I say)

ब्रवीति
bravīti (he says)

but: ब्रूमः
brūmaḥ (we say)

ब्रूते
brūte (Ā) (he says)
The consonant व् (v) is inserted before endings beginning with a vowel and the root vowel is shortened.
Examples:
ब्रुवन्ति
bruvanti (they speak)

ब्रुवते
bruvate (Ā) (they speak) (see 4.22.e)

This root does not occur outside the present system.

c. The roots रुद् (√*rud*—weep) and स्वप् (√*svap*—sleep) insert इ (i) before consonant initial endings.
Examples:
स्वपिति नृपः ।
svapiti nṛpaḥ. (The king sleeps.)

कस्माद्रोदिषि देवि ।
kasmād rodiṣi devi (Why are you weeping, lady?)

d. The common root हन् (√*han*—kill) is rather peculiar in that before consonant initial endings (except म् [m] and व् [v]), the weak stem loses its न् (n), while before vowel initial endings, the weak stem loses its vowel अ् (a). In the latter case the initial ह् (h) is changed to घ् (gh). The paradigm is as follows:

हन् (√*han*) (2P)

वचन vacana →	एक° eka°	द्वि° dvi°	बहु° bahu°
पुरुष puruṣa			
प्रथम° prathama°	हन्ति hanti	हतः hataḥ	घ्नन्ति ghnanti
मध्यम° madhyama°	हंसि haṃsi	हथः hathaḥ	हथ hatha
उत्तम° uttama°	हन्मि hanmi	हन्वः hanvaḥ	हन्मः hanmaḥ

7.21 **The third, or हु गण (√*hu gaṇa*)**

The third गण (*gaṇa*) is unique in that its गण (*gaṇa*) sign is prefixed to the root. The sign is even more striking in that it has no fixed form for the whole class but takes its form from the phonological structure of each root. It is in fact a sort of echo syllable or "reduplication," which the Indian grammarians call अभ्यास (*abhyāsa*), or repetition.

7.22 **General Rules of अभ्यास** (*Abhyāsa*)

The basic rules of "reduplication" (which also apply to a number of forms outside the present system) are that the अभ्यास (*abhyāsa*) syllable represents a part of the root. A root beginning with a vowel will have an अभ्यास (*abhyāsa*) syllable consisting of that vowel, or of the vowel and a following consonant. For a root beginning with a consonant or consonant cluster, the अभ्यास (*abhyāsa*) will consist of that consonant or the first consonant of that cluster, and the following vowel.

7.23 **Specific Rules for the हु गण** (*√hu gaṇa*)

a. A root vowel generally appears in its short form in अभ्यास (*abhyāsa*).

   Example:

   दा (*√dā*—give) → ददा (*dadā*) = present stem, *but*

b. Root vowel ऋ (ṛ) is changed to इ (i) in अभ्यास (*abhyāsa*).

   Example:

   भृ (*√bhṛ*—bear) → बिभृ (*bibhṛ*) = present stem.

c. As is evident in the previous example, an initial aspirated consonant is represented in अभ्यास (*abhyāsa*) by its non-aspirated counterpart:

   Example:

   धा (*√dhā*—put) → दधा (*dadhā*) = present stem.

d. An initial कण्ठ्य (*kaṇṭhya*—velar) is represented by the तालव्य (*tālavya*—palatal) corresponding to it in voicing, while initial ह् (h) is replaced by ज् (j).

   Example:

   हु (*√hu*—sacrifice) → जुहु (*juhu*) = present stem.

7.24 Strong forms of the present stem show गुण (*guṇa*) of the root vowel.

Examples:

भृ (√*bhṛ*—bear) → बिभर्ति (*bibharti*—he bears)

बिभृमः (*bibhṛmaḥ*—we bear)

हु (√*hu*—offer as a sacrifice) → जुहोमि (*juhomi*—I offer)

जुहुमः (*juhumaḥ*—we offer)

7.25 It is an important peculiarity of this गण (*gaṇa*) that its roots regularly require the loss of the न् (n) of the प्रथम° बहु° परस्मैपद (*prathama° bahu° parasmaipada*) ending, not only (as with other non-a गण-s [*gaṇa*-s]) in the आत्मनेपद (*ātmanepada*).

Examples:

जुहोति

juhoti (he offers)

जुह्वति

juhvati (they offer)

बिभेति

bibheti (he is afraid)

बिभ्यति

bibhyati (they are afraid)

7.26 **Irregular roots of the हु गण** (√*hu gaṇa*)

There are two extremely common roots belonging to the हु गण (√*hu gaṇa*) that require special attention and with which you must become familiar.

a. These roots दा (√*dā*—give) and धा (√*dhā*—place, put) are alike in completely losing their root vowel in all weak forms.

Examples:

ददाति

dadāti (he gives) (strong)

दद्मः
dadmaḥ (we give) (weak)

दधाति
dadhāti (he puts) (strong)

दधति
dadhati (they put) (weak)

b. When the ध् (dh) of the weak stem दध् (*dadh*) comes directly before the त् (t), थ् (th), or स् (s) of an ending, it becomes त् (t) and **its lost aspiration reappears** in the initial of the अभ्यास (*abhyāsa*) syllable.
Example:
धत्तः
dhattaḥ (the two place)

7.27 **The fourth, or दिव् गण** (*√div gaṇa*)

The गण (*gaṇa*) sign is य (ya). It is suffixed to the root, which takes no strength.

Examples:

नश् नश्यति
√naś → naśyati (he is destroyed)

नश्यामि
naśyāmi (I am destroyed)

Some common roots of this गण (*gaṇa*) are:

कुप् → कुप्यति
√kup (P) (be angry) kupyati (he is angry)

क्रुध् → क्रुध्यति
√krudh (P) (be angry) krudhyati (he is angry)

मन् → मन्ये
√man (Ā) (think) manye (I think)

7.28 **The fifth, or सु (√*su*) and eighth, or तन् (√*tan*) गण-s (*gaṇa*-s)**

These two गण-s (*gaṇa*-s) are treated very similarly. The गण (*gaṇa*) sign of the सु (√*su*) class is नु (nu), and that of the तन् (√*tan*) class is उ (u); but, as almost all of the roots of the latter end in न् (n), the two conjugations show few differences.

7.29 **Rules for the सु (√*su*) and तन् गण-s (√*tan gaṇa*-s)**

a. The final vowel of the stem उ (u) is subject to गुण (*guṇa*) in the strong forms.

Examples:

सु	सुनोति	सुनुमः
√su (press) →	sunoti	sunumaḥ
तन्	तनोति	तनुमः
√tan (stretch) →	tanoti	tanumaḥ

b. The उ (u) of the weak forms of either गण (*gaṇa*) may be dropped optionally before the म् (m) or व् (v) of द्वि° (*dvi*°) and बहु° (*bahu*°) endings. सु गण (√*su gaṇa*) roots with final consonants are an exception to this.

Examples:

तन्	तनुमः / तन्मः
√tan →	tanumaḥ or tanmaḥ
सु	सुनुवः / सुन्वः
√su →	sunuvaḥ or sunvaḥ
but आप्	आप्नुमः
√āp →	āpnumaḥ (we obtain)

7.30 The most important roots of these गण-s (*gaṇa*-s) to learn are:

कृ	√kṛ (8P) (do, make)
श्रु	√śru (5P) (hear, hear about, listen)
आप्	√āp (5P) (get, obtain)

The first two are somewhat irregular.

a. कृ (√*kṛ*) is one of the most common and useful roots in the language and, like भू (√*bhū*) and अस् (√*as*), must be memorized. It is somewhat irregular in that:

i. It is the only root of the तन् गण (√*tan gaṇa*) that does not have a root-final न् (n).

ii. Both its strong and weak forms are irregular in that:

a) Strong forms involve गुण (*guṇa*) of *both* the root vowel ऋ (ṛ) and the गण (*gaṇa*) sign vowel उ (u). The strong stem, then, is करो (*karo*).

Examples:
करोति
karoti (he does)

करोषि
karoṣi (you do)

करोमि
karomi (I do)

b) In weak forms, the root changes to कुर् (*kur*). The weak stem, then, is कुरु (*kuru*).
Example:
कुरुतः
kurutaḥ (the two do)

iii. As a corollary to rule 7.29.b, weak forms of कृ (√*kṛ*) **always** lose the उ (u) vowel of the गण (*gaṇa*) sign before म् (m) and व् (v) of द्वि° (*dvi*°) and बहु° (*bahu*°) endings.
Example:
कुर्मः
kurmaḥ (we do)

b. The root श्रु (√*śru*) becomes शृ (√*śṛ*) before the गण (*gaṇa*) sign. Thus the paradigm is शृणोति (*śṛṇoti*), शृणुतः (*śṛṇutaḥ*), शृण्वन्ति (*śṛṇvanti*), etc.

7.31 **The sixth, or तुद् गण** (*√tud gaṇa*)

This गण (*gaṇa*), like the भू गण (*√bhū gaṇa*), has अ (a) as its गण (*gaṇa*) sign and behaves just like that गण (*gaṇa*) except that its roots never take गुण (*guṇa*) before the गण (*gaṇa*) sign.

Example:

नुद्	नुदति
√nud (push) →	nudati (he pushes)

7.32 a. A few relatively common roots of this गण (*gaṇa*) are strengthened before the गण (*gaṇa*) sign by the infixation of a nasal before, and corresponding to, the root final consonant.

Examples:

मुच्	मुञ्चति
√muc (release) →	muñcati
सिच्	सिञ्चति
√sic (sprinkle) →	siñcati
विद्	विन्दति
√vid (find) →	vindati

b. The common root इष् (*√iṣ*—wish, want) forms the present stem इच्छ (*iccha*).

Example:

इच्छामि

icchāmi (I want)

7.33 **The seventh, or रुध् गण** (*√rudh gaṇa*)

Roots of this गण (*gaṇa*) are relatively few in number and all end in consonants. The गण (*gaṇa*) sign is a nasal consonant, homorganic with the root-final consonant and infixed immediately before it. In the strong forms, the sign is strengthened to the syllable न (na).

7.34 **Internal Consonant सन्धि** *(Sandhi)*

The seventh गण (*gaṇa*), like the second, presents a few problems of internal consonant सन्धि (*sandhi*). The following rules are applicable:

a. A nasal immediately preceding a स्पर्श (*sparśa*) is changed to the nasal of the same वर्ग (*varga*) as that स्पर्श (*sparśa*).
Example:
युज्
√yuj (yoke, join) + infix न् (n) → (weak stem) युञ्ज् (*yuñj*);

युञ्ज् -तः युङ्क्तः
yuñj + -taḥ → yuṅktaḥ (the two join)

b. Root final ज् (j) of several roots that belong to this गण (*gaṇa*) is treated exactly like root final च् (c). (See 7.18.e)
Example:
युज् -थः युङ्क्थः
√yuj + -thaḥ → yuṅkthaḥ (you two join)

c. i. An aspirated स्पर्श (*sparśa*) loses its aspiration when it occurs immediately before any स्पर्श (*sparśa*) or ऊष्मन् (*ūṣman*).
Example:
रुध् रुन्त्से
rudh (Ā) → runtse (you block)

ii. If a root final voiced aspirate स्पर्श (*sparśa*) (except as in 7.26.b) precedes initial त् (t) or थ् (th) of an ending, the त् (t) or थ् (th) is voiced *and* aspirated.
Examples:
रुध् √rudh (block, prevent)
strong stem रुणध् (*ruṇadh*) + ति (ti) →
रुणद्धि (*ruṇaddhi*—he blocks)

weak stem रुन्ध् (*rundh*) + तः (*taḥ*) →
रुन्द्धः (*runddhaḥ*—the two block)

7.35 **Some Examples of रुध् गण (√*rudh gaṇa*) roots:**

A few relatively common रुध्गण (√*rudh gaṇa*) roots, with some examples are:

युज् (√*yuj*—join)	युनक्ति	(*yunakti*—he joins)
	युञ्ज्मः	(*yuñjmaḥ*—we join)
भुज् (√*bhuj*—eat)	भुनक्षि	(*bhunakṣi*—you eat)
	भुञ्जन्ति	(*bhuñjanti*—they eat)
छिद् (√*chid*—cut)	छिनत्ति	(*chinatti*—he cuts) (See 7.18.a)
	छिन्दन्ति	(*chindanti*—they cut)

7.36 **The ninth, or क्री गण** (√*krī gaṇa*)

This गण (*gaṇa*) has relatively few roots of common occurrence. The गण (*gaṇa*) sign is the syllable नी (nī) suffixed to the unstrengthened root. In the strong forms, the suffix is ना (nā). The ई (ī) of the weak stem is lost before endings beginning with a vowel.

Examples:

क्री क्रीणाति

√krī krīṇāti (he buys)

क्रीणीमः

krīṇīmaḥ (we buy)

क्रीणन्ति

krīṇanti (they buy)

7.37 The most important and common root of the गण (*gaṇa*), ज्ञा (√*jñā*—know), is irregular in that it loses its own root-nasal ञ् (ñ) before the गण (*gaṇa*) sign or, in other words, throughout its entire present conjugation.

Example:

ज्ञा	जानाति	जानीमः	जानन्ति
√jñā,	jānāti,	jānīmaḥ,	jānanti, etc.

जानामि धर्मं न च मे प्रवृत्तिः ।
जानाम्यधर्मं न च मे निवृत्तिः ॥
jānāmi dharmaṃ na ca me pravṛttiḥ.
jānāmy adharmaṃ na ca me nivṛttiḥ.
(I know what's right, but I don't do it.
I know what's wrong, but I don't stop.)
Memorize this example and the forms of this useful root.

7.38 **The tenth, or चुर् गण** (√*cur gaṇa*)

This गण (*gaṇa*) has very few roots. Its गण (*gaṇa*) sign is अय (aya), which is suffixed to the root. It is thus like the other "a" गण-s (*gaṇa*-s). The root vowel is strengthened by गुण (*guṇa*). Perhaps the most common root in this गण (*gaṇa*) is चिन्त् (√*cint*—think) (see 7.16.2).

Example:

चिन्तयति चिन्तयामि चिन्तयन्ति

EXERCISES

A. Translate the reading into English.

B. Translate the following sentences into Sanskrit (number in brackets indicates गण (*gaṇa*) to which root belongs).

1. Where is the demon? (use वृत्—√*vṛt* 1Ā); I think he is in the ashram (*āśramaḥ*) (use स्था—√*sthā* 1P).
2. How does the hero cut off the limbs of the demon? I know! He does it with the arrow.
3. How do you know? Since the lady says it, therefore I know it.
4. Whenever Rāma comes, the demons are afraid (use भी—√*bhi* 3P), but Rāma is never afraid.
5. Lady! In this region there is another forest.
6. Then the sages of the hermitage obtained permission from the goddess (देवी–*devī*).
7. The rākṣasas sit (सद्—√*sad* 1P) on the ground and perform (कृ—√*kṛ* 8P) meditation.

8. When Rāma picks up an arrow, the demons all flee.
9. The descendants of Raghu assembled for the protection of the city of Mithilā.
10. The women of that region do not understand the bliss of marriage.
11. Hail, daughter! Where does the sage go?
12. He went to Mithilā; and now, a rākṣasa is harassing me here in the forest.

C. Write out and learn the (P/Ā) paradigm of कृ (√*kṛ*) (8).

D. Memorize the following verse.

इतो न किंचित् परतो न किंचिद्
यतो यतो यामि ततो न किंचित् ।
विचार्य पश्यामि जगन्न किंचित्
स्वात्मावबोधादधिकं न किंचित् ॥

There is nothing whatever here, nothing elsewhere.
Wherever I go there is nothing there either.
When I think about it, I see that the world itself is nothing.
There is nothing greater than understanding one's Self.

READING

यदा नृपस्यानुज्ञामाप्नोति रामस्तदा मुनिना सह सो ऽरण्यं गच्छति । तत्र वने बहव ऋषयो वसन्त्याश्रमेषु । ते सर्वदा ध्यानमाचरन्ति यज्ञान्कुर्वन्ति च । तस्मिन्नेव काले बहवो राक्षसास्तान्मुनीन्बाधन्ते । राक्षसेभ्यो मुनीनां रक्षणायागच्छति रामः । बालको ऽपि स वीरो बहून्राक्षसानिषुभिर्हन्ति । यत्र यत्रायाति राघवस्ततस्ततो निशाचरा बिभ्यति पलायन्ते च । यत्र कुत्रापि राक्षसान्पश्यतो रामो लक्ष्मणश्च तत्र तेषां गात्राणि छिन्त्तः । यदा सर्वे निशाचरा हता निर्गता वा सन्ति तदा रामो वनं जहाति मिथिलां चागच्छति । तस्मिन्देशे ऽतीव पण्डितो नृपो जनको नाम राज्यं करोति । जनकस्यातीव रमणीया कन्या सीता नाम । सर्वासां नारीणां श्रेष्ठा सेति चिन्तयन्ति जनाः । सीतया सह विवाहं करोमीति चिन्तयन्ति सर्वे नृपाः । ततस्ते मिथिलायां समागच्छन्ति ॥

GLOSSARY

अनुज्ञा
anujñā (f)—permission

अरण्यम्
araṇyam (n)—forest

आ + चर् → आचरति
ā + √car (1P) → ācarati—practice

आप् → आप्नोति
√āp (5P) → āpnoti—obtain

आ + या → आयाति
ā + √yā (2P) → āyāti—come

इदानीम्
idānīm (ind)—now

इषुः
iṣuḥ (m)—arrow

इह
iha (ind)—here

कन्या
kanyā (f)—daughter

कुप् → कुप्यति
√kup (4P) → kupyati—be angry; become angry

क्रुध् → क्रुध्यति
√krudh (4P) → krudhyati—be angry; become angry

गत
gata (adj)—gone

गात्रम्
gātram (n)—limb

छिद् → छिनत्ति
√chid (7P) → chinatti—cut, cut off

जनकः
janakaḥ (prop. noun)—name of Sītā's father

ततः
tataḥ (ind)—hence, then

देवी
devī (f)—lady, queen

देशः
deśaḥ (m)—place, region

ध्यानम्
dhyānam (n)—meditation

निर्गत
nirgata (adj)—departed

निशाचरः
niśācaraḥ (m)—Lit. "night roamer," a rākṣasa

पण्डितः
paṇḍitaḥ (adj)—wise, (m)—learned man

पला + इ → पलायते
palā + √i (1Ā) → palāyate—flee (conjugate like an a-गण root from stem पलाय—*palāya*)

बहु
bahu (adj)—many

बाध् → बाधते
√bādh (1Ā) → bādhate—harass

भी → बिभेति (बिभ्यति)
√bhī (3P) → bibheti (bibhyati = 3rd pl.)—fear

भूमिः
bhūmiḥ (f)—land, earth

मिथिला
mithilā (f prop)—city of Mithilā

यत् (-द्)
yat (-d)—used to introduce direct or indirect discourses, used with or without इति at the end

रक्षणम्
rakṣaṇam (n)—protection

रमणीय
ramaṇīya (adj)—beautiful

राघवः
rāghavaḥ (m)—descendant of Raghu = Rāma

वा
vā (ind)—or (placed after words like *ca*)

विवाहः
vivāhaḥ (m)—marriage

सद् → सीदति
√sad (1P) → sīdati—sit (See 7.15.c)

सम् + आ + गम् → समागच्छति
sam + ā + √gam (1P) → samāgacchati—assemble

सर्वदा
sarvadā (ind)—always

स्था → तिष्ठति
√sthā (1P) → tiṣṭhati—remain

हा → जहाति
√hā (3P) → jahāti—abandon

LESSON 8

Noun Stem Strength; Noun Stems in -अन् (-an); अनद्यतन भूते लङ् (Anadyatana Bhūte Lañ) The Imperfect; उपसर्ग-s (Upasarga-s)

8.0 All the noun stems introduced thus far have ended in vowels. This is not the case, however, with all nouns. Several classes of nouns have stems with consonant finals. These stems (and some vowel stems—see below, 10.0), unlike the nouns so far learned, have a distinction of stem strength.

8.1 **Noun Stem Strength**

a. Of पुंलिङ्ग and स्त्रीलिङ्ग stems, the only strong forms are प्रथमा विभक्ति, एकवचन, द्विवचन, and बहुवचन; and the द्वितीया विभक्ति, एकवचन, and द्विवचन. The rest are weaker. Some stems further distinguish, among the weaker forms, a weak and a weakest, depending upon whether the inflectional ending begins with a consonant (weak) or a vowel (weakest).

b. Of नपुंसकलिङ्ग stems, only the प्रथमा and द्वितीया बहुवचन are strong. If the stem distinguishes degree of weakness, the प्रथमा and द्वितीया एकवचन are weak while the same cases of the द्विवचन are the weakest. Other cases are, as usual, the same as the corresponding पुंलिङ्ग stems.

8.2 **Noun Stems in** -अन् (-an)

An important class of consonant stems ends in -अन् (-an). These stems are all पुंलिङ्ग or नपुंसकलिङ्ग. Try to learn these nouns in both stem and nominative singular form. If only the first is learned, you will not know the gender; if only the second, you are apt to forget the stem ending and confuse the nouns with those of the -अ (-a) or -आ (-ā) classes.

8.3 **Strength in** -अन् (-an) **Stems**

The strong forms show the last vowel of the stem as -आ (-ā), the weak as -अ (-a), and the weakest as Ø (i.e., the vowel is lost). The difference in the degree of the strong-weak distinction has to do with the place of accentual strength at an earlier stage of the language. This also accounts for the strength in the present system. This type of accentuation is absent in classical Sanskrit, although its effects are clearly seen. In dealing with this class of nouns, it is wise to learn the paradigms of the important items thoroughly. As an aid to memory, however, keep in mind a short sentence incorporating the instrumental singular form of each item. This case shows the weakest form if there is one. For practical purposes keep in mind that stems whose second consonant is part of a conjunct (e.g., आत्मन् [*ātman*], कर्मन् [*karman*]) show the strong/weak alternation while others (e.g., राजन् [*rājan*], नामन् [*nāman*]) show the strong/weak/weakest alternation.

Examples:

राज्ञा विना राज्यं नश्यति ।

rājñā vinā rājyaṃ naśyati.

(Without a king, the kingdom perishes.)

कर्मणा विना न कश्चन जीवति ।

karmaṇā vinā na kaścana jīvati. (Nobody lives without karma.)

आत्मनात्मानं जानाति पण्डितः ।

ātmanātmānaṃ jānāti paṇḍitaḥ.

(The wise man knows the Self by means of the Self.)

अयोध्यायां राजा वर्तते दशरथो नाम्ना ।

ayodhyāyāṃ rājā vartate daśaratho nāmnā.

(There is a king in Ayodhyā, Daśaratha by name.)

8.4 **Typical Case Endings**

Note the case endings of these nouns. Although these and other stems are statistically outnumbered by the -अ (-a) and -आ (-ā) classes, these endings are really the "typical" ones for each case. This is especially important to note in the एकवचन

weak cases. The proper endings then, for consonant and many vowel stems are:

तृतीया—आ
चतुर्थी—ए
पञ्चमी—अः
षष्ठी—अः
सप्तमी—इ

Memorize these endings as quickly as possible.

8.5 Paradigms of -अन् (-an) stems

a. i. पुंलिङ्ग; आत्मन् (*ātman*—the soul, self) (strong/weak)

वचन vacana →	एक° eka°	द्वि° dvi°	बहु° bahu°
विभक्ति ↓ vibhakti			
1.	आत्मा ātmā	आत्मानौ ātmānau	आत्मानः ātmānaḥ
2.	आत्मानम् ātmānam	आत्मानौ ātmānau	आत्मनः ātmanaḥ
3.	आत्मना ātmanā	आत्मभ्याम् ātmabhyām	आत्मभिः ātmabhiḥ
4.	आत्मने ātmane	आत्मभ्याम् ātmabhyām	आत्मभ्यः ātmabhyaḥ
5.	आत्मनः ātmanaḥ	आत्मभ्याम् ātmabhyām	आत्मभ्यः ātmabhyaḥ
6.	आत्मनः ātmanaḥ	आत्मनोः ātmanoḥ	आत्मनाम् ātmanām
7.	आत्मनि ātmani	आत्मनोः ātmanoḥ	आत्मसु ātmasu
सम्° sam.	आत्मन् ātman	आत्मानौ ātmānau	आत्मानः ātmānaḥ

ii. पुंलिङ्ग; राजन् (*rājan*—king) (strong/weak/weakest)

वचन vacana →	एक° eka°	द्वि° dvi°	बहु° bahu°
विभक्ति ↓ vibhakti			
1.	राजा rājā	राजानौ rājānau	राजानः rājānaḥ
2.	राजानम् rājānam	राजानौ rājānau	राज्ञः rājñaḥ
3.	राज्ञा rājñā	राजभ्याम् rājabhyām	राजभिः rājabhiḥ
4.	राज्ञे rājñe	राजभ्याम् rājabhyām	राजभ्यः rājabhyaḥ
5.	राज्ञः rājñaḥ	राजभ्याम् rājabhyām	राजभ्यः rājabhyaḥ
6.	राज्ञः rājñaḥ	राज्ञोः rājñoḥ	राज्ञाम् rājñām
7.	राज्ञि / राजनि rājñi / rājani	राज्ञोः rājñoḥ	राजसु rājasu
सम्° sam.	राजन् rājan	राजानौ rājānau	राजानः rājānaḥ

b. i. नपुंसकलिङ्ग; कर्मन् (*karman*—action) (strong/weak)

वचन vacana →	एक° eka°	द्वि° dvi°	बहु° bahu°
विभक्ति ↓ vibhakti			
1.	कर्म karma	कर्मणी karmaṇī	कर्माणि karmāṇi
2.	कर्म karma	कर्मणी karmaṇī	कर्माणि karmāṇi
3.	कर्मणा karmaṇā	कर्मभ्याम् karmabhyām	कर्मभिः karmabhiḥ

4.	कर्मणे karmaṇe	कर्मभ्याम् karmabhyām	कर्मभ्यः karmabhyaḥ
5.	कर्मणः karmaṇaḥ	कर्मभ्याम् karmabhyām	कर्मभ्यः karmabhyaḥ
6.	कर्मणः karmaṇaḥ	कर्मणोः karmaṇoḥ	कर्मणाम् karmaṇām
7.	कर्मणि karmaṇi	कर्मणोः karmaṇoḥ	कर्मसु karmasu
सम्° sam.	कर्मन् / कर्म karman/karma	कर्मणी karmaṇī	कर्माणि karmāṇi

ii. नपुंसकलिङ्ग; नामन् (*nāman*—name) (strong/weak/weakest)

वचन vacana →	एक° eka°	द्वि° dvi°	बहु° bahu°
विभक्ति ↓ vibhakti			
1.	नाम nāma	नामनी / नाम्नी nāmanī/nāmnī	नामानि nāmāni
2.	नाम nāma	नामनी / नाम्नी nāmanī/nāmnī	नामानि nāmāni
3.	नाम्ना nāmnā	नामभ्याम् nāmabhyām	नामभिः nāmabhiḥ
4.	नाम्ने nāmne	नामभ्याम् nāmabhyām	नामभ्यः nāmabhyaḥ
5.	नाम्नः nāmnaḥ	नामभ्याम् nāmabhyām	नामभ्यः nāmabhyaḥ
6.	नाम्नः nāmnaḥ	नाम्नोः nāmnoḥ	नाम्नाम् nāmnām
7.	नाम्नि / नामनि nāmni/nāmani	नाम्नोः nāmnoḥ	नामसु nāmasu
सम्° sam.	नामन् / नाम nāman/nāma	नामनी / नाम्नी nāmanī/nāmni	नामानि nāmāni

8.6 **अनद्यतनभूते लङ्** (*Anadyatanabhūte Laṅ*); **The Imperfect**

This is one of the several verbal (and nominal-verbal) forms used to indicate preterite or "past" time in Sanskrit. All of these forms are best translated as "simple past" tenses in English. Keep clearly in mind that terms like "imperfect" have been given by Western grammarians as classifiers on the basis of parallels with grammars of classical languages. **They do not indicate anything** with regard to the "aspect" or degree of duration or repetition of the action or state suggested by a verbal root. Even the Sanskrit name अनद्यतनभूते (past time prior to today) serves now only as a classifier. The form is by no means actually restricted in its application as the name would suggest.

8.7 The लङ् is formed mechanically from the present stems of the previous lesson. Once these are learned, the लङ् is quite simple and so has the virtue of greatly expanding your ability to use the language with a minimum of new memorization.

8.8 **Formation of the लङ्**

The लङ् is formed from the appropriate present stems by two simple steps:

1. A preterite augment: the syllable अ (a) is prefixed to the stem. This augment, or आगम (*āgama*), which is used with some other past tenses, is peculiar phonologically in that it combines with root initial vowels to form the वृद्धि of the initial instead of the expected (3.7) गुण.

   Example:

   इ

   √i (2P) (go)

   अ + इ → ऐ

   a (augment) + i (weak stem) → ai (weak stem of लङ्)

2. To the appropriate लङ् stems (strong or weak as at 7.10.1) are directly suffixed the appropriate "secondary" endings.

8.9 The Secondary Endings for the लङ् (*lañ*) are:

	परस्मैपद			आत्मनेपद		
	एक°	द्वि°	बहु°	एक°	द्वि°	बहु°
प्रथम°	त् -t	ताम् -tām	अन् / उः -an/uḥ	त -ta	आताम् -ātām	अन्त / अत / रन् -anta/ata/ran
मध्यम°	स् -s	तम् -tam	त -ta	थाः -thāḥ	आथाम् -āthām	ध्वम् -dhvam
उत्तम°	अम् -am	व -va	म -ma	इ / ए -i/e	वहि -vahi	महि -mahi

It is evident that they are often closely related to the "primary" endings but are shorter or lighter. The उत्तम° एक° आत्मनेपद ending इ (i) regularly combines with the अ (a) of a preceding गण sign to form ए (e).

8.10 "अ" गण-s

For the "a" गण-s the situation is quite simple and regular.

Root	प्रथम°एक°लट्	प्रथम°एक°लङ्	*Meaning*
भू √bhū	भवति bhavati	अभवत् abhavat	he was
गम् √gam	गच्छति gacchati	अगच्छत् agacchat	he went
मन् √man	मन्यते manyate	अमन्यत amanyata	he thought
कुप् √kup	कुप्यति kupyati	अकुप्यत् akupyat	he was angry

Rules for adding the terminations are the same as those given at 4.22 above. The प्रथम° बहु° परस्मैपद takes the ending -अन् (-an). The प्रथम° बहु° आत्मनेपद takes the ending -अन्त (-anta).

Before these endings, and before the उत्तम° एक° परस्मैपद ending -अम् (-am), the अ (a) of the गण signs is lost.

अगच्छन्	(*agacchan*)	they went
अभवन्	(*abhavan*)	they were
अवदम्	(*avadam*)	I said
अमन्यन्त	(*amanyanta*)	they thought

8.11 **"Non-अ" गण-s** (*gaṇa-s*)

The "non-अ" गण-s are also generally regular, but there are a few points that require mention.

a. The third, हु, गण takes the ending उः (uḥ) in प्रथम° बहु° परस्मैपद. Before this ending the final vowel of the stem is subject to गुण.

Examples:

हु अजुहोत् अजुहुताम्
√hu → ajuhot (he offered), ajuhutām (those two offered),
अजुहवुः
but ajuhavuḥ (they offered).

b. The seventh, रुध्, गण is quite regular, but note that the प्रथम° and मध्यम° of the strong forms present what appear to be anomalous endings because of the fact that their stem-final consonants form, with the single consonants of the endings, conjuncts that must be resolved (see 3.25.f) by the loss of what are, here, the actual endings.

Examples: भुज् (√*bhuj*—eat) (7P)

प्रथम°	मध्यम°
(अभुनक्त्) → अभुनक्	(अभुनक्ष्) → अभुनक्
(abhunakt) → abhunak	(abhunakṣ) → abhunak

c. The important root अस् (be) inserts the vowel ई (ī) between the stem and the endings त् (t) and स् (s) of the लङ् yielding आसीः (*āsīḥ*—you were) and the enormously common narrative आसीत् (*āsīt*—he, she, it was; or there was).

Example:

आसीद्राजा दशरथो नाम । राज्ञो राज्ये बहवो मुनय आसन् ।

āsīd rājā daśaratho nāma. rājño rājye bahavo munaya āsan.

(There was a king by the name of Daśaratha. There were many sages in the king's realm.)

8.12 उपसर्ग-s (*Upasarga*-s): **Verbal Prefixes**

उपसर्ग-s, or verbal prefixes, are one of a number of factors accounting for the flexibility and richness of Sanskrit. The use of these simple, easily memorized prefixes greatly enhances the connotative power of the various verbal roots without anything like the mental effort that would be required to memorize wholly different verbs for each meaning.

8.13 The उपसर्ग-s function basically in three ways, although these functions frequently overlap and are not consistent for all उपसर्ग-s or even for the same one with different roots. We may classify their function as:

a. **pleonastic:** This is the case in which the prefixation of an उपसर्ग does not substantially alter the basic meaning of a verbal root.

Example:

उप + लभ् → उपलभते = लभते

upa + √labh (1Ā) (obtain) → upalabhate = labhate (gain, obtain, acquire)

b. **analytic:** Here the उपसर्ग has a particular semantic value of its own, by which it modifies or qualifies the meaning of a verbal root.

Example:

अव + तॄ → अवतरति

ava (down) + √tṝ (1P) (cross) → avatarati (he descends)

c. **idiomatic:** Here the combination of an उपसर्ग and a root yields a meaning not clearly related to either.

Examples:
अव + गम् → अवगच्छति
ava (down) + √gam (1P) (go) → avagacchati
(he understands)

अनु + ज्ञा → अनुजानाति
anu (after) + √jñā (9P) (know) → anujānāti (he permits)

8.14 In any given case, the same combination of उपसर्ग and verbal root may be used in any of these three ways. The context and usage must always be considered.
Examples:
अव + गम् → अवगच्छति
ava (down) + √gam (go) → avagacchati—(a) he understands; (b) he goes down

उप + लभ् → उपलभते
upa + √labh (obtain) → upalabhate—(a) he obtains; (b) he learns, knows

8.15 The following is a list of the major उपसर्ग-s with their basic meanings. Examples are provided of their nominal analytic use and in some case, of important idiomatic usages.

Basic Meanings	"Analytic Examples"	"Idiomatic" Examples
अति (*ati*—beyond, exceeding, surpassing)	√क्रम् (1P) (step) अतिक्रामति (he oversteps, transgresses) [irregular length of अ (a)] √पत् (1P) (jump, fly) अतिपतति (he skips over)	

Basic Meanings	"Analytic Examples"	"Idiomatic" Examples
अधि (*adhi*—over, superiority)	√कृ (8P) (do) अधिकरोति (he appoints, authorizes)	√गम् (1P) (go) अधिगच्छति (he attains)
अनु (*anu*—after, successive, following)	√सृ (1P) (move) अनुसरति (he follows) √वद् (1P) (speak) अनुवदति (he repeats, translates) √कृ (8P) (do) अनुकरोति (he imitates)	√ज्ञा (9P) (know) अनुजानाति (he permits)
अन्तर् (*antar*—within, inward)	√धा (3P) (place) अन्तर्दधाति (he hides, conceals) √गम् (1P) (go) अन्तर्गच्छति (he goes in, insinuates)	
अप (*apa*—away; bad moral or value judgment)	√नी (1P) (lead) अपनयति (he leads away) √नुद् (6P) (push) अपनुदति (he drives away)	

Basic Meanings	"Analytic Examples"	"Idiomatic" Examples
अप	√वद् (1P) (speak) अपवदति (he speaks ill of, reviles) √हृ (1P) (take) अपहरति (he kidnaps, abducts)	
अभि (*abhi*—to, for, towards, fully)	√गम् (1P) (go) अभिगच्छति (he approaches sexually) √जि (1P) (win) अभिजयति (he triumphs) √ज्ञा (9P) (know) अभिजानाति (he recognizes)	√धा (3P) (place) अभिदधाति (he says, tells)
अव (*ava*—down)	√तॄ (1P) (cross) अवतरति (he descends) √लोक् (1Ā) (look) अवलोकते (he looks down)	√गम् (1P) (go) अवगच्छति (he understands)
आ (*ā*—back, return [in motion verbs];	√गम् (1P) (go) आगच्छति (he comes)	

Basic Meanings	"Analytic Examples"	"Idiomatic" Examples
आ (with non-motion verbs, an intensifier or used pleonastically)	√हृ (1P) (take) आहरति (he fetches)	
उद् (*ud*—up, rising, arising)	√स्था (1P) (stand) उत्तिष्ठति (he stands up) √भू (1P) (be) उद्भवति (he arises, originates, is born) √पत् (1P) (fly) उत्पतति (he flies up) √हृ (1P) (take) उद्धरति (he lifts, rescues)	
उप (*upa*—towards)	√गम् (1P) (go) उपगच्छति (he approaches)	√दिश् (6P) (point out) उपदिशति (he teaches, instructs) √जीव् (6P) (live) उपजीवति (he lives off, subsists on or by)
नि (*ni*—down, into, in)	√वस् (1P) (dwell) निवसति (he inhabits, settles in)	

Basic Meanings	"Analytic Examples"	"Idiomatic" Examples
निः (*niḥ*—out, out from)	√क्रम् (1P) (step) निष्क्रामति (he goes out) √वस् (1P) (dwell) निर्वसति (he lives abroad in exile)	
परा (*parā*—away, forth)	√गम् (1P) (go) परागच्छति (he returns) √जि (1P) (win) पराजयति (he defeats)	
परि (*pari*—around, about)	√अट् (1P) (wander) पर्यटति (he wanders about)	
प्र (*pra*—onward; often used pleonastically)	√चल् (1P) (move) प्रचलति (he goes on, moves along) √कृष् (1P) (drag) प्रकर्षति (he drags along)	√भू (1P) (be) प्रभवति (he is powerful, has mastery over, rules) √हृ (1P) (take) प्रहरति (he strikes)
प्रति (*prati*—back, against, reciprocal action)	√गम् (1P) (go) प्रतिगच्छति (he goes back)	√ज्ञा (9P) (know) प्रतिजानाति (he promises, vows)

Basic Meanings	"Analytic Examples"	"Idiomatic" Examples
वि (*vi*—opposition, against, reciprocal action)	√स्मृ (1P) (remember) विस्मरति (he forgets) √युज् (7P) (join) वियुनक्ति (he disjoins)	√हृ (1P) (take) विहरति (he diverts himself, takes pleasure)
सम् (*sam*—together)	√गम् (1P) (go) संगच्छति (he comes together with) √वद् (1P) (speak) संवदति (he converses) √हृ (1P) (take) संहरति (he puts together, collects)	√भू (1P) (be) संभवति (it is possible, he comes into existence)

8.16 It should be kept in mind that the above examples are by no means intended to be exhaustive of the uses of the उपसर्ग-s. Rather they are to suggest some of the common applications of these important prefixes.

8.17 There is no restriction as to the number of उपसर्ग-s that may precede a given verbal form or its derivatives. Two and sometimes three may be strung together before a root to give some additional shade of meaning.

Examples:

उद् + आ + हृ → उदाहरति

ud + ā + √hṛ (1P) → udāharati (he gives an illustration)

सम् + आ + गम् → समागच्छन्ति

sam + ā + √gam (1P) → samāgacchanti (they convene)

अभि + उप + आ + इ → अभ्युपैति

abhi + upa + ā + √i (2P) → abhyupaiti (he approaches, agrees)

8.18 **Placement of उपसर्ग-s** (*upasarga-s*)

An उपसर्ग or series of उपसर्ग-s is placed immediately before the verbal form that it modifies. However, in the case of preterite tenses such as the लङ्, which require the preterite augment (आगम), it is the augment that immediately precedes the verbal stem, while the उपसर्ग-s, if any, must precede the augment.

Examples:

	लट्	लङ्
उप + विश् upa + √viś (6P) (sit)	उपविशति upaviśati (he sits)	उपाविशत् upāviśat (he sat)
नि + वस् ni + √vas (1P) (inhabit)	निवसति nivasati (he inhabits)	न्यवसत् nyavasat (he inhabited)
अभि + उप + इ abhi + upa + √i (2P) (agree)	अभ्युपेमः abhyupemaḥ (we agree)	अभ्युपैम abhyupaima (we agreed)

EXERCISES

A. Translate the reading into English.

B. Rewrite the reading, changing all the लट् forms into their corresponding लङ् forms, and all the लङ् forms into their corresponding लट् forms.

C. Translate the following sentences into Sanskrit:

1. When Rāma came for Sītā's स्वयंवर (*svayaṃvara*), all the kings ridiculed him.
2. None of the kings (lit., no king at all) lifted Śiva's bow.
3. The sages did not understand what you said. (Put relative clause first.)
4. Janaka stood up in the assembly (सभा—*sabhā*) of the kings and said, "Rāma has won." (Use इति [*iti*]).
5. Finally the proud king became very angry (क्रुध्—√*krudh*).
6. But the hero did not exert himself and did not break the bow.
7. The proud queen forgot the name of the angry sage.
8. "O, Śambhu! You promised me a kingdom!" he said.
9. That woman never forgot her स्वयंवर (*svayaṃvara*).
10. The king's son, by name Devadatta, reviled Śambhu.
11. A fool does not easily obtain the Self.
12. "Why did he eat grass?" they thought.

D. Memorize the following verse.

केयूरा न विभूषयन्ति पुरुषं हारा न चन्द्रोज्ज्वला
न स्नानं न विलेपनं न कुसुमं नालंकृता मूर्धजाः ।
वाण्येका समलंकरोति पुरुषं या संस्कृता धार्यते
क्षीयन्ते खलु भूषणानि सततं वाग्भूषणं भूषणम् ॥

Bracelets do not adorn a person, nor necklaces shining like the moon, not baths and ointments, flowers or jewelled coiffures. Only that speech which is refined (*saṃskṛta*) adorns a person. Mere ornaments will always fade; the ornament of speech is the only true ornament.

READING

यदा रामः सीतामपश्यत्तदा तस्यामन्वरज्यत । तस्मिन्काले बहवो राजानः सीतायाः स्वयंवरायागच्छन् । जनको राजैवमवदच्च । यः को ऽपि राजा शिवस्य चापे बाणं संदधाति स मम कन्यां परिणयतीति । नृपा अचिन्तयन् । अहो एतेन* सुलभेन कर्मणा सोत्तमा नारी ममैव भार्या भवतीति । गर्वितास्ते मूर्खा नाजानन्यच्छम्भोश्चापो ऽतीव गुरुरिति । अथापि सर्वे प्रायतन्त । न कश्चन राजा तस्मिन्कर्मणि समर्थ आसीत् । अन्ततः श्रीरामो बालको ऽपि तं चापमुपागच्छत् । राजानस्तमपश्यन्प्राहसंश्च । अहो एष* बालको वीराणां कर्मणि प्रयतत इति । स न किमप्यवदत् । किंतु चापं पत्रमिव लीलयोदहरदभनक्च । राजानो ऽक्रुध्यन्किंतु जनकः सीता चातुष्यताम् ॥

---

* See 5.6

GLOSSARY

अति + क्रम् → अतिक्रामति
ati + √kram (1P) → atikrāmati—transgress

अथापि
athāpi (ind)—(equals अथ in most cases) moreover, however, even so

अनु + रञ्ज् → अनुरज्यते
anu + √rañj (4Ā) → anurjyate—be fond of, like

अन्ततः
antataḥ (ind)—finally

अप + वद् → अपवदति
apa + √vad (1P) → apavadati—revile

अभि + गम् → अभिगच्छति
abhi + √gam (1P) → abhi-gachati—approach

अभि + जि → अभिजयति
abhi + √ji (1P) → abhijayati—win

आत्मन्
ātman (m)—self, Self, commonly used as reflexive

इष् → इच्छति
√iṣ (6P) → icchati—desire, wish, want

उत्तम
uttama (adj)—supreme, excellent

उद् + था (= उद् + स्था)→ उत्तिष्ठति
ud + √thā (= ud + sthā)(1P) → uttiṣṭhati—stand up

उप + गम् → उपगच्छति
upa + √gam (1P) → upagacchati—approach

कर्मन्
karman (n)—activity, religious act, grammatical object

गर्वित
garvita (adj)—proud

गुरु (f—गुर्वी)
guru (adj; f—gurvī)—heavy; (m)—teacher

चापः
cāpaḥ (m)—bow

जनकः
janakaḥ (m prop)—king of Mithilā

तथापि
tathāpi (ind)—even so

तुष् → तुष्यति
√tuṣ (4P) → tuṣyati—be happy

तुष्ट
tuṣṭa (adj)—content, happy

तृणम्
tṛṇam (n)—blade of grass, a straw, often used metaphorically for something of little consequence or value.

नामन्
nāman (n)—name

पत्रम्
patram (n)—leaf

परि + नी → परिणयति
pari + √nī (1P) → pariṇayati—marry

प्र+ ज्ञा → प्रतिजानाति
prati + √jñā (9P) → pratijānāti—promise, vow

प्रभावः
prabhāvaḥ (m)—power

प्र+ यत् → प्रयतते
pra + √yat (1Ā) → prayatate—attempt, try, exert oneself

प्र+ हस् → प्रहसति
pra + √has (1P) → prahasati—ridicule

भञ्ज् → भनक्ति
√bhañj (7P) → bhanakti—break

भुज् → भुनक्ति
√bhuj (7P) → bhunakti—eat

यत्
yat (see Glossary, Lesson 7)

राजन्
rājan (m)—king

लीला
līlā (f)—play, sport

शम्भुः
śambhuḥ (m prop)—Śiva

सम् + धा → संदधाति
saṃ + √dhā (3P/Ā) →saṃdadhāti—join, bring together

सभा
sabhā (f)—assembly

सुलभ
sulabha (adj)—easy

स्वयम्
svayam (ind)—oneself, used reflexively and applicable to all persons, i.e., himself, herself, yourself, etc.

स्वयंवरः
svayaṃvaraḥ (m)—lit., "self-choice," the name of a ceremony at which a princess chooses a husband, or has one chosen by contest.

LESSON 9

Noun Stems in अः (aḥ); The कर्मणि प्रयोग (Karmaṇi Prayoga)

9.0 **Noun Stems in अः** (aḥ)

There is another important class of nouns whose stems end in अः (aḥ). They are mostly नपुंसकलिङ्ग nouns, and their declension is a good example of a regular consonantal paradigm.

9.1 a. नपुंसकलिङ्ग; तपः (*tapaḥ*—act of austerity)

	एक°	द्वि°	बहु°
1.	तपः tapaḥ	तपसी tapasī	तपांसि tapāṃsi
2.	तपः tapaḥ	तपसी tapasī	तपांसि tapāṃsi
3.	तपसा tapasā	तपोभ्याम् tapobhyām	तपोभिः tapobhiḥ
4.	तपसे tapase	तपोभ्याम् tapobhyām	तपोभ्यः tapobhyaḥ
5.	तपसः tapasaḥ	तपोभ्याम् tapobhyām	तपोभ्यः tapobhyaḥ
6.	तपसः tapasaḥ	तपसोः tapasoḥ	तपसाम् tapasām
7.	तपसि tapasi	तपसोः tapasoḥ	तपःसु tapaḥsu
sam.	तपः tapaḥ	तपसी tapasī	तपांसि tapāṃsi

b. पुंलिङ्ग nouns ending in अः (aḥ) are not at all common, while स्त्रीलिङ्ग nouns with this ending are virtually nonexistent. However, by a process to be discussed at length later on (13.9.a), it is rather common for the नपुंसकलिङ्ग stems to be treated as adjectives. When this happens they must, of course, be declined in the gender of whatever they modify.

For this reason it is necessary to learn the appropriate paradigm. In this instance the पुंलिङ्ग and स्त्रीलिङ्ग forms are the same. They are, moreover, different from the नपुंसकलिङ्ग forms only in the first two cases.

पुंलिङ्ग; अङ्गिरः (*aṅgiraḥ*—name of a sage)

	एक°	द्वि°	बहु°
1.	अङ्गिराः aṅgirāḥ	अङ्गिरसौ aṅgirasau	अङ्गिरसः aṅgirasaḥ
2.	अङ्गिरसम् aṅgirasam	अङ्गिरसौ aṅgirasau	अङ्गिरसः aṅgirasaḥ

(other forms same as नपुंसकलिङ्ग)

9.2 There are a few nouns whose stems end in -उः (-uḥ) and -इः (-iḥ). Their paradigms closely parallel those of the stems in -अः (-aḥ).

a. नपुंसकलिङ्ग; हविः (*haviḥ*—oblation)

	एक°	द्वि°	बहु°
1.	हविः haviḥ	हविषी haviṣī	हवींषि havīṃṣi
2.	हविः haviḥ	हविषी haviṣī	हवींषि havīṃṣi
3.	हविषा haviṣā	हविर्भ्याम् havirbhyām	हविर्भिः havirbhiḥ
4.	हविषे haviṣe	हविर्भ्याम् havirbhyām	हविर्भ्यः havirbhyaḥ
5.	हविषः haviṣaḥ	हविर्भ्याम् havirbhyām	हविर्भ्यः havirbhyaḥ
6.	हविषः haviṣaḥ	हविषोः haviṣoḥ	हविषाम् haviṣām
7.	हविषि haviṣi	हविषोः haviṣoḥ	हविःषु haviḥṣu
sam.	हविः haviḥ	हविषी haviṣī	हवींषि havīṃṣi

b. नपुंसकलिङ्ग; धनुः (*dhanuḥ*—bow)

	एक°	द्वि°	बहु°
1.	धनुः dhanuḥ	धनुषी dhanuṣī	धनूंषि dhanūṃṣi
2.	धनुः dhanuḥ	धनुषी dhanuṣī	धनूंषि dhanūṃṣi
3.	धनुषा dhanuṣā	धनुर्भ्याम् dhanurbhyām	धनुर्भिः dhanurbhiḥ
4.	धनुषे dhanuṣe	धनुर्भ्याम् dhanurbhyām	धनुर्भ्यः dhanurbhyaḥ
5.	धनुषः dhanuṣaḥ	धनुर्भ्याम् dhanurbhyām	धनुर्भ्यः dhanurbhyaḥ
6.	धनुषः dhanuṣaḥ	धनुषोः dhanuṣoḥ	धनुषाम् dhanuṣām
7.	धनुषि dhanuṣi	धनुषोः dhanuṣoḥ	धनुःषु dhanuḥṣu
sam.	धनुः dhanuḥ	धनुषी dhanuṣī	धनूंषि dhanūṃṣi

Adjectival application of these stems (13.9.a) take, in पुंलिङ्ग and स्त्रीलिङ्ग the same strong endings as do the stems in -अः (-aḥ), except in the प्रथमा एक° where they show no strength.

9.3 It is helpful to learn the important nouns of this class with the original final स् (s), the प्रथमा एक°, and another case, preferably the तृतीया एक° so that the absolute final, ः (ḥ), is not confused with that of the प्रथमा एक° ending of पुंलिङ्ग stems with final अ (a).

9.4 Some of the important nouns of these classes are listed here with a) original stem final, b) प्रथमा एक° and c) तृतीया एक°. Learn them.

(a)		(b)	(c)	
चक्षुस् cakṣus	→	चक्षुः cakṣuḥ	चक्षुषा cakṣuṣā	eye, faculty of sight
मनस् manas	→	मनः manaḥ	मनसा manasā	mind, mental faculty

तपस् →	तपः	तपसा	
tapas	tapaḥ	tapasā	austerity
तमस् →	तमः	तमसा	
tamas	tamaḥ	tamasā	darkness
धनुस् →	धनुः	धनुषा	
dhanus	dhanuḥ	dhanuṣā	bow
वपुस् →	वपुः	वपुषा	
vapus	vapuḥ	vapuṣā	body
नमस् →	नमः	नमसा	
namas	namaḥ	namasā	homage, a bow of respect
चेतस् →	चेतः	चेतसा	
cetas	cetaḥ	cetasā	mind, thought
यशस् →	यशः	यशसा	
yaśas	yaśaḥ	yaśasā	fame, glory
तेजस् →	तेजः	तेजसा	
tejas	tejaḥ	tejasā	splendor

Examples:

साधारणाः पुरुषाश्चक्षुषा लोकं पश्यन्ति । साधवः परमं सत्यं मनसा पश्यन्ति ।
sādhāraṇāḥ puruṣāś cakṣuṣā lokaṃ paśyanti. sādhavaḥ paramaṃ satyaṃ manasā paśyanti
(Ordinary men perceive the world with the eye, sages see the highest truth with the mind.)

शिवस्य धनुर्नोद्धरन्ति राजानः ।
śivasya dhanur noddharanti rājānaḥ
(Kings do not lift the bow of Śiva.)

9.5 **कर्मणि प्रयोग** (*Karmaṇi Prayoga*): **The Sanskrit 'Passive'**

[Note: Before proceeding with this section it is advisable to refer back for a moment to the sections on the uses of the प्रथमा, द्वितीया, and तृतीया विभक्ति-s (4.28) and to make sure that you clearly understand the concepts of कर्तृ (subject) and कर्मन् (direct object) of a verbal root (4.40-42)]. All the clauses and sentences that we have thus far encountered have two important and related points in common:

a. The कर्तृ (subject) of any धातु (verbal root) is in the प्रथमा विभक्ति (nominative case).
b. The क्रियापद (verb) of any clause always agrees in number and person with the कर्तृ (subject).

9.6 For example, in the sentence पण्डितो मूर्खांस्त्यजति । (*paṇḍito mūrkhāṃs tyajati*—A wise man abandons fools), the verbal ending -ति (-ti) tells us that the कर्तृ is एकवचन. It also tell us that the "person" of the subject is प्रथमपुरुष. In fact, it is so specific that except for the actual name, type, or identity of the कर्तृ, nothing else need be provided. This is especially clear in the case of the उत्तम and मध्यमपुरुष where the identity of the subject is already clear from the context. Thus, the -मि (-mi) of गच्छामि (*gacchāmi*—I go) is so specific that the inclusion of the कर्तृ (अहम्) is optional. The same would be true for the second sentence of the sequence: रामो नगरं त्यजति । ततो वनं गच्छति । (*rāmo nagaraṃ tyajati. tato vanaṃ gacchati*—Rāma leaves the city. Then he goes to the forest.)

9.7 In all of these sentences, then, the verbal ending alone specifies everything we need to know about the कर्तृ except its name and gender. Therefore, when that name is provided, it is in the प्रथमा or nominative (naming) case.

9.8 In the first sentence if we change the number of the कर्तृ, the verbal ending also changes. Thus:

पण्डितो मूर्खांस्त्यजति ।	(*paṇḍito mūrkhāṃs tyajati*)
पण्डितौ मूर्खांस्त्यजतः ।	(*paṇḍitau mūrkhāṃs tyajataḥ*)
पण्डिता मूर्खांस्त्यजन्ति ।	(*paṇḍitā mūrkhāṃs tyajanti*)

On the other hand, a change in the number of the कर्मन् (direct object) makes no difference whatsoever to the verbal ending or the कर्तृ governed by it. In short, then, the क्रियापद (verb) tells us nothing about the कर्मन् (direct object), not even its objectness. Therefore, everything about the कर्मन्, its number and its very objectness, must be provided. This is done by the appropriate द्वितीया (accusative) case ending.

9.9 Such a usage of the finite verb to refer exclusively to the कर्तृ is called the कर्तरि प्रयोग, which means, the verbal usage, प्रयोग, with respect to the कर्तृ (subject). It is similar to the English "active voice," but, as noted above, it must not be confused with the परस्मैपद ("active" voice).

9.10 There is, however, another type of sentence, which differs from the कर्तरि प्रयोग in that the finite verb refers to (or agrees with) the कर्मन् (direct object) instead of the कर्तृ. This is called the कर्मणि प्रयोग, or verbal usage with respect to the direct object.

9.11 Just as in the कर्तरि प्रयोग, the verbal ending specifies the number and person of the कर्तृ, so in the कर्मणि प्रयोग, it varies with the number and person of the कर्मन्.

9.12 In the sentence मूर्खास्त्यज्यन्ते । (*mūrkhās tyajyante*—Fools are abandoned), note that the ending -अन्ते (-ante), which specifies the number and person of the कर्मन्, and the य (ya) sign of the कर्मणि प्रयोग, which specifies its objectness, obviate the need for the special object marker (the द्वितीया ending). All that needs to be supplied is the "name" of the object. Therefore, like the कर्तृ in the कर्तरि प्रयोग, it is put in the प्रथमा (nominative/naming case).

9.13 On the other hand, there is now nothing to specify the subjectness of the कर्तृ. This must now be shown explicitly by means of the agentive case, the तृतीया (instrumental) case.

9.14 So to complete the transformation of the example at 9.6, the कर्तृ or the subject of the action of the verbal root त्यज् (√*tyaj*), must be in the तृतीया : मूर्खास्त्यज्यन्ते पण्डितेन । (*mūrkhās tyajyante paṇḍitena*—Fools are abandoned by the wise man.) = (The wise man abandons fools.)

9.15 Note that just as the verb in the कर्तरि प्रयोग takes no account of the number, etc., of the कर्मन्, so in the कर्मणि प्रयोग it is independent of the कर्तृ.

Examples:

मूर्खास्त्यज्यन्ते पण्डितेन ।
mūrkh*ās* tyajy*ante* paṇḍitena

मूर्खास्त्यज्यन्ते पण्डिताभ्याम् ।
mūrkh*ās* tyajy*ante* paṇḍitābhyām

मूर्खास्त्यज्यन्ते पण्डितैः ।
mūrkh*ās* tyajy*ante* paṇḍitaiḥ

मूर्खस्त्यज्यते पण्डितेन । (-आभ्याम् ; -ऐः)
but mūrkh*as* tyajy*ate* paṇḍitena (-ābhyām ; -aiḥ)

9.16 To recapitulate, then, in traditional terminology:

a. In the कर्तरि प्रयोग (i.e., कर्तृ in प्रथमा; क्रियापद agrees with कर्तृ), the कर्मत्व (objectness) of the कर्मन् is अनभिहित (unspecified) by the क्रियापद. Therefore, the कर्मन् is in the द्वितीया विभक्ति.

b. In the कर्मणि प्रयोग (i.e., कर्मन् in प्रथम; क्रियापद agrees with कर्मन्), the कर्तृत्व (subjectness) of the कर्तृ is अनभिहित by the क्रियापद. Therefore, the कर्तृ is in the तृतीया विभक्ति.

9.17 The भावे प्रयोग (*Bhāve Prayoga*): **Abstract Construction**

It is clear from the very terminology used to name these constructions that the distinction should apply only to सकर्मक धातु-s (transitive verbs)(4.38), i.e., to verbs that can take कर्मन्-s (direct objects). In fact, however, the freedom and frequency with which the कर्मणि प्रयोग is used has led to the creation of a parallel construction used with अकर्मक धातु-s (intransitive verbs). This construction, for which English has no real equivalent, is called the भावे प्रयोग, the abstract construction.

9.18 This construction, a *sort of* "passive" of intransitive verbs, is actually a sort of analog to the कर्मणि प्रयोग constructed in the absence of a कर्मन्. Since every verb has a कर्तृ, one can proceed with the भावे प्रयोग as far as the कर्तृ with no difficulty. The कर्तृ

is put into the तृतीया, just as it is in the कर्मणि प्रयोग. But whereas the verb of the कर्मणि प्रयोग agrees with the कर्मन्, in the भावे प्रयोग there is no कर्मन् with which to make it agree. Here, then, the "कर्मन्" is taken to be the abstract तत् (it *or* that). Accordingly the verb in a भावे construction must always be प्रथमपुरुष एकवचन.

Examples:

The कर्तरि sentences:

मुनयो वने वसन्ति ।

munayo vane vasanti. (The sages live in the forest.)

and

राजानः सुखं जीवन्ति ।

rājānaḥ sukhaṃ jīvanti. (Kings live happily.)

could be transformed into the following भावे sentences:

मुनिभिर्वन उष्यते ।

munibhir vana uṣyate. (See 3.18 for सन्धिद्व)

(Literally, "It is lived in the forest by the sages.")

and

राजभिः सुखं जीव्यते ।

rājabhiḥ sukhaṃ jīvyate.

(Literally, "It is lived happily by kings.")

9.19 To transform a कर्तरि to a कर्मणि प्रयोग sentence:

1. Put the कर्तृ in the तृतीया.
2. Put the कर्मन् in the प्रथमा.
3. Use the कर्मणि form of the verb in agreement with the कर्मन्.

Example:

रामो राक्षसान्हन्ति ।

rām*o* rākṣas*ān* hant*i*. (Rāma kills the demons.)

1. रामः → रामेण । rāmaḥ → rāmeṇa
2. राक्षसान् → राक्षसाः । rākṣasān → rākṣasāḥ
3. हन्ति → हन्यन्ते । hanti → hanyante

रामेण राक्षसा हन्यन्ते ।

rāmeṇa rākṣasā hanyante.

(Rāma kills the demons [lit., the demons are killed by Rāma].)

9.20 To transform a कर्मणि to a कर्तरि प्रयोग simply reverse the above procedure.

Example:

मया त्वं राजा क्रियसे ।

mayā tvaṃ rājā kriya*se*. (You are made king by me.)

reverse	1. मया → अहम् ।	mayā → aham
"	2. त्वम् → त्वाम् ।	tvam → tvām
"	2. राजा → राजानम् ।	rājā → rājānam
"	3. क्रियसे → करोमि ।	kriyase → karomi

अहं त्वां राजानं करोमि ।

ahaṃ tvāṃ rājānaṃ karomi. (I make you king.)

9.21 The कर्मणि and भावे प्रयोग-s may be formed in the लङ् as well as the लट्. They are formed just as though from a fourth गण verb with the prefixed augment. They must of course always have the आत्मनेपद versions of the "secondary endings" (see 8.9).

Examples:

राक्षसो ऽहन्यत रामेण ।

rākṣaso 'hanyata rāmeṇa. (The demon was killed by Rāma.)

नगरमगम्यत राज्ञा ।

nagaram agamyata rājñā. (The king went to the city.)
(Literally: "It was gone to the city by the king.")

9.22 Remember that in transforming a sentence from or to the कर्मणि प्रयोग the only parts of speech that must be changed are the कर्तृ, कर्मन्, and the क्रियापद. Of course, any adjectives that modify the कर्तृ and कर्मन् and any nouns or pronouns in apposition with them must remain in agreement or apposition and must then change accordingly. Adverbs and other nouns that are not the कर्तृ or कर्मन् and not in agreement or apposition with them do not change. This latter includes nouns in cases other than the प्रथमा, द्वितीया, and तृतीया. Be careful of words in the तृतीया that are not the कर्तृ in कर्मणि constructions. This case may mark the instrument (करण) of an action and may appear to be in agreement or apposition with the true कर्तृ. For example, in the sentence दशरथेन शरेण ब्राह्मणो हन्यते । (*daśarathena śareṇa brāhmaṇo hanyate*—The brāhman is killed with an arrow by Daśaratha), the कर्तृ is Daśaratha while the arrow is the करण, despite their seeming agreement. The correct कर्तरि transformation would be: दशरथः शरेण ब्राह्मणं हन्ति । (*daśarathaḥ śareṇa brāhmaṇaṃ hanti*).

9.23 These constructions, the कर्मणि and भावे प्रयोग-s, are extremely common in Sanskrit but do not always have any special force that sets them apart in meaning from their कर्तरि प्रयोग counterparts. When translating into English, then, it is generally advisable to render them into active sentences if the passive sounds awkward or forced. Certainly this should always be done in the case of भावे sentences.

9.24 **The Formation of the** कर्मणि प्रयोग (*karmaṇi prayoga*)

The formation of this complicated-sounding, but actually rather simple, construction is quite mechanical and is easily learned.

9.25 The कर्मणि (and भावे) प्रयोग is not part of the present system. It is formed by two simple steps.

a. To the धातु (verbal root), **absolutely without reference to its** गण, is added य, the कर्मणि marker to form the कर्मणि stem.
b. To this stem are then added the appropriate आत्मनेपद endings.

Example:

धातु	कर्तरि	कर्मणि	Meaning
त्यज्	त्यजति	त्यज्यते	(he, she, it . . .)
√tyaj (1)	tyajati	tyajyate	is abandoned
ज्ञा	जानाति	ज्ञायते	
√jñā (9)	jānāti	jñāyate	is known
छिद्	छिनत्ति	छिद्यते	
√chid (7)	chinatti	chidyate	is cut

9.26 Keep two points clearly in mind:

a. The य of the कर्मणि प्रयोग is not to be confused with the य of the fourth गण, even though there are cases where the two forms might be identical. The कर्मणि प्रयोग is formed from roots of all गण-s and is **not derived from the present stems.**

b. Although the कर्मणि प्रयोग **always** takes the आत्मनेपद endings, it is **not true** that those endings always indicate कर्मणि प्रयोग. (See 4.16)

9.27 The following are important exceptions to the basic rule of कर्मणि stem formation:

a. Root final इ (i) or उ (u) is lengthened,

धातु	कर्तरि	कर्मणि	*Meaning of* कर्मणि
जि	जयति	जीयते	(he, she, it . . .)
√ji (1)	jayati	jīyate	is conquered
हु	जुहोति	हूयते	
√hu (3)	juhoti	hūyate	is offered
स्तु	स्तौति	स्तूयते	
√stu (2)	stauti	stūyate	is praised

b. Root final आ (ā) (or any complex vowel) almost always becomes ई (ī).

दा	ददाति	दीयते	
√dā (3)	dadāti	dīyate	is given
स्था	तिष्ठति	स्थीयते	
√sthā (1)	tiṣṭhati	sthīyate	is stood
पा	पिबति	पीयते	
√pā (1)	pibati	pīyate	is drunk
गै	गायति	गीयते	
√gai (1)	gāyati	gīyate	is sung

हा	जहाति	हीयते	
√hā (3)	jahāti	hīyate	is abandoned

but	ज्ञा	जानाति	ज्ञायते	
	√jñā (9)	jānāti	jñāyate	is known

c. Root final ऋ (ṛ) becomes रि (ri). This takes place most significantly with:

कृ	करोति	क्रियते	
√kṛ (8)	karoti	kriyate	is done

but, if ऋ (ṛ) is preceded by a conjunct, it is subject to गुण:

स्मृ	स्मरति	स्मर्यते	
√smṛ (1)	smarati	smaryate	is remembered

d. Certain roots beginning with व (va) or य (ya) and ending in a consonant undergo a reduction, called संप्रसारण (*saṃprasāraṇa*), of the initial semivowel *and* its vowel अ (a) to उ (u) or इ (i) respectively:

वद्	वदति	उद्यते	
√vad (1)	vadati	udyate	is spoken
वच्	वक्ति	उच्यते	
√vac (2)	vakti	ucyate	is said
वस	वसति	उष्यते	
√vas (1)	vasati	uṣyate	is lived
यज्	यजति	इज्यते	
√yaj (1)	yajati	ijyate	is sacrificed

e. Some roots, especially the important roots अस् (√*as*—be), ब्रू (√*brū*—speak), and अर्ह् (√*arh*—be worthy, capable) have no कर्मणि forms.

f. The root पश् (√*paś*—see) is replaced in the कर्मणि and all other forms not formed from the present stem by दृश् (√*dṛś*). Example:

दृश्यते (he, she, it is seen)

EXERCISES

A. Translate the reading into English.

B. Translate the following sentences and transform them from कर्तरि to कर्मणि or भावे, or from कर्मणि or भावे to कर्तरि प्रयोग, as is applicable.

1. यदा साधवो वनं गच्छन्ति तदा ते भार्याः परित्यजन्ति ।
   yadā sādhavo vanaṃ gacchanti, tadā te bhāryāḥ parityajanti.

2. यः पुरुष आत्मानं जानाति स एव सर्वाँल्लोकाञ्जयति ।
   yaḥ puruṣa ātmānaṃ jānāti, sa eva sarvāṃl lokāñ jayati.

3. येन लोको ऽक्रियत तस्मै नमस्करोम्यहम् ।
   yena loko 'kriyata, tasmai namaskaromy aham.

4. यच्चक्षुषा दृश्यते तन्मिथ्या । यच्छान्तेन मनसा ज्ञायते तत्सत्यम् ।
   yac cakṣuṣā dṛśyate tan mithyā, yac chāntena (see 3.45 for सन्धि) manasā jñāyate tat satyam.

5. राज्ञः सभायां सर्वे वीराः शत्रूनपावदन् ।
   rājñaḥ sabhāyāṃ sarve vīrāḥ śatrūn apāvadan.

6. यदा रामो ऽनुज्ञामुपलभते तदारण्यं गच्छति ।
   yadā rāmo 'nujñām upalabhate tadāraṇyaṃ gacchati.

7. यदा मुनिर्लोकं पर्यत्यजत्तदा तपो ऽकरोत् ।
   yadā munir lokaṃ paryatyajat tadā tapo 'karot.

8. मुनेस्तेजसा सूर्यो ऽप्यन्तर्धीयते ।
   munes tejasā sūryo 'py antardhīyate.

9. या नार्यो निशाचरेभ्यः पलायन्ते ता एव बिभ्यति ।
   yā nāryo niśācarebhyaḥ palāyante tā eva bibhyati.

10. तदनन्तरं वृद्धो राजा हविरजुहोदपि चाभिषेकमकरोत् ।
    tadanantaraṃ vṛddho rājā havir ajuhod api cābhiṣekam akarot.

C. Memorize the following verse.

पूज्यते यदपूज्यो ऽपि यदगम्यो ऽपि गम्यते ।
वन्द्यते यदवन्द्यो ऽपि स प्रभावो धनस्य हि ॥

The dishonorable one is honored, the one who should be shunned is now approached, the blameworthy one is praised, for such is the power of wealth.

READING

यदा जनकस्य कन्या पर्यणीयत दशरथस्य पुत्रेण तदा साधु साध्वित्यभाष्यत सर्वैः । जनकस्यापरा कन्या पर्यणीयत लक्ष्मणेन । ततो रामेण लक्ष्मणेन च सुखमन्वभूयत । अनन्तरं तौ द्वौ वीरावयोध्यां प्रत्यागच्छताम् । तत्र च सुखमुष्यते ताभ्याम् । कालेन राजा दशरथ आत्मानं जरया पीडितं जानाति । अपि च स स्वस्य ज्येष्ठं पुत्रं रामं राज्ये क्षमममन्यत । अहो वृद्धो ऽस्मि । राज्यं न पुनरिष्यते मया । वनं मया गम्यते तत्र च तपः क्रियते । मम राज्यस्य भारः पुत्रे निक्षिप्यत इति पुनरचिन्तयन्नृपः । तदा रामस्याभिषेकायाज्ञा राज्ञादीयत ॥

GLOSSARY

अधि + गम् → अधिगच्छति
adhi + √gam (1P) → adhigacchati —attain

अनन्तरम्
anantaram (ind)—after

अनु + ज्ञा →अनुजानाति
anu + √jñā (9P) → anujānāti— permit

अन्तर् + धा → अन्तर्दधाति
antar + √dhā (3P) → antardadhāti —hide

अपर
apara (adj)—other, another (declined like पर, see 5.7)

अपि च
api ca (ind.)—moreover

अभिषेकः
abhiṣekaḥ (m)—consecration, coronation

आज्ञा
ājñā (f)—order, command

उप + लभ् →उपलभते
upa + √labh (1Ā) → upalabhate— attain

क्षम
kṣama (adj)—able, competent

चक्षुः
cakṣuḥ (n)—eye

चेतः
cetaḥ (n)—intellect

जरा
jarā (f)—old age

जि →जयति
√ji (1P) →jayati—win

तदनन्तरम्
tadanantaram (ind)—after that

तपः
tapaḥ (n)—asceticism

तेजः
tejaḥ (n)—splendor

दा →ददाति
√dā (3P) → dadāti—give

द्वि (stem = द्व)
(number)—two, treated as an अ stem noun, in dual only (see 19.6.b)

धनुः
dhanuḥ (n)—bow

नमः
namaḥ (n)—reverence, homage, bow of respect

नि + क्षिप् → निक्षिपति
ni + √kṣip (6P) → nikṣipati— throw down, entrust, place

परि + त्यज् → परित्यजति

pari + √tyaj (1P) → parityajati—abandon

प्रति + आ +गम् → प्रत्यागच्छति

prati +ā +√gam (1P) → pratyāgacchati—go back

ब्रह्मन्

brahman (n)—Brahma, absolute reality; (m)—the god Brahmā

भारः

bhāraḥ (m)—load, weight, burden

मनः

manaḥ (n)—mind, mental faculty

मिथ्या

mithyā (ind)—false

लोकः

lokaḥ (m)—world

वृद्ध

vṛddha (adj)—old

शान्त

śānta (adj)—calm

साधुः

sādhuḥ (m)—sage, holy man; sādhu! (ind)—(exclamation) "wonderful!"

सूर्यः

sūryaḥ (m)—sun

स्तु → स्तौति

√stu (2P) → stauti—praise

स्व

sva (adj)—one's own (declined like पर, see 5.7, but optionally follows masculine in -a)

हु → जुहोति

√hu (3P) → juhoti—offer

LESSON 10

Nominal Stems in -ऋ (-ṛ); Verbal Adjectives; The भूते कृदन्त (Bhūte Kṛdanta)

10.0 There is relatively small but important group of nouns whose stems end in the vowel -ऋ (ṛ). This group is divisible into two closely similar subgroups with slightly different declensions. Nouns of these declensions are unlike other nouns in final vowels in that they show the system of stem strength typical of consonant final stems.

i. The first, and much more restricted, of these subgroups consists almost wholly of terms for kinship relations such as:

दुहितृ (*duhitṛ*) (f) daughter
पितृ (*pitṛ*) (m) father
भ्रातृ (*bhrātṛ*) (m) brother
मातृ (*mātṛ*) (f) mother

ii. The second, and larger, group consists of a series of quasi-adjectival agent nouns formed from many verbal roots by the addition of the suffix -तृ (-tṛ), similar in meaning to the English agentive suffix -er. This suffix is either added directly to the verbal root or in some cases, is separated from the root by the vowel इ (i). (See 13.1.a, 16.1.) In either case the root vowel takes गुण if possible.

Examples:

root	**agent noun**
कृ (√*kṛ*) (8P) do	कर्तृ (*kartṛ*) doer, grammatical subject
जि (√*ji*) (1P) win	जेतृ (*jetṛ*) winner, victor
गम् (√*gam*) (1P) go	गन्तृ (*gantṛ*) goer
भुज् (√*bhuj*) (7P) eat	भोक्तृ (*bhoktṛ*) eater
रक्ष् (√*rakṣ*) (1P) protect	रक्षितृ (*rakṣitṛ*) protector

This group also contains two kinship terms: नप्तृ (*naptṛ* [m]—grandson) and स्वसृ (*svasṛ* [f]—sister).

10.1 Gender of Stems in -ऋ (-ṛ)

a. The stems of group one (kinship terms) are पुंलिङ्ग or स्त्रीलिङ्ग according to the natural gender of the family member named. This group contains no nouns of the नपुंसकलिङ्ग.

b. The agentive nouns of group two, however, are quasi-adjectival in that they may take on the gender of a person or thing with which they are in apposition. When स्त्रीलिङ्ग forms occur the ending -तृ (-tṛ) is replaced by the ending -त्री (-trī). These forms are then declined regularly according to the paradigm for stems in -ई (ī) given at 7.1. Thus, one has to learn new declensions only for पुंलिङ्ग and the less common नपुंसकलिङ्ग. The kinship term स्वसृ (*svasṛ*—sister) is, of course, स्त्रीलिङ्ग.

10.2 Declension of Stems in -ऋ (-ṛ)

a. All stems of group one and पुंलिङ्ग stems (plus स्वसृ—*svasṛ*) of group two have very similar declensions with only two basic differences:

   i. Except for the प्रथम एक°, where all these forms show the ending -आ (-ā), the two groups differ in the strong forms (8.1); nouns of group one showing गुण of the stem final -अर् (-ar), nouns of group two showing वृद्धि -आर् (-ār).

   ii. स्त्रीलिङ्ग nouns of group one and the noun स्वसृ (*svasṛ*—sister) of group two have as their द्वितीया बहु° ending -ॠः (-ṝḥ) in contrast to the corresponding ending -ॠन् (ṝn) for पुंलिङ्ग nouns of both groups.

b. Final -ऋ (-ṛ) of नपुंसकलिङ्ग nouns of group two is treated (as regards length) exactly as is the final -उ (-u) of the नपुंसकलिङ्ग nouns in final -उ (-u) (see 6.1.d).

10.3 Paradigms of -ऋ (-ṛ) Stem Nouns

a. The following paradigm shows the declension of पितृ (*pitṛ*—father) a typical पुंलिङ्ग noun of group one. In addition the प्रथमा and द्वितीया विभक्ति-s of कर्तृ (*kartṛ*—doer), a पुंलिङ्ग noun of group two, and of मातृ (*mātṛ*—mother) representing a स्त्रीलिङ्ग noun of group one are given. Their तृतीया through सप्तमी forms will follow the paradigm for पितृ.

i. पुंलिङ्ग; पितृ (*pitṛ*—father)

	एक°	द्वि°	बहु°
1.	पिता pitā	पितरौ pitarau	पितरः pitaraḥ
2.	पितरम् pitaram	पितरौ pitarau	पितॄन् pitṝn
3.	पित्रा pitrā	पितृभ्याम् pitṛbhyām	पितृभिः pitṛbhiḥ
4.	पित्रे pitre	पितृभ्याम् pitṛbhyām	पितृभ्यः pitṛbhyaḥ
5.	पितुः/पितुर् pituḥ/pitur (see 3.40)	पितृभ्याम् pitṛbhyām	पितृभ्यः pitṛbhyaḥ
6.	पितुः/पितुर् pituḥ/pitur	पित्रोः pitroḥ	पितॄणाम् pitṝṇām
7.	पितरि pitari	पित्रोः pitroḥ	पितृषु pitṛṣu
सम्°	पितः/पितर् pitaḥ/pitar (see 3.40)	पितरौ pitarau	पितरः pitaraḥ

ii. पुंलिङ्ग; कर्तृ (*kartṛ*—doer, agent, grammatical subject)

	एक°	द्वि°	बहु°
1.	कर्ता kartā	कर्तारौ kartārau	कर्तारः kartāraḥ
2.	कर्तारम् kartāram	कर्तारौ kartārau	कर्तॄन् kartṝn

iii. स्त्रीलिङ्ग; मातृ (*mātṛ*—mother)

	एक°	द्वि°	बहु°
1.	माता mātā	मातरौ mātarau	मातरः mātaraḥ
2.	मातरम् mātaram	मातरौ mātarau	मातॄः mātṝḥ

b. नपुंसकलिङ्ग; दातृ (*dātṛ*—giver, giving)

	एक°	द्वि°	बहु°
1.	दातृ dātṛ	दातृणी dātṛṇī	दातॄणि dātṝṇi
2.	दातृ dātṛ	दातृणी dātṛṇī	दातॄणि dātṝṇi
3.	दातृणा dātṛṇā	दातृभ्याम् dātṛbhyām	दातृभिः dātṛbhiḥ
4.	दातृणे dātṛṇe	दातृभ्याम् dātṛbhyām	दातृभ्यः dātṛbhyaḥ
5.	दातृणः dātṛṇaḥ	दातृभ्याम् dātṛbhyām	दातृभ्यः dātṛbhyaḥ
6.	दातृणः dātṛṇaḥ	दातृणोः dātṛṇoḥ	दातॄणाम् dātṝṇām
7.	दातृणि dātṛṇi	दातृणोः dātṛṇoḥ	दातृषु dātṛṣu
सम्°	दातृ dātṛ	दातृणी dātṛṇī	दातॄणि dātṝṇi
or	दातः/दातर् dātaḥ/dātar (see 3.40)		

10.4 Verbal Adjectives: Sanskrit Participles

Despite its possession of a rich and complex system of verbal conjugations, or perhaps because of this, Sanskrit shows a marked proclivity for nominalization—the substitution of nominal forms (सुबन्त-s) for finite verbal forms (तिङन्त-s). This is done through the use of a variety of declinable and indeclinable words, which are derived from the verbal roots. Perhaps the most versatile and useful of these words are the participles (कृदन्त-s). These words are remarkable in that they are adjectival in form but verbal in function. As a result of this peculiar dual nature it is often possible for one word, formally a simple adjective, to replace virtually an entire clause. Beginning students are particularly fond of these forms as, through their use, they are frequently able to substitute an easily declinable adjective for a possibly obscure and almost certainly forgotten finite verb. Participles, like any nominal forms, may be negated by the prefixing of -अ or before initial vowels, -अन् (see 6.21).

Example:

श्रु (√*śru*) (5P) hear	श्रुत (*śruta*) heard
	अश्रुत (*aśruta*) unheard

10.5 **The भूते कृदन्त (*Bhūte Kṛdanta*): Past-passive Participle**

Now that the कर्मणि प्रयोग has been introduced, it is advisable to learn, in conjunction with it, the so-called past-passive participle of Sanskrit. This participle is very common and useful. It is formed from virtually any धातु , or verbal root, and depending mainly on the transitivity of the root, has two basic applications.

10.6 a. From सकर्मक (transitive) roots, it forms adjectives that indicate that the nouns that they modify are the कर्मन्-s (direct objects) of the action expressed by the धातु , or verbal root. Such a verbal adjective, agreeing (here as regards case, number, and gender) with the कर्मन् of its root, is of course a nominalization of the कर्मणि प्रयोग. As such, its subject, if expressed, must be in the तृतीया विभक्ति.

Examples:

हन्	राक्षसो हतो रामेण ।
√han (2P) (kill)	rākṣaso *hato* rāmeṇa.
	(The demon is [was] *killed* by Rāma.)
पठ्	तत्पुस्तकं न मया पठितम् ।
√paṭh (1P) (read)	tat pustakaṃ na mayā *paṭhitam.*
	(That book is [was] not *read* by me.)
	(I didn't read the book.)

	तानि पुस्तकान्यपठितानि ।
	tāni pustakāny *apaṭhitāni*.
	(Those books have not been *read*.)
त्यज्	त्यक्तां कन्यां पश्यामि ।
√tyaj (1P)	*tyaktām* kanyāṃ paśyāmi.
(abandon);	(I see the abandoned girl.)
छिद्	किं नश्छिन्नम् ।
√chid (7P) (cut)	kiṃ naś *chinnam*? (What of ours is *cut*? [i.e., What's it to me?])

Note that the action expressed by this usage of the भूते कृदन्त is not necessarily "past." Rather one might say that it is "perfective" in that it is completed and not still in process regardless of the tense of the clause in which it appears.

b. From अकर्मक (intransitive) धातु -s, or verbal roots, it forms adjectives that indicate that the nouns modified are the कर्तृ-s (subjects) of the action of the धातु, verbal root. This action is frequently in the past. In other words, the participle serves as a nominalization of a simple past tense (e.g., लङ्) in the कर्तरि प्रयोग.

Examples:

i. This usage is especially common with verbs of motion, which, although they have their locus of motion in the द्वितीया विभक्ति (see 4.38, 41), are treated as अकर्मक धातु -s (intransitive roots).

गम्	रामो वनं गतः । सीतापि तत्र गता ।
√gam (1P) (go)	rāmo vanaṃ *gataḥ*. (Rāma *went* to the forest.) sītāpi tatra *gatā*. (Sītā also *went* there.)
आ + या	अहमप्यायातः ।
ā + √yā (2P) (come)	aham apy āyātaḥ. (I also came.)

ii. From other अकर्मक roots the participle may be an adjective with no particular reference to time.

स्था √sthā (1P) (stand)	बहवो मुनयो वने स्थिताः । bahavo munayo vane *sthitāḥ*. (Many sages are *standing* (*located*) in the forest.)
कुप् √kup (4P) (be angry)	अतीव कुपितौ तौ द्वौ मुनी । atīva *kupitau* tau dvau munī. (The two muni-s are extremely *angry*.)
मृ √mṛ (6Ā) (die)	सर्वे वीरा मृताः । sarve vīrā mṛtāḥ. (All the heroes are dead.)
जन् √jan (4Ā) (be born)	त्वं कुत्र जातः । tvaṃ kutra jātaḥ. (Where were you born?)

By extension, such adjectives may come to be used as nouns in their own right.

Examples:

बुध् √budh (1P) (be enlightened)	बुद्ध । बुद्धस्य नाम गौतम इति । buddha (enlightened); *buddhasya* nāma gautama iti. (The *Buddha's* name was Gautama.)
वृध् √vṛdh (1Ā) (grow)	वृद्ध । वृद्धा किमवदत् । vṛddha (fully grown, old); vṛddhā kim avadat. (What did the old woman say?)

10.7 The formation of this useful participle is generally quite simple. The participle is invariably an -अ stem adjective. It is usually formed by the suffixation of the syllable -त directly to the धातु, or verbal root.

a. The root normally shows no strength.

कृ	किं त्वया कृतम् ।
√kṛ (8)	kiṃ tvayā *kṛtam.*
	(What have you *done*?)
श्रु	एवं मया श्रुतम् ।
√śru (5)	evaṃ mayā *śrutam.*
	(Thus have I *heard.*)
वि + स्मृ	अद्यापि सा न मया विस्मृता ।
vi + √smṛ (1)	adyāpi sā na mayā *vismṛtā.*
	(Even today, I don't *forget* her.)
अभि + भू	शिवः कथमभिभूतः पार्वत्या ।
abhi + √bhū (1)	śivaḥ katham *abhibhūtaḥ* pārvatyā.
	(How was Śiva overcome by Pārvatī?)

b. If the root has a weaker form, the suffix is added to that (cf. 7.1.5.a).

Examples:

दंश्	दशति	दष्ट
√daṃś (1)	daśati (bite)	daṣṭa (bitten) 7.18.c
बन्ध्	बध्नाति	बद्ध
√bandh (9)	badhnāti (bind)	baddha (bound)

This applies also to those roots which are weakened in the कर्मणि प्रयोग (9.27.d).

Examples:

यज्	इष्ट
√yaj (1) (sacrifice)	iṣṭa (sacrificed)

वच्	उक्त
√vac (2) (speak)	ukta (spoken, said)

NOTE: The extremely common root √वच् is especially common in कर्मणि forms, and its भूते कृदन्त, उक्त, may refer either to something that was said or to a person addressed. This is often confusing. A good clue is that when the former is meant (something said), it is usually in the नपुंसकलिङ्ग whereas a person addressed will require the participle to be in the gender proper to that person (पुंलिङ्ग, स्त्रीलिङ्ग).

Examples:

यत्त्वयोक्तं तदसत्यमेव ।

yat tvay*oktaṃ,* tad asatyam eva.

(What you said, is surely false.)

एवमुक्ता राक्षसेन सीता भीताभवत् ।

evam *uktā* rākṣasena sītā bhītābhavat.

(Addressed thus by the demon, Sītā became frightened.)

c. A group of roots, some of them very common, ending in nasals, lose the final nasal before the ending -त.

Examples:

गम् (√*gam*) (1) go	गत (*gata*) went
यम् (√*yam*) (1) restrain	यत (*yata*) restrained
नम् (√*nam*) (1) bend, bow	नत (*nata*) bent
रम् (√*ram*) (1) delight, be content	रत (*rata*) delighted
हन् (√*han*) (2) kill	हत (*hata*) killed

10.8 The following sound changes should be learned:

a. In general, root final -आ or complex vowels become -ई before the ending -त.

Examples:

पा (√*pā*) (1) drink	पीत (*pīta*) drunk
गै (√*gai*) (1) sing	गीत (*gīta*) sung;
	गीता (*gītā*) song

But, the following important exceptions must be memorized:

i. ज्ञा (√jñā) (9) know ज्ञात (*jñāta*) known
ii. स्था (√*sthā*) (1) stand स्थित (*sthita*) stood
iii. दा (√*dā*) (3) give दत्त (*datta*) given
iv. धा (√*dhā*) (3) place हित (*hita*) placed

b. A root final voiced aspirate is deaspirated before त, and the त् is voiced and aspirated. (7.26.b)
Examples:
बुध् (√*budh*) (1) awaken + त (*ta*) → बुद्ध (*buddha*) awakened
क्षुभ् (√*kṣubh*) (4) shake + त (*ta*) → क्षुब्ध (*kṣubdha*) shaken
लभ् (√*labh*) (1) obtain + त (*ta*) → लब्ध (*labdha*) obtained

c. The roots दह् (1) (√*dah*—burn) and दुह् (2) (√*duh*—milk) are treated as if they were दघ् (*dagh*) and दुघ् (*dugh*) respectively, and the root नह् (4) (√*nah*—bind) as if it were नध् (*nadh*).
दह् (√*dah*) burn + त (*ta*) → दग्ध (*dagdha*) burned
दुह् (√*duh*) milk + त (*ta*) → दुग्ध (*dugdha*) milked
नह् (√*nah*) bind + त (*ta*) → नद्ध (*naddha*) bound

d. Several other roots with final ह् are treated peculiarly: The root final ह् before -त becomes ढ् and the त् is lost. A preceding इ or उ vowel is lengthened. In the roots सह् (1) (√*sah*—endure, bear), and वह् (1) (√*vah*—carry), the अ vowel becomes ओ. (See 20.6.i.)
Examples:
लिह् (√*lih*) (2) lick → लीढ (*līḍha*) licked
रुह् (√*ruh*) (1) climb, mount → रूढ (*rūḍha*) climbed, mounted
सह् (√*sah*) (1) endure → सोढ (*soḍha*) endured
वह् (√*vah*) (1) carry → वोढ (*voḍha*) carried

e. See 7.18.e and 34.b for the treatment of the तालव्य root finals च् and ज् before -त. Note also the change of त् to ट् after ष् (7.18.b). श् before त् or थ् everywhere becomes ष्.
Examples:

युज् (√*yuj*) (7) join → युक्त (*yukta*) joined
द्विष् (√*dviṣ*) (2) hate → द्विष्ट (*dviṣṭa*) hated
दृश् (√*dṛś*) see → दृष्ट (*dṛṣṭa*) seen

10.9 Certain roots are set off from the -त ending by the vowel इ. There is no comprehensive set of rules covering all cases of this use of इ. There are, however, certain root finals which generally require it.

a. Root final conjuncts.
Examples:

निन्द् (√*nind*) (1) blame → निन्दित (*nindita*) blamed
चुम्ब् (√*cumb*) (1) kiss → चुम्बित (*cumbita*) kissed
शङ्क् (√*śaṅk*) (1) doubt → शङ्कित (*śaṅkita*) doubted

b. Root final मूर्धन्य consonants.
Examples:

पठ् (√*paṭh*) (1) read → पठित (*paṭhita*) read
भाष् (√*bhāṣ*) (1) speak → भाषित (*bhāṣita*) spoken
वस् (√*vas*) (1) → (उष्—*uṣ*) → उषित (*uṣita*) dwelt
dwell

c. Root final ल् (l) or व् (v).
Examples:

चल् (√*cal*) (1) move → चलित (*calita*) moved
जीव् (√*jīv*) (1) live → जीवित (*jīvita*) lived, enlivened
सेव् (√*sev*) (1) serve → सेवित (*sevita*) served

d. Root final nonvoiced aspirates.
Examples:

लिख् (√*likh*) (6) write → लिखित (*likhita*) written

e. All 10th गण roots take इ, which is added to the strengthened stem.

चिन्त् (√*cint*) (10) think → चिन्तित (*cintita*) thought
चुर् (√*cur*) (10) steal → चोरित (*corita*) stolen

10.10 Many other finals **may** require इ. These should simply be learned as they are encountered. The following are important examples:

पत् (√*pat*) (1) fall → पतित (*patita*) fallen
खाद् (√*khād*) (1) eat → खादित (*khādita*) eaten
कुप् (√*kup*) (4) be angry → कुपित (*kupita*) angry
बाध् (√*bādh*) (1) oppress → बाधित (*bādhita*) oppressed

10.11 The root ग्रह् (9P) (√*grah*—take hold of) inserts ई before the ending. The correct form, then, is गृहीत (*gṛhīta*—taken).

10.12 A few roots form the भूते कृदन्त with the suffix -न. The largest class of these are roots ending in द्. The द् before the न् of the ending is peculiar in that it assimilates completely and becomes न्.

Examples:

छिद् (√*chid*) (7) cut → छिन्न (*chinna*) cut
भिद् (√*bhid*) (7) split → भिन्न (*bhinna*) separated, split
पद् (√*pad*) (4) move → पन्न (*panna*) moved

There are other roots which take this ending and which are simply learned as encountered.

Examples:

पॄ (√*pṝ*) (9) fill → पूर्ण (*pūrṇa*) full, filled
जॄ (√*jṝ*) (4) waste away → जीर्ण (*jīrṇa*) wasted, aged
ली (√*lī*) (4) cling → लीन (*līna*) attached
हा (√*hā*) (3) abandon → हीन (*hīna*) abandoned
तॄ (√*tṝ*) (1) cross → तीर्ण (*tīrṇa*) crossed

EXERCISES

A. Translate the reading into English.

B. Translate the following into Sanskrit using the भूते कृदन्त wherever possible.

1. I think that Śiva and Viṣṇu are the (two) fathers of the world.
2. If all the rākṣasas are slain by Rāma, how then do we see them in the hermitage?
3. Lakṣmaṇa never abandons his dear brother. If a brother is slain, whence comes another?
4. Sītā said, "If I am abandoned by my husband, how will I stay in Ayodhyā?"
5. Gautama's daughter is desired by the aged victor.
6. Bound and bowed, he was abandoned in the prison by mother and daughter, like an old pot.
7. The jewel was acquired by my brother, but in the course of time, it was forgotten by him.
8. The land was shaken by Indra's thunder, and the people were overcome with fear.
9. The words were spoken to her father, but their truth was doubted by him.
10. The queen was served by my mother, and to her was given a gem as brilliant as the sun.

C. Memorize the following verse.

चितां प्रज्वलितां दृष्ट्वा वैद्यो विस्मयमागतः ।
नाहं गतो न मे भ्राता कस्येदं हस्तलाघवम् ॥

Seeing the blazing funeral pyre, the doctor is greatly astonished, "I didn't attend him, nor did my brother. Whose skill, then, has accomplished this?"

READING

यदा दशरथस्याज्ञा जनैः श्रुता तदायोध्यानन्देन पूर्णेवाभवत् । नगरस्य मार्गेषु लोका गायन्ति नृत्यन्ति च । तेन च स्वर्गे ऽपि देवास्तुष्टा अभवन् । अहो वृद्धेन पित्रा राघवो राजा कृत इत्युक्तं तैः । किं बहुना । अभिषेकस्य श्रवणादयोध्यानन्दस्य सागरे निमग्नेवाभवत् । पितुर्वचनं श्रूयते रामेणापि । तेन वचनेन प्रमुदितो ऽपि स दुःखस्य लेशमन्वभवत् । यदि राज्यं मया क्रियते तर्हि प्रियः पिता वनं गच्छति । तदा भ्रातृभिः सह कथमिह तिष्ठाम्यहमिति ॥

GLOSSARY

अभि + भू
abhi + √bhū (1P)—overcome

अभिभूत
abhibhūta (adj)—overcome

इन्द्रः
indraḥ (m prop)—Indra

इष्ट
iṣṭa (adj)—desired

इह
iha (ind)—here

उक्त
ukta (adj)—spoken, spoken to, addressed (see 10.7.b)

कर्तृ
kartṛ (m)—doer, agent, grammatical subject

किं बहुना
kiṃ bahunā (idiom)—'why continue on' (e.g., किं बहुना प्रलापेन—'what is the use of prattling on,' see 4.42.b)

कृत
kṛta (adj)—done, made

कुम्भः
kumbhaḥ (m)—pot

क्षुब्ध
kṣubdha (adj)—agitated, shaken

गर्जनम्
garjanam (n)—thunder

गै (गायति)
√gai (1P) (gāyati)—sing

गौतमः
gautamaḥ (m prop)—Gautama

जीर्ण
jīrṇa (adj)—old, aged

जीवित
jīvita (adj)—living

जॄ
√jṝ (1P)—waste away, age (also 4P जीर्यति—*jīryati*)

जेतृ
jetṛ (m)—victor, conqueror

त्यज्
√tyaj (1P)—abandon

त्यक्त
tyakta (adj)—abandoned

दीप्त
dīpta (adj)—shining, brilliant

दुहितृ
duhitṛ (f)—daughter

नगरम्
nagaram (n)—city

नत
nata (adj)—bowed, bent

नद्ध
naddha (adj)—bound

नम्
√nam (1P)—bow, bend

नह्
√nah (4P)—bind

निमग्न
nimagna (adj)—sunk

नी
√nī (1P)—lead

नृत्
√nṛt (4P/Ā)—dance

नेतृ
netṛ (m)—leader

पत्
√pat (1P)—fall

पितृ
pitṛ (m)—father

पूर्ण
pūrṇa (adj)—full

प्रमुदित
pramudita (adj)—delighted, pleased

बन्धनागारः
bandhanāgāraḥ (m)—prison

बुद्ध
buddha (adj)—awake, enlighten; -ḥ (m)—the Buddha

भर्तृ
bhartṛ (m)—husband, lord (belongs to the class of agent nouns despite the fact that it seems like a kinship term)

भ्रातृ
bhrātṛ (m)—brother

भीतिः
bhītiḥ (f)—fear

भूमिः
bhūmiḥ (f)—land, earth

मणिः
maṇiḥ (m)—jewel

मातृ
mātṛ (f)—mother

मार्गः
mārgaḥ (m)—path, road

लभ्
√labh (1Ā)—acquire, gain

लब्ध
labdha (adj)—acquired, gained

लेशः
leśaḥ (m)—little, small bit, trace

शङ्क्
√śaṅk (1Ā)—doubt

शङ्कित
śaṅkita (adj)—doubted

श्रवणम्
śravaṇam (n)—hearing

श्रुत
śruta (adj)—heard

सत्य
satya (adj)—real, true; -m (n)—reality, truth

सागरः
sāgaraḥ (m)—ocean

सेव्
√sev (1Ā)—attend on, serve

सेवित
sevita (adj)—served

LESSON 11

Stems in -अन्त्; Adjectival Suffixes in -मन्त् and -वन्त्; The क्तवतु (Past Active Participle); The त्वान्त/ल्यबन्त (Gerund); The लोट् (Imperative)

11.0 **Stems in -अन्त्**

There are a number of nominal and adjectival stems in Sanskrit that end in the vowel अ followed by the conjunct -न्त्. These words fall into a very few fairly significant categories.

1. Adjectives formed with the possessive suffixes -मन्त् and -वन्त् (traditionally called मतुप् and वतुप् respectively by the grammarians).
2. The वर्तमाने कृदन्त (present participle). See Lesson 15.
3. A small number of anomalous forms which appear to have belonged originally to 1 or 2.

11.1 The following paradigms are for stems belonging to 1 and 3 above. The present participles (2), whose paradigm differs slightly, will be treated separately (Lesson 15).

a. पुंलिङ्ग । भगवन्त् (blessed)

	एक°	द्वि°	बहु°
प्र°	भगवान्	भगवन्तौ	भगवन्तः
द्वि°	भगवन्तम्	भगवन्तौ	भगवतः
तृ°	भगवता	भगवद्भ्याम्	भगवद्भिः
च°	भगवते	भगवद्भ्याम्	भगवद्भ्यः
प°	भगवतः	भगवद्भ्याम्	भगवद्भ्यः
ष°	भगवतः	भगवतोः	भगवताम्
स°	भगवति	भगवतोः	भगवत्सु
सम्°	भगवन्	भगवन्तौ	भगवन्तः

b. As usual, the नपुंसकलिङ्ग differs from the पुंलिङ्ग only in the प्रथमा and द्वितीया.

नपुंसकलिङ्ग । भगवन्त् (blessed)

	एक°	द्वि°	बहु°
प्र°	भगवत्	भगवती	भगवन्ति
द्वि°	भगवत्	भगवती	भगवन्ति
सम्°	भगवत्	भगवती	भगवन्ति

Note that stem strength and weakness is shown by the presence or absence of the stem nasal न् (see 8.1).

c. The स्त्रीलिङ्ग, or feminine, of the stems is formed by adding ई to the weak stem (-अत्) and is then declined like any noun of that stem final (see 7.1).

Example:

भगवती (blessed lady)

11.2 There are two stems that end in -अन्त् ,which are very useful and should be learned.

a. The important adjective महन्त् (large, great) is declined like the above, but its stem vowel अ is long (आ) in *all* the strong forms.

Examples:

महानृषिर्दृश्यते न दृश्यते वा कलौ युगे ।

(Does a great ṛṣi appear or not in the kali age?)

राक्षसा महान्तौ वीरौ न कदापि घ्नन्ति ।

(The rākṣasa-s never kill the two great heroes.)

b. The word भवन्त् (स्त्रीलिङ्ग—भवती), perhaps a shortened form of भगवन्त् ,is regularly used as a polite or respectful equivalent of the मध्यमपुरुष pronoun. It construes with the verb in the प्रथमपुरुष and may be used in the बहुवचन to show still greater respect.

Examples:

भवान्कस्माद् देशादागतवान् ।

(From what country have you come?) (See 11.4)

भवन्तः कुत्र वसन्ति ।
(Where do you live?)

यद्भवत्या कृतं तन्मह्यमतीव रोचते ।
(What you [my lady] have done pleases me very much.)

तत्कथं ज्ञातं भवद्भिः ।
(How do you know this?)

11.3 The Adjectival Suffixes -मन्त् and -वन्त्.

The most common forms of this type are adjectives made by suffixation of the possessive affix -मन्त् (मतुप्) to the stem form of most nouns.

Examples:

बुद्धिः (f) (intelligence)	बुद्धिमन्त् (wise)
स्मृतिः (f) (memory, sacred knowledge)	स्मृतिमन्त् (possessed of memory)
धनुः (n) (bow)	धनुष्मन्त् (having a bow) (m) (archer)
मधु (n) (honey)	मधुमन्त् (sweet)

रामो बुद्धिमान्स्मृतिमानित्युक्तं रामायणे ।
(It is said in the *Rāmāyaṇa* that Rāma is wise and possessed of memory.)

The suffix -मन्त् is changed to -वन्त् when:

1. The stem ends in a म् or an अ or आ, or if any one of the preceding occurs as the penultimate.

   Examples:

विद्या (f) (knowledge)	विद्यावन्त् (possessed of knowledge)
लक्ष्मी (f) (fortune)	लक्ष्मीवन्त् (possessed of fortune)
यशस् (n) (fame)	यशस्वन्त् (famous)

2. The stem originally ends in a स्पर्श.

   Example:

विद्युत् (n) (lightning)	विद्युत्वन्त् (possessed of lightning)

NOTE: The stem to which the -मन्त् or -वन्त् suffix is added is not considered word final. Therefore, the addition of these affixes do not require external सन्धि.

11.4 **The क्तवतु (Past Active Participle)**

Such possessive usages are fairly limited. However, the suffixation of -वन्त् (स्त्रीलिङ्ग—-वती) to a भूते कृदन्त, whether its verbal root is सकर्मक or अकर्मक, yields a useful and common verbal adjective modifying the कर्तृ, which functions as yet another simple past tense in the कर्तरि प्रयोग.

Examples:

√गम् (go) । रामो वनं गतवान् । सीतापि गतवती ।

(Rāma went to the forest. Sītā went too.)

√भक्ष् (10P) (eat); √वच् (2P) (say)

नाहं भक्षितवानम्बेत्युक्तवाञ्छ्रीकृष्णो भागवते ।

("I didn't eat [it] mummy," so said Śrīkṛṣṇa in the *Bhāgavata Purāṇa*.)

11.5 **The त्वान्त/ल्यबन्त् (Gerund)**

The gerund, or indeclinable participle in -त्वा or -य, is one of the most frequently encountered and useful items in the language. The gerund is used, often profusely, to mark successive dependent clauses, the actions of which are meant to be prior to, or, in some cases, simultaneous with, the action of an independent clause. In most cases the कर्तृ of the dependent clause is the same as that of the independent clause. In this way, a complex sentence may have only one finite verb or its syntactic equivalent.

Examples:

पौत्रान्दृष्ट्वा कुटुम्बं परित्यज्य वनं गत्वा वृक्षस्य समीप उपविश्येन्द्रियाणि विजित्य परमं ध्यात्वा च मोक्षं लभते मनुष्यः ।

(Having seen his grandchildren, having left his family, having gone to the forest, having sat down near a tree, having subdued his senses, and having meditated on the highest, a man obtains liberation.)

कपेस्तद्वचनं श्रुत्वा सीता सुखिताभवत् ।
(Having heard the monkey's speech, Sītā became happy.)

उक्त्वा भुक्त्वा गता गृहम् ।
(Having talked and eaten, she went home.)

11.6 Since it is always an अव्ययपद (indeclinable) the त्वान्त or ल्यबन्त is not subject to agreement of any kind with कर्तृ, कर्मन्, or anything else. Because of this it may be used freely in both कर्तरि and कर्मणि clauses with reference generally to the कर्तृ regardless of its case.

Example:
रामेण तत्र गत्वा सर्वे राक्षसा हताः ।
(Rāma, having gone there, killed all the rākṣasa-s.)

11.7 The त्वान्त/ल्यबन्त is formed in different ways, depending upon whether the verbal root is preceded by an उपसर्ग. (See 8.12.)

a. i. If there is no उपसर्ग, the suffix -त्वा is added directly to a weak form of the root, in general the same form which precedes the -त of the भूते कृदन्त. (See 10.7-9.) These forms are called त्वान्त.

Examples:

√गम्	(1P)	→	गत्वा	(having gone)
√हन्	(2P)	→	हत्वा	(having slain)
√दृश्	(4P)	→	दृष्ट्वा	(having seen)
√श्रु	(5P)	→	श्रुत्वा	(having heard)
√वच्	(2P)	→	उक्त्वा	(having said)
√त्यज्	(1P)	→	त्यक्त्वा	(having abandoned)
√कृ	(8P)	→	कृत्वा	(having done)
√स्था	(1P)	→	स्थित्वा	(having stood)
√पा	(1P)	→	पीत्वा	(having drunk)
√दा	(3P)	→	दत्त्वा	(having given)
√धा	(3P)	→	हित्वा	(having placed)

ii. A number of roots require the insertion of the vowel इ before the ending. Others take the vowel optionally. The root √ग्रह् (9P) (गृह्णाति) requires the vowel ई (cf. 10.9-11).

Examples:

√वस्	(1P)	→	उषित्वा	(having dwelt)
√विद्	(2P)	→	विदित्वा	(having known)
√ग्रह्	(9P)	→	गृहीत्वा	(having taken)

iii. Roots of the tenth गण (7.38) require that the ending -त्वा, which must be preceded by the vowel इ, replace the final अ of the *present stem.*

Example:

√चिन्त् (10P)—चिन्तयित्वा (having thought)

b. Roots preceded by उपसर्ग-s form the gerund in two ways, depending upon whether or not the root ends in a short vowel. These forms are called ल्यबन्त.

i. If the root does not end in a short vowel (by far the most common case), the ल्यबन्त is formed by adding the suffix -य directly to the root. Before this suffix (and the suffix -त्य; see ii below) the roots generally take the weakened forms appropriate before the -त of the भूते कृदन्त. (See 10.7-9.)

Examples:

परि + √त्यज्	→	परित्यज्य	(having abandoned)
आ + √गम्	→	आगम्य	(having come)
अनु + √ज्ञा	→	अनुज्ञाय	(having permitted)

ii. If a root ends in a short vowel **and** is preceded by an उपसर्ग the suffix is -त्य.

Examples:

वि + √जि	→	विजित्य	(having conquered)
अनु + √कृ	→	अनुकृत्य	(having imitated)
प्र + √इ	→	प्रेत्य	(having died)

11.8 Note that some roots in -अम् or -अन् that form weakened past भूते कृदन्त-s (गम् → गत; हन् → हत) (see 10.7.c) are sometimes treated as short अ stems after उपसर्ग-s. So, आ + गम् may form आगम्य or आगत्य (having come), while नि + हन् **always** forms निहत्य (having killed).

11.9 **The लोट् (Imperative)**

The लोट् is the mode of instruction or command. Since it occurs most commonly in direct address, मध्यम पुरुष forms are the most frequently used, although for various reasons, including politeness, the प्रथम पुरुष forms are also quite common.

11.10 The लोट् has no mode-sign of its own and simply adds its own distinctive endings to the present stems of the various roots.

11.11 The scheme of personal endings is as follows:

	परस्मैपद			आत्मनेपद		
	एक°	द्वि°	बहु°	एक°	द्वि°	बहु°
प्र°	तु	ताम्	अन्तु/अतु	ताम्	आताम्	अन्ताम्/अताम्
म°	Ø/धि/हि	तम्	त	स्व	आथाम्	ध्वम्
उ°	आनि	आव	आम	ऐ	आवहै	आमहै

11.12 मध्यम पुरुष **Endings:**

a. The मध्यम° एक° परस्मैपद ending for roots of the 'अ' गण-s (1,4,6,10) is Ø (zero). In other words, this most important लोट् form, is identical with the present stem.

Examples:

√भू (1P) (be) हे शकुन्तले भर्तुर्बहुमता भव ।

(O Śakuntalā, *be* well respected by your husband!)

√स्था (1P) (stay); √गम् (1P) (go)

राम नगरे मा तिष्ठ वनमेव गच्छ ।

(Rāma! Don't *stay* in the city, *go* to the forest.)

परि + √व्रज् (1P) (wander)

वने परिव्रजेति श्रुत्वा परिव्राजको ऽभवत् ।

(Having heard, "*wander* in the forest," he became a wandering mendicant.)

√भज् (1P) (worship)

भज गोविन्दं भज गोविन्दं गोविन्दं भज मूढमते ।

(*Worship* Govinda [Kṛṣṇa], *Worship* Govinda, *Worship* Govinda, O you fool!)

b. The non-अ गण-s (2, 3, 5, 7, 8, 9) have, for this form, the endings -हि or धि, depending upon whether the verbal stem ends in a vowel or a consonant. Note that this particular form is unusual in that for the non-अ गण-s it is made from the weak form of the stem, even in those गण-s that require root strength in all other एक° परस्मैपद forms.

Examples:

	लट्	लोट्
√इ (2)	एति	इहि (go!)
√दुह् (2)	दोग्धि	गां दुग्धि पयः (*Milk* the cow for milk!)
√ब्रू (2)	ब्रवीति	ब्रूहि ब्रूहि मित्र (*Speak*! *Speak*, friend!)

c. Some roots of the third (हु) गण present irregularities.

i. The root √हु itself violates rule b., in that it takes the ending -धि, despite the fact that its stem ends in a vowel.

Example:

जुहुधि (offer!)

ii. Far more important are the two common roots √दा and √धा. Here they form देहि (give) and धेहि (place).

Example:

भोजनं देहि राजन् (*Give* [me] food, O King!)

d. Since all roots of the seventh (रुध्) गण end in consonants and the गण sign **precedes** the final consonant, all the present stems of the गण likewise end in consonants. Therefore, the मध्यम° एक° परस्मैपद ending in the लोट् of roots of this गण is always -धि.

Example:

√युज् । युङ्ग्धि, "yoke!"

e. Roots of the fifth and eighth (सु and तन्) गण-s take the ending -हि when the **root itself** ends in a consonant.

Example:

√आप् । सुखमाप्नुहि (*Attain* happiness!)

But, when the roots end in vowels, this form is identical with the weak stem itself.

Examples:

√कृ (8P) यत्पित्रोक्तं तत्कुरु तात ।

(*Do* what your father says, my dear boy!)

√श्रु (5P) गुरोर्वचनं शृणु ।

(*Hear* the words of the guru.)

f. 9th गण roots ending in vowels take -हि, but those ending in consonants lose their class sign and take the special ending -आन.

Example:

√ग्रह् । गृहाण "take"

11.13 The मध्यम° एक° आत्मनेपद is formed by adding the ending -स्व to the present stem in all cases.

Examples:

√युध् (4Ā)	युध्यस्व ।	(fight!)
√क्षम् (1Ā)	क्षमस्व मां देव ।	(*Forgive me*, O God.)
√आस् (2Ā)	आस्स्व ।	(sit!)

11.14 After मध्यम° एक° forms, the most important are the प्रथम° एक°.

a. The परस्मैपद adds -तु to present stems. The non-अ गण-s show normal strength.

Examples:

√गम् । रामो वनं गच्छतु ।

(*Let* Rāma *go* to the forest.)

√कृ । भरतो राज्यं करोतु ।

(*Let* Bharata *rule* the kingdom.)

b. This form is very frequently used, especially in dramas as a polite or respectful equivalent of the मध्यम°.

Examples:

√जि (1P) जयत्वार्यः ।

(*May* my lord [i.e., "you"] *be victorious*.)

प्र + √विश् प्रविशत्वार्यः ।

(*Please enter*, my lord.)

c. This form of the roots √अस् (2P) (be), and √भू (1P) (be) (अस्तु, भवतु) is often used in the senses, "Okay.," "very well," "Let it be," etc.

11.15 The प्रथम°, बहु°, परस्मैपद ending -अन्तु behaves exactly like the indicative ending -अन्ति in that it causes the loss of the -अ of an अ गण stem and loses its nasal after stems of the third गण. (See 7.25.)

Examples:

√पश् (4P) सर्वे भद्राणि पश्यन्तु ।

(*May* everyone *see* auspicious things.)

√तॄ (1P) सर्वे दुर्गाणि तरन्तु ।

(*May* everyone *overcome* difficulties.)

√दा (3P) ब्राह्मणेभ्यो धनं ददतु ।

(*Let* them *give* wealth to the brāhmans.)

√भी (3P) न कस्मादपि बिभ्यतु ।

(*Let* them *fear* nothing at all.)

11.16 **The कर्मणि प्रयोग of the लोट् :**

The लोट् may be used in the कर्मणि and भावे प्रयोग-s as well as in the कर्तरि प्रयोग. It is formed, like the कर्मणि प्रयोग of the लट् , by the addition of the appropriate आत्मनेपद लोट् ending to the कर्मणि stem. (See 9.24-27.)

11.17 This form functions as a very formal or polite imperative and is very freely used in conversation. In actual use, the कर्तृ (in the तृतीया—here usually त्वया, भवता, or भवद्भिः, "by you") is generally unexpressed, and the कर्मन् (in the प्रथमा) is frequently (necessarily in the भावे प्रयोग) (see 9.17) not made explicit.

Examples:

√वच् (2P) उच्यताम् Lit.,"*Let it be spoken* (by you)." "Please speak."

√लिख् (6P) लिख्यताम् Lit.,"*Let it be written* (by you)." "Please write (it)."

√आस् (2Ā) आस्यताम् Lit., "*Let it be sat* (by you)." "Please sit down."

आ√गम् (1P) मया सहागम्यताम् Lit., "*Let it be come* (by you) with me." = "Please come with me."

अलं√कृ (8P) आसनम् अलंक्रियताम् Lit.,"*Let* the seat *be adorned* (by you)." = "Please sit down."

√क्षम् (1Ā) क्षम्यतामयं पुरुषः Lit., "*Let* this person *be pardoned*." = "Pardon me." (For अयम्, see 19.1)

11.18 Note that the negative particle मा is used instead of न to negate लोट् forms.

Examples:

नगरं मा गच्छ । (*Don't go* to the city.)

तन्मा कुरु । (*Don't do* that.)

EXERCISES

A. Translate the reading into English and be prepared to answer questions about it in Sanskrit.

B. Rewrite all the gerunds in the reading, removing उपसर्ग-s from those that have them and adding the उपसर्ग अनु to those that have none. (Don't worry about the meaning of the forms thus generated.)

C. Translate the following sentences into Sanskrit.

1. Having entered the house and having sat on the ground, he said to me, "Give me some food!"
2. Upon hearing the words, "Mother, having left home, I am going to the forest," Kausalyā said, "Let it not be!" (Use √भू.)
3. Ah! Rāma, I am oppressed by great sorrow. Do not go, having left me!
4. My daughter is extremely intelligent and well-versed in the स्मृति-s. (Use -मन्त् suffix.) Therefore let her be the wife of the king.
5. Stand up, you old fool! Does a man sit when the king enters? (Use अपि as question marker.)

D. Transform the लोट् clauses or sentences in "A" and "C" above into कर्मणि or भावे प्रयोग forms.

E. Memorize the following verse.

तृष्णां छिन्द्धि भज क्षमां जहि मदं पापे रतिं मा कृथाः
सत्यं ब्रूह्यनुयाहि साधुपदवीं सेवस्व विद्वज्जनान् ।
मान्यान्मानय विद्विषो ऽप्यनुनय प्रच्छादय स्वान् गुणान्
कीर्तिं पालय दुःखिते कुरु दयामेतत्सतां लक्षणम् ॥

Cut off your desires, cultivate tolerance, put an end to your drunken ways, take no pleasure in evil, tell the truth, follow the path of the virtuous, serve the wise, honor those who deserve to be honored, conciliate even your enemies, conceal your own virtues, preserve your good name, have compassion for those in trouble; this is the mark of the virtuous.

READING

श्रीरामस्याभिषेकं श्रुत्वा सर्वे जना नन्दिता अभवन् । वस्तुतो ऽयोध्यानन्दस्य सागरे निमग्नेवादृश्यत । दशरथस्य ज्येष्ठा भार्या कौसल्या नाम मम पुत्रो राजेति मत्वा परमं सुखमन्वभवत् । अथ वृद्धस्य राज्ञो ऽन्या भार्या कैकेयी नामासीद् यस्याः पुत्रो भरतः । पुरा कस्मिंश्चित्समये सा दशरथस्य महान्तमुपकारं कृत्वा राज्ञो द्वौ वरौ प्राप्तवती । ततस्तु तौ वरौ न कदापि कैकेय्या वृतावास्ताम् । अधुना तु सा वरावनुस्मृत्य दशरथस्य समीपं गत्वा वचनमब्रवीत् । जयत्वार्यपुत्रः । अप्यनुस्मरत्यार्यपुत्रो मद्द्वौ वरौ वृणीष्वेत्यात्मनो वचनमिति । राजा क्षणमेक चिन्तयित्वावदत्स्मरामि प्रिये स्मरामि यदिच्छसि तद्ब्रूहीति । प्रथमेन वरेण मम पुत्रो भरतो राज्ये ऽभिषिक्तो भवतु । द्वितीयेन च रामो ऽयोध्यां परित्यज्य वनं गच्छत्वित्युक्तवती कैकेयी । तस्यास्तद्वचनं श्रुत्वा दशरथो मूढ इव क्षणमुपविश्याशन्या हतो वृक्ष इव भूमावपतत् ॥

GLOSSARY

अधुना
(ind)—now, at present

अनु + √स्मृ
(1P)—recall, remember

अम्बा
(f)—mother (irreg. संबोधनम् = अम्ब)

अभिषिक्त
(adj)—consecrated

अशनिः
(f)—bolt of lightning

आर्यः
(m)—noble person, lord; as term of address—sir.

आर्यपुत्रः
(m)—"my lord"; used by wife to husband

उपकारः
(m)—assistance, favor

उप + √विश्
(6P)—sit

कैकेयी
(f prop)—Kaikeyī, Bharata's mother

क्षणः
(m)—a moment, instant (see 4.41)

तु
(ind)—but

√दृश्
see (non-present equivalent of पश्)

द्वि (stem = द्व)
(number)—two, treated as an अ stem noun, in dual only (see 19.6.b)

द्वितीय
(adj)—second

नन्दित
(adj)—overjoyed

पाल्
(10P)—protect

पुरा
(ind) previously, long ago

प्रथम
(adj)—first

प्र + √विश्
(6P)—enter

प्र√आप्
(5P)—obtain

बुद्धिः
(f)—wit, intelligence

बुद्धिमन्त्
(adj; f -अती)—wise

√ब्रू
(2Ā)—speak, tell

भोजनम्
(n)—food

महन्त्
(adj)—great, large

मा
(ind)—negative used with imperative

मूढ
(adj)—stupefied

वरः
(m)—boon, wish

वस्तुतः
(ind)—in fact

√वृ (वृणीते)
(9Ā)—choose (as a boon)

वृक्षः
(m)—tree

वृत
(adj)—chosen

समयः
(m)—time, period of time

समीपम्
(n)—nearness, vicinity

√स्मृ
(1P)—remember

स्मृतिमन्त्
(adj)—possessed of memory, well-versed in स्मृति

LESSON 12

Nominal Stems in -इन्; समास (Nominal Composition)

12.0 The suffix -इन् is used freely in Sanskrit to form adjectives or nouns that indicate that the thing denoted by the word to which the suffix is added is possessed by, or in some way an attribute of, the word that the newly formed adjective modifies.

a. The suffix is normally used with noun stems in -अ or -आ and replaces the final vowel.

Examples:

हस्तः (hand) + इन् → हस्तिन् (possessing a "hand"= elephant)

योगः (yoga) + इन् → योगिन् (yogi)

b. A number of stems in -अस् form a similar adjective by the suffixation of -विन्, which is added to the stem.

Examples:

तपः (asceticism) + विन् → तपस्विन् (ascetic)

मनः (mind) + विन् → मनस्विन् (wise)

c. These forms are all पुंलिङ्ग or नपुंसकलिङ्ग, as the context requires. The corresponding स्त्रीलिङ्ग-s are formed with the suffixes -इनी and -विनी and are then declined according to the -ई paradigm (7.1).

Examples:

योगिनी (female yogi)

तपस्विनी (female ascetic, a wretched woman)

12.1. The declension of the पुंलिङ्ग and नपुंसकलिङ्ग forms is as follows:

a. पुंलिङ्ग; योगिन् (yogin)

विभक्ति	एक°	द्वि°	बहु°
प्र°	योगी	योगिनौ	योगिनः
द्वि°	योगिनम्	योगिनौ	योगिनः
तृ°	योगिना	योगिभ्याम्	योगिभिः
च°	योगिने	योगिभ्याम्	योगिभ्यः
प°	योगिनः	योगिभ्याम्	योगिभ्यः

ष°	योगिनः	योगिनोः	योगिनाम्
स°	योगिनि	योगिनोः	योगिषु
सम्°	योगिन्	योगिनौ	योगिनः

b. नपुंसकलिङ्ग; रूपिन् (possessed of form)

प्र°	रूपि	रूपिणी	रूपीणि
द्वि°	रूपि	रूपिणी	रूपीणि
सम्°	रूपि	रूपिणी	रूपीणि

The remainder of the declension is the same as the पुंलिङ्ग.

12.2 This paradigm is quite regular. The only point that should be stressed and watched for is that the प्रथमा एक° पुंलिङ्ग ends in ई. Do not on this account confuse these forms with those of the -इ or -ई declensions. This confusion is best avoided, as with the other consonant stems, by memorizing the stem form as well as the प्रथमा.

Example:

योगिन् → योगी

12.3 समास: Nominal Composition

Now that you have learned most of the major nominal declensions in all their confusing variety of stems and endings, we come to a feature of Sanskrit that almost makes one wonder why one ever had to learn all this. The feature is समास, nominal compounding, and is one of the most significant and distinctive characteristics of the classical language. It is the variety of nominal compounds that lends to classical Sanskrit much of its characteristic density, terseness, sonorousness, subtlety, and power.

12.4 There is nothing about the formation of most Sanskrit समास-s that should present any great difficulty to a speaker of English. What sets Sanskrit compounds off from those of English and similar languages is the great freedom allowed in compound formation and in literary and scientific texts, the extraordinary number of words that may be brought together into a single compound.

12.5 Nominal compounding is a technique whereby nouns may be related to one another without need for the conventional markers of syntactic relation (i.e., the nominal case-endings). Thus composition normally entails लुक् (loss) of सुप्-s (case-endings). Now, as mentioned above (4.44), it is precisely the presence of these सुप्-s, specifiers of syntactic relations, that makes word order a matter of considerably less significance than it is in English. Therefore, if the सुप्-s are lost, one would expect that some other factor, such as fixed word order, would be required to prevent confusion. This is exactly the case in समास whenever there is a syntactic relation or some degree of subordination between two nouns. Except for one type of समास (see Lesson 14), then, word order is rigidly fixed in the formation of समास-s.

12.6 **Word Order in समास-s**

The word order is always the same. The principal noun (or adjective), i.e., the one which itself does not modify, and is not subordinated to, any other word *in the compound* (or potential compound), is always placed last, with the immediately subordinated word preceding it. A few examples from English may serve to clarify this. In the compound "bluebird" (assume for a moment that it refers to any blue bird), it is clearly the word *bird* that is principal and the modifier *blue* that is secondary. Therefore, in the sentence, "He sees the bluebird," *bird* serves as the direct object of the verb *sees*; it is directly related to something *outside* the compound. *Blue* merely specifies something about bird. In the same way, in the sentence, "I took the horsecart," it is *cart* and not *horse* that is the direct object of *take*. If we reverse the order of the members of the compound, as in, "I took the carthorse," we have a completely different sentence. In the first, *horse* is subordinated to *cart* and serves merely to specify a kind of cart. In the second, *cart* specifies a kind of horse. Thus, in both sentences only the final member has any reference *outside the compound*. This is the general rule in Sanskrit with respect to the two most important kinds of compounds.

12.7 Analysis of समास-s

Analysis of compounds in Sanskrit, then, proceeds from the last member back to the first by a series of word-pairs. The technique is to establish the relation of the final member to the preceding member, and next, regarding the last pair as a single unit, to determine its relationship to the preceding member; and then to consider the relationship between the final triplet and the preceding member, and so on. Thus, the great length of some compounds should not be a cause for alarm. No compound relation refers to more than two words. The following diagrams will illustrate how this is done. Each roman letter indicates one compound relation.

Examples:

जनकतनयास्नानपुण्योदकम् (n) (See 12.14.)

(Water sanctified by the bath of the daughter of Janaka.)

जनक — तनया — स्नान — पुण्य — उदकम्

janaka — daughter — bath — holy — water

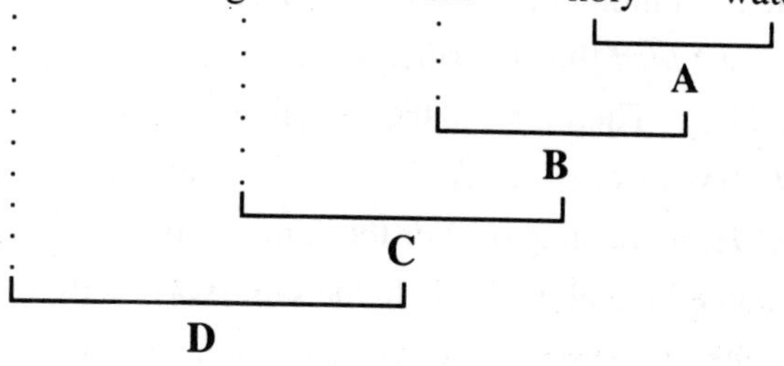

गोपीपीनपयोधरमर्दनचञ्चलकरयुगशालिन् (adj.)
(Having two hands trembling to knead the swelling breasts of the cowgirls.)

गोपी — पीन — पयोधर — मर्दन — चञ्चल — कर — युग — शालिन्
cowgirl-swelling-breast-kneading-trembling-hand-pair-having

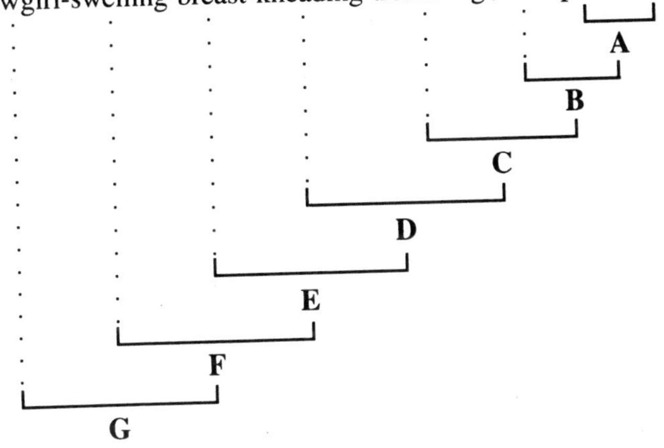

12.8 **Techniques of Compounding**

In almost all types of समास, there is लुक्, or loss of the case-number ending, in all members **except the last.** The last member relates to things outside the समास and is treated **in general** as though it were uncompounded. Prior members of समास-s usually appear in their stem forms or in some alteration of these stem forms and do not show any change for number or case.

Example:
देवमित्रम् (=देवस्य मित्रम्)
(The friend of god)

If we assume that the unspecified case-relation here is षष्ठी (genitive), the समास could equally well stand for देवस्य मित्रम्, देवयोर्मित्रम्, or देवानां मित्रम् (the friend of the god, two gods, or gods). Despite the लुक्, or loss of the case-number ending, the word देव has not lost its power (शक्ति) to express syntactic relation and number. However, here, as with most composition, we must rely on the context to determine what the lost ending was.

12.9 **Types of समास-s**

There are several types of समास-s in Sanskrit. These are distinguished according to their विग्रह, 'analysis,' which enables us to "dissolve" the compounds or paraphrase them by restoring what has been lost in composition.

12.10 The two most important types of समास-s for the beginning student to master are called कर्मधारय and तत्पुरुष.

a. **The कर्मधारय समास** is extremely common. Its formation and विग्रह (analysis) are extremely simple.

   i. In its most common form, it is composed simply of a noun (or nominal item) to which is prefixed a modifying adjective in its **stem form**. सन्धि at all compound junctures is external.

   Examples:

समास	**Meaning**	विग्रह
तुङ्गवृक्षः	tall tree	तुङ्गो वृक्षः
सुन्दरमृगः	beautiful deer	सुन्दरो मृगः
प्रियमित्रम्	dear friend	प्रियं मित्रम्
हतराक्षसाः	slain rākṣasa-s	हता राक्षसाः
त्यक्तभार्या	abandoned wife	त्यक्ता भार्या
वृद्धतपस्विनी	aged ascetic woman	वृद्धा तपस्विनी
अभिज्ञातशूरौ	two recognized heroes	अभिज्ञातौ शूरौ

   Notice that the noun modified is in no way altered. It retains its usual gender and proper number and **is used exactly like an uncompounded noun.**

   Examples:

   तुङ्गवृक्षे वसन्ति बहुशुकाः । (तुङ्गे वृक्षे वसन्ति बहवः शुकाः ।)
   (Many parrots live in the tall tree.)

   मृतराक्षसेषु तिष्ठति रामः । (मृतेषु राक्षसेषु . . .)
   (Rāma stands amidst the dead rākṣasa-s.)

b. A less common but still frequently occurring kind of कर्मधारय समास is that in which one noun is equated with another.

Here again it is the prior member, which is subordinate, that "qualifies" the latter.

Examples:

समास	विग्रह	**Meaning**
वाग्द्वारम्	वाग् द्वारम्	(speech-door) a doorway which is of the form of a speech
सागरमेखला	सागरो मेखला	(ocean-girdle) a girdle which is the ocean
राजर्षिः	राजा ऋषिः	(king-sage, a royal sage)
नरसिंहः	नरः सिंहः	(man-lion)

In this type of समास, which is called the **appositional** or **equational** कर्मधारय, the two elements, being nouns, retain their inherent genders, just as when any two nouns are equated. Thus, in the compound वाग्द्वारम्, वाग् is स्त्रीलिङ्ग while द्वारम् is नपुंसकलिङ्ग.

12.11 समानाधिकरण : **Case Agreement**

In either of the two types of कर्मधारय समास, the members, when subjected to विग्रह must be in the same case. This is because these members, whether their relationship is that of adjective and noun or of apposition, always stand in the same grammatical relationship to a verb or other part of speech. Thus, for example in the sentence:

दशरथो महान् राजा महान्तं हस्तिनं महति वने हन्ति ।

(The great King Daśaratha kills the great elephant in the great forest.)

a. दशरथः, महान् and राजा are in apposition and so must be in the same case (प्रथमा) as कर्तृ of √हन्.
b. महान्तम् modifies हस्तिनम्, which is the कर्मन् of √हन्, so they must agree.
c. महति modifies वने, the अधिकरण (locus) of the action of √हन्, so they too must agree.

The sentence could be rewritten using कर्मधारय समास-s each one including a group of words in agreement:

दशरथमहाराजो महाहस्तिनं महावने हन्ति ।

The Sanskrit term for this kind of equal governance of several words by a verb, etc., is called समानाधिकरण This is not to be confused with the apparent agreement such as we saw in the sentence of the type:

रामेण शरेण राक्षसो हन्यते ।

(Rāma kills the rākṣasa with an arrow.)

in which there is no समानाधिकरण relating रामेण, the कर्तृ, and शरेण, the करण (instrument), of the action of √हन्. A कर्मधारय समास then, is one whose members are governed by the relationship of समानाधिकरण.

12.12 **The तत्पुरुष समास : Syntactic Compound**

The other major compound type which must be mastered thoroughly is the so-called तत्पुरुष, or **syntactic compound**. The तत्पुरुष contrasts sharply with the कर्मधारय in that, as appears when subjected to विग्रह, there **must not** be case agreement (समानाधिकरण) between the two members. If in विग्रह, the last member is cited in its प्रथमा form, the prior member will be in any other case. The तत्पुरुष may then be identified by the number of the case of the prior member. In fact, the षष्ठी and तृतीया are, in that order, the most common types of तत्पुरुष.

Type	समास		विग्रह	**Meaning**
षष्ठी	देवपुत्रः	(m)	देवस्य पुत्रः	son of the god
षष्ठी	रामदूतः	(m)	रामस्य दूतः	Rāma's messenger
षष्ठी	राक्षसकन्या	(f)	राक्षसस्य कन्या	daughter of the rākṣasa
षष्ठी	सीतापुस्तकम्	(n)	सीतायाः पुस्तकम्	Sītā's book
षष्ठी	नरोत्तमः	(m)	नराणामुत्तमः	best of men
तृतीया	निद्राबाधित	(adj)	निद्रया बाधित	oppressed by sleep
तृतीया	नृपहत	(adj)	नृपेण हत	slain by the king
पञ्चमी	मरणभयम्	(n)	मरणाद्भयम्	fear of death

सप्तमी	वनवासः	(m)	वने वासः	dwelling in the forest
सप्तमी	जलक्रीडा	(f)	जले क्रीडा	sport in the water
चतुर्थी	पादोदकम्	(n)	पादाभ्यामुदकम्	water for the feet
द्वितीया	स्वर्गगमनम्	(n)	स्वर्गं प्रति गमनम्	going to heaven

12.13 **Notes on the formation of तत्पुरुष and कर्मधारय समास-s**

a. कर्मधारय or तत्पुरुष समास-s may either be nouns or adjectives, as their final members are nouns or adjectives.

Examples:

	समास	विग्रह		
(तृतीया तत्पुरुष)	नृपोक्त	नृपेणोक्त	(adj)	spoken by the king
(षष्ठी तत्पुरुष)	नृपवचनम्	नृपस्य वचनम्	(n)	the speech of the king
(कर्मधारय)	तुङ्गवृक्षः	तुङ्गो वृक्षः	(n)	the tall tree
(कर्मधारय)	वृक्षतुङ्ग	वृक्ष इव तुङ्ग	(adj)	tall as a tree

In fact, however, the placement of certain types of adjectives in a समास can very often tell us a lot even before we have understood the compound.

i. The भूते कृदन्त functions most generally as an adjective. Its placement in a समास can be particularly helpful.

a. If any भूते कृदन्त or other adjective occurs as the *prior* member of a समास, the समास is almost certain to be a कर्मधारय of the type discussed in 12.10.a.i.

Examples:

हतपुत्रः	= हतः पुत्रः	(m)	slain son
क्रुद्धब्राह्मणः	= क्रुद्धो ब्राह्मणः	(m)	angry brāhman

क्रुद्धब्राह्मणो हतपुत्रं पश्यति ।

(The angry brāhman sees the slain son.)

b. If, on the other hand, the भूते कृदन्त of a सकर्मक root occurs as the final member of a समास, one is most likely dealing with a तत्पुरुष functioning as an adjective. Moreover, since such a भूते कृदन्त is a कर्मणि form, the समास is most likely to be तृतीया तत्पुरुष.

Examples:

रामहत (adj) = रामेण हत slain by Rāma

शिष्यपठितानि (पुस्तकानि) = शिष्यैः पठितानि (पुस्तकानि) (books) read by students

ii. Since there is no limit to the number of members in a समास nor any restriction as to the types of compound functions possible within any one समास, there is no reason why a तत्पुरुष adjective so formed cannot then precede another noun and make a new compound and so on.

Example:

नृपहतपुत्रं पश्यति क्रुद्धब्राह्मणः ।

(The angry brāhman sees the son slain by the king.)

शिष्यपठितपुस्तकानि न कदापि पठ्यन्ते ऽन्यैः जनैः ।

(Other people never read the books read by students.)

iii. A समास in which an adjective other than a भूते कृदन्त of a सकर्मक root occurs as final member following a noun is very likely to be a कर्मधारय adjective comparing something to the prior member in regard to the quality expressed by the final member. The word इव (like) frequently appears in the विग्रह of such compounds.

Examples:

वृक्षतुङ्ग	वृक्ष इव तुङ्ग	tall as a tree
काककृष्ण	काक इव कृष्ण	black as a crow

12.14 Remember that the विग्रह of compounds of whatever length is carried out from right to left, one juncture at a time.

Examples:

(क°= कर्मधारय; त°= तत्पुरुष; तृ°= तृतीया; ष°= षष्ठी)

समास विग्रह

नृप — हत — पुत्र → नृपेण हतः पुत्रः

(हत — पुत्र: क°)

(नृप — हत-पुत्र: तृ° त° (a son killed by a king))

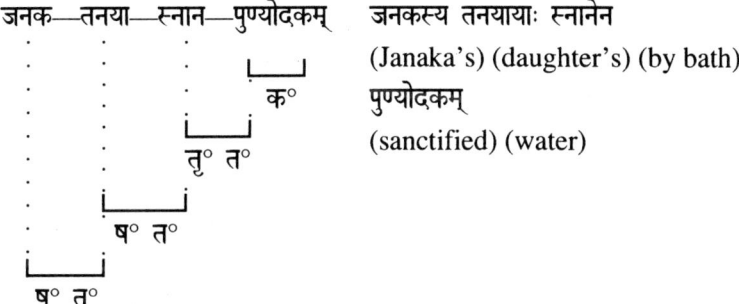

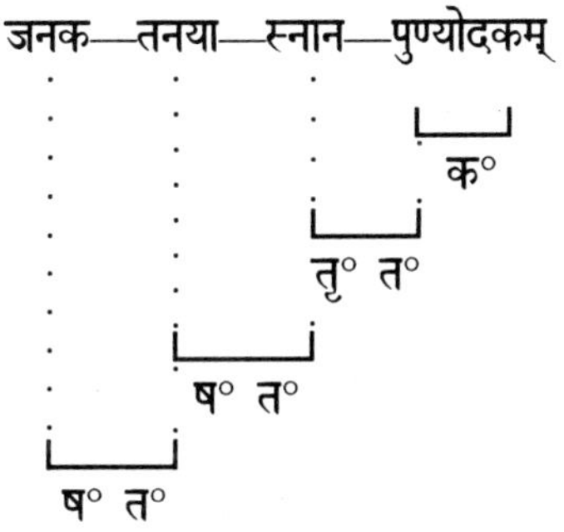

जनकस्य तनयायाः स्नानेन
(Janaka's) (daughter's) (by bath)
पुण्योदकम्
(sanctified) (water)

(Water sanctified by the bath of the daughter of Janaka.)

12.15 One may refer to a compound as a whole by the term describing its final juncture.

12.16 Certain words have reduced or altered forms when they occur in समास-s. Following are a few important examples.

a. Stems in -अन् and -इन् lose their final न् when they are prior members of समास-s and appear as -अ or -इ stems respectively.

Examples:

समास	विग्रह	
राजपुरुषः	राज्ञः पुरुषः	(king's man)
आत्महत्या	आत्मनो हत्या	(suicide)
हस्तिनासा	हस्तिनो नासा	(elephant's trunk)
राजर्षिः	राजा ऋषिः	(king-sage)

b. The word राजन् (m) (king) loses its final न् when it is at the end of most कर्मधारय and तत्पुरुष समास-s, thereby falling into the -अ declension.

Examples:

दशरथराजः	दशरथो राजा	(King Daśaratha)
राजराजः	राज्ञां राजा	(king of kings)

अनुचरो राजराजस्य (servant of the king of kings [Kubera])

c. Stems in -अन्त् take their weak form (-अत्) when they are prior members of समास-s.

Examples:

भगवद्गीता	भगवतो गीता	(the song of the Lord)
हनूमत्सन्देशः	हनूमतः सन्देशः	(Hanūmān's message)

When the very important adjective महन्त् (see 11.2.a) is the prior member of a कर्मधारय, it always takes the irregular form महा.

समास		विग्रह	**Meaning**
महाराजः	(m)	महान्राजा	(great king)
महामुनयः	(m)	महान्तो मुनयः	(great sages)
महादेवी	(f)	महती देवी	(great goddess)
महामिथुनम्	(n)	महन्मिथुनम्	(great sexual union of Śiva and Pārvatī)
महायानम्	(n)	महद्यानम्	(great vehicle)

d. The pronouns have special forms when they occur as prior members of तत्पुरुष समास-s (their only use in compounds).

i. The उत्तम पुरुष and मध्यम पुरुष pronouns अहम् and त्वम् are represented by their पञ्चमी forms for the number intended, regardless of the case-relation intended.

Examples:

मन्मनः (मत् + मनः)	मम मनः	(my mind)
अस्मद्वियोगः	अस्मद् वियोगः	(separation from us)
युष्मन्मित्रम्	युष्माकं मित्रम्	(your friend)
त्वत्कृते	तव कृते	(for your sake)
त्वत्स्नेहः	त्वयि स्नेहः	(love for you)

ii. The प्रथमा पुरुष demonstrative pronouns सः, तत्, and सा always appear in the एक° नपुंसकलिङ्ग, प्रथमा form तत् regardless of the number, case, or gender intended.

Examples:

तत्पुरुषः	तस्य पुरुषः	(his man [servant])
तत्पतिः	तस्याः पतिः	(her husband)
तद्व्रतः	तस्मिन्व्रतः	(devoted to that)

12.17 **उपपद समास : "Reduced-word" Compounds**

Several द्वितीया तत्पुरुष-s end in reduced forms of bare verbal roots, which signify the agent of the action of the verbal root. The prior member is often the कर्मन् of this root. Since these final members are उपपद-s, "reduced words," in that they have no forms independent of such compounds, the विग्रह-s require the substitution of a finite verbal form for the last member. This form is usually the प्रथमपुरुष वर्तमाने लट् in the number and voice required.

Examples:

Root		समास		विग्रह	**Meaning**
√विद्	(2P)	वेदवित्*	(m)	वेदान्वेत्ति ।	(knower of the Vedas)
√ज्ञा	(9P)	शास्त्रज्ञः	(m)	शास्त्राणि जानाति ।	(knower of the *śāstras*)
√हन्	(2P)	वृत्रहन्	(m)	वृत्रं हन्ति ।	(slayer of Vṛtra)
√पा	(1P)	सोमपः	(m)	सोमं पिबति ।	(drinker of soma)

As the above examples show, the long vowels of roots are shortened to make the stem forms. Roots ending in short vowels have a final त् added in generating these forms.

Examples:

√जि	(1P)	इन्द्रजित्*	(m)	इन्द्रं जयति ।	(conqueror of Indra)
√कृ	(8P)	लोकक्षयकृत्*	(m)	लोकानां क्षयं करोति ।	(destroyer of the worlds)

*(for declensions see 21.1.b., c.)

12.18 This formation occurs with case relations other than द्वितीया, notably with the roots √गम्, √स्था and √जन्. √गम् is reduced to ग.

Examples:

खगः	खे गच्छति	(sky-goer [bird])
गृहस्थः	गृहे तिष्ठति	(householder)
पादपः	पादेन पिबति	(foot-drinker [tree])
ब्रह्मजः	ब्रह्मणो जायते	(born from Brahman)

EXERCISES

A. Translate the reading into English.

B. Identify and give विग्रह for all the compounds in the reading.

C. Form कर्मधारय compounds from the following.

1. महान्तो मुनयः (great muni-s)
2. लम्बमुदरम् (pot-belly)
3. विवाहिता नारी (married woman)
4. बहवो ब्राह्मणाः (many brāhmans)

D. Form तत्पुरुष compounds from the following:

1. राज्ञां शत्रवः (enemies of the kings)
2. आत्मनो ज्ञानम् (knowledge of the Ātman)
3. भगवतो गीता (song of God)
4. मूर्खाणां राजा (king of fools)
5. निद्रया बाधितः (overcome with sleep)
6. रामे रतः (devoted to Rāma)
7. विश्वं जयति (√जि) (conqueror of all)
8. तस्या वचनम् (her speech)

E. Translate the following sentences into Sanskrit, using कर्मधारय and तत्पुरुष compounds, whenever possible.

1. Daśaratha, having heard the speech of the cruel woman, was overcome with grief.
2. Ah! Let not the son of the old king go to the great forest.
3. You are a knower of truth, O sage-king, therefore do that which you previously promised.

F. Memorize the following verse.

द्वन्द्वो द्विगुरपि चाहं मद्गृहे नित्यमव्ययीभावः ।
तत्पुरुष कर्म धारय येनाहं स्यां बहुव्रीहिः ॥

I am a married man (*dvandvaḥ*) with a measly two cows (*dviguḥ*) (i.e., a poor man); in my household there is never any money to spend (*avyayībhāvaḥ*). My good man, please do something (*tat puruṣa karma dhāraya*) so that I can be a rich man (*bahuvrīhiḥ*).

READING

कैकेयीवचनं श्रुत्वा महाराजो महावज्रहतवृक्ष इव पतितो भूमितले । सेवकैः संज्ञां कथमपि प्रापितः सो ऽवदत् । भरतमातस्तादृशं क्रूरकर्म मा क्रियताम् । ज्येष्ठपुत्रो वनं मा गच्छतु । यदि मम सुकुमारसुतो घोरारण्यं गच्छति तर्ह्यहं यमसदनमचिराद्गच्छामीति । किंतु सा राजपत्नी शोकाकुलस्य राज्ञः करुणवचनं श्रुत्वा केवलमहसदवदच्च । भो धर्मज्ञराज । पूर्वं स्वयं प्रतिज्ञाते वरे ऽधुना कथं विचारः । अस्मद्वंशे तन्न कदापि क्रियत इति । पुनः पुनर्निषण्णो नृपस्तच्चित्तपरिवर्तने प्रयत्नातिशयमकरोत् । अन्ततः स धर्मजालबद्धनृपो भवतु पापे मत्पुत्रो राम आहूयतामित्युक्त्वा पुनस्तीक्ष्णशरहतखगवद्धरातले पतति स्म ॥

---

*वद् (वत्)—at end of word = इव.

GLOSSARY

अचिरात्
(ind)—shortly, soon

अतिशयः
(m)—great degree, excess

अधुना
(ind)—now

आकुल
(adj)—distressed, agitated, disordered

आह्वे → आह्वयति
(1P)—call, summon

उदरम्
(n)—belly

करुण
(adj)—pitiful, tender

केवलम्
(ind)—only

क्रूर
(adj)—cruel, terrible

खम्
(n)—air, sky

खगः
(m)—bird

-ग
(adj)—going, moving (in, on, to) (from √गम्; see 12.17-18)

घोर
(adj)—terrible, frightful

चित्तम्
(n)—heart, mind

जालम्
(n)—net, snare

-जित्
(adj)—conquering (from √जि; see 12.17-18)

-ज्ञ
(adj)—knowing (from √ज्ञा; see 12.17-18)

ज्ञानम्
(n)—knowledge

तपस्विन्
(m; f -विनी)—ascetic

तलम्
(n)—surface, plane

तादृश
(adj)—such

धरा
(f)—earth

धर्मः
(m)—law, duty, right, etc.

निद्रा
(f)—sleep

निषण्ण
(adj)—dejected

पतिः
(m)—lord, husband
(irregular declension, see 21.3.b)

पत्नी
(f)—wife

परिवर्तनम्
(n)—change, reversal

पापा
(f)—wicked woman

प्रतिज्ञात
(adj)—promised, vowed

प्रयत्नः
(m)—effort

प्रापित
(adj)—restored to

प्रासादः
(m)—palace

ब्रह्मन्
(m)—the god Brahmā

यमः
(m prop)—god of Death

राजर्षिः
(m)—royal sage, royal seer

लम्ब
(adj)—hanging

वंशः
(m)—race, lineage

वज्रः (वज्रम्)
(m,n)—thunderbolt, Indra's weapon

विचारः
(m)—deliberation, hesitation

विवाहित
(adj)—married

शत्रुः
(m)—enemy

संज्ञा
(f)—consciousness

सदनम्
(n)—palace

सुकुमार
(adj)—tender

सुतः
(m)—son

सेवकः
(m)—attendant

√हस्
(1P)—laugh

LESSON 13

तुमन्नन्त (The Infinitive); समास Continued; बहुव्रीहि Application of कर्मधारय and तत्पुरुष समास-s; The द्विगु समास

13.0 An extremely useful and simple indeclinable of an "infinitive" or dative "infinitive" value may be formed freely from virtually all roots in the language.

13.1 a. **Formation of the Infinitive**

The characteristic and invariable marker of this formation is the suffix -तुम्. Before this suffix, the root vowel is subject to गुण. Between the root and the suffix the vowel इ is inserted in some cases. The pattern for the occurrence of this इ and the stem itself is the same in each case as with the agentive suffix तृ (10.0.ii; see too, 16.1).

Examples:

√कृ	कर्तुम्	(to do)
√गम्	गन्तुम्	(to go)
√श्रु	श्रोतुम्	(to hear)
√इ	एतुम्	(to go)
√पठ्	पठितुम्	(to read)
√पत्	पतितुम्	(to fall)
√भू	भवितुम्	(to be)
√वच्	वक्तुम्	(to say)
√ग्रह्	ग्रहीतुम्	(to take)

b. The common root √दृश् (to see) irregularly forms द्रष्टुम् (to see) (instead of the expected गुण form). √सृज् (1P) (create) forms स्रष्टुम्. (See 16.5.b.i.)

c. The suffix -तुम् preceded by the vowel इ replaces, as in the formation of the gerund (11.7.a.iii), the final अ of the present stem of roots of the tenth गण.

Example:

√चिन्त्	चिन्तयितुम्	(to think)

13.2 As in English, the infinitive may be used with an auxiliary verbal or nominal-verbal form. It serves as an infinitive in the sense of "to + verb." It frequently occurs with auxiliary verbs indicating desire, will, intent, capability, undertaking, etc.

√श्रु	तच्छ्रोतुमिच्छामि ।	*I want to hear* that.
√गम्	तत्र गन्तुं नेच्छन्ति ।	*They don't want to go* there.
√हन्	रावणं हन्तुं व्यवसायं करोति ।	*He resolves to kill* Rāvaṇa.
√त्यज्	तां त्यक्तुमारभते ।	*He starts to leave* her.

Note that this अव्ययपद can take a कर्मन्, like a finite verb or verbal adjective.

a. An extremely common occurrence of this usage is with the fifth or √सु गण root √शक् (5P) (be able). This root rarely occurs except as an auxiliary to an infinitive. It should be memorized at once.

Examples:

अव + √गम् तत्पुस्तकमवगन्तुं न शक्नोति ।
(*He is* not *able to understand* that book.)

√गम् स्वर्गं गन्तुं कथं शक्नुमः ।
(How *are we able to go* to heaven?)

√जीव् रामेण विना न जीवितुं शक्नुवन्त्ययोध्यावासिनः ।
(The inhabitants of Ayodhyā *are not able to live* without Rāma.)

b. The form also occurs freely with verbs of motion in a "dative-infinitive" sense of "in order to," "for the purpose of," etc.

Examples:

√दृश् अपि मां द्रष्टुं भवानागतवान् ।
(*Did* you come *to see* me?)

√कृ निशाचराणां विनाशनं कर्तुं वनं गतो लक्ष्मणपूर्वजः ।
(Lakṣmaṇa's elder brother [Rāma] went to the forest *to bring about* the destruction of the *niśācara*-s.)

c. The infinitive occurs frequently with the auxiliary verb √अर्ह् (1P) "to be worthy *or* capable." The phrase (infinitive + finite form of √अर्ह्) generally serves as a polite imperative.

Examples:

आ + √गम् भवानागन्तुमर्हति ।

(*You ought to come* = Please come.)

√श्रु मद्वचनं श्रोतुमर्हसि कैकेयि ।

(Kaikeyī, *you ought to hear* my words. = Please listen Kaikeyī.)

√भू रामो राजा भवितुमर्हति ।

(Rāma *should be king*.)

13.3 The infinitive may be used "passively," with no change in form, if its auxiliary verb is in the कर्मणि प्रयोग.

Examples:

√वच्	तन्न वक्तुं शक्नोमि ।	I can't *say* that.
√वच्	तन्न वक्तुं शक्यते (मया) ।	That can't *be said* (by me).
√गम्	रामेण तद्धननं कर्तुं गम्यते ।	Rāma goes *to kill* him. (See 4.38.)

13.4 बहुव्रीहि **Application of** कर्मधारय **and** तत्पुरुष समास-s

The बहुव्रीहि is one of the most characteristically Sanskrit applications of nominal compounds. It is basically simple and even delightful in its conception, but often confuses students because they fail initially to grasp the idea. Before attacking these compounds it is necessary that a few points be understood.

13.5 Absolutely the most important thing to understand is that the बहुव्रीहि is **not a type of compound** in the sense in which the कर्मधारय and तत्पुरुष समास-s are. To identify a compound as a बहुव्रीहि does not, as in the case of the कर्मधारय and तत्पुरुष, tell one anything about the relationship between the members of the compound. Rather, the term बहुव्रीहि indicates a secondary application of a compound of the कर्मधारय or तत्पुरुष types. The term suggests the relationship of the **whole compound** (whose internal structure we must determine as discussed in Lesson 12) to some other word outside the compound.

13.6 The usage of बहुव्रीहि-s is based on the fact that, in Sanskrit, any noun may function as an adjective with no special adjectival marker, **when and only when** it occurs as the last member of a कर्मधारय or तत्पुरुष समास. In other words, unless its last member is already an adjective (see 12.13), any कर्मधारय or तत्पुरुष compound can do double service both as a noun in its own right or, when used as a बहुव्रीहि, as an adjective.

13.7 English has several examples that may illustrate this interesting usage.

a. When Paul Revere cried, "The redcoats are coming!", he was not really referring to coats at all. What he really meant to say was that the men whose coats were red were on their way. The issue was of more than purely sartorial significance. In the same way, when we refer to someone as a loudmouth, bluestocking, blue-blood, yellow-belly, fathead, or redhead, we are not talking about mouths, stockings, blood, etc. We mean people who possess the things mentioned. When we talk of paperbacks, redwings, largemouths, or sulphur-bottoms, we are speaking of books, birds, fish, and whales. In all of these cases, the compounds (mostly कर्मधारय-s) serve as adjectives (विशेषण-s) modifying some other noun, which may be implied or expressed. In none of these cases would it be possible simply to use the uncompounded final noun as an adjective. We can call a man a redcoat or redcap, but not just coat or cap.

b. The same situation prevails in Sanskrit. The only difference is that whereas in English this usage is restricted to a few compounds, most of which are internally of the कर्मधारय

type, in Sanskrit the usage may be applied freely to almost any कर्मधारय or तत्पुरुष compound whose final member is a noun.

13.8 The structure of बहुव्रीहि-s is no different from that of the underlying compound in each case. It is only the विग्रह that, in explaining both the underlying compound relation and the relation of the whole compound to something outside it, differentiates the forms. The विग्रह must of course be supplied by us.

13.9 बहुव्रीहि समास-s can be easily identified by contextual criteria, and in many cases by formal criteria.

a. The formal criteria are quite simple. Since the essence of the बहुव्रीहि function is that certain nouns serve as adjectives, then such nouns must behave as adjectives. They must take on the gender of the noun (outside the compound) that they modify. If, as is often, but (alas!) not always the case, the final member is of a different inherent gender than that of the noun being modified, then it must lose its inherent gender and be treated as an adjective of its own stem final. Thus, we may take the कर्मधारय समास "पीताम्बरम्" (विग्रह—पीतमम्बरम्) ("yellow clothing"), which is नपुंसकलिङ्ग (neuter), and make it serve as an adjective modifying a पुंलिङ्ग (masculine) noun (e.g., पुरुषः) in the sense of the man **whose clothes are yellow**, **the man with the yellow clothes.** But in order to do this, the neuter अम्बरम् must be brought into agreement with पुरुषः. This is done by treating it as an adjective in -अ (its proper stem final). Thus, while पीताम्बरम् means, "yellow clothes," पीताम्बरः can only mean, "the man or god with yellow clothes." By the same token, पीताम्बरा can only mean "the woman with yellow clothes." In the same way, the षष्ठी तत्पुरुष—गजाननम् (विग्रह—गजस्याननम्,"the face of an elephant") must, if it appears as गजाननः, mean "the man *or* god who has the face of an elephant." The adjectival treatment of बहुव्रीहि final nouns is occasionally confusing since nouns may take forms that they never have in their regular paradigms.

Examples:

रामो महातेजाः (brilliant Rāma)

हनुमान् कृतकर्मा (Hanumān having accomplished his duty)

Here the नपुंसक nouns तेजः and कर्मन् must be declined as पुंलिङ्ग nouns to agree with रामः and हनुमान्. Thus तेजः is treated like the पुंलिङ्ग stems ending in अः (e.g., अङ्गिरः [9.1.b]), while कर्मन् is declined like the पुंलिङ्ग stems ending in -अन् (e.g., आत्मन् [8.5.a.i]). Thus, when a final noun of a compound appears with a gender other than its inherent gender, you can be virtually certain that the compound is a बहुव्रीहि.

b. If the inherent gender of the compound-final member is the same as that of the noun being modified, we are still able to identify the बहुव्रीहि by the context, just as we know that in the sentence, "His father was a black-shirt," we do not intend to propagate a theory of spontaneous generation from filthy laundry. Take as an example the बहुव्रीहि compound "बहुव्रीहिः" ("man with a lot of rice"). This is a बहुव्रीहि application of the कर्मधारय समास—"बहुव्रीहिः" (m) (विग्रह—बहुव्रीहिः), "much rice." Now if the compound is to serve as an adjective modifying, or referring to, a man, there will be no formal distinction between the two usages, since व्रीहिः is पुंलिङ्ग to begin with. Even so, in the sentence अस्माकं ग्रामे बहुव्रीहिर्वसति भार्यया सह। ("In our village a *bahuvrīhi* lives with his wife"), it is clear that a person, not rice, is being referred to. However, since only rice appears to be mentioned as the subject of the sentence, there can be no doubt that the compound is used in a बहुव्रीहि application. By the same token, in the sentence सा बहुव्रीहिं पचतीति श्रुत्वा बहुब्राह्मणास्तं खादितुमागच्छन् । (Having heard,

"She is cooking *bahuvrīhi*," many brahmans come to eat it.), it is clear that the simple कर्मधारय is meant.

13.10 विग्रह of बहुव्रीहि समास-s

a. The analysis of a बहुव्रीहि application of a समास must provide two levels of information:

   i. It must serve as a विग्रह of the underlying form (or forms) i.e., कर्मधारय or तत्पुरुष.

   ii. It must clarify the relation of the समास as a whole to whatever it modifies and, at the same time, indicate clearly that the compound is a बहुव्रीहि.

b. This information is provided by a conventionalized procedure for विग्रह of बहुव्रीहि-s. The steps of this procedure are as follows:

   i. Give the विग्रह of the underlying compound in the same order in which the members appear in the compound. This is to establish, as in Lesson 12, whether the underlying compound form is a कर्मधारय or तत्पुरुष. It is very important to note here that this step is done without reference to the बहुव्रीहि, or adjectival application of the compound. Therefore, the final member and any preceding adjective are given in their proper inherent gender.

   ii. Immediately after this विग्रह appears a form of the relative pronoun—यः, यत्, or या. This is the unmistakable marker of the बहुव्रीहि's विग्रह. The number and gender of this form are determined by the number and gender of the noun that the बहुव्रीहि समास modifies. The case of the form is determined by the relationship of the underlying members of the compound to the noun modified. This relative form, then, specifies the way in which the बहुव्रीहि is to be understood. As in the case of the विग्रह forms of prior members of तत्पुरुष समास-s, this relative form may be in any case but the प्रथमा.

Again, however, as with तत्पुरुष, the षष्ठी and तृतीया विभक्ति-s, in that order, are most common, with the सप्तमी running a poor third, and the rest occurring less frequently.

iii. After this relative form, its correlative appears either in the case in which it actually occurs in the sentence in question, or in the प्रथमा followed by this case. Often the प्रथमा is replaced or supplemented by a repetition of the whole (now completely analyzed) बहुव्रीहि समास in the प्रथमा.

iv. So in the example पीताम्बरः ("he whose clothes are yellow," epithet of Viṣṇu), the विग्रह would proceed as follows:

पीतम् अम्बरं यस्य सः (पीताम्बरः)

(yellow) (clothing) (of whom) (he) (is *pītāmbaraḥ*)

This is, "whose clothing is yellow is *pītāmbaraḥ*." Here, the first stage is the विग्रह of the simple underlying कर्मधारय, with the adjective पीत modifying and agreeing with the neuter अम्बरम्. Since the noun which the compound modifies (Viṣṇu) is पुंलिङ्ग and since the relation of this noun to the final member (अम्बरम्) is possessive, the relative is in the षष्ठी° एक°, पुंलिङ्ग. If the same form occurred in another case, we could, to be meticulously correct, add the appropriate case form of the correlative as the final step, but we could omit the प्रथमा form.

Example:

॥ पीताम्बराय नमः ॥ (Homage to Viṣṇu!)

A typical विग्रह would be:

पीतमम्बरं यस्य तस्मै . . .

If the phrase were:

पीताम्बरस्य भक्तः (a devotee of Viṣṇu)

The विग्रह could read: पीतमम्बरं यस्य तस्य . . ., but it would have to be clearly understood that the तस्य and the यस्य

are neither in apposition nor agreement. The यस्य refers to the relationship between अम्बरम् and विष्णुः and defines the बहुव्रीहि relation. The तस्य, on the other hand, is simply a reference to the quite accidental fact that the compound happens to be in the षष्ठी in this sentence.

v. An appositional कर्मधारय would be analyzed as follows: सागरमेखला (having the ocean for a girdle) = पृथिवी (f) (the earth). विग्रह—सागरो (m). मेखला (f), यस्याः सा (सागरमेखला) (she whose girdle is the ocean).

13.11 a. As noted above (12.13.a.i), it is very common for कर्मधारय समास-s to have भूते कृदन्त-s of सकर्मक roots as prior members. When such compounds are applied as बहुव्रीहि-s, it is usual for the relative pronoun of the विग्रह (13.10.b.ii) to be in the तृतीया and to construe with the prior member.

Examples:

जितेन्द्रियः (one who has conquered the senses)
(conquered) (sense)
विग्रहः
जितानीन्द्रियाणि येन सः (जितेन्द्रियः)
(he by whom the senses are conquered)

कृतकर्मा (one who has performed an action)
(performed) (action)
विग्रहः
कृतं कर्म येन सः (कृतकर्मा)
(he by whom the action is performed)

पीतोदकी (one [f] who has drunk water,
(drunk) (water) *or* whose water is drunk)
विग्रहः
पीतमुदकं यया सा (पीतोदकी)
(she by whom the water is drunk)
or
पीतमुदकं यस्याः साः (पीतोदका)
(she whose water is drunk)

बहुव्रीहि समास-s of this type may be used like the भूते कृदन्त itself to denote a perfective or completed action (10.6.a).
Example:
हतमृगान् सिंहान्पश्यामि ।
(I see the lions who have killed the deer.)
विग्रहः
हता मृगा यैस्तान्

b. When the भूते कृदन्त is of an अकर्मक root or has no clear कर्मणि application, it is normally treated as any other adjective and the relative construes with the last member.
Example:
स्थितप्रज्ञस्य का भाषा ।
(What is the description of the man of established intellect?)
विग्रहः
स्थिता प्रज्ञा यस्य तस्य ।

13.12 बहुव्रीहि application may also be easily made of तत्पुरुष compounds.
Example:
गजाननः (elephant-faced one = Gaṇeśa)
विग्रहः
गजस्याननं यस्य सः ।

13.13 बहुव्रीहि-s may be of any length and may occur, like any other adjective, as members of other compounds.
Examples:
बहुशोणितलिप्तशरीरः
(whose body is covered with lots of blood)
विग्रहः
बहुना शोणितेन लिप्तं शरीरं यस्य सः

हतपुत्रब्राह्मणः
(brahman whose son has been killed *or* who has killed his son)

विग्रहः

हतः पुत्रो यस्य/ येन स ब्राह्मणः

13.14 As is clear from the विग्रह, a बहुव्रीहि समास may replace an entire relative clause.

Example:

शुद्धमना मे प्रियः । यस्य मनः शुद्धं स मे प्रियः ।

(The man of pure mind is dear to me.)

13.15 बहुव्रीहि-s are extremely common as names and epithets.

Examples:

Name/Epithet		विग्रह
बृहदश्वः	(having great horses)	बृहन्तो ऽश्वा यस्य सः
नीलकण्ठः	(having a blue throat = Śiva)	नीलः कण्ठो यस्य सः
हलायुधः	(having a plowshare for a weapon = Balarāma)	हलमायुधं यस्य सः
वीरसेनः	(having an army of heroes)	वीराणां सेना यस्य सः
मूषिकवाहनः	(having a rat for a mount = Gaṇeśa)	मूषिको वाहनं यस्य सः

13.16 **The द्विगु समास**

The द्विगु ("two cow") समास is a kind of कर्मधारय of which the first member is a numeral. (For declension of numerals see 19.6.) This type of compounding is not normally used simply to enumerate things. Its major uses are:

a. To denote aggregates or sets of things of which the number is well known. The एकवचन is always used regardless of the numeral involved.

Examples:

त्रिभुवनम्	(n)	(the three worlds)
सप्तपदी	(f)	(the seven steps of a marriage ceremony)
त्रिलोकम्	(n)	(the three worlds)
पञ्चरात्रम्	(n)	(the five nights of a certain rite)

b. As बहुव्रीहि-s in the sense of names or epithets:

Name/Epithet		विग्रह
दशरथः	(having ten chariots)	दश रथा यस्य सः
दशग्रीवः	(having ten necks = Rāvaṇa)	दश ग्रीवा यस्य सः
त्रिलोचनः	(having three eyes = Śiva)	त्रीणि लोचनानि यस्य सः
दशबलः	(having ten powers = Buddha)	दश बलानि यस्य सः

EXERCISES

A. Translate the reading into English.

B. Identify and provide विग्रह-s for all the समास-s in the reading up until the sentence beginning with एवमुक्ता.

C. Do the same for the remainder of the reading.

D. Translate the following sentences into Sanskrit, using बहुव्रीहि-s and infinitives wherever possible. Provide the विग्रह for each बहुव्रीहि.

1. He whose mind is pure does not want to stay in the city.
2. The demon with the face of a monkey is unable to kill the king.
3. I am unable to understand the meaning of those many-paged books.
4. Please tell (use √अर्ह् plus infinitive 13.2.c) me that, lady. I am one whose curiosity is great.
5. "Today the king's son must go (use √अर्ह् plus infinitive 13.2.c) to the forest." Hearing that, all the inhabitants of Ayodhyā became (such that) their minds were afflicted with grief (use बहुव्रीहि).

E. Memorize the following verse.

गोष्पदीकृतवाराशिं
मशकीकृतराक्षसम् ।
रामायणमहामाला-
रत्नं वन्दे ऽनिलात्मजम् ॥

I praise the son of the wind, that jewel in the great necklace of the *Rāmāyaṇa*, who treated the mighty *rākṣasa*-s like so many mosquitoes and the vast ocean like a puddle in the hoof print of a cow.

READING

नृपं द्रष्टुमागच्छत्वार्यपुत्र इत्याज्ञां श्रुत्वा श्रीरामः समुत्पन्नकौतूहलो वायुवेगेन राजभवनमागच्छत् । आगत्य च विवर्णमुखं राजानं दृष्ट्वा जातचिन्तो वचनमब्रवीत् । जयत्वार्यः । भवदाज्ञयागतो ऽस्मि । कुतो भवानश्रुपूर्णलोचनः। मयि जातक्रोध इव भवान् भाति । अप्यहं कृतापराध इति । पुत्रवचनं श्रुत्वा दशरथः कृतप्रयत्नो ऽपि किमपि भाषितुं नाशक्नोत् । तदा राजकुमारः कैकेयीमपृच्छत् । देवि किमिति नृपतिरद्य विषण्णमनाः । सर्वदा मां दृष्ट्वा मम पिता कुपितो ऽपि प्रसीदति । अद्य तु मां संप्रेक्ष्य राज्ञस्तस्य खेदः कुतः प्रवर्तत इति । एवमुक्ता तु महात्मना राघवेण सा पुनरतिदारुणं वचनमुक्तवती । हे राम श्रूयताम् । पुरा तव पित्रा मह्यं द्वौ वरौ दत्तौ । प्रथमेन भरताभिषेको वृतो मया द्वितीयेन च तव दण्डकारण्यगमनम् । यदि पितरं सत्यप्रतिज्ञं कर्तुमिच्छसि तर्हि मम वचनेन भवान्वनवासी भवतु भरतश्च राज्यं प्रशास्तु । रामस्तु तस्या वज्रोपमं वचः श्रुत्वा क्षणमपि नाव्यथत । शान्तमना एवमस्तु देव्यद्यैव वनं गच्छामीत्यभाषत ॥

GLOSSARY

अति
(ind)—a prefix used with adjectives and adverbs meaning 'very,' 'too,' 'excessively'

अद्य
(ind)—today

अपराधः
(m)—sin, offense

अर्थः
(m)—meaning

√अर्ह्
(1P)—be fit, worthy; auxilliary with infinitive forms polite imperative (see 13.2.c)

अश्रु
(n)—tear

आननम्
(n)—face

उत्पन्न
(adj)—arisen, sprung up

उद् + √दिश्
(6P)—point out

उद्दिश्य
ल्यबन्त (of उद् +√ दिश्)—pointing out, with reference to . . .

उपमा
(f)—similarity; simile

कपिः
(m)—monkey

किमिति
(ind)—why

कुमारः
(m)—boy

कौतूहलम्
(n)—curiosity

क्रोधः
(m)—anger

खेदः
(m)—depression, sadness

गमनम्
(n)—going

जात
(adj)—born, arisen

दण्डकम् , दण्डकः
(n, m prop)—Daṇḍaka, name of a forest

दारुण
(adj)—harsh, cruel, severe

नृपतिः
(m)—king

पत्रम्
(n)—page, leaf

पुस्तकम्
(n)—book

प्रतिज्ञा
(f)—vow, promise

प्र + √वृत्
(1Ā)—proceed, take place, continue

प्र + √शास्
(2P)—rule, reign

प्र + √सद्
(1P)—be pleased, appeased, be pacified

भगवन्त्
(adj) (f -अती)—blessed one

भवनम्
(n)—palace

√भा
(2P)—appear, seem

मुखम्
(n)—face

लोचनम्
(n)—eye

वचः
(n)—speech

वानरः
(m)—monkey

वायुः
(m)—wind

वासिन्
(m; f -इनी)—dweller, inhabitant

विवर्ण
(adj)—devoid of color

विषण्ण
(adj)—dejected

वेगः
(m)—speed

√व्यथ्
(1Ā)—be agitated

√शक्
(5P)—be able

शुद्ध
(adj)—pure

समुत्पन्न
(adj)—arisen

सम् + प्र+ √ईक्ष्
(6Ā)—see, regard

LESSON 14

समास Concluded; The द्वन्द्व and अव्ययीभाव समास-s; The विधि लिङ् (Optative)

14.0 There remain two basic types of compounds to be examined. These are rather different from the preceding two types and their बहुव्रीहि applications, but they are extremely simple and require only the briefest treatment.

14.1 **The द्वन्द्व समास**

The first of these is the द्वन्द्व समास, sometimes given the racy title of "copulative compound." This compound differs from the basic कर्मधारय and तत्पुरुष types in that it does not consist of sets of pairs but is simply a stringing together of any number of nouns, which in ordinary syntax would be connected by the conjunctive particle च or, in rare cases, the disjunctive particle वा. Since the items are simply listed, there is no grammatical subordination of one member to another. Still, the formation of the द्वन्द्व is the same as that of the others insofar as prior members lose their सुप्-s or case endings.

14.2 a. The gender of a द्वन्द्व is the same as that of its final member. Thus:

सीतारामौ = सीता च रामश्च
(Sītā and Rāma)

सुतकन्ये = सुतश्च कन्या च
(son and daughter)

b. Number is determined not by the number of members of the compound but by the number of things represented by these members, thus देवपुरुषौ (the god and the man), **but** देवपुरुषाः (gods and men).

c. There is no limit to the number of members in a द्वन्द्व, e.g., देवासुरगन्धर्वपिशाचराक्षसाः
(The gods, asuras, gandharvas, piśācas, and rākṣasas).

14.3 In some cases, especially when a pair (द्वन्द्व) of nouns is closely associated, it may be represented by a द्वन्द्व with the नपुंसकलिङ्ग एकवचन ending.

Examples:

सुखदुःखम् (pleasure and pain)

This a common technique for linking pairs of opposites.

श्रुताश्रुतम् (what is heard and what is not heard)

कृताकृतम् (what is done and what is not done)

14.4 द्वन्द्व-s may be included in extended समास-s. In the विग्रह of such compounds, the द्वन्द्व-s are left intact.

Examples:

a. वीर्यबुद्धिसंपन्न (endowed with valor and intelligence)

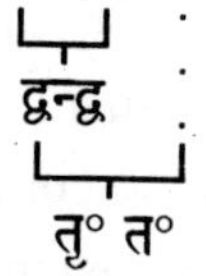

विग्रह = वीर्यबुद्धिभ्यां संपन्न

b. सुखदुःखद (causing pleasure and pain)

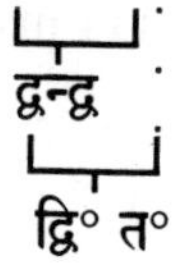

विग्रह = सुखदुःखे ददाति

c. रक्तलिप्तहस्तमुखः (having hands and face smeared with blood)

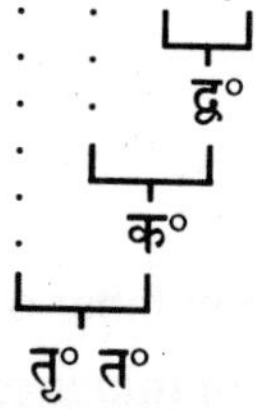

विग्रह = रक्तेन लिप्तानि हस्तमुखानि यस्य सः

14.5 The order of words in a द्वन्द्व is not, as in other types of समास, of any syntactic significance. There are, however, a number of rules laid down by the grammarians that regulate word order. The two most important such rules, in order of precedence are:

a. A word signifying a person or thing of greater importance or entitled to greater honor or precedence precedes one signifying someone or something less worthy.
   Example:
   ब्राह्मणक्षत्रियवैश्यशूद्राः
   (brāhmans, kṣatriyas, vaiśyas, and śudras) (the four classes of Indian society in descending order)

b. If rule 'a' does not apply, a word with fewer syllables precedes one with more.
   Example:
   अहिनकुलम् (14.3) (snake and mongoose)

14.6 When a kinship term ending in -ऋ (10.0.i) precedes another such term or the word पुत्रः in a द्वन्द्व, its stem vowel is changed to आ.
Example:
मातृ + पितृ → मातापितरौ (mother and father)

14.7 एकशेष द्वन्द्व : **Elliptical Dual**
In a few cases, when two nouns, especially kinship terms, are extremely closely associated as a natural pair, the द्विवचन of one of them may be used to express the द्वन्द्व.
Example:
पितरौ (=मातापितरौ) (mother and father)

14.8 The द्वन्द्व, then, is perhaps the most rudimentary form of nominal compound. There is only one point worth stressing: despite the fact that when a द्वन्द्व is subjected to विग्रह, all the members are in the same case, this type of समास should clearly be distinguished from a कर्मधारय समास, for which this is also the case due to समानाधिकरण.

14.9 अव्ययीभावसमास : **Indeclinable Compound**

Another relatively common type of समास is called अव्ययीभावसमास, or indeclinable (अव्यय) nominal compound. As the name implies, these compounds function as adverbs. They are formed by the junction of an अव्ययपद (as prior member) and a nominal stem (as final member).

14.10 The endings of the final members of these compounds are usually changed so as to conform to the प्रथमा-द्वितीया एक° नपुंसकलिङ्ग endings of nouns of the various stem finals. Some stem finals are, however, reduced.

a. Final members ending in -अन् take the ending -अम् though नपुंसक nouns may take -अ.

b. Final long vowels are shortened.

Examples:

यथा + कामः → यथाकामम् (according to desire)
प्रति + अग्निः → प्रत्यग्नि (facing the fire)
अधि + राजन् → अधिराजम् (upon the king)

14.11 The prior member, or अव्ययपद, most often belongs to one of three categories:

a. उपसर्ग

Examples:

प्रति + दिनः (m) (day) → प्रतिदिनम् (every day)

अनु + लोमन् (n) (hair) → अनुलोम (lit., with hair, or fur, i.e., in the proper manner)

सम् + अक्षन् (n) (eye) → समक्षम् (before the eyes)

b. the form स (=सह) (together).

Examples:

स + कोपः (m) (anger) → सकोपम् (with anger)
स + कामः (m) (desire) → सकामम् (with desire)
स + आदरः (m) (respect) → सादरम् (with respect)

c. a relative अव्ययपद, especially यथा (just as) and यावत् (to the extent that).

Examples:

यथा + शास्त्रम्	(authoritative text)
यथाशास्त्रम्	in accordance with the śastras
यथा + कामः	(desire)
यथाकामम्	in accordance with desire
यथा + विधिः	(rule, custom)
यथाविधि	in accordance with established practice
यावत् + जीवः	(life)
यावज्जीवम्	for one's whole life
यावत् + संवत्सरः	(year)
यावत्संवत्सरम्	as long as a year, for the duration of a year

Sentences:

समक्षं पश्य मे मुखम् ।

Look at my mouth which is *before* (*your own*) *eyes.*

सर्वे सर्वदा यथाशक्ति कर्म कर्तुमर्हन्ति ।

Everyone should always work *according to* (*his*) *ability.*

एतत्सर्वं मया यथाशास्त्रं कृतम् ।

I did all this *in accordance with the śāstras.*

14.12 विधि लिङ् : The Optative Mode

The विधि लिङ् is the last important conjugation to be based on the गण-s of the present system. It is a mode of the present system, just as the लोट्, or imperative, is a mode, and it had two major uses.

1. **Prescription.** In this usage, the लिङ् indicates that the subject *should, ought,* must generally, or had better, per-

form the action or undergo the state expressed by the verbal root. As such, it serves a similar (injunctive) function as that of the लोट्. The difference is that here the "command" is usually of a general sort.

Examples:
अपण्डितः पण्डितसभायां मौनं समाश्रयेत् ।
(In an assembly of the wise, a fool *should resort to* silence.)

यो मोक्षमिच्छति स वनं गच्छेत् ।
(He who wishes liberation *should go* to the forest.)

स्थितधीः* किं प्रभाषेत किमासीत व्रजेत किम् ।
(How would a man of firm intelligence *speak*, how *sit*, and how *move about*?)

न वदेद्यावनीं भाषां प्राणैः कण्ठगतैरपि ।
(One *should not speak* a Western language even to save one's life.)
*See 21.3.h

2. **Hypothesis.** In this usage, the लिङ् is used conditionally to indicate either a state contrary to fact, or one which is probable but not certain. The first of these usages is most common in relative clauses, while the second is common in the sense of "might," "may," or "would."
Examples:
रामो यदि वनाज्झटिति नागच्छेत्तर्ह्यहं यमलोकं गच्छेयम् ।
(If Rāma *should not return* at once from the forest, then *I would* die.) (Literally, "would go to Yama's realm.")

रामो वीरो न स्यात्कथं जीवेयुः पुरुषाः ।
(If Rāma *were not* a hero, how would *men live*?)

यः को ऽपीदं पुस्तकं पठेत्स शतयज्ञफलं प्राप्नुयात् ।

(Whoever *should read* this book, he *would attain* the fruit of a hundred sacrifices.)

यथा काष्ठं च काष्ठं च समेयातां महोदधौ ।
समेत्य च व्यपेयातां तद्वद्भूतसमागमः ॥

(Just as two bits of driftwood *might come together* in the ocean, and, having met, *might go their separate ways*, just so is the coming together of living beings.)

यदहरेव विरजेत्तदहरेव प्रव्रजेत् ।

(On the very day that one *turns away* from the things of this world, one *should wander* forth [as an ascetic]).

14.13 The विधि लिङ् is unlike the other modes of the present system (लट्, लङ्, लोट्) in that it is distinguished not by particular personal endings but by a special **mode-sign** that is inserted between the present stem (7.5) and, for the most part, the secondary endings (8.9).

14.14 **Mode Sign of the** विधि लिङ्

The optative mode-sign is basically ई for all forms except the परस्मैपद forms of roots belonging to the non-अ गण-s (2, 3, 5, 7, 8, 9). For these roots, the mode-sign is या. In the case of the अ गण-s (1, 4, 6, 10), the mode-sign ई coalesces with the preceding अ of the गण-sign to form ए.

14.15 The various cases are best considered individually by voice and by type of गण.

a. परस्मैपद

i. अ गण-s

a. The mode-sign ई plus the अ of the गण-sign yield ए, which is then the characteristic sign of the विधि लिङ् of the roots of these गण-s. The endings are the normal secondary endings, but the प्रथम° बहुवचन

ending is always -उः and never -अन्.

b. The ए (गण-sign + mode-sign) is never allowed to come into contact with an initial vowel of a personal ending (e.g., -अम्, -उः). Such contact is avoided by the insertion of य् between them.

Examples:

गच्छ + ई + अम् → गच्छेयम्

(I would, should, might go.)

वद + ई + उः → वदेयुः

(They would, should, might say.)

c. Thus, the conjugation of √भू (1P) in the विधि लिङ् would be:

	एक°	द्वि°	बहु°
प्र°	भवेत्	भवेताम्	भवेयुः
म°	भवेः	भवेतम्	भवेत
उ°	भवेयम्	भवेव	भवेम

ii. non-अ गण-s

The mode-sign या is added to the weak form of the stem regardless of the usual strong-weak distinction of present stems. The endings are the same as for the अ गण-s, but the mode-sign loses its आ before the ending उः.

Example:

प्र + √आप् (5P) (attain)

	एक°	द्वि°	बहु°
प्र°	प्राप्नुयात्	प्राप्नुयाताम्	प्राप्नुयुः
म°	प्राप्नुयाः	प्राप्नुयातम्	प्राप्नुयात
उ°	प्राप्नुयाम्	प्राप्नुयाव	प्राप्नुयाम

iii. You should learn the paradigms of the two important roots √अस् (2P) and √कृ (8P). In accordance with (ii) above, the लिङ् of √अस् is based on the weak stem, which is स्. Thus, the paradigm is:

प्र° स्यात् स्याताम् स्युः etc.

These forms are useful. स्यात् means "maybe," "perhaps," etc. √कृ is, as always, irregular. Here it loses its final stem vowel उ before the mode-sign.

प्र° कुर्यात् कुर्याताम् कुर्युः etc.

Fill out and memorize both paradigms.

b. आत्मनेपद

i. अ गण-s

The mode-sign is as at 14.15.a.i.a above. The endings are the regular आत्मनेपद secondary endings, except that the उत्तम° एक° has अ and the प्रथम° बहु° has -रन्, instead of ए and -अन्त, respectively. The गण-sign plus mode sign (=ए) is, as in 14.15.a.i.b., not permitted to come into contact with an initial vowel of an ending.

Examples:

लभ् + ई + अ → लभेय

(I should, would, might get.)

भाष् + ई आताम् → भाषेयाताम्

(They [two] might speak.)

ii. non-अ गण-s

The mode-sign ई is always added to the weak stem. Since most आत्मनेपद forms are weak anyway, this is not as surprising as it is in the परस्मैपद forms. As in i. above, the mode-sign is set off from a following vowel by य्.

Example:

भुञ्ज् + ई + अ → भुञ्जीय

(I would, should, etc., eat.)

14.16 The आशीर् लिङ् , or the Benedictive

Grouped by the grammarians with the विधि लिङ् , but not formed from the present stem, is a somewhat rare conjugational mode known as the आशीर् लिङ्, or optative of blessing. It is used as the name implies mainly for uttering blessings or prayers. Its detailed formation is complicated and need not concern the beginning student. However, its परस्मैपद प्रथम° forms may be encountered occasionally.

Examples:

भूयात्	भूयास्ताम्	भूयासुः
May it be!	May those two be!	May they be!

EXERCISES

A. Translate the reading into English.

B. List and identify all लिङ् (optative) forms and substitute for them the corresponding लोट् (imperative) forms.

C. Translate the following into Sanskrit (See English-Sanskrit Glossary at end of lesson):

1. If a man would experience bliss, let him go to the forest and there sit long in meditation.
2. Having left the city and become a muni, how then should I speak to you, friend.
3. Are all brāhmans men of stabilized mind? How should I know? It is not known to me whether they are all sages or not (use यत् and न वा and इति).
4. Having done what, might men attain liberation? A man should do what is written in the *śāstras*. Thereby he may become liberated.
5. If I should not see the faces of Rāma and Lakṣmaṇa (use द्वन्द्व) again, I should surely be afflicted by great sorrow.
6. Let Lakṣmaṇa go with Sītā and Rāma (use द्वन्द्व) if he wishes to fulfill (use √कृ) truth and duty (धर्मः, use द्वन्द्व).
7. If they were not afflicted by birth, old age, and fear of death (use द्वन्द्व), men might be happy. Moreover, (अपि च) having experienced disease, poverty, sorrow, and disas ters (use द्वन्द्व), they would be of agitated minds.

D. Memorize the verse beginning यथा काष्ठम् (from 14.12) and be prepared to recite it in class.

READING

जितेन्द्रियः सुखदुःखसमो रामो मातरं द्रष्टुं गच्छेयमिति मत्वान्तःपुरमगच्छत् । तं शोकावहवृत्तान्तं श्रुत्वा राममाता परशुच्छिन्नकदलीव पृथिव्यां पतिता । ततो बाष्पपूर्णनयना साब्रवीत् । पुत्र यदि त्वं शोकावहो न जायेथास्तर्ह्यहमप्रजा न तादृशं दुःखमनुभवेयम् । या माता पुत्रस्य पूर्णेन्दुसदृशं मुखं न पश्येत्सा कथं जीवेत् । कथमहं जीवेयमिति । तच्छ्रुत्वा सर्वे जना भृशं व्यलपन् । किंतु लक्ष्मणस्तद्भ्रातुर्दुःखं दृष्ट्वाजितक्रोधः कोपरक्तनयन इदं * वचो ऽब्रवीत् । भो भ्रातरिदं सोढुं न शक्नोमि । भवतो वनगमनं मह्यं न रोचते । श्रूयतां तावत् । आवयोर्जराहतबुद्धिः पिता नारीवशगतः किं न ब्रूयात् । भवतो ऽपराधं विना नृपस्त्वां राज्यं त्यक्त्वा वनं गच्छेरिति कथं भाषते । कः पुत्रो भार्याजितस्य पितुर्वचनं हृदये कुर्यात् । आगच्छत्वार्यः । अहं सर्वामयोध्यां तीक्ष्णशरैर्निर्जनां कुर्याम् । राजानं पितरमपि हन्तुं समर्थो ऽस्मीति । कुपितस्य भ्रातुर्वचः श्रुत्वा रामो ऽब्रवीत्तात मास्तु कोपः । पुत्रो न कदापीदृशं वाक्यं ब्रूयात् । अपि च पुरुषो न कदापि क्रोधवशं गच्छेत् । विगतक्रोधो भवितुमर्हति भवानिति । अन्ततो लक्ष्मणस्तथास्त्वित्युक्त्वा मन्युं पराजित्य यत्र यत्र त्वं गच्छेस्तत्र तत्र गच्छेयमहमपीत्युक्तवान् ॥

---

*See 19.1

GLOSSARY

अ-; अन्-
(negative prefix for nominal or indeclinable forms. अ- precedes consonants, अन्- precedes vowels—un-, non-, without-, -less)

अजित
(adj)—unconquered

अन्तःपुरम्
(n)—inner apartment, esp., women'schambers

आवह
(adj)—bringing, conveying (common at end of compound)

इन्दुः
(m)—moon

इन्द्रियम्
(n)—sense, organs of sense

ईदृश
(adj)—such, of this kind

उदधिः
(m)—ocean

कदली
(f)—plantain or banana tree, often an object of comparison due to its frailty and its transitory nature

काष्ठम्
(n)—log

कोपः
(m)—anger, rage

गमनम्
(n)—going

छिन्न
(adj)—cut

√जन् → जायते (प्रथम° एक° लट्)
(4Ā)—be born, arise

जित
(adj)—conquered, subdued

तातः
(m)—1) father; 2) a term of affection applied to any person, but usually to inferiors or juniors, 'my child,' 'my son,' 'dear one,' etc.

-द
(adj)—giving, causing, giving rise to (at end of compound only)

नयनम्
(n)—eye

निः-
(ind)—without, devoid of (only as first member of compound)

नीत
(adj)—led

परशुः
(m)—axe

परा + √जि
(1P)—conquer, subdue

पृथिवी
(f)—earth

प्रति
(ind)—1) as postposition following द्वितीया : to,with respect to; 2) as first member of अव्ययीभाव : every, each

बाष्पः
(m)—tears

भृशम्
(adv)—extremely

मन्युः
(m)—anger, rage

मित्रम्
(n)—friend

मोक्षः
(m)—liberation

यत्
(ind)—in that (neut. rel. pronoun used adverbially)

रक्त
1) (adj)—reddened
2) (n -म्)—blood

√रुच्
(1Ā)—to be pleasing [to . . . (object in चतुर्थी)]

वशः
(m)—power, control, influence

वशगत
(adj)—under the influence (of)

वाक्यम्
(n)—speech

विगत
(adj)—gone, departed

वि + √लप्
(1P)—lament

वीर्यम्
(n)—valor

वृत्तान्तः
(m)—report, news, story

शास्त्रम्
(n)—scholarly text

स-
(ind)—with, having (used only as prior member of compound)

संवत्सरः
(m)—year

सदृश
(adj)—like, fit, suitable

सम
(adj)—same, equal

समागमः
(m)—meeting, coming together

सम् + आ + √इ
(2P)—come together, meet

√सह्
(1Ā)—bear, endure

हृदयम्
(n)—heart

हृदये + √कृ
(idiom)—take seriously, take to heart

ENGLISH-SANSKRIT GLOSSARY

agitated	आकुल	(adj)
birth	जन्मन्	(n)
death	मृत्युः	(m)
disaster	व्यसनम्	(n)
disease	रोगः	(m)
for a long time	चिरम्	(ind)
liberated	मुक्त	(adj)
liberation	मोक्षः	(m)
moreover	अपि च	(ind)
old age	जरा	(f)
poverty	दारिद्र्यम्	(n)
stabilized	स्थिर	(adj)
surely, certainly	निश्चितम्	(ind)
written	लिखित	(adj)

LESSON 15

वर्तमाने कृदन्त (The Present Participle)

15.0 With the विधि लिङ् (optative) we learned the last verbal conjugation of the present system. However, there is still one participial (i.e., nominal) form based on the present stem. This form, the present participle, is of very common occurrence and great usefulness. It is, like the भूते कृदन्त and other non-conjugational verbal forms, an excellent example of classical Sanskrit's tendency to depart from the तिङन्त forms. It functions like the भूते कृदन्त in that it, too, is both adjectival (in that it must agree in case, number, and gender with the noun to which it refers) and verbal (in that it must have a कर्तृ [grammatical subject]) and may, if formed from a सकर्मक root, have a कर्मन् (direct object). Its relation to the भूते कृदन्त is very much like that of the कर्तरि to the कर्मणि प्रयोग. That is, it is subject-referent, i.e., is in grammatical agreement with its कर्तृ, while the भूते कृदन्त (of a सकर्मक root) is object-referent, i.e., in agreement with its कर्मन्. Its use, however, is rather different.

15.1 **The use of the वर्तमाने कृदन्त.**

The वर्तमाने कृदन्त is basically a simple formation. Nevertheless, the use of this form, like that of बहुव्रीहि समास-s, and the कर्मणि प्रयोग, is sometimes confusing to the beginner. Therefore, it requires some explanation.

15.2 There are basically two reasons for confusion regarding this participle, one conceptual and significant, the other mechanical and trivial.

a. The latter, trivial reason is nothing more than the fact that certain common forms of the participle are identical with some common finite verbal forms. This, however, is rarely the cause of real ambiguity. This minor issue will be discussed below (15.12).

b. The major reason for misunderstanding the function of the वर्तमाने कृदन्त is a failure to understand that the participle is limited, unlike the भूते कृदन्त, to a status in a sentence subordinate to another finite verb or its equivalent. The present participle can never substitute for the principal verb of a sentence or an independent clause. In this it is rather like the gerund (see 11.5).

Thus, although रामो वनं गतः । (or गच्छति, अगच्छत्, गतवान्, गच्छतु etc.) is a complete sentence, the phrases

i. रामो वनं गत्वा (त्वान्त)

ii. रामो वनं गच्छन् (वर्तमाने कृदन्त)

require an independent verbal phrase just as clearly as do their English equivalents:

i. Rāma, having gone to the forest, . . . and

ii. Rāma, going to the forest, . . .

The "resolution" of these sentence fragments must be a finite verb or some nominal equivalent. For example, the phrases i. and ii. could be resolved by the clause मुनिमपश्यत्. The sentences would now read:

i. रामो वनं गत्वा मुनिमपश्यत् ।

ii. रामो वनं गच्छन्मुनिमपश्यत् ।

which would mean:

i. Having gone to the forest, Rāma saw a sage.

ii. [While] going to the forest, Rāma saw a sage. [or] Rāma, [who was] going to the forest, saw a sage.

15.3 As the above sentences show. the major difference with regard to usage, between त्वान्त and the वर्तमाने कृदन्त, is that the action expressed by the former is more or less perfective while the action expressed by the latter is more or less imperfective. The त्वान्त is used to indicate an action that is **completed** by the time of the action expressed by the finite verb of the complementary independent clause. The वर्तमाने कृदन्त, on the other hand, generally expresses an action that is in **process** at the time of the action of the independent verb so the two actions (or states) are more or less simultaneous. Thus in sentence (i) above we would understand that Rāma had already completed his journey to the forest before he saw the sage. In (ii) he sees the sage while he is still on his way.

15.4 a. This expression of simultaneous actions maybe otherwise accomplished by the compound sentences of the type यदा . . . तदा etc., (6.5 ff.) that have been introduced earlier. Examples:

i. यदा रामो वनमगच्छत्तदा स मुनिमपश्यत्

(When Rāma went to the forest, he saw a sage.)

ii. यः पुरुषः कृष्णं भजति स मोक्षं लभते ।

(The man who worships Kṛṣṇa, [he] attains liberation.)

An important function of the वर्तमाने कृदन्त is to serve as a substitute for such relative clauses. The above examples might be paraphrased as follows:

i. वनं गच्छन्रामो मुनिमपश्यत् ।

ii. कृष्णं भजन्पुरुषो मोक्षं लभते ।

b. If you always remember first to translate a वर्तमाने कृदन्त **regardless of its case**, as a subordinate or relative **clause**, you will have no difficulty with the form. Afterwards, if you feel the result is not always the best English, you may change the English wording; but you will have understood the sentence. It is impossible to stress this point too strongly because the वर्तमाने कृदन्त, like the भूते कृदन्त, is a **verbal adjective** and must, therefore, agree in case, number, and gender with the noun it modifies. If, however, you try to express the case of this adjective separately, **you will not understand the sentence**.

15.5 a. Consider the following sentence:

वनं गच्छता रामेण मुनिर्दृश्यते ।

(Rāma, going to the forest, sees the sage.)

Here we see the वर्तमाने कृदन्त of the root √गम् in its तृतीया, एक, पुंलिङ्ग form. Now the structure of the finite phrase of the sentence is clear:

रामेण मुनिर्दृश्यते ।

(The sage is seen by Rāma.)

b. The remainder of the sentence, वनं गच्छता, requires some explanation.

i. Two specific questions arise:

a. Why is गच्छता in the तृतीया?

b. What is the syntactical role of वनम् in the sentence?

ii. The answers to these questions are:

a. गच्छता is in the तृतीया because, being an adjective, it must agree in case, number, and gender with the noun it modifies. Since रामेण is तृतीया, एक, पुंलिङ्ग and गच्छता modifies रामेण, it must be the same. **This does not mean that the action of "going" is to be understood or translated as being agentive or instrumental!**

b. वनम् is द्वितीया, एक, नपुंसक and is the locus of motion of the action of the root √गम् as expressed in the form गच्छता (see 4.38).

iii. In these two questions (and answers) lies the whole explanation of the function of the वर्तमाने कृदन्त. It is nominal in that it is an adjective and it is verbal in that it can (if formed from a सकर्मक root) have a direct object. As such, it can serve as a transition between two separate clauses by serving as an adjective in one and as a verb in the other.

iv. Thus, in our example the words वनम् and रामेण each relate in a different way to the key word गच्छता—the first as locus of motion of a verb and the second as the governing noun of an adjective. It is as though रामेण were the subject of two different clauses, of which the verbs were derived from √गम् and √दृश् respectively.

v. Because of this dual nature of the present participle, we should translate it as a verb of a subordinate or relative clause.

vi. We should then translate
वनं गच्छता रामेण मुनिर्दृश्यते as:
(The sage is seen by Rāma, **who is going to the forest**.) (or) (Rāma, **while going to the forest**, sees a sage.)

a. Remember that the वर्तमाने कृदन्त is a verbal adjective and not a verbal noun. Therefore it is no more proper to attempt to give its own case relation than it is with an ordinary (nonverbal) adjective. Thus if (as many beginning Sanskritists do) one were to translate the phrase: रामेण गच्छता as "by Rāma's going . . .," it would be as great an error as to translate रामेण श्यामेन as "by the dark of Rāma . . ."

b. There are indeed many true nouns derived from the verbal roots (Lesson 20). The वर्तमाने कृदन्त, however, may be easily distinguished from these (and all other verbal adjectives) by the fact that it is formed from the present stems of the various roots, rather than from the roots themselves.

15.6 Formation of the वर्तमाने कृदन्त

The वर्तमाने कृदन्त has one feature more characteristic of verbal than of nominal forms. Unlike the other participial formations learned thus far (the भूते कृदन्त [Lesson 10] and -तवन्त् [11.4] constructions), it distinguishes *voice*. Like finite verbs it has different endings according to whether its verbal root is conjugated in the आत्मनेपद or परस्मैपद.

a. The परस्मैपद participle may be formed quite mechanically. The stem form is discovered in each case by dropping the final इ of the प्रथम, बहु, परस्मैपद form of वर्तमाने लट् (present indicative).

i. Thus, the "active" participle of the following roots may be generated as follows:

root	प्रथम°बहु°लट्	participle stem
√गम् (1)	गच्छन्ति	गच्छन्त्
√श्रु (5)	शृण्वन्ति	शृण्वन्त्
√कृ (8)	कुर्वन्ति	कुर्वन्त्
√भी (3)	बिभ्यति	बिभ्यत्
√अस् (2)	सन्ति	सन्त्
√छिद् (7)	छिन्दन्ति	छिन्दन्त्

ii. The forms thus generated are ones with a strong/weak alternation of -अन्त्/-अत्. The only exception to this is that roots of the third गण (which have no न् in their प्रथम बहु परस्मैपद लट् forms [see 7.25]), therefore have a participial stem form in -अत्, which then has no strong/weak alternation. All its forms are in this sense "weak."

iii. The paradigm is thus the same as that given at 11.1, with the single important exception that the पुंलिङ्ग, एक, प्रथमा is always formed without length of the final अ. Examples:

√पश् (4) सीतां पश्यन्रामो मुदितो ऽभवत् ।
(*Seeing* Sītā, Rāma became happy.)

√श्रु (5) मधुराञ्छब्दाञ्छृण्वन्सुखितो ऽपि पर्युत्सुको भवेत् ।
(Even a happy man, *when he hears* sweet sounds, might be stricken by longing.)

√भी (3) राक्षसेभ्यो बिभ्यदृषिर्घोरवनमत्यजत् ।
(*Fearing* the rākṣasa-s, the *ṛṣi* left the terrible forest.)

आ + √गम् (1) भवन्तमागच्छन्तं दृष्ट्वा सर्व उत्तिष्ठन्तु ।
(Seeing you *coming*, let everyone rise.)

√वस् (1), सम् + √वद् (1) वने वसद्भिर्मुनिभिः सह संवदतो जनान् रामलक्ष्मणौ सस्नेहं पश्यतः ।
(Rāma and Lakṣmaṇa view with affection the people, *who are conversing* with the sages dwelling in the forest.)

iv. The स्त्रीलिङ्ग forms of the participle are formed by the suffixation of ई to either the strong or weak stem (depending on the गण) and are declined regularly according to 7.1.

The ई is added:

a. to the strong stem in गण-s 1,4 and 10.

Examples:

root	**m. stem**	**f. stem**
√वद् (1)	वदन्त्	वदन्ती

b. to the strong **or** weak stem for गण 6 and for roots of the 2nd गण ending in आ, although the strong stem is perhaps more common.

Examples:

root	**m. stem**	**f. stem**
√तुद् (6)	तुदन्त्	तुदन्ती/तुदती
√या (2)	यान्त्	यान्ती/याती

c. to the weak stem for all others.

Examples:

root	**m. stem**	**f. stem**
√कृ (8)	कुर्वन्त्	कुर्वती
√छिद् (7)	छिन्दन्त्	छिन्दती

v. The नपुंसकलिङ्ग is formed in general from the weak stem -अत् and its declension is the same as that of neuter stems in -वन्त् or -मन्त् (11.1.b) except in the प्रथमा, द्वितीया and संबोधन द्विवचन forms where stem-strength occurs in accordance with the pattern of the feminine.

For example:

√गम्	एक°	द्वि°	बहु°
प्र°	गच्छत्	गच्छन्ती	गच्छन्ति
द्वि°	गच्छत्	गच्छन्ती	गच्छन्ति
सम्°	गच्छत्	गच्छन्ती	गच्छन्ति

15.7 The आत्मनेपद stem form of the वर्तमाने कृदन्त, which, as with the finite verbs, **has no semantic value** to distinguish it from the परस्मैपद, is generated simply by:

a. adding -मान to present stems of roots of the अ गण-s (1,4,6, and 10).

Examples:

root	**stem form**	
√भाष् (1Ā)	भाषमाण	(See 3.59 for सन्धि.)
√मन् (4Ā)	मन्यमान	

b. adding -आन to the weak present stems of the non-अ गण-s (2,3,5,7,8,9).

Examples:

root	**stem form**	
√द्विष् (2)	द्विषाण	(See 3.59 for सन्धि.)
√कृ (8)	कुर्वाण	
√हु (3)	जुह्वान	

c. Since the आत्मनेपद forms are all -अ stems, their declension is of no difficulty. The प्रथमा एक endings are:

पुंलिङ्गः -अः

नपुंसकलिङ्गः -अम्

and स्त्रीलिङ्गः -आ

d. The use of the आत्मनेपद is just like that of the परस्मैपद.

Example:

अहं कामान्न कदापि त्यजेयमिति मन्यमानेषु पुरुषेषु वैराग्यं कथमुद्भवेत् ।

(How could *vairāgya* arise among men *who think*, "I would never abandon sensual pleasures?")

15.8 A कर्मणि (or भावे) equivalent of the वर्तमाने कृदन्त may be formed from the कर्मणि stem of any verbal root. As in the case of finite verbs, this participle is formed with the आत्मनेपद ending, which, for this form, is invariably -मान.

15.9 As with any कर्मणि प्रयोग form, this participle agrees with the कर्मन् or object of the action expressed by its verbal root, if the root is सकर्मक, or transitive.

Examples:

रामेण हन्यमाना राक्षसा दूरं गच्छन्ति यथा वायुना नुद्यमानानि पर्णानि ।

(The rākṣasa-s, *being slain* by Rāma, go far away, like leaves driven by the wind.)

मया दृश्यमानासु कन्यासु सीतोत्तमेति मन्ये ऽहम् ।

(I think that among the girls I *see* (lit., *being seen* by me), Sītā is the best.)

15.10 There are a number of special or idiomatic applications of the वर्तमाने कृदन्त which, if studied carefully, greatly increase one's ability to understand and generate sophisticated Sanskrit sentences:

a. The वर्तमाने कृदन्त of the root √अस् (सन्त् सत् सती), "being," is quite useful. One of its regular idiomatic applications is with the निपात (particle) अपि to indicate a situation contrary to normal expectation.

Examples:

ब्राह्मणः सन्नपि स न वेदज्ञः ।

(*Even though he is* a brāhman, he is not a knower of the Vedas.)

सुन्दरी सत्यपि दुर्गा न विवाहिता ।

(*Even though she is* beautiful, Durgā is not married.)

i. This sense of "even though" may be conveyed by अपि and the वर्तमाने कृदन्त of any other root as well.

Example:

पुस्तकं पठन्नप्यर्थं नावगच्छामि ।

(*Even though I read t*he book, I don't understand the meaning.)

b. The वर्तमाने कृदन्त of the आत्मनेपद roots √वृत् (1Ā) and √विद् (4Ā), "to be, exist," (वर्तमान and विद्यमान) in the sense of "existing," "going on," "present," have several common uses.

i. The participle वर्तमान can be used as an adjective meaning "present" or even as the noun "the present." It is from this form that we have the grammatical term वर्तमाने लट्, or the लट् (indicative) used in the present.

ii. The negative of the participle of √विद्, अविद्यमान is used in order to provide the विग्रह of a particular kind of बहुव्रीहि समास. In this kind of समास, the prior member is the negative particle अ, which here serves as a sort of adjective meaning not-existing. When such a compound is subjected to विग्रह, however, a real word is required. The word is usually supplied by the participle अविद्यमान. Example:

समास	विग्रह	**meaning**
अपुरुषम् (राज्यम्)	अविद्यमानाः पुरुषा यस्मिंस्तत्	a (realm) having no men

c. Another common use of this participle is as a true continuative or "imperfective." This is done by making use of the simultaneity of the participial action with a finite form of a verb of motion or of standing still.
Examples:

√गै	(1P)	(sing)	गायन्नागच्छति । (He *comes singing*.)
सम् + √भाष्	(1Ā)	(speak)	तया सह संभाषमाण आस्ते । (He *is speaking* with her [lit., He sits speaking with her.])
√हस्	(1P)	(laugh)	हसंस्तिष्ठति । (He *goes on laughing* [lit., He stands laughing.])

15.11 सति सप्तमी and सतः षष्ठी : Absolute Constructions

Two of the most common and characteristic idiomatic uses of the participles, especially the present participles, are the सति सप्तमी and सतः षष्ठी or locative and genitive absolute constructions. By the use of these constructions, a noun and its participle may, by being placed either in the सप्तमी or षष्ठी case, form a special kind of relative clause that conveys a sense of concurrent or immediately contiguous time relative to that of an independent clause.

a. By far the more common of these usages is in the सप्तमी or locative case. Its meaning is simply "while" or "when," and it may be formed freely with both active and passive participles.

Examples:

रामे वनं गच्छति सर्वे जना दुःखिता अभवन् ।

(*When Rāma was going to the forest*, all the people were unhappy.)

सीतायां तं पश्यन्त्यां कैकेय्यहसत् ।

(*While Sītā was watching him*, Kaikeyī laughed.)

सर्वेषु जनेषु दुःखितेषु सत्सु देवा अपि विषण्णा भवन्ति ।

(*When all the people are unhappy*, even the gods become dejected.)

रामेण हन्यमानेषु राक्षसेषु वानरा आनन्देनानृत्यन् ।

(*When the demons were being killed by Rāma*, the monkeys danced for joy.)

i. The same construction may be used with other participles, for example;

तस्मिन्हते राक्षसे सर्वे जना भयमुक्ता अभवन् ।

(*When that rākṣasa was killed*, all people became free from fear.)

b. An exactly parallel usage to the सति सप्तमी may be formed from the षष्ठी, or genitive case. This usage, called the सतः षष्ठी, is somewhat less common than the सति सप्तमी although its function is quite similar. It too indicates simultaneous action. Its occurrence, however, is occasionally restricted to cases in which the action expressed by the genitive participle is carried on not only at the same time as the action expressed by a finite verb (or equivalent) but in spite of it. As this construction is used to indicate action that is in some way disrespectful or contemptuous, it is called अनादरषष्ठी, or genitive of disrespect.

Examples:

पश्यतो रावणस्य रामो राक्षसान्हन्ति ।

(Rāma kills the rākṣasas [*despite the fact that*] *Rāvaṇa is looking on*; i.e., Rāma kills the rākṣasa-s right before Rāvaṇa's eyes.)

राज्ञो भाषमाणस्य कैकेय्यहसत् ।

(Kaikeyī laughed *while the king was speaking*.)

c. Note that both absolutive constructions are used only when the subjects of the two clauses are not the same.

15.12 **Special problems**

One of the most elementary but frequently occurring errors that students commit with regard to the वर्तमाने कृदन्त is due to the fact that in many instances the various cases of a participle of a given root may be homonymous with finite forms of the same root. A glance through the paradigm will indicate where confusion is possible.

a. The most common instance of this should be considered separately. It happens that the सप्तमी, एकवचन, पुंलिङ्ग or नपुंसकालिङ्ग of the परस्मैपद वर्तमाने कृदन्त of roots belonging to the अ गण-s has exactly the same form as the extremely common प्रथमपुरुष, एकवचन, परस्मैपद of the वर्तमाने लट्.

Since, because of the common occurrence of the सति सप्तमी (15.11.a), the former form occurs relatively frequently, the opportunities for confusion are not rare. To avoid this confusion, be sure, when dealing with an apparently finite verbal form, that you can identify the subject of the verb and that there are no "suspicious locatives" in its vicinity. Example:

रामे वनं गच्छति सर्वे दुःखिता भवन्ति ।

Do not simply assume that गच्छति is a finite form. If it were, you would have to find a subject. रामे, of course, cannot be the subject of **any finite form**. Even if you were to assume an unexpressed subject, you would have to explain रामे. Keeping in mind the सति सप्तमी eliminates the difficulty.

i. One should note in this connection that the confusion, common among beginners, of the post-consonantal forms of ए and ओ (viz., े and ो) can prove particularly troublesome here.

EXERCISES

A. Translate the reading up until the sentence beginning एवं वदति रामे.

B. Identify all the वर्तमाने कृदन्त-s in A. Rewrite the reading, substituting relative clauses or other paraphrases for the वर्तमाने कृदन्त-s.

C. Translate the remainder of the reading and carry out the same procedure as in B.

D. Translate the following sentences into Sanskrit, using वर्तमाने कृदन्त-s and absolute constructions whenever possible.

1. Rāma and Lakṣmaṇa killed rākṣasa-s in the forest while (despite the fact that) the king of the rākṣasa-s was watching. (√पश् [4P])

2. When the king speaks, everyone stands listening.
3. The guru stands among the students who are reading books.
4. I cannot see the book that is being read by you.
5. When who is slain, do the people become free from fear?

E. Now rewrite the sentences of D., substituting relative clauses for the participles.

F. Translate and memorize the following two verses.

कूजन्तं राम रामेति मधुरं मधुराक्षरम् ।
आरुह्य कविताशाखां वन्दे वाल्मीकिकोकिलम् ॥

वाल्मीकेर्मुनिसिंहस्य कवितावनचारिणः ।
शृण्वन्रामकथानादं को न याति परां गतिम् ॥

Note: These two verses are based upon figures of speech called समस्तरूपक-s, or compound-metaphors, in which the subject of comparison (e.g., वाल्मीकिः) is compared to the object of comparison (e.g., कोकिलः) by making an appositional कर्मधारय compound (see 12.10.b) of which the former is the prior and the latter the final, member. Thus, the word वाल्मीकिकोकिलः means the "Vālmiki cuckoo," or "Vālmīki viewed poetically as a cuckoo." There are two such समस्तरूपक-s in the first verse and three in the second.

READING

अहमपि वनं गच्छामीति वदन्तं लक्ष्मणं परिष्वजमानो रामो ऽमन्यत । प्रियां वनगमनात्पूर्वं पश्यामीति । एवं चिन्तयित्वा सीतापतिः सीतां द्रष्टुं गतः । सीताप्यागच्छन्तं विवर्णवदनं भर्तारं दृष्ट्वा चिन्तया बाध्यमानैवमब्रवीत् । एतादृशस्य शोकस्य कारणमुच्यतामिति । एवमुक्तो दशरथतनयो ऽब्रवीत् । पुरा राज्ञा सत्यप्रतिज्ञेन दशरथेन कैकेय्यै महावरौ दत्तौ । अद्य ममाभिषेके क्रियमाणे सा वदति । प्रथमवरेण चतुर्दशवर्षाणि रामेण दण्डकारण्य उष्यताम् । द्वितीयेन भरतो यौवराज्ये ऽभिषिच्यतामिति । ततो

ऽहमद्यैव पितृप्रतिज्ञामनुसृत्यायोध्यां परित्यजन्वनं गच्छेयम् । त्वयात्रैव स्थीयताम् । देवपूजां यथाविधि सर्वदा कुर्वती भरतशत्रुघ्नौ सेवस्वेति । एवं वदति रामे जनकतनया संक्रुद्धा सत्युपहासमकरोत् । आर्यपुत्र किं भाषसे । ईदृशं वचनं न कदापि त्वादृशा वीरा वक्तुमर्हन्ति । भर्तुर्वनं गच्छतः कथं भार्या नगरे तिष्ठेदिति । एवं ब्रुवतीं सीतां न नेतुमैच्छद्रामो वनदुःखानि चिन्तयन् । सो ऽवदत् । शृणु सीते । वने वसता जनेन बहुदुःखान्यनुभूयन्ते । वने सिंहादयो* हिंस्रजन्तवश्चरन्ति यथाकामम् । तत्र च सन्ति बहून्यन्यानि मार्गश्रमादीनि दुःखानीति । तद्वचनं श्रुत्वा दुःखिता सीताश्रुपूर्णनयना पुनरब्रवीत् । हे राम । त्वया निरूप्यमाणानि दुःखानि सुखान्येव भवेयुस्त्वया सह संचरन्त्या मम । त्वयि वनं गते कथमिह जीवेयम् । त्वया त्यक्ताहं विषं पिबेयमग्निं वा प्रविशेयम् । अलमनेन वचनेन । दण्डकारण्यं गच्छता त्वया सहाहमागच्छामीति । रामो ऽपि तां शोचन्तीं परिष्वज्य सान्त्वयन्नेवावदत् । साधु प्रिये साधु । यदि मया सहागन्तुमिच्छसि तर्ह्यागच्छेति ॥

---

* See “आदिः” in the glossary

GLOSSARY

अक्षरम्

(n)—syllable, sound, word

अग्निः

(m)—fire

अलम्

(ind)—enough, sufficient; with तृतीया, 'enough of . . .'

आदिः

(m)—beginning; this word is very frequently used as the final member of a *bahuvrīhi* application of appositional *karmadhāraya* compounds of the meaning 'having . . . for a beginning.' This is the typical Sanskrit way of saying '. . . etc.,' indicating a known group by its first or foremost member. Example: इन्द्रादयो देवाः (the gods) having Indra foremost,i.e., Indra, etc.

आ + √रुह्

(1P)—ascend (to)

उपहासः

(m)—satirical laughter, ridicule

एतादृश

(adj)—such

कथा

(f)—story, tale

कविता

(f)—poetry

कामः

(m)—desire

कारणम्

(n)—reason, cause

√कूज्

(1P)—warble

कोकिलः

(m)—koil, Indian cuckoo

चतुर्दश

(adj)—fourteen (see 19.3)

√चर्

(1P)—move, wander

चारिन्

(m)—roamer, wanderer

जन्तुः

(m)—creature, living being

तनयः

(m)—son

तनया

(f)—daughter

त्वादृश

(adj)—like you

दुर्गा

(f prop)—Durgā, woman's name

नादः

(m)—roar

नि + √रूप्
(10P)—see, perceive, foresee, describe

पर
(adj)—highest (see 5.7)

परि + √स्वज् → परिष्वजते
(1Ā)—embrace

√पा → पिबति (see 7.15.d)
(1P)—drink

पूजा
(f)—worship, reverence

पूर्वं + (पञ्चमी विभक्ति)
(ind)—before 'X'

प्र + √विश्
(6P)—enter

मधुरम्
(ind)—sweetly

यथाकामम्
(ind)—in accordance with desire, at will

यथाविधि
(ind)—in accordance with custom

√या
(2P)—go

यौवराज्यम्
(n)—state of being heir apparent

√वन्द्
(1Ā)—praise, extol

वर्षम्
(n)—year; in द्वितीया 'for a year' (see 4.41)

वदनम्
(n)—face

वाल्मीकिः
(m prop)—the *ṛṣi* Vālmīki, first poet (*ādikaviḥ*), and traditional author of the Rāmāyaṇa

विधिः
(m)—rule, custom

विषम्
(n)—poison

शाखा
(f)—branch

√शुच्
(1P)—grieve

श्रमः
(m)—toil, effort

संक्रुद्ध
(adj)—angry

सं + √चर्
(1P)—go, walk

√सान्त्व्
(10P)—pacify, appease

सिंहः
(m)—lion

हिंस्र
(adj)—injurious, harmful

हिंसा
(f)—violence

ENGLISH-SANSKRIT GLOSSARY

book	पुस्तकम्	(n)
fear	भयम्	(n)
free	मुक्त	(adj)
listen	√श्रु	(5P)
people	जनः	(m) (use sing. or pl.)
read	√पठ्	(1P)
slain	हत	(adj)
stand	√स्था	(1P)
student	शिष्यः	(m)

LESSON 16

Non-गण Conjugations;
The लृट्, लृङ्, and लुट्
(Future System and the Conditional);
The कृत्य (Gerundive)

16.0 Thus far, all the finite verbal forms you have learned, with the exception of the कर्मणि प्रयोग, have involved knowledge of the गण, or conjugation class, to which each धातु, or verbal root, belongs. These forms, the लट्, लङ्, लोट् and लिङ् are, moreover, the only finite forms generated according to these गण-s. The remaining verbal conjugations, then, whatever their own peculiarities, do not require that you know the गण of a root in order to generate their forms.

16.1 **सेट्, वेट्, and अनिट् Roots**

With regard to the non-गण conjugations, all Sanskrit roots may be classified according to whether or not they require the vowel इ between themselves and tense markers or endings that begin with any consonant except य्. Since य् is an exception, the issue does not arise with regard to the कर्मणि प्रयोग.

a. This particular इ is called इट् by the Sanskrit grammarians, and all roots are then classified as सेट् (with इट्) or roots that require the इ wherever possible, अनिट् (without इट्), roots that do not require इ, and वेट्, or roots that optionally take the इ. The अनिट् roots are rather more numerous than the others.

b. It is this distinction that explains the seemingly sporadic occurrence of the इ before the agentive suffix -तृ and the infinitive ending -तुम्.

c. The rules for which roots belong to which categories are complex and need not be learned at this point. The distinction, however, is an important one. Its existence should therefore be kept in mind. If this is done, the verbal forms themselves, when learned, will show clearly the presence or absence of the इट्. This will be seen, for example, in the case of the ऌट् conjugation introduced below.

16.2 **सामान्यभविष्यत्काले ऌट् : The Simple Future**

Thus far, although you have learned several modes of verbal forms indicating "present time" and numerous ways of indicating preterite or "past" time, you have learned no straightforward way of expressing future time. Sanskrit has several ways of doing this. The simplest, which may be used to indicate immediate future, is simply to use the लट्, or present indicative.

Example:

भो बालक वनं गच्छ । तथास्तु गच्छामि ।

(Hey boy! Go to the forest. So be it. I [shall] go.)

On the other hand, for more general expression of future time, Sanskrit has two distinct verbal conjugations. The most important of these and the one more frequently used is also the simplest. It is called सामान्यभविष्यत्काले ऌट्, or "ऌट् in the sense of general future time." The term सामान्य, "ordinary, general," is used by the grammarians in an attempt to distinguish the usage of this form from that of the other future (see 16.11), but in fact no such distinction is observed in the literature.

16.3 **Formation of the ऌट्**

a. The ऌट् stem is formed by the suffixation to a verbal root, of the tense marker -स्य-.

   i. Before this marker a root vowel takes गुण if capable of it.

   ii. In case of सेट् roots, and optionally in the case of वेट् roots, the tense marker is preceded by the vowel इ. In this case the स् of the marker is changed to ष् (3.58). The future stems of such roots then typically end in -इष्य.

   iii. To the future stems thus formed are added the same primary endings used with the लट्.

iv. The final अ of a लृट् stem is treated just like the final अ of any अ-गण stem.

Examples:

Root	लृट् **forms**	
√दा (P) (give)	दास्यति	(he will give)
√गम् (P) (go)	गमिष्यामि	(I shall go)
√मन् (Ā) (think)	मंस्यन्ते	(they will think)
√कृ (P) (do)	करिष्यामः	(we shall do)

v. 10th गण roots form the लृट् from the present stem. All 10th गण roots are सेट्.

Examples:

√चुर् (P) (steal)	चोरयिष्यति	(he will steal)
√चिन्त् (P) (think)	चिन्तयिष्यामि	(I shall think)

16.4 **कर्मणि प्रयोग of the लृट्**

The लृट्, like most conjugations, has corresponding कर्मणि and भावे प्रयोग-s. But, like all conjugations not formed from the present stem, the लृट् has no special कर्मणि or भावे stem. The कर्मणि and भावे प्रयोग-s then, are distinguished only by the fact of their always requiring the आत्मनेपद endings. In the case of roots (धातु-s) ordinarily conjugated in the आत्मनेपद, there is no difference between corresponding कर्तरि and कर्मणि or भावे प्रयोग forms.

Examples:

Root

√स्था (1P)(stay) रामो वने स्थास्यति (कर्तरि)
रामेण वने स्थास्यते (भावे)
(Rāma *will stay* in the forest)

√लभ् (Ā) (gain) न किमपि लप्स्यते (कर्तरि) (कर्मणि)
(*He will gain* nothing; Nothing *will be gained*.)

16.5 **सन्धि and the लृट्**

The formation and usage of the लृट् are so simple and regular that they present few difficulties. There are, however, a few

सन्धि rules and other sound changes that should be noted here. Some of these have been introduced before but are repeated so as to refresh your memory.

a. अनिट् roots ending in consonants present a number of instances of internal consonant सन्धि since no vowel intervenes between their final consonants and the स् of the लृट् marker. Before स् of the future tense marker:

i. Voiced स्पर्श-s change to their corresponding non-voiced स्पर्श-s.

Example:

Root	लृट्
√भिद् (split)	भेत्स्यति (he will split)

ii. Aspirate स्पर्श-s are changed to their corresponding non-aspirates and rule i., if necessary, applies.

Example:

Root	लृट्
√लभ् (obtain, gain)	लप्स्यते (he will obtain)

iii. तालव्य consonants and ह् are changed to क् and the स् is changed to ष् (7.18.c).

Examples:

Root	लृट्	
√त्यज् (abandon)	त्यक्ष्यति	(he will abandon)
√दृश् (see)	द्रक्ष्यति	(he will see) (see 16.5.b.i)
√वच् (say)	वक्ष्यति	(he will say)
√दह् (burn)	धक्ष्यति	(compare 7.26.b) (he will burn)

iv. स् of several roots, most notably √वस् (1P) (dwell), is changed to त्.

Example:

Root	लृट्
√वस् (dwell)	वत्स्यति (he will dwell)

b. Several other sound changes are to be noted.

i. In the लृट् and some other forms requiring vowel strength, like the infinitive (13.1.a), a few roots with medial ऋ show र instead of the regular गुण (i.e., अर्).
Examples:

Root	लृट्	
√दृश् (see)	द्रक्ष्यति	(he will see)
√सृज् (emit, create)	स्रक्ष्यति	(he will create)
√सृप् (move, creep)	स्रप्स्यति	(he will move)

ii. A few roots are strengthened by a penultimate nasal.
Example:

Root	लृट्	
√नश् (4P) (perish)	नङ्क्ष्यति	(he will perish)

16.6 लृट् of Some Important Roots

Learning the following examples will give a sense of the easily recognizable form of the लृट् of some common roots.

a. अनिट् roots are more common than सेट् (and वेट्) roots. Some typical examples are:

√दा (give)	दास्यति	(he will give)
√स्था (stand)	स्थास्यति	(he will stand)
√ज्ञा (know)	ज्ञास्यति	(he will know)
√त्यज् (leave)	त्यक्ष्यति	(he will leave)
√दृश् (see)	द्रक्ष्यति	(he will see)
√लभ् (get)	लप्स्यते	(he will get)

b. सेट् roots, however, are quite common and include some that you must remember.

√कृ (do)	करिष्यति	(he will do)
√भू (be)	भविष्यति	(he will be)
√गम् (go)	गमिष्यति	(he will go)
√हन् (kill)	हनिष्यति	(he will slay)

For वेट् roots, of course, two forms are possible. Thus:

√नश् (perish)	नङ्क्ष्यति/नशिष्यति	(he will perish)
√क्षम् (pardon)	क्षंस्यति/क्षमिष्यति	(he will pardon)

16.7 The following sentences illustrate the use of the future:

किं भविष्यति किं भविष्यतीति चिन्तयन्तः सर्वे शिष्याः परीक्षाशालामुद्विजन्त आगमिष्यन्ति ।

(Thinking, "What *will be*? What *will be*?" all the students *will come*, trembling, to the examination hall.)

यद्यहं जनकतनयां त्यक्ष्यामि तर्हि कस्मिन्नगरे स्थास्यतीत्यवश्यं मंस्यते रघुकुलनन्दनः ।

(The bringer of joy to Raghu's race *will* certainly *think*, "If I abandon the daughter of Janaka, in what city *will she stay*?")

मरणानन्तरं कुत्र गमिष्यति राक्षसः । यत्र न किमपि द्रक्ष्यति श्रोष्यति वा तत्र गमिष्यति ।

(Where *will* the rākṣasa *go* after death? *He will go* where *he will* neither *see* nor *hear* anything.)

16.8 **भविष्यत्काले कृदन्त : Future Participle**

A future participle may be made from the ऌट् stem in a way precisely analogous to the formation of the present participle of an अ गण stem (15.6).

Examples:

Root		**Participle Stem**
√दा	(P)	दास्यन्त्
√भू	(P)	भविष्यन्त्
√युध्	(Ā)	योत्स्यमान

Example:

ग्रामं गमिष्यन् पुरुषो व्याघ्रमपश्यत् ।

(The man *about to set off* for the village saw the tiger.)

16.9 **अतिपत्तौ ऌङ् : The Conditional**

Classical Sanskrit has a special tense formation specifically reserved for hypotheses or situations contrary to fact. This is called अतिपत्तौ ऌङ्, or "ऌङ् in the sense of nonexistence, non-coming to pass (अतिपत्तिः)." This is actually of rather rare occurrence and is included here only because its formation, once the ऌट् is learned, presents no difficulty whatever.

16.10 The ऌङ् is formed from the future stem, exactly as the लङ् (imperfect) is formed from the present stem. The stem is preceded by the augment अ and followed by the appropriate secondary ending (8.9). A few examples will suffice:

Root	ऌट्	ऌङ्	
√गम् (P) (go)	गमिष्यति	अगमिष्यत्	(he would have gone)
√भाष् (Ā) (speak)	भाषिष्यते	अभाषिष्यत	(he would have spoken)
√त्यज् (P) (leave)	त्यक्ष्यति	अत्यक्ष्यत्	(he would have left)

The form, when it occurs, is used in reference to situations that are hypothetical or that are flatly contrary to fact.

Example:

रामश्चेत्तत्राभविष्यद्रावणः सीतां नैवाहरिष्यत् ।

(If Rāma *had been* there, Rāvaṇa *would* not *have abducted* Sītā.)

16.11 **अनद्यतन (श्वस्तन) भविष्यत्काले लुट् : The Periphrastic Future**

The second of the two future formations is considerably less common. Its formation is peculiar in that it is periphrastic, or made up of two distinct forms. One of these forms is nominal and one verbal. This peculiarity is enhanced by the fact that in the most frequently used person, the **प्रथमपुरुष**, the finite verbal form is omitted.

16.12 **Formation of the लुट्**

a. The लुट् of a given verbal root, except in the **प्रथमपुरुष** form, consists of a sequence of:

   i. an agentive noun derived from the root,

   ii. the लट् form of the root √अस् (2P) (be) agreeing in number and person with the **कर्तृ** of the root.

b. The agentive noun is formed by the addition of the suffix -तृ to the root, strengthened by गुण. The formation of the noun is discussed at 10.0-3. Its use is as follows.

i. Its प्रथमा° एक° पुंलिङ्ग form (ending in- ता) is used for all मध्यम and उत्तमपुरुष forms regardless of number and gender.

a. Examples:

Root	Agentive		Noun
√कृ (8P) (do)	कर्तृ	→	कर्ता
√गम् (1P) (go)	गन्तृ	→	गन्ता
√भू (1P) (be)	भवितृ	→	भविता

b. मध्यम and उत्तमपुरुष forms:

Root			
√कृ	कर्तास्मि	(कर्ता + अस्मि)	(I shall do)
√गम्	गन्तासि	(गन्ता + असि)	(you will go)
√भू	भवितास्वः	(भविता + स्वः)	(we two shall be)

ii. प्रथमपुरुष forms differ from those of the other persons in that the finite form of अस् is normally omitted. Since without this form it is impossible to indicate number, the remaining agentive noun normally takes its proper number.

Examples:

Root		लुट्
√कृ	कर्ता	(he will do)
√गम्	गन्तारौ	(they [2] will go)
√भू	भवितारः	(they will be)

Only context can help you distinguish these future forms from the normal use of the agentive nouns.

16.13 The complete paradigm of √भू would be:

	एक°	द्वि°	बहु°
प्रथम°	भविता	भवितारौ	भवितारः
मध्यम°	भवितासि	भवितास्थः	भवितास्थ
उत्तम°	भवितास्मि	भवितास्वः	भवितास्मः

16.14 The लुट् has no modes and occurs only in the परस्मैपद , regardless of the conjugation of the underlying root.

16.15 The लुट् is called अनद्यतन ("not today") or श्वस्तन ("pertaining to tomorrow") to distinguish it from the more general लृट्. This distinction, however, has not remained clear in the classical language.

Example:

हे सीते रामलक्ष्मणौ श्वो वनं गन्तारौ ।
त्वमपि गन्तासि वा न वा ।

(Oh Sītā, Rāma and Lakṣmaṇa *will go* to the forest tomorrow. *Will you* too *go* or not?)

16.16 **कृत्य : The "Gerundive" or Prescriptive Passive Participle**

The "gerundive" (not to be confused with the "gerund" of 11.5) is yet another of those extremely useful "verbal adjectives" that we call participles. This particular participle is like the भूते कृदन्त of a कर्मणि or भावे application as it requires the कर्तृ of the action or state expressed by its verbal root to be in the तृतीया विभक्ति. It is not uncommon, however, to find the कर्तृ of a gerundive in the षष्ठी. The participle, itself, is, when formed from a सकर्मक root, in agreement with its कर्मन्. Moreover, it is "prescriptive" in that the form indicates that the विशेष्य (thing modified) of this adjectival form **is to be, should be, ought to be** the object (where an object is possible) of the action or state expressed by the verbal root. Its force is very similar to that of the विधि लिङ् or optative mode.

Examples:

ब्राह्मणो न केनापि हन्तव्यः ।

(A brāhman is not *to be killed* by anyone.)

नार्यपि न कदापि हन्तव्या ।

(A woman, too, is never *to be killed*.)

रामेण राज्यं करणीयम् ।

(Rāma *should rule* the kingdom.)

महाभारतं दुर्विज्ञेयं देवैरपि ।
(The *Mahābhārata* is *hard to understand*, even for the gods.)

तन्न वक्तव्यं न मन्तव्यमपि ।
(That is not *to be said*, not even *thought*.)

तन्न मम कार्यम् ।
(I don't *have to do* that.)

a. The gerundive of अकर्मक roots is a participial equivalent of the भावे प्रयोग. As such, its कर्तृ, if expressed, must be in the तृतीया (or षष्ठी) while the form itself, having no कर्मन् with which to agree, must be प्रथमा, एक, नपुंसकलिङ्ग.
Examples:
अत्र मया स्थातव्यम् ।
(Lit.,) (*It is to be stayed* here by me.) (I *ought to stay* here.)

भवतु । मया गन्तव्यम् ।
(Very well, I *must go*.)

न कस्यापि गन्तव्यम् । सर्वेषां स्थातव्यम् ।
(No one *is to leave*. Everyone *must stay*.)

i. The gerundive of the root √भू is used idiomatically to indicate likelihood or probability. Here, as in other uses of the copula, the subject must be in the same case as its predicates. The case here is तृतीया.
Example:
तेन राज्ञा भवितव्यम् ।
(He *must be* king.)

ii. The form भवितव्यम् by itself is frequently used in conversation and dramatic dialogue in the sense of "very likely," "probably," "undoubtedly," etc.

16.17 The gerundive, because of its prescriptive nature, can be used as a polite imperative with a तृतीया form of one of the 2nd person pronouns expressed or implied.

Examples:

आगन्तव्यम् ।

(*Come*!)

गन्तव्यं यदि नाम निश्चितम् ।

(*Go*! If you have made up your mind.)

न भेतव्यं न भेतव्यम् । मयीह तिष्ठति न को ऽपि भयमनुभवतु ।

(*Do not fear, do not fear*. While I stand here, let no one experience fear.)

यद्यद्रोचते तद्ग्राह्यम् । यद्यन्न रोचते तत्त्याज्यम् ।

(*Take* what you like, *leave* what you don't.)

16.18 Gerundives, like other adjectives, may sometimes become nouns.

Examples:

√कृ → कार्यम्

(duty, what is to be done)

√पा → पेयम्

(beverage, what is to be drunk.)

16.19 **Formation of the Gerundive**

The gerundive may be formed from most roots by the addition of one of the following three suffixes:

-य -तव्य -अनीय

The rules for treatment of roots before these suffixes are as follows:

a. **The suffix -य**

The rules for the treatment of root vowels before -य are complex and, unusually for Sanskrit, allow a good deal of freedom.

i. **Root final vowels**

a. final आ always becomes ए.

Examples:

√ज्ञा	ज्ञेय	(to be known)
√पा	पेय	(to be drunk)

b. final vowels other than आ are treated variously. They may be unchanged, subject to गुण, or (less commonly) to वृद्धि. In some cases, the same root may show optionally any of these alternatives.

c. If the vowel is subjected to गुण or वृद्धि, then the strengthened vowel may if ए or ऐ and must if ओ or औ be treated as though it preceded a vowel (see 3.11). Thus:

ए	→	ए or अय्
ऐ	→	ऐ or आय्
ओ	→	अव्
औ	→	आव्

Examples:

Root	**Gerundive**		
√जि	जेय / जय्य	(गुण)	(to be conquered)
√भू	भव्य	(गुण)	(to be)
	भाव्य	(वृद्धि)	

d. If a final short vowel is not strengthened then the consonant त् often intervenes between the vowel and the suffix -य (cf. 11.7.b.ii).

Examples:

√जि	जित्य	(to be conquered)
√कृ	कृत्य	(to be done)

ii. **Root medial vowels**

a. medial अ is unchanged in some roots and lengthened in others.

Examples:

Root	**Gerundive**	
√गम्	गम्य	(to be gone [to])
√त्यज्	त्याज्य	(to be abandoned)

b. medial इ, उ, or ऋ vowels are unchanged in some roots and subjected to गुण in others.

Examples:

√द्विष्	द्वेष्य	(to be hated)
√युध्	योध्य	(to be fought)
√गुह्	गुह्य	(to be hidden)

Don't worry about the vagueness of these rules. You will come to recognize the common forms with practice.

b. **The suffix** -तव्य

This extremely common suffix is added in each case to the same stem that precedes the -तुम् of the infinitive (13.1), or the agentive suffix -तृ (10.0).

Examples:

√भू	भवितव्य	(probably)
√कृ	कर्तव्य	(to be done)
√वच्	वक्तव्य	(to be said)
√मन्	मन्तव्य	(to be thought)
√गम्	गन्तव्य	(to be gone)
√पठ्	पठितव्य	(to be read)
√दा	दातव्य	(to be given)
√भुज्	भोक्तव्य	(to be eaten)

c. **The suffix** -अनीय

In general, root vowels are subject to गुण before this suffix, which is rather less common than the other two.

Examples:

√कृ	करणीय	(to be done)

√गम्	गमनीय	(to be gone)
√रक्ष्	रक्षणीय	(to be protected)

Many roots, especially those ending in long आ, do not form gerundives with this suffix.

16.20 The difference of suffix does not change the meaning or use of the form. As can be seen from the above, one root may have several gerundives because of the three suffixes and the variety of forms possible before the suffix. On the other hand, not all roots actually occur with all suffixes, and in any case particular forms are often preferred.

Examples:

√कृ	कृत्य, कार्य, कर्तव्य, करणीय
√जि	जित्य, जेय, जय्य, जेतव्य
√भू	भव्य, भाव्य, भवितव्य

16.21 Roots that only occur in the present system (e.g., √पश् [1P] [see] and √ब्रू [2P] [say]) do not form gerundives or other non-present participles.

EXERCISES

A. Translate the reading into English.

B. Translate the following sentences into English:

॥१॥ रामेणाहं त्याज्येति चिन्तयित्वा सीता भीता भविष्यतीत्येवं मन्ये ऽहम् ।

॥२॥ रामश्चेद्राक्षसान्नाहनिष्यद्ध्रुवं सर्वे नष्टा अभविष्याम । ततस्तस्मै लोकरक्षकाय रामचन्द्राय नमः ।

॥३॥ पश्यत । त्यक्तराज्यौ राघवौ मुनिभ्यः सर्वं धनं दातारौ । साधु साधु । अहमपि सर्वं त्यक्तास्मि । ततस्तापसवस्त्रं गृहीत्वा वने वत्स्यामि ।

॥४॥ दशरथभार्या कस्मादकर्तव्यं कर्म करोति । तत्पापकर्मणः कारणं दुर्विज्ञेयम् । कैकेयी प्रष्टव्या ।

॥५॥ हा हा नगरसुखानि कथं कोमलबालकाभ्यामतिकोमलया सीतया च त्याज्यानि । किं तैः कार्यं कर्कशवनेषु ।

॥६॥ रामचन्द्रस्य चन्द्रमुखं सर्वदा सर्वैर्दर्शनीयम् । तस्य मधुरवाक्यानि श्राव्याणि । तदानन्दकारणचरितं ध्यातव्यमपि ।

C. Translate the following sentences into Sanskrit:

1. If I do not see the moon-face of the beloved son of the king, I shall abandon my body.
2. Who gives what is to be given, who says what is to be said, he is one whose duty (i.e., what is to be done) is done. (Use a बहुव्रीहि.)
3. Listen! I shall go wherever the son of the king goes. If I have to go (use a gerundive) to the dreadful forest, the abode of deer, monkeys, and rākṣasa-s, then I shall not stay in Ayodhyā.

D. Compose five simple Sanskrit sentences using लृट् forms of the following roots:

√हन् √कृ √भू √गम् √दृश्

- Now substitute in your sentences the लुट्.

- Compose five sentences using gerundives of these same roots.

E. Translate and memorize the following verse.

धन्या द्रक्ष्यन्ति रामस्य ताराधिपसमं मुखम् ।
सदृशं शारदस्येन्दोः फुल्लस्य कमलस्य च ॥

READING

हा रामलक्ष्मणौ वनं गन्तारौ । ताभ्यां सह वैदेह्यपि गमिष्यति । हा रघुकुलनन्दनेन विना कथं जीवितव्यमिति विलपन्तो ऽयोध्यावासिनो जनाः शुष्कजले सरसि मत्स्या इवादृश्यन्त । भयशोकपीडितराजो ऽप्यनुज्ञार्थमागच्छन्तं सुतं दृष्ट्वा पुत्ररहितो ऽचिरान्मरिष्यामीति चिन्तयन्नवदत्स्थातव्यं वत्स न त्वया गन्तव्यम् । हे राघव मम वाक्यं न केवलं त्वया श्रोतव्यं हृदये ऽपि धातव्यम् । कैकेयीवरदानमोहितस्य मम वचनेन त्वया राज्यं न त्याज्यम् । अहं निग्रहणीय इति । तच्छ्रुत्वा सत्यवादी रामो ऽञ्जलिं कृत्वावदत् । न वक्तव्यमिदं वचनं न मन्तव्यमपि । राज्यं करोतु भरतः । अहं वनवासमाचरिष्यामि । प्रतिज्ञान्ते भवत्पादौ पुनर्ग्रहीष्यामि । अपि च

यान्गुणानद्य प्राप्स्यामि कः श्वो मह्यं दास्यति तान् । अतो ऽहं सराष्ट्रजनधनधान्यां पृथिवीं विसृष्टास्मि । भरताय सा देया । अद्य वनं गन्तास्मीति । ततः पितरं त्यक्त्वा ससीतालक्ष्मणो रामस्त्यक्तभोगस्य मे वने वन्येन जीवतः किं कार्यं धनेनेति चिन्तयन्सर्वं धनं ब्राह्मणेभ्यो दत्त्वा मुनिवस्त्रं गृहीत्वा वनं गन्तुं प्रारभत । ततो विगतानन्दा जना रामविरहितनगरं चन्द्रहीनमिवाकाशं तोयहीनमिवार्णवमपश्यन् । दशरथो ऽपि प्रियपुत्रं वनगतं विज्ञाय शोकशल्यहतमना मुनेः शापमनुस्मृत्य हा हा लभे ऽहं मुनिशापफलमिति वदन्नेव महाराजः प्राणानत्यजत् ॥

GLOSSARY

अञ्जलिः
(m)—gesture of reverence or supplication made by placing the palms together

अधिपः
(m)—ruler

अर्णवः
(m)—the sea

अर्थम्
(ind)—(at end of a compound) for the purpose of, for the sake of

अन्तः
(m)—end

आकाशम्
(n)—sky

कमलम्
(n)—lotus

कर्कश
(adj)—rough, harsh

कुलम्
(n)—family

कोमल
(adj)—tender

√ग्रह्
(9P)—seize, grasp

चन्द्रः
(m)—moon

जरा
(f)—old age

जलम्
(n)—water

ताराधिपः
(m)—lord of the stars; the moon

तोयम्
(n)—water

दानम्
(n)—giving, granting

√दृश्
to see, to look upon, regard, consider (supplements पश् in non-present conjugations)

धनम्
(n)—wealth

धन्य
(adj)—fortunate

√धा
(3P)—to put *or* place (16)

धान्यम्
(n)—grain

नन्दनः
(m)—causer of joy

नि + √ग्रह्
(9P)—imprison

पादः
(m)—foot

प्र + आ + √रभ्
(1Ā)—start, undertake

प्राणः
(m)—the breath; प्राणान्+√त्यज् [1P] = "abandon life breaths," die

प्र + √आप्
(5P)—receive, get

फलम्
(n)—fruit

फुल्ल
(adj)—blooming

भयम्
(n)—fear, alarm

भोगः
(m)—sensual enjoyment

मत्स्यः
(m)—fish

√मृ
(1P)—die

मोहित
(adj)—deluded

रहित
(adj)—devoid of, missing (esp. at end of compound); example:
जलरहित—without water

राष्ट्रम्
(n)—kingdom

वत्सः
(m)—calf, son; in सम्बोधन as term of endearment, 'my dear child'

वन्यम्
(n)—forest-food; i.e., gathered food as opposed to cultivated

वस्त्रम्
(n)—garment, clothing

वादिन्
(m)—speaker

वासः
(m)—clothing

वि + √ज्ञा
(9Ā)—realize

विरहित
(adj)—deserted, separated from

वि + √सृज्
(6P)—release, give-up

वैदेही
(f prop)—Vaidehī ("lady from Videha"), Sītā

शल्यम्
(n)—arrow, spear

शारद
(adj)—autumnal

शाला
(f)—room, chamber, house, hut

शुष्क
(adj)—dried up

श्वः
(ind)—tomorrow
सरः
(n)—lake
सहस्रम्
(n)—a thousand

√सृज्
(6P)—release
√सृप्
(1P)—move
हीन
(adj) = रहित

ENGLISH-SANSKRIT GLOSSARY

abode	वासनम्	(n)
body	शरीरम्	(n)
deer	मृगः	(m)
dreadful	घोर	(adj)
face	मुखम्	(n)
monkey	वानरः	(m)
oppressed	पीडित	(adj)

LESSON 17

परोक्षभूते लिट् (The Perfect); The Perfect Participle

17.0 The लिट्, or "perfect," is the last of the finite verbal conjugations in very frequent use. Like the लङ्, it functions as a simple narrative past. The term "perfect," like the term "imperfect," was given to the form by Western philologists and has no significance with regard to "aspect" or duration of action or states expressed.

17.1 The traditional Indian grammatical texts do attempt to distinguish the functions of the two forms (लङ् and लिट्). They say that the लङ् expresses अनद्यतनभूतकाल, or past time (not today) that was witnessed directly by the speaker, while the लिट् expresses परोक्षभूतकाल, (past time not directly perceived) an action not witnessed by the speaker. In fact, however, as is the case with all parts of the verbal system (cf. 16.15, etc.), such distinctions are not generally maintained in actual usage.

17.2 The लिट्, then, is used as yet another simple preterite tense. Thus, the following sentences all mean the same thing. (No translation, it is to be hoped, is necessary.)

रामो वनं गच्छति स्म ।	(लट्)
रामो वनमगच्छत् ।	(लङ्)
रामो वनं गतः ।	(भूते कृदन्त)
रामो वनं गतवान् ।	(क्तवतु or 'past active participle')
रामो वनं जगाम ।	(लिट्)

17.3 **Use of the लिट्**

The general use of the लिट्, then, requires no particular comment.

a. It might, however, be noted here that by an extension of the grammarians' prescription of the form for परोक्ष time, poetic (and pedantic) usage may reserve the उत्तमपुरुष forms of the लिट् for actions of which the speaker (who is also the subject) has no clear recollection, or is unconscious. Such usage is, of course, rare.

Example:

उन्मत्त इव बहु प्रललप राजसमीपे ।

(I prattled on like a drunkard in the presence of the king.)

b. The लिट् also has a few stereotyped usages. When in epic or *purāṇic* texts a new speaker is introduced, this is generally marked by his or her name or title and the appropriate लिट् of the root √वच्.

Examples:

राम उवाच (Rāma said)

ऋषय ऊचुः (the *ṛṣi*-s said)

c. Commentators on texts often use the root √अह् (say), which occurs only in the लिट्, to suggest or paraphrase what the author on whose work they are commenting is going to say. Thus: वनगमनानन्तरं रामः किमकरोदित्याह । ("What did Rāma do after going to the forest?" He [i.e., the author] now *says*.)

d. At the end of some *purāṇic* texts, the प्रथमा° एक° लिट् of √अस् is used to indicate the end of a narrative. The phrase used is इति हास (इति + ह + आस) (Thus it was. . .). The phrase in time has become a noun इतिहासः (m) (history, chronicle, legend, or story).

17.4 Formation of the लिट्

The forms of the लिट्, however, present a wide and initially intimidating variety of phonological and morphological contingencies. These need not be memorized immediately. It is important, however, to learn to recognize लिट् forms and how to generate some of the more important ones. This is made much simpler by the fact that, within certain limits of variation, most लिट् forms exhibit one or more of a number of typical and easily recognizable characteristics. These signs are:

a. The use of अभ्यास (reduplication) in the formation of the लिट् stem.

b. Characteristic strong-weak alternation in the लिट् stem.

c. Special personal endings.

17.5 All of these features involve a certain amount of irregularity which will be discussed separately under each heading.

17.6 **अभ्यास : Reduplication**

The most characteristic feature of the "perfect" system is that virtually all its stems are formed by the peculiar process known as अभ्यास. This is the same process introduced in connection with the third गण of the present system (7.22-25). In fact, the particular rules for लिट् अभ्यास are much the same as those for the third गण. There are, however, some differences and some additional rules. Only the latter are detailed below, so review **carefully** the rules for the formation of present stems of the third गण.

a. **Treatment of consonants**

Root consonants are treated just as in the present stems of the third गण. Note, however, that the consonant ज् of the root √जि (conquer) and the consonant ह् of the root √हन् (kill) are changed to कण्ठ्य (velar) sounds in the root portion of the लिट् stems.

Examples:

root	लिट्	
√जि (1P)	जिगाय	(he conquered)
√हन् (2P)	जघान	(he killed)

b. **Treatment of root medial and final vowels**

i. Root vowel ऋ always becomes अ in the अभ्यास syllable (cf.7.23.b).

Examples:

root	लिट्	
√कृ (do)	चकार	(he did)
√भृ (bear)	बभार	(he bore) (cf. बिभर्ति [लट्])

ii. Other non-initial root vowels reduplicate as in the present stems of the third गण, but a very important exception, which must be learned immediately, is that the root √भू has ब as its अभ्यास, so that its लिट् stem is बभू (see 17.9.a below).

iii. Certain common roots beginning with व (and in the case of यज्, य) followed by a single final consonant (cf. 9.27.d) are subject in several forms to a distinctive weakening. This process is known as संप्रसारण These roots, e.g., √वच्, √वद्, √वप्, √वश्, √वस्, √वह्, and √यज्, take respectively their संप्रसारण vowel (i.e., उ or इ) as their अभ्यास syllables. This, in turn, is prefixed to the full (or strengthened) grade of the root in strong forms (see 17.8.f). In weak forms, however, the root, too, is subject to संप्रसारण and the contact of the two similar short vowels yields the corresponding long vowel (3.3).

Root	**Strong लिट् form**	**Weak लिट् form**
√वच् (P) (say)	उवाच (he said)	ऊचुः (they said)
√यज् (P) (sacrifice)	इयाज (he sacrificed)	ईजुः (they sacrificed)

c. **Treatment of root initial vowels**

i. Roots with initial vowels may form the reduplicated लिट् only if the syllable of the root is लघु (light). Sanskrit syllables are considered either लघु (light) or गुरु (heavy) depending on the nature of their vowel.

a. Long vowels, संयुक्त vowels, and any vowels that immediately precede a consonant cluster, अनुस्वार, or विसर्ग are गुरु (cf. 7.16).

b. Short vowels, unless they precede a cluster, अनुस्वार, or विसर्ग , are लघु. Roots with a गुरु vowel (as in i. above) in initial position do not form a reduplicated लिट् but have a corresponding form, the periphrastic perfect, which is treated below (17.18). The only exception to this rule is the root √आप्(5P) (obtain), which forms a reduplicated लिट् as though from a root √*अप्.

ii. Root initial short vowels

a. The vowel अ (and the आ of √आप्) are reduplicated, and the result of the contact of the two vowels is, of course, आ.

Examples:

√अस् (P)	(be)	आस	(he was)
√अह् (P)	(say)	आह	(he said)
√आप् (P)	(obtain)	आप	(he obtained)

b. Initial इ and उ are likewise reduplicated, but the coalescence of the two short vowels to a long occurs **only** in weak forms (see 17.13). In strong forms:

1. the root vowel is subject to गुण, and
2. the अभ्यास is separated from it by its corresponding semi-vowel.

Example:

Root	**Strong लिट्**	**Weak लिट्**
√इष् (wish)	इयेष (wished)	ईषुः (they wished)

c. Do not worry about roots beginning with ऋ.

17.7 There are two important exceptions to the rules regarding अभ्यास.

a. If a root fulfills all of the criteria listed below, then **in weak forms only** (see 17.13), it is subject to the phenomena of

i. अभ्यासलोप (loss of reduplication), and

ii. एत्वम् (change of medial अ to ए).

The criteria are:

1. The root must be of the form consonant-vowel-consonant with both consonants simple (i.e., not part of a cluster).

2. The vowel must be अ.
3. In general, the first consonant must be one which is not altered in अभ्यास (i.e., it must not be aspirate, कण्ठय [velar] or ह्).

   Examples:

Root	**Strong**	**Weak**
√तप् (be hot)	ततापा (he was heated)	तेपुः (they were heated)
√शप् (curse)	शशाप (he cursed)	शेपुः (they cursed)
√पत् (fall)	पपात (he fell)	पेतुः (they fell)

4. Some roots, however, will optionally undergo अभ्यासलोप and एत्वम्, even though they do not conform to the rules above.

   Examples:

√फल्	(to bear fruit)	फेलिरे (they bore fruit)
√भज्	(to share)	भेजुः (they shared)

b. The root √विद् (2P), "know," has no अभ्यास in its लिट् forms. Furthermore, the form is commonly used as a present tense; सर्वं खल्विदं ब्रह्मेति । य एवं वेद स एव तत्त्वज्ञः । स मोक्षं लभते । (All this [world] is truly Brahman. Who *knows* this, he alone is a knower of essential truth. He will gain liberation.)

17.8 **Stem strength in the लिट्**

The perfect is exactly like the non-अ गण-s of the present system in its general distinction of strong and weak forms (7.9, 10). Here, too, the एकवचन परस्मैपद forms are strong, while the others (द्विवचन and बहुवचन परस्मैपद and all the आत्मनेपद forms) are weak.

a. In general, as with the present system, the distinction is maintained by a strengthening of the root vowel of the strong forms while the weak forms retain the root vowel in its original grade.

i. This does not pertain to root initial अ. For the rules governing other root initial vowels, see 17.6.c.ii.

17.9 It is characteristic of roots with a final vowel that among the strong forms themselves there is a regular alternation of root vowel strength. The system of root final vowel strength in the strong forms is:

Form	**Vowel Strength**
प्रथमपुरुष	वृद्धि
मध्यमपुरुष	गुण
उत्तमपुरुष	गुण or वृद्धि

Examples:

	प्रथम°	मध्यम°	उत्तम°
√कृ (do)	चकार	चकर्थ	चकर / चकार
√भी (fear)	बिभाय	बिभेथ	बिभय / बिभाय

a. The extremely important root √भू, however, is irregular in this regard. Its root vowel is unstrengthened and is set off from vowel endings by its corresponding semi-vowel -व् (for irregular अभ्यास, see17.6.ii above).

Example:

	प्रथम°	मध्यम°	उत्तम°
√भू (be)	बभूव	बभूविथ	बभूव

b. For the treatment of root final आ, see 17.14.b.

17.10 Root medial अ, which occurs very frequently, follows the analogy of root-final vowels in the strong forms. That is, it takes वृद्धि (=length) in the प्रथमपुरुष, गुण (=no change) in the मध्यम° and optionally, गुण or वृद्धि in the उत्तम°. Since roots with medial अ are so common, their forms are among the most typical of the लिट्. The rhythm of the strong forms, particularly of the प्रथमपुरुष short-long-short (अ-आ-अ), is an easily recognizable sign of the perfects of the roots.

Examples:	प्रथम°	मध्यम°	उत्तम°
√गम् (go)	जगाम	जगमिथ	जगम / जगाम
√शक् (be able)	शशाक	शशक्थ	शशक / शशाक
√पत् (fall)	पपात	पपतिथ	पपत / पपात
√हन् (kill)	जघान	जघन्थ	जघन / जघान

17.11 Other medial vowels are subject to गुण in all strong forms.

Examples:

Root	प्र° एक°
√भिद् (split)	बिभेद
√कुप् (be angry)	चुकोप

17.12 The above rules of stem strength in strong forms do not apply to vowels which are गुरु (see 17.6.c.i). Such vowels take no strength and so their perfects do not exhibit the strong-weak distinction.

Examples:

Root	प्र° एक°	प्र° बहु°
√चुम्ब् (kiss)	चुचुम्ब	चुचुम्बुः (they kissed)
√नन्द् (rejoice)	ननन्द	ननन्दुः (they rejoiced)

17.13 The weak forms usually show the root vowel with no change.

Examples:

Root	**Strong**	**Weak**
√कृ (do)	चकार	चक्रुः (they did)
√छिद् (cut)	चिच्छेद	चिच्छिदिम (we cut)

However, a few roots with medial -अ-, but which, by reason of their first consonant's being subject to change in अभ्यास, do not qualify for अभ्यासलोप and एत्वम् (17.7.a), show a weakening of their root vowel in the weak forms. This weakening, which has no bearing on the variable strength of the strong forms as shown at 17.10, involves the complete loss of the root vowel. The four most important roots that exhibit this phenomenon are √हन् (kill), √जन् (be born), √गम् (go), and √खन् (dig):

Examples:

	प्रथम° एक°		प्रथम° बहु°	
√गम् (P)	जगाम	(he went)	जग्मुः	(they went)
√हन् (P)	जघान	(he killed)	जघ्नुः	(they killed)
√जन् (Ā)	जज्ञे	(he was born)	जज्ञिरे	(they were born)
√खन् (P)	चखान	(he dug)	चख्नुः	(they dug)

17.14 The लिट् endings are as follows:

	परस्मैपद			आत्मनेपद		
	एक°	द्वि°	बहु°	एक°	द्वि°	बहु°
प्र°	-अ [औ]	-अतुः	-उः	-ए	-आते	-[इ] रे
म°	-थ	-अथुः	-अ	-से	-आथे	-ध्वे
उ°	-अ [औ]	-व	-म	-ए	-वहे	-महे

a. The परस्मैपद endings are generally peculiar to the perfect. Only -व, -म, and -उः are the same as the corresponding secondary (e.g., लङ् or लिङ्) endings. On the other hand, the आत्मनेपद endings are the same as the corresponding primary (e.g., लट्) endings—with the exception of the प्रथम° एक° and बहुवचन. It is important that you learn the प्रथमपुरुष endings at once.

b. The bracketed ending -औ is the regular प्रथम° and उत्तम°, एक° परस्मैपद ending for roots with final आ (and, more rarely, संयुक्त vowels).

Examples:

Root	प्रथम° / उत्तम° एक° परस्मैपद	
√या (go)	ययौ	(he/ I went)
√स्था(stand)	तस्थौ	(he/ I stood)
√ज्ञा (know)	जज्ञौ	(he/ I knew)
√दा (give)	ददौ	(he/ I gave)
√पा (drink)	पपौ	(he/ I drank)
√गै (sing)	जगौ	(he/ I sang)
√धा (place)	दधौ	(he/ I placed)

c. These roots are also peculiar in that they lose their root vowels before any ending beginning with a vowel or preceded by the vowel इ.

Example:

Root	प्रथम° बहु° परस्मैपद
√स्था	तस्थुः

These forms, particularly those ending in औ are also typical and easily recognizable "perfect" forms.

17.15 The लिट् endings that begin with consonants (-थ, -व, -म, -रे, -से, -ध्वे, -वहे, and -महे) are, moreover, frequently separated from the perfect stem by the vowel इ. The application of this vowel, which is not wholly dependent upon whether the root in question is अनिट्, सेट्, or वेट्, is summarized as follows:

a. The प्रथमपुरुष, बहुवचन, आत्मनेपद ending is **always** preceded by इ. Since this rule has no exceptions, it is useful to remember this ending as -इरे.

Examples:

√भाष्	→	बभाषिरे	(they spoke)
√मन्	→	मेनिरे	(they thought) (See 17.7.a.)

b. The मध्यमपुरुष, एकवचन, परस्मैपद ending -थ takes the इ sporadically. Many roots take it optionally, and in the case of those in final -आ, the root vowel is lost before it (17.14.c).

For example:

Root		
√दा	→	ददाथ/ददिथ (you gave)

c. The remaining six consonant-initial endings (-व, -म, -से, -ध्वे, -महे, and -वहे) may or may not take इ **but in practice almost always do so**.

Examples:

Root	**consonant endings**
√भाष् (Ā)	बभाषिमहे (we spoke)

√गम् (P) जग्मिव (we two went)
√वच् (P) ऊचिव (we two spoke)
√मन् (Ā) मेनिध्वे (you thought) (See 17.7.a.)

d. Several roots ending in the vowels उ and ऋ do not take the इ except, of course, before -रे. These roots are:

(in उ)	(in ऋ)
√स्तु (praise)	√कृ (do)
√द्रु (run, flow)	√भृ (bear)
√स्रु (flow)	√वृ (choose)
√श्रु (hear)	√सृ (move)

All of these roots are fairly common and some, like √कृ and √श्रु, are extremely so.

Examples:

चकर्थ (you did)
चकृम (we did)
शुश्रुव (we two heard)

17.16 These, then, are the basic rules for the formation of the लिट्. Do not attempt at this point to memorize them all. Do, however, familiarize yourself with the varieties of formation and strength of the various perfect stems. Pay special attention to the basic types of लिट् sound patterns. Review these paragraphs several times. You **should** memorize all the प्रथमपुरुष endings with their typical forms for the types of roots mentioned above.

17.17 Some examples of the लिट्:

वाल्मीकिरुवाच ।
यदा पिता स्वसुतविवर्णमुखं ददर्श तदा निःश्वसन्भूमौ निपपात।
(Vālmīki *said*: "When the father *saw* the pale face of his own son, he *fell* sighing to the ground.")

भरतो राजा भविष्यतीत्युक्त्वा रामलक्ष्मणौ वनं जग्मतुः ।
(Having said "Bharata will be king," Rāma and Lakṣmaṇa *went* to the forest.)

वनं गत्वा श्रीरामचन्द्रो मुनिभ्यो ऽभयं ददौ । ततो दुष्टराक्षसानां शिरांसि सर्पदन्ततीक्ष्णशरैश्चिच्छेद ।

(Having gone to the forest, Śrī Rāma *gave* fearlessness to the *munis*. Then he *cut off* the heads of the wicked *rākṣasas* with arrows as sharp as serpents' teeth.)

तत एव राक्षसानां महाभयमुद्बभूव । यत्र यत्र तस्थतुर्वीरौ राघवौ तत्र तत्र निशाचरा बहु विलेपुः ।

(Because of that, great dread *sprang up* among the *rākṣasas*. Wherever the two Rāghava heroes *stood*, there the rangers of the night [*rākṣasas*] *lamented* greatly.)

तदनन्तरमन्यद्वनं जगाम रघुपतिः । तत्र च महातपस्तेपे सः ।

(Then the lord of the Raghus [Rāma] *went* to another forest. There he *performed* great *austerities*.)

17.18 लिट् Continued: The Periphrastic Perfect

As mentioned at 17.6.c.i, roots of a certain phonological type do not form the ordinary reduplicated perfect. These are roots that have an initial vowel which is गुरु either by nature (long or संयुक्त) or by position (preceding a conjunct consonant). Such roots are, in fact, relatively rare and of no great consequence. The form that they take that corresponds to the reduplicated लिट्, however, is of considerable interest because of its other applications. This form is also called लिट् by the grammarians. Western grammarians call it the periphrastic perfect. Like the periphrastic future (लुट्), it is made up of a fixed nominal and a variable verbal form.

17.19 Formation of the Periphrastic Perfect

The formation of the periphrastic perfect is quite simple. The nominal element is formed by suffixing -आम् directly to the root. This form is then followed in the परस्मैपद by the appropriate लिट् of the roots √अस्, √कृ, or less often √भू. In the आत्मनेपद, the auxiliary verb is the आत्मनेपद form of √कृ only.

17.20 Thus, for example, for the roots √आस् (2Ā), "sit," and √एध् (1Ā), "grow," the प्रथम°, एक°, आत्मनेपद forms would be आसां चक्रे and एधां चक्रे. In the epic, √आस् is sometimes taken as परस्मैपद, and so its लिट् form could be आसामास, आसांचकार, or आसांबभूव. The प्रथम°, बहु°, परस्मैपद would then be आसामासुः (-चक्रुः, -बभूवुः). The root √आप् is exempt from this formation (17.6.c.i.b).

17.21 This form is also used instead of the reduplicated लिट् for roots of the tenth गण. Here, however, the syllable -आम् is added, not to the root, but to the present stem.

Examples:

Root		**Periphrastic perfect**	
√चुर्	(steal)	चोरयामास	(he stole)
√चिन्त्	(think)	चिन्तयामास	(he thought)

17.22 By this last technique (i.e., suffixation of -आम् to the present stem) are formed the most significant occurrences of the periphrastic लिट्, the perfects of the secondary conjugations. These will be discussed in the following lesson.

17.23 **The Perfect Participle**

The लिट्, like लट् and the लृट्, has associated with it a verbal adjective. This one serves as a past active participle but is of extremely rare occurrence, being restricted in actual usage to a very few verbal roots.

17.24 Its masculine stem is formed by adding the suffix -वांस् to the weak form of the perfect stem. Thus, √कृ → चकृवांस्. If this stem is monosyllabic, the -वांस् is set off from the stem by the vowel इ (but see a.):

√स्था → तस्थिवांस् (stood)
√तप् → तेपिवांस् (heated)

a. In fact, this form and its peculiar declension is of interest mainly because a fairly common word, विद्वांस् (learned *or* wise man), is, in form, a perfect participle. Like the finite लिट् of the root √विद्, it loses both its reduplication and its past sense.

b. The paradigm is as follows:

i. पुंलिङ्ग—विद्वांस् (learned *or* wise man)

	एक°	द्वि°	बहु°
प्र°	विद्वान्	विद्वांसौ	विद्वांसः
द्वि°	विद्वांसम्	विद्वांसौ	विदुषः
तृ°	विदुषा	विद्वद्भ्याम्	विद्वद्भिः
च°	विदुषे	विद्वद्भ्याम्	विद्वद्भ्यः
प°	विदुषः	विद्वद्भ्याम्	विद्वद्भ्यः
ष°	विदुषः	विदुषोः	विदुषाम्
स°	विदुषि	विदुषोः	विद्वत्सु
सम्°	विद्वन्	विद्वांसौ	विद्वांसः

Note the संप्रसारण grade in the weak forms that occur before vowel initial terminations.

ii. नपुंसकलिङ्ग

प्र°, द्वि°, सम्°—विद्वत्	विदुषी	विद्वांसि

The remaining cases are the same as पुंलिङ्ग.

iii. स्त्रीलिङ्ग

ई is suffixed to the weakest stem (=विदुषी), and the declension follows (7.1).

EXERCISES

A. Translate the reading up to the line beginning हे पुत्रक.

B. Isolate all the लिट् forms in the passage translated for A, and give for each the प्रथमपुरुष, बहुवचन form.

C. Repeat A. and B. for the remainder of the reading.

D. Give the प्रथमपुरुष, एक° and बहुवचन लिट् of the following roots (Ā or P as indicated):

√शप्	(1P)	(curse)	√क्रुध्	(4P)	(be angry)
√कृ	(8P)	(do)	√भू	(1P)	(be)
√अस्	(2P)	(be)	√वस्	(1P)	(dwell)
√एध्	(1Ā)	(grow)	√यज्	(1P)	(sacrifice)
√आप्	(5P)	(obtain)	√चिन्त्	(10P)	(think)

√लभ्	(1Ā)	(obtain)	√धा	(3P)	(place)
√गम्	(1P)	(go)	√हन्	(2P)	(kill)

E. For review of the गण-s, provide the लङ् (imperfect) forms corresponding to those generated in D.

F. Translate the following into Sanskrit, using the लिट् whenever a preterite is called for:

1. When the sons of the aged king saw the students of the sages, they gave them fruits.
2. The leader of the army of the *rākṣasas*, his eyes red with anger, seized (√ग्रह्) the trembling daughter of the yogi and said, "Today you will be my wife, O one of the beautiful face (use बहुव्रीहि)."
3. When that supreme yogi, whose senses were subdued, heard the terrible news, he stood up and wept like a boy.

G. Read, translate, and memorize the following two verses. Note that the syntax here has nothing to do with the verse boundaries. (The last word of the first verse construes grammatically with the first word of the second.)

राजा दशरथः स्वर्गं जगाम विलपन्सुतम् ।
गते तु तस्मिन्भरतो वसिष्ठप्रमुखैर्द्विजैः ॥ १ ॥
नियुज्यमानो राज्याय नैच्छद्राज्यं महाबलः ।
स जगाम वनं वीरो रामपादप्रसादकः ॥ २ ॥

READING

ससीतालक्ष्मणे श्रीरामचन्द्रे दण्डकारण्यं गच्छति कैकेयीपुत्रो भरतो राजगृहे मातुलभवने कंचित्कालमुषित्वा सर्वं वृत्तमविज्ञाय पुनरयोध्यां प्रत्याययौ । स रथस्थः सँल्लक्ष्मीहीनं नगरं पश्यन्दुःखितमना राजमन्दिरं राजहीनं सिंहहीनं कन्दरमिव प्रविवेश । आदितो वृत्तान्तं कैकेयीवदनादेव श्रुत्वा

पितरं मृतं भ्रातरौ निर्वासितौ च ज्ञात्वा दशरथात्मजो ऽतीव शुशोच चुकोप च । भरत उवाच । धिक् त्वां पापे । किं कृतवती त्वम् । कुतः पुरुषव्याघ्रौ वनं जग्मतुः । ब्रूहि ब्रूहि किमक्रियत त्वया । एवमुक्ता स्वपुत्रेण सा रघुकुलाशनिरुत्तरं ददौ । हे पुत्रक त्वत्कृत एव मया सर्वमेतत्कृतम् । मा शोकमाश्रय वीर । अद्यप्रभृति राज्यं त्वया कर्तव्यमिति । स शोकपीडितमनास्तस्या विपरीतवचनं शुश्राव सकोपश्च बभाषे । किं मया कार्यं राज्येन । ज्येष्ठपुत्रो रामो यथाविध्यभिषिच्यताम् । अहमद्य वनं गन्तास्मि रामचन्द्रवदनं द्रष्टुम् । मया सह पुनरागमिष्यत्ययोध्यां रघुकुलनन्दनः । त्वं तावद्वनं गच्छ । अग्निं प्रविश्य रज्जुं कण्ठे बद्ध्वा वा नरकं प्राप्नुहि । तवान्या गतिर्नास्तीति । यदि रामं वनादानेतुं न शक्नोमि तर्हि लक्ष्मणवत्तत्रैव स्थास्यामीति चिन्तयामास । अन्ततः स रामानुजो दशरथस्य चतुर्थपुत्रेण शत्रुघ्नेन सह महत्या सेनया परिवृतो दण्डकारण्यगमनमारेभे ॥

GLOSSARY

अनुजः
(m)—'born after,' i.e., younger brother

अभि + √सिच् → अभिषिञ्चति
(6P)—anoint, consecrate

आदितः
(ind)—from the beginning

आ + √नी
(1P)—bring, fetch

आ + √श्रि
(1P)—have recourse to

उत्तरम्
(n)—reply

√एध्
(1Ā)—grow

कण्ठः
(m)—throat

कन्दरम्
(n)—cave

कृते
kṛte (ind)—on account of, for the sake of (used with genitive or at end of compound)

चतुर्थ
(adj)—fourth

तावत्
(ind)—meanwhile

धिक्
(ind)—particle expressing anger or contempt, "damn!"; may be used singly as an interjection. Example: हा धिक् "damn!" or to condemn or revile some particular person or object that must then be in the द्वितीया विभक्ति. Example: धिक् त्वाम् "damn you!"

नरकः
(m)—hell

नि + युज्
(7P)—install, appoint (with चतुर्थी or सप्तमी विभक्ति)

निर्वासित
(adj)—exiled

परिवृत्त
(adj)—surrounded

पुत्रकः
(m)—boy, son

प्रति + आ + √या
(2P)—come back to, return

प्रभृति
(ind)—(at end of cmpd., after ind., or the पञ्चमी) starting from. . . Examples: जन्मप्रभृति from birth on, अद्यप्रभृति from today onward

बद्ध
(adj)—bound

√बन्ध् → बध्नाति
(9P)—bind

मन्दिरम्
(n)—house, palace

मातुलः
(m)—maternal uncle

मृत
(adj)—dead

रज्जुः
(f)—rope

रथः
(m)—chariot

राजगृहम्
(n prop)—Rājagṛha, capital city of the Kekeyas

लक्ष्मी
(f)—fortune, prosperity, the goddess Lakṣmī

वदनम्
(n)—mouth

विपरीत
(adj)—perverse, contrary, false

वृत्त
(adj)—happened, occurred; -m (n)—news report

व्याघ्र
(m)—tiger (at end of cmpd. = "best of")

सेना
(f)—army

स्व
(adj)—(normally declined like pronoun) one's own; commonly used as prior member of a कर्मधारय. Example: स्वपुत्र his, (her) son, etc.

-स्थ
(adj)—standing (at end of cmpd. only)

ENGLISH-SANSKRIT GLOSSARY

anger	कोपः	(m)
beautiful, excellent	वर	(adj)
boy	बालकः	(m)
eye	नयनम्	(n)
face	आननम्	(n)
fruit	फलम्	(n)
leader	नायकः	(m)

news	वृत्तान्तः	(m)
red	रक्त	(adj)
sense	इन्द्रियम्	(n)
student	शिष्यः	(m)
subdued	जित	(adj)
supreme	परम	(adj)
tremble	उद् + √विज्	(6Ā)
weep	√रुद् → रोदिति	(2P) (see 7.20.c)

GLOSSARY FOR VERSES

(In order of occurrence)

वसिष्ठः
(m prop)—one of the great brahman *ṛṣi*-s of Indian tradition

स्वर्गः
(m)—heaven

वि + √लप्
(1P)—lament

प्रमुख
(adj)—foremost

द्विजः
(m)—'twice-born,' a brahman

नि + √युज्
(7P)—install, appoint (with चतुर्थी or सप्तमी)

बलम्
(n)—power, strength

पादः
(m)—foot, esp., as part of the body touched in veneration of someone; hence after a name or title in a compound it means that person referred to with reverence. For example: 'the foot of Rāma,' i.e., the venerable Rāma

प्रसादक
(adj)—propitiating

LESSON 18

णिजन्त, सन्नन्त, and यङन्त Secondary Conjugations; नामधातु (The Denominative)

18.0 With one exception, the characteristic signs of the various conjugated systems introduced thus far are alike in that they are markers only of tense or mode. In other words, the ten signs of the गण-s (7.4ff.), the -स्य of the future (16.2ff.), and the अभ्यास (reduplication) of the perfect (17.0ff.) suffice only to mark the general conjugation to which a verbal form belongs. They do not tell us anything about the action expressed by a verbal root except, in general, the relative time of the action.

18.1 The one exception is the य, characteristic of the कर्मणि प्रयोग (9.5ff.). This, unlike the others, tells us that the sentence or clause in which it appears is "passive." This special "passive" sign, however, is applicable only to forms which mirror the present system.

18.2 **Secondary Conjugations**

In addition to the conjugations discussed so far, Sanskrit has four special conjugations that, like the कर्मणि प्रयोग, indicate something about the action of a verbal root other than its tense.

18.3 These forms are also like the कर्मणि stems in -य in that they have a distinctive sign that is suffixed to a special form of the root to form a distinctive stem. They differ from the कर्मणि stems in -य and other present stems in that, in many cases, this distinctive secondary stem may serve as the basis for formations outside the present system. The secondary conjugations, then, are not tenses but special derivative stem formations that in turn are used, like verbal roots, as the basis for various conjugations. It is for this reason that these forms are said to be "secondary" conjugations. It is also for this reason that the forms are identified in Sanskrit by their special stem-forming suffixes:

णिजन्त (ending in णिच्),
यङन्त (ending in यङ्),
सन्नन्त (ending in सन्).

The forms are discussed below in order of decreasing importance.

18.4 णिजन्त (प्रेरक): **The Causative**

This is by far the most frequently used and important of the secondary conjugations. It is referred to either by its characteristic suffix (-अय्), which is called णिच् by the grammarians, or by the name प्रेरक ("causer," "impeller") for its function.

a. A णिजन्त verbal form indicates that its grammatical subject causes someone or something to carry out or undergo the action or state expressed by the underlying verbal root. Causative sentences, then, involve two कर्तृ-s: the subject of the causative (i.e., derivative) verb **and** the subject of the simple verb or the action or state expressed by the underlying verbal root. Take, for example, two sentences: रामो वनं गच्छति । (Rāma goes to the forest.) and दशरथो रामं वनं गमयति । (Daśaratha sends Rāma [causes Rāma to go] to the forest). In the first sentence रामः is, of course, the कर्तृ of the root √गम् (go) as he is the agent, the goer. In the second sentence, however, the finite verb is गमयति, which is formed not from √गम् but rather from गमय् (cause to go), the णिजन्त derivative of √गम्. The कर्तृ of this form is दशरथः. Rāma remains the कर्तृ of the underlying root √गम् as he is still the one who does the actual going.

18.5 **कर्तृ-s of Underlying Roots**

The कर्तृ of a finite णिजन्त form is treated exactly like that of any other finite verbal form. It is in the प्रथमा विभक्ति if the form is a कर्तरि प्रयोग and in the तृतीया if it is a कर्मणि प्रयोग. The treatment of the कर्तृ of the underlying or simple verbal root, however, requires some explanation, especially as it is different depending on the transitivity of the underlying root.

a. अकर्मक धातु-s

With णिजन्त forms of अकर्मक धातु-s, including verbs of motion (see 4.38,41), the कर्तृ of the underlying root is placed in the द्वितीया विभक्ति. The णिजन्त forms even of अकर्मक धातु-s are themselves सकर्मक.

Examples:

Underlying root

√गम्	(go)	दशरथो रामं वनं गमयति । (Daśaratha makes Rāma go to the forest.)
√स्था	(stand)	सेवकः फलं स्वामिनो हस्ते स्थापयति । (The servant places a fruit in his master's hand.)
√पत्	(fall)	वानरा महावृक्षान्पातयन्ति । (The monkeys fell the great trees.)
√वस्	(dwell)	को मां वने वासयिष्यति । (Who will make me dwell in the forest?)
√भू	(be)	दशरथो रामं राजानं भावयति । (Daśaratha makes Rāma king.)

b. In the case of सकर्मक धातु-s, the कर्तृ of the underlying root is generally placed in the तृतीया विभक्ति, although the द्वितीया is sometimes encountered.

Examples:

Underlying root

√हन्	(kill)	सुग्रीवो रामेण वालिनं घातयति । (Sugrīva has Rāma kill Vālin.)
√कृ	(do)	रामो भरतेन राज्यं कारयामास । (Rāma had Bharata rule the kingdom.)

√दा (give) राजानुचरैर्धनं जनेभ्यो दापयेत् ।
(*Let* the king *cause* his attendants *to give* money to the people.)

i. Roots whose णिजन्त stems convey the senses of teaching, or feeding, are exceptions. With them the कर्तृ of the underlying root is placed in the द्वितीया. (See 18.10.a.iii.)
Examples:
गुरुः शिष्यान्पुस्तकानि पाठयति ।
(The guru has his students read the books.)

राजा ब्राह्मणं भोजयति ।
(The king feeds the brāhman.)

ii. The roots √अद् (2P) (eat) and √खाद् (1P) (eat) are exceptions to the exception. The subjects of their णिजन्त derivatives, आदय् (feed) and खादय् (feed) are in तृतीया.
Example:
हे सूत नृपाश्वैः खादय ।
(O charioteer, feed the king's horses.)

18.6 **Formation of the णिजन्त**

The formation of the णिजन्त is quite simple. In general the causative marker इ (णिच्) is suffixed directly to the root, which is usually strengthened. Because of additional strength of the इ in various forms, it is simplest to regard the causative marker as -अय्.

18.7 The rules for root-strength are as follows:

a. Initial or medial short vowels (except अ), if in a लघु syllable (see 17.6.c.i), usually take गुण.
Examples:

Root		णिजन्त	
√बुध् (1)	(be awake)	बोधय्	(awaken)
√विश् (6)	(enter)	वेशय्	(cause to enter)
√क्लृप् (1)	(be arranged)	कल्पय्	(arrange)

Some roots, however, have गुण only optionally.

Examples:

√शुभ् (1)	(shine, be beautiful)	शुभय् / शोभय् (make beautiful)

b. Initial or medial vowels in गुरु syllables (except अ) remain, as elsewhere, unstrengthened.

Example:

Root		णिजन्त	
√चुम्ब् (1)	(kiss)	चुम्बय्	(cause to kiss)

c. Medial or initial अ, if in a लघु syllable, is usually lengthened. For example:

Root		णिजन्त	
√त्यज् (1)	(abandon)	त्याजय्	(cause to abandon)
√पठ् (1)	(read)	पाठय्	(teach)
√अद् (2)	(eat)	आदय्	(feed)
√हन् (2)	(kill)	घातय्	(cause to kill)
		(Note irregular form)	

i. But a number of roots show no lengthening.

Examples:

√गम् (1)	(go)	गमय्	(cause to go)
√जन् (4)	(be born)	जनय्	(give birth to)

ii. In some cases both forms (i.e., with अ and आ) are citable from the same root.

Examples:

√क्रम् (1)	(step)	क्रमय् / क्रामय् (cause to step)
√शम् (4)	(be still)	शमय् / शामय् (calm, extinguish)

d. Final simple vowels, except आ, are nomrally subject to वृद्धि.

Examples:

Root		णिजन्त	
√भू (1)	(be)	भावय्	(cause to be)

√कृ (8)	(do)	कारय्	(cause to do)
√श्रु (5)	(hear)	श्रावय्	(cause to hear, teach)

e. Final आ (and संयुक्त vowels) are generally set off from the causative marker by the consonant प्. This is a characteristic sign of the णिजन्त forms of roots with such finals. For example:

Root		णिजन्त	
√स्था (3)	(stand)	स्थापय्	(place)
√दा (3)	(give)	दापय्	(cause to give)
√स्ना (2)	(bathe [intransitive])	स्नापय्	(bathe [transitive])
√ज्ञा (9)	(know)	ज्ञापय्	(inform)

A few roots show not the प्, but य्, before the णिच्.

Root		णिजन्त	
√पा (1)	(drink)	पायय्	(cause to drink)

f. The root √इ (2) (go), which would form आयय् by rule d., instead forms आपय् (a common verb meaning teach) when preceded by the उपसर्ग अधि.

18.8 **Forms of the णिजन्त**

Since the णिजन्त is a secondary or derivative verbal root, it is not restricted to any one conjugation but may be used fairly freely as the base for the various verbal systems. Note that except for the कर्मणि प्रयोग (18.10), the परस्मैपद endings are generally used for the causative, regardless of the voice of the simple root.

18.9 **The Present System**

The णिजन्त may serve as the base for a complete present system, exactly analogous to those of the अ गण roots of the present stem, formed by suffixing अ to the णिच् suffix -अय्. Therefore, the णिजन्त present stem is characterized by the sign -अय and is conjugated exactly like roots of the tenth (√चुर्) गण. प्रथमपुरुष

एकवचन forms of the णिजन्त of the root √स्था (stand) (stem स्थापय्) will suffice as an example:

लट्	स्थापयति	(he places)
लङ्	अस्थापयत्	(he placed)
लोट्	स्थापयतु	(let him place)
विधि लिङ्	स्थापयेत्	(he should place)
वर्तमाने कृदन्त	स्थापयन्त्	(placing)

18.10 The कर्मणि प्रयोग

A regular कर्मणि प्रयोग stem may be formed from the णिजन्त by replacing the causative sign -अय् with the regular कर्मणि प्रयोग sign -य. This is added to the root strengthened as for the causative (18.7), including the consonant प् where required (18.7.e). As usual with the कर्मणि प्रयोग, the आत्मनेपद endings are used.

Examples:

Root	कर्तरि णिजन्त	कर्मणि णिजन्त
√स्था	स्थापयति	स्थाप्यते
√गम्	गमयति	गम्यते
√लभ्	लाभयति	लाभ्यते
√श्रु	श्रावयति	श्राव्यते

a. When transforming कर्तरि प्रयोग into कर्मणि प्रयोग, it is necessary to be aware of the different treatment accorded the कर्तृ-s of सकर्मक and अकर्मक धातु-s (18.5).

i. अकर्मक धातु-s

णिजन्त forms of अकर्मक धातु-s are themselves सकर्मक. The कर्मणि प्रयोग is formed just as for a simple सकर्मक verbal form. For example:

कर्तरि—कन्या पक्षिणं पञ्जरे स्थापयति ।
कर्मणि—कन्यया पक्षी पञ्जरे स्थाप्यते ।
(The girl places the bird in the cage.)

ii. सकर्मक धातु-s

सकर्मक धातु-s are treated similarly. Here the कर्मन् of the णिजन्त (= the कर्तृ of the underlying root) is put into the प्रथमा विभक्ति, while the कर्तृ of the णिजन्त goes into the तृतीया विभक्ति.

Example:

कर्तरि—सुग्रीवो रामेण [रामं वा] वालिनं घातयति ।

कर्मणि—सुग्रीवेण रामो वालिनं घात्यते ।

(Sugrīva has Rāma kill Vālin.)

iii. Roots whose णिजन्त stems convey the senses of teaching or feeding, may optionally take their causal object (कर्मन् of the णिजन्त) in the प्रथमा विभक्ति or द्वितीया विभक्ति. In the first option, the कर्मन् of the underlying root is placed in the द्वितीया विभक्ति; in the second option, it is placed in the प्रथमा विभक्ति. (See 18.5.b.i.)

Examples:

कर्तरि— गुरुः शिष्यान्वेदान् पाठयति ।

कर्मणि— गुरुणा शिष्या वेदान् पाठ्यन्ते ।

कर्मणि—गुरुणा शिष्यान्वेदाः पाठ्यन्ते ।

(The guru has the students study the Vedas.)

कर्तरि—राजा ब्राह्मणमोदनं भोजयति ।

कर्मणि— राज्ञा ब्राह्मण ओदनं भोज्यते ।

कर्मणि— राज्ञा ब्राह्मणमोदनो भोज्यते ।

(The king feeds the brāhman rice.)

18.11 Other Formations

In conjunction with the following forms, it is important to note that causative stems are *always* सेट् (16.1.a). That is, they *always* have the vowel इ between them and the endings of the non-present forms for which the अनिट्—सेट् distinction is relevant.

18.12 भूते कृदन्त

The भूते कृदन्त and its counterpart the past active participle (in -तवन्त्) are formed by the suffixation of the ending directly to the root, strengthened according to 18.7, plus the इट्.

Examples:

Root		भूते कृदन्त	
√स्था	(stand)	स्थापित	(placed)
√दृश्	(see)	दर्शित	(shown)
√गम्	(go)	गमित	(banished)
√कृ	(do)	कारित	(caused to be done)
√कुप्	(be angry)	कोपितवन्त्	(angered [transitive])

18.13 **Gerund**

a. Without उपसर्ग

The normal ending -त्वा, preceded by the इट्, is added directly to the causative sign -अय्.

Examples:

Root		Gerund	
√स्था	(stand)	स्थापयित्वा	(having placed)
√कृ	(do)	कारयित्वा	(having caused to do)
√दृश	(see)	दर्शयित्वा	(having shown)
√गम्	(go)	गमयित्वा	(having banished)

b. With उपसर्ग

The normal ending -य replaces the causative sign.

Examples:

Root		Gerund	
अनु + कृ	(imitate)	अनुकार्य	(having caused to imitate)
प्रति + स्था	(be firm)	प्रतिष्ठाप्य	(having established)

c. When roots with medial अ that show no strength in the णिजन्त (18.7.c.i) are preceded by an उपसर्ग, the ending is added directly to the णिजन्त marker.

Examples:

Root		Gerund	
अव + गम्	(understand)	अवगमय्य	(having caused to understand)
अनु + जन्	(be born after)	अनुजनय्य	(having caused to be born after)

18.14 Infinitive

As with the gerund without उपसर्ग, the infinitive ending -तुम् preceded by the इट् is added to the causative marker.

Examples:

Root		Infinitive	
√स्था	(stand)	स्थापयितुम्	(to place)
√हन्	(kill)	घातयितुम्	(to kill)
√गम्	(go)	गमयितुम्	(to go)

18.15 Gerundive

a. -तव्य

Like -तुम् and -त्वा, the ending -तव्य preceded by इट् is added to the causative sign.

Examples:

Root		Gerundive	
√स्था	(stand)	स्थापयितव्य	(to be placed)
√गम्	(go)	गमयितव्य	(to be made to go)

b. -य

Like the -य of the कर्मणि प्रयोग the ending -य replaces the causative marker.

Examples:

Root		Gerundive	
√स्था	(stand)	स्थाप्य	(to be placed)
√गम्	(go)	गम्य	(to be made to go)

c. -अनीय

The ending -अनीय, like -य, replaces the causative marker:

Examples:

Root		Gerundive	
√स्था	(stand)	स्थापनीय	(to be placed)
√गम्	(go)	गमनीय	(to be made to go)

18.16 लृट्

The future sign -स्य preceded by the इट् (→ इष्य) is added to the causative marker.

Examples:

Root		लृट्	
√स्था	(stand)	स्थापयिष्यति	(he will place)
√गम्	(go)	गमयिष्यति	(he will cause to go)
√कृ	(do)	कारयिष्यति	(he will cause to do)

18.17 लुट्

The nominal suffix -तृ preceded by इट् is added to the causative sign. For example:

Root		लुट्	
√स्था	(stand)	स्थापयिता	(he will place)
√गम्	(go)	गमयितास्मि	(I will cause to go)

The nominal element may also serve as an agentive noun.

18.18 लिट्

The causative may form **only** the periphrastic perfect and in fact, accounts for the great majority of the occurrences of this form in the language. The periphrastic perfect is formed from the causative stem exactly as from the few simple roots that must take this form (17.18).

Examples:

Root		लिट्	
√स्था	(stand)	स्थापयामास (बभूव/चकार)	(he placed)
√कृ	(do)	कारयामास (बभूव/चकार)	(he caused to do)
√श्रु	(hear)	श्रावयामास (बभूव/चकार)	(he caused to hear, he taught)

18.19 **Uses of the णिजन्त**

As can easily be seen, it is extremely useful to have a simple grammatical form that can remove the subject of a verb one step from the action of a verbal root by making that subject the agent who impels another subject to act. This useful form is exploited often in Sanskrit. Keep in mind that, in many cases, the णिजन्त may be translated by a simple verb in English. Try to translate in this way whenever possible, avoiding such phrases "cause to" unless you feel that they are either stylistically sound, or unavoidable in English.

Examples:

√कुप्	(4)	(be angry)	कोपयति	(he angers)
√पत्	(1)	(fall)	पातयति	(he fells)
√स्वप्	(2)	(sleep)	स्वापयति	(he puts to sleep)
√पठ्	(1)	(read)	पाठयति	(he teaches)
√श्रु	(5)	(hear)	श्रावयति	(he announces, he teaches)
√स्था	(3)	(stand)	स्थापयति	(he puts, places)
√भुज्	(7)	(eat)	भोजयति	(he feeds)
√ज्ञा	(9)	(know)	ज्ञापयति	(he informs)

a. The णिजन्त of the common root √दृश् (दर्शयति) may, without change of form, be used both actively and passively in the senses of:

i. to cause to see;

ii. to show (i.e., cause to be seen).

The second usage may or may not take the आत्मनेपद endings and is especially common when the idea of one's showing oneself or something of one's own is intended.

Example:

ऋषिभ्यः स्वं विश्वरूपं दर्शयित्वा महेश्वरः कैलासं ययौ ।

(Having *manifested* his cosmic form to the *ṛṣis*, Maheśvara went to Kailāsa.)

18.20 सन्नन्त : The Desiderative

The सन्नन्त, or desiderative, is another derivative stem formed quite freely from most roots and causative derivatives. The form is considerably less common than the णिजन्त and is, in fact, chiefly represented by two derivative nominal forms.

18.21 The सन्नन्त indicates that the subject of the form desires to do or experience the action or state expressed by the underlying root. It may be paraphrased by the infinitive of the simple root with an appropriate form of √इष्, etc.

Examples:

रामो वनं जिगमिषति ।

= रामो वनं गन्तुमिच्छति ।

(Rāma wants to go to the forest.)

भवतां सेवां चिकीर्षामि ।

= भवतां सेवां कर्तुमिच्छामि ।

(I want to serve you [lit., do your service].)

18.22 **Formation of the सन्नन्त**

The form is made by suffixing the characteristic desiderative sign -स (called सन् by the grammarians), preceded in some cases by the इट् to a verbal root. The इट् occurs more or less as it does with the infinitive. The rules regarding formation are for your reference. You need not memorize them.

a. Before this sign (-स or -इष), the root is subject to अभ्यास.
   i. The reduplication of consonants is mostly the same as with the third गण and लिट् (7.22).
   ii. The treatment of vowels is somewhat different:
      a. अ, आ, ऋ, ॠ, (see a.ii.b.and b.ii and iii below) and इ, ई vowels all appear in the अभ्यास syllable as इ.
      Examples:

Root		**सन्नन्त Stem**	
√कृ	(do)	चिकीर्ष	(wish to do)
√गम्	(go)	जिगमिष	(wish to go)
√जि	(conquer)	जिगीष	(wish to conquer)
		(See 18.22.b.v.)	

b.Before स, ऋ or ॠ vowels when preceded by a labial consonant reduplicate as उ (see b.ii and iii below).

Example:

√मृ (die) मुमूर्ष (wish to die)

c. उ, ऊ, vowels appear as उ in the अभ्यास syllable.

Example:

√भू (be) बुभूष (wish to be)

b. The root syllable itself is usually unchanged, but:

i. Final इ and उ are lengthened before स.

Example:

√जि (conquer) जिगीष (wish to conquer)

ii. Final ऋ or ॠ becomes ईर् or ऊर् before स.

Examples:

√कृ (do) चिकीर्ष (wish to do)

√तॄ (cross) तितीर्ष (wish to cross)

√मृ (die) मुमूर्ष (wish to die)

iii. इ, उ, and ऋ vowels always, when final, and optionally when medial, take गुण before -इष.

Example:

√वृध् (grow) विवर्धिष (wish to grow)

iv. Some roots with final -अन् or -अम् lengthen their root vowel.

Examples:

√मन् (think) मीमांस (wish to think)

(Note irregular lengthening of reduplicated vowel.)

√हन् (kill) जिघांस (wish to kill)

(See 18.22.b.v)

v. Some initial तालव्य-s and ह् show reversion in the root syllable to कण्ठय-s after the अभ्यास syllable.

Examples:

√हन् (kill) जिघांस (wish to kill)

(See 1.22.b.iv.)

√जि	(conquer)	जिगीष	(wish to conquer)
but			
√ज्ञा	(know)	जिज्ञास	(wish to know)

vi. A few roots, notably √आप् (obtain), √दा (give), and √धा (place), have peculiarly contracted forms of अभ्यास and root. These forms are ईप्स (desire tc obtain), दित्स (desire to give), and धित्स (desire to place), respectively.

c. All सन्नन्त stems end in अ and are treated exactly like अ गण stems in the present system.

Examples:

Root	लट्	लोट्	लङ्
√कृ (do)	चिकीर्षति (he wishes to do)	चिकीर्षतु (let him wish to do)	अचिकीर्षत् (he wished to do)
	विधि लिङ्	वर्तमाने कृदन्त	
	चिकीर्षेत् (he should wish to do)	चिकीर्षन्त् (wishing to do)	

d. Like the other secondary stems, the सन्नन्त always forms its future with इट्.

Examples:

√कृ (do) चिकीर्षिष्यति । (he will wish to do) चिकीर्षितास्मि (I will wish to do)

e. Like the other derivative stems, it forms only the periphrastic perfect.

Example:

√कृ (do) चिकीर्षामास (he wished to do)

18.23 The most frequently encountered forms of the सन्नन्त are two nominal forms that are peculiar to it. These are:

1. an adjective ending in -उ that indicates that the person or thing modified by it is desirous of doing the action or undergoing the state expressed by the simple root.

2. a स्त्रीलिङ्ग noun in -आ that indicates the actual desire to do or undergo what is expressed by the simple root.

a. Both forms are derived by substituting the proper ending उ or आ for the final अ of the सन्नन्त stem.

Examples:

Root		**Stem**	**Adjective**	**Meaning**
√कृ	(do)	चिकीर्ष	चिकीर्षु	(wishing to do)
√युध्	(fight)	युयुत्स	युयुत्सु	(wishing to fight)
√ज्ञा	(know)	जिज्ञास	जिज्ञासु	(wishing to know, curious)

धर्मक्षेत्रे कुरुक्षेत्रे समवेता युयुत्सवः ।
मामकाः पाण्डवाश्चैव किमकुर्वत सञ्जय ॥
श्रीमद्भगवद्गीता १.१

(What did my sons and the sons of Pāṇḍu do, gathered on the Kuru field, the field of dharma, *eager for battle*, O Sañjaya.) (MEMORIZE THIS VERSE) (See 20.11.j.)

Examples:

Root	**Stem**	**Nominal form**	**Meaning**
√ज्ञा (think)	जिज्ञास	जिज्ञासा	(the desire to know curiosity)
√कृ (do)	चिकीर्ष	चिकीर्षा	(the desire to do)

b. A number of these nouns of type 2. take somewhat restricted meanings.

Examples:

Root	**Noun**	**Meaning**
√मन् (think)	मीमांसा	(inquiry, name of a philosophical school of vedic speculation)
√आप् (get)	ईप्सा	(desire [esp. to get])
√श्रु (hear)	शुश्रूषा	(obedience)
√बाध् (drive off)	बीभत्सा	(loathing, repulsion)
√पा (drink)	पिपासा	(thirst)
√भुज् (eat)	बुभुक्षा	(hunger)

18.24 A कर्मणि प्रयोग may be based on the सन्नन्त stem. The form is generated by substituting the कर्मणि marker य for the final अ of the desiderative stem and using, of course, the आत्मनेपद endings.

Examples:

√कृ (do)	मया चिकीर्ष्यते ।	(It is desired to be done by me [i.e., I want to do it].)
√आप् (obtain)	शुभमीप्स्यते सर्वैः ।	(Everyone wants the good.)

18.25 **सन्नन्त of णिजन्त**

It is possible to form a secondary verbal derivative based on another such derivative. An example would be बिभावयिषति, the प्रथम° एक° परस्मैपद लट् of the सन्नन्त derivative of the णिजन्त derivative of the root √भू (be). This would mean "he wishes to cause to be." Such tertiary forms are not at all common and need not be studied here.

18.26 **यङन्त, यङ्लुगन्त : The Intensive**

The last of the secondary verbal derivatives has two forms, the यङन्त and the यङ्लुगन्त. Called in English the intensive, or the frequentative, it indicates that the action or state signified by the verbal root is either repeated or of great force or intensity. Its characteristic is a reduplication marked by particularly strong forms of the अभ्यास syllable. It may (यङन्त) or may not (यङ्लुगन्त) have the stem sign य, called यङ् by the grammarians. The intensive can be made from nearly every root in the language except roots of more than one syllable, roots that begin with a vowel, and roots belonging to the tenth गण.

Examples:

चेक्रियते	(he does repeatedly)
देदीयते	(he gives generously)

a. **Stem Formation**

Both the यङन्त and the यङ्लुगन्त require अभ्यास (reduplication) to form their stems. The rules for अभ्यास are generally the same as those found for the third गण roots (7.22) and for the लिट् (perfect) (17.6). However, in the यङन्त the य is added to the root prior to reduplication and the root is subjected to the same changes that are found with the passive (9.25) stem formation. In the यङ्लुगन्त the reduplication is based on the root alone. In the intensive the reduplicated syllable is unusually strong. The strengthening of the reduplicated syllable is accomplished in one of three ways.

i. Like the third गण roots and the लिट्, the first consonant of a root is reduplicated. But unlike these, the root vowel in the reduplicated syllable is strong: अ and ऋ reduplicate as आ, इ and ई reduplicate as ए, and उ and ऊ reduplicate as ओ.

Examples:

	Root	Stem
यङ्लुगन्त		
	√वद्	वावद्
	√हु	जोहु
यङन्त		
	√दा	देदीय
	√भू	बोभूय

ii. The entire root is reduplicated. This type usually involves roots that end in र् or ल् or a nasal and that have अ or ऋ as their root vowels. Note that the final nasal of the reduplicated syllable assimilates to the following consonant and the root vowel ऋ is strengthened to either अर् or इर्.

Examples:

	Root	Stem
यङ्लुगन्त		
	√चर्	चर्चर्
	√हन्	जङ्घन्

√नम् नन्नम्
√कृ चर्कर् or चर्किर्

यङन्त

√जन् जञ्जन्य or जाजाय (following i.)

iii. This type of reduplication is seen in about thirty roots, most having final or penultimate न् or in roots with final or medial ऋ. Here the entire root is reduplicated, as in ii. above, but between the reduplicated syllable and the root and ई is inserted. Note here that the general rules of reduplication are for the most part ignored. Example:

	Root	**Stem**
यङ्लुगन्त		
	√गम्	गनीगम्
यङन्त		
	√वृत्	वरीवृत्य

b. **The यङ्लुगन्त**

This form of the intensive is similar to third गण roots of the present system (7.21 ff.), although it is conjugated only in the परस्मैपद. While in theory any verbal form in the language can be made from the यङ्लुगन्त, its occurrences are most commonly found in the present system. When conjugated in the present system, the reduplicated stem of the intensive will take strengthening where necessary (7.9). In strong forms, between the stem and consonant initial terminations, an ई may optionally be inserted (except when the reduplication follows type iii. above). Before this ई, root final vowel will take गुण, but a root medial vowel remains unchanged. Note that, like the conjugation of the 3rd गण, the प्रथम° बहु° लट्° ending is -अति and the प्रथम° बहु° लङ्° will take उः.

Examples:

√विद्	वेविद्	**weak stem**	(to really know)	
	वेवेद्	**strong stem**		
	एक°		द्वि°	बहु°
लट्	वेवेत्ति / वेविदीति		वेवित्तः	वेविदति
	वेवेत्सि / वेविदीषि		वेवित्थः	वेवित्थ
	वेवेद्मि / वेविदीमि		वेविद्वः	वेविद्मः
लङ्	अवेवेत् or अवेविदीत्			
लोट्	वेवेत्तु or वेविदीतु			
विधि लिङ्	वेविद्यात्			
वर्तमाने कृदन्त	वेविदत्			

√भू	बोभू	**weak stem**	
	बोभो	**strong stem**	
	प्रथम°एक°	प्रथम°द्वि°	प्रथम°बहु°
लट्	बोभोति /बोभवीति	बोभूतः	बोभुवति

c. **The यङन्त**

The यङन्त is the more common form of the intensive in the later language. To its reduplicated stem, the आत्मनेपद endings are added. From this form of the intensive all verbal forms of the language can be made.

Examples:

Root	**Stem**	
√दा	देदीय	प्रथम° एक°
लट्		देदीयते
लङ्		अदेदीयत
लोट्		देदीयताम्
विधि लिङ्		देदीयेत
periphrastic perfect		देदीयां चक्रे
लृट्		देदीयिष्यते
कर्मणि लट्		देदीय्यते

18.27 **नामधातु : The Denominative**

Another source of verbal forms in Sanskrit is the नामधातु, or noun-root, which, as its name implies, is a technique for deriving verbal forms from nouns. This technique is common in English. Consider such sentences as: "Stop clowning!"; "We're just kidding around"; "I wish he would stop badgering me"; and so forth. No doubt you can think of many others. In each of these sentences a verb is generated from a noun as opposed to a "verbal" infinitive (in English). In the examples, the subject of the action is either behaving like the signified noun in question or treating the object like that thing.

18.28 Forms such as these, not directly derived from a धातु (verbal root) but from a नामन् (noun), are common in classical Sanskrit. The basic meaning of these forms may be summarized as follows, in decreasing order of importance, letting X stand for any nominal item (noun or adjective):

1. a. become X (especially if X is an adjective);
   b. act like, imitate X (especially if a noun)
2. a. turn into X;
   b. regard or treat as X
3. desire X
4. do or perform X (especially if X is a noun expressing an action)

Meanings 1 and 2 are by far the most important.

18.29 **Formation of नामधातु Stems**

The characteristic sign of the नामधातु is य, which is suffixed to nominal stems. Therefore, like the णिजन्त and सन्नन्त, नामधातु-s are treated just like the present stems of अ गण roots.

a. As one would expect, nominal stems with final अ form the bulk of नामधातु stems. Here य is added to the stem whose final अ is either unchanged or lengthened.
   i. In practice, examples with lengthening are more common, tend to take the आत्मनेपद endings, and are generally used in meaning 1.

Examples:

Noun	नामधातु लट्	**Meaning**
काकः (m) (crow)	काकायते	(He acts like a crow.)
शुक्ल (adj) (white)	शुक्लायते	(It becomes [turns] white.)
सिंहः (m) (lion)	सिंहायते	(He plays the lion [i.e., is brave, etc.])
तरुण (adj) (young)	तरुणायते	(He becomes [or acts] young.)

ii. Where the final अ is unchanged, the forms tend to take the परस्मैपद endings and are generally used in meaning 2.

Examples:

Noun	नामधातु लट्	**Meaning**
तरुण (adj) (young)	तरुणयति	(He makes [someone] young.)
शुक्ल (adj) (white)	शुक्लयति	(He makes [paints] [something] white.)
सिंहः (m) (lion)	सिंहयति	(He treats or regards [something] as a lion.)

This distinction is a general one and not absolute. However, it is a fair generalization that stems with आ and the आत्मनेपद endings are अकर्मक and are used reflexively while stems with अ and the परस्मैपद endings are सकर्मक.

Examples:

सुवचनेन शत्रुर्मित्रायते ।

(Through kind words an enemy *becomes a friend.*)

सुवचनेन स शत्रुं मित्रयति ।

(Through kind words *he makes* his enemy *a friend.*)

b. Nouns with other stem finals are relatively less common. They are treated as follows:

i. आ usually remains unchanged.

Example:

कन्या (f) (girl) कन्यायते (becomes a girl)

ii. इ, ई or उ, ऊ become ई or ऊ.

Example:

नारी (f) (woman) नारीयते (becomes a woman)

iii. Consonant endings usually remain unchanged.

Example:

नमः (n) (homage) नमस्यति (do homage)

iv. But final consonants may be lost, especially when the आत्मनेपद endings are used in meaning 1. Here, the preceding vowel is treated as the final.

Examples:

राजन् (m) (king) राजायते (he plays the king, acts like the king)

अप्सरस् (f) (nymph) अप्सरायते (seems to be *an apsaras*)

18.30 **Use of the नामधातु**

A common and characteristic application of the नामधातु injects irony into meaning 1. to indicate the fact that a person or thing is either incapable of acting like another, is foolishly acting like another, or in some way (ironically) appears to be another. Learn these two examples:

1. प्रासादशिखरस्थो ऽपि सन्न काको गरुडायते ।

(Even though perched on the pinnacle of a palace, a crow does not *become an eagle*. [i.e., No matter how high a fool may rise, he remains a fool.])

2. संप्राप्ते षोडशवर्षे सूकर्यप्यप्सरायते ।

(When she attains sixteen years of age, even a sow becomes a nymph. [i.e., Any girl seems beautiful in the first blush of youth.])

EXERCISES

A. Translate the reading up to the sentence beginning with रामस्तु and identify by simple root and form all forms from secondary roots.

B. Do the same for the reading from रामस्तु to अन्ततो भरतो.

C. Do the same for the remainder of the reading. Then translate into Sanskrit the sentences that follow using the णिजन्त and सन्नन्त wherever possible. Avoid, however, forming the सन्नन्त of णिजन्त-s.

D. Translate the following into Sanskrit (for vocabulary, see English-Sanskrit glossary below).

1. Having caused Rāma to dwell in the forest, Kaikeyī will wish to make Bharata king.
2. Thinking, "The prince wants to kill me," Lakṣmaṇa was desirous of fighting.
3. Bharata, the knower of dharma, had his army bathe in the Ganges. (Use periphrastic perfect.)
4. Lakṣmaṇa wanted to fight Bharata but was unable to anger Rāma.
5. A donkey does not become a lion by a roar; a man does not become a hero by boasting.
6. The boy places the fruit at his teacher's feet.
7. The two boys should inform their mother and father of all that happened.
8. Let the old sage teach (णिजन्त of √श्रु) us the *Ṛgveda*.
9. Angering his father, the young child wanted to see his mother.
10. His curiosity made him follow Rāma to the forest.

E. Translate and memorize the following two verses (see vocabulary for verses, below).

1. The first verse, from the *Rāmāyaṇa*, is a charming description of the monkey Hanumān's delight upon thinking that he has found the kidnapped Sītā. It is especially valuable to memorize as it provides a fine drill for the perfect (लिट्), periphrastic perfect, imperfect (लङ्), and causative (णिजन्त).

आस्फोटयामास चुचुम्ब पुच्छं ननन्द चिक्रीड जगौ जगाम ।
स्तम्भानरोहन्निपपात भूमौ निदर्शयन्स्वां प्रकृतिं कपीनाम् ॥

2. The second verse, from भर्तृहरि-s "वैराग्यशतक" (hundred verses concerning withdrawal from the worldly life), illustrates two things, the aging poet's battle with craving and the नामधातुः.

वलिभिर्मुखमाक्रान्तं पलितैरङ्कितं शिरः ।
गात्राणि शिथिलायन्ते तृष्णैका तरुणायते ॥

READING

त्वमद्य भव नो राजा पुत्रात्मानमभिषेचय । पाहि चास्मान्नरर्षभेत्युक्तो राजकर्तृभिर्धर्मं चिकीर्षुर्भरतः सर्वं जनं प्रत्युवाच । नास्मि स्थापयितव्यो ऽहं सिंहासने । सूर्यवंशे राज्यं सदा शासनीयं ज्येष्ठेन । अतो ऽहं महासेनां योजयित्वा ज्येष्ठभ्रातरं तेजस्विनं सीतापतिं वनादागमयिष्यामीति । एवं भाषमाणे भरते सर्वेषां शृण्वतां विगतशोकानां जनानां नयनेभ्यः प्रहर्षजबाष्पबिन्दवो निपेतुः । तदनन्तरं बहूञ्छिल्पिनः समाज्ञाप्य राजमार्गं कारयित्वा

यदि त्वार्यं न शक्ष्यामि विनिवर्तयितुं वनात् ।
वने तत्रैव वत्स्यामि यथार्यो लक्ष्मणस्तथेति ॥ १ ॥

वदन्स वनगमनाय प्रतस्थौ । एकदा दण्डकारण्यगते रामे सीतया वनरमणीयतां दर्शयति सौमित्रिरुपगच्छन्त्या भरतसेनाया रेणुशब्दौ निरूप्य महाशालमारुह्य चमूं दिधक्षन्निव वचनं बभाषे ।

अग्निं संशमयत्वार्यः सीता च भजतां गुहाम् ।
सज्जं कुरुष्व चापं च शरांश्च कवचं तथा ॥ २ ॥

व्यक्तं यत्संप्राप्ताभिषेको भरत आवां घातयितुमिहागतः । एहि भ्रातः । अद्य राज्यमिच्छन्ती कैकेयी मया हतं पुत्रं द्रक्ष्यति गजभग्नं द्रुममिवेति । रामस्तु क्रोधमूर्च्छितं लक्ष्मणं परिसान्त्वयन्वाक्यमब्रवीत् । मास्तु कोपो लक्ष्मण । किमत्र धनुषा कार्यमसिना कवचेन वा । भरतं भ्रातरं हत्वा किं करिष्यामि राज्येन ।

यद्द्रव्यं बान्धवानां वा मित्राणां वा क्षये भवेत् ।
नाहं तत्प्रतिगृह्णीयां भक्षान्विषमयानिव ॥ ३ ॥

भरतं दिदृक्षामि । आवां न्यस्तशस्त्राविह प्रतिपालयावः । तदनन्तरमुपगते सशत्रुघ्ने भरते सर्वेषां दशरथपुत्राणां सानन्दं समागमो ऽभवत् । भरतो रामं वृद्धराजमरणं ज्ञापयामास । ततो ऽयोध्यां पुनरागत्य सर्वलोकं शास्त्वार्य इति बहुवारमुक्तः श्रीरामचन्द्रः पितुः प्रतिज्ञां हृदये स्थापयन् यदुक्तं जीवता मम पित्रा तन्न लोपयितुं शक्यते मयेत्यचिन्तयत् । संपूर्णवनवासानन्तरमयोध्यां मया गमिष्यते लोकशासनं च करिष्यते । यावन्मया वन उष्यते तावद्राज्यं क्रियतां धर्मज्ञेन भरतेनेत्युक्तवान् । अन्ततो भरत एवमुवाच । भवतां हेमभूषिते पादुके मह्यं दातव्ये । ते भवत्स्थाने राज्यं करिष्यत इति । तथास्त्विति रामेणानुज्ञातो भरतो भ्रातृपादुके शिरसि स्थापयित्वाभाषत । एते पादुके राज्यं कुरुताम् । अहं नगराद्बहिर्भवत्पादौ दिदृक्षुर्वत्स्यामि । संपूर्णे चतुर्दशे वर्षे यदि त्वां न द्रक्ष्यामि तर्ह्यग्निं प्रवेक्ष्यामीति । ततो ऽयोध्यां च शोकार्तः प्रतिनिववृते ॥

GLOSSARY

असिः
asiḥ (m)—sword

आर्त
(adj)—afflicted with, suffering from (usually at end of cmpd.)

आसनम्
(n)—seat

√इ
(2P)—go

उपगत
(adj)—drawn near

ऋषभः
(m)—bull (fig. at end of cmpd., bull among. . .; i.e., 'best of. . .')

कवचः
(m)—armor

क्षयः
(m)—destruction

गजः
(m)—elephant

गुहा
(f)—cave

चमूः
(f)—army

चिकीर्षु
(adj)—desirous of doing

-ज
(adj)—(at end of cmpd.) born from, produced

तेजस्विन्
(adj)—(f -इनी) glorious

√दह्
(1P)—burn

द्रुमः
(m)—tree

द्रव्यम्
(n)—thing, thing of value, wealth

नरः
(m)—man

निदर्शय्
(णिजन्त of नि + √दृश्)—show, point out

नि + √पत्
(1P)—fall or sink down

नि + √रूप्
(10P)—perceive, notice

न्यस्त
(adj)—set down

परिसान्त्व् परि + √सान्त्व्
(10P)—calm, soothe

√पा
(2P)—protect

पादुका
(f)—sandal

पिपासा
(f)—thirst

प्रति + √ग्रह्
(9P)—take

प्रति + नि + √वृत्
(1Ā)—return

प्रतिपाल् प्रति + √पाल्
(10P)—wait, watch, protect

प्रति + √वच्
(2P)—answer

प्रति + √स्था
(1P)—establish

प्र + √स्था
(1P)—set out

प्रहर्षः
(m)—joy

बहिः
(ind)—outside

बहुवारम्
(ind)—many times

बान्धवः
(m)—friend, relative

बिन्दुः
(m)—drop, spot

भक्षः
(m)—food

भग्न
(adj)—broken

√भज्
(1Ā)—have recourse to, betake oneself to

भूषित
(adj)—ornamented

-मय
(adj)—(f -मयी) (affix) consisting of, made of

मरणम्
(n)—dying, death

मूर्च्छित
(adj)—stupefied, senseless

√युज्
(7Ā)—join

रमणीयता
(f)—beauty, charm

राजकर्तृ
(m)—king-maker

रेणुः
(m)—dust

√लुप् → लुम्पते
(6Ā)—break, destroy: णिजन्त—neglect, violate

संपूर्ण
(adj)—filled

संप्राप्त
(adj)—arrived

सिंहासनम्
(n)—lion-seat, throne

लोपः
(m)—loss, damage, violation

वासनम्
(n)—dwelling, abode

वि + नि + √वृत्
(1Ā)—turn back, return

व्यक्त
(adj)—clear

शब्दः
(m)—sound

शस्त्रम्
(n)—weapon

शालः
(m)—a kind of tree

√शास्
(2Ā)—rule

शासनम्
(n)—sovereignty, rule

शिखरः
(m)—peak, pinnacle

शिरः
(n)—head

शिल्पिन्
(m)—artisan

सं + √शम्
(4Ā)—be extinguished

सज्ज
(adj)—ready

सम् + अव + √इ
(2P)—convene, come together

समागमः
(m)—meeting

सम् + आ + √ज्ञा
(9P)—know; णिजन्त = order, command

सौमित्रिः
(m prop)—Saumitri, son of Sumitrā, Lakṣmaṇa

स्थानम्
(n)—place

हेमम्
(n)—gold

ENGLISH-SANSKRIT GLOSSARY

bathe	√स्ना	(2P)
boasting	कत्थनम्	(n)
donkey	गर्दभः	(m)
Ganges	गङ्गा	(f)
roar	नादः	(m)

GLOSSARY FOR VERSES

(In order of appearance)

आ + √स्फुट्
(6P)—burst, make a loud noise; णिजन्त = clap the hands on the chest, strike the arms

√चुम्ब्
(1P)—kiss

पुच्छम्
(n)—tail

√क्रीड्
(6P)—play

√गै
(4P)—sing

स्तम्भः
(m)—post

√नन्द्
(1P)—rejoice

√रुह्
(1P)—climb up

नि + √पत्
(1P)—fall

स्व
(adj)—one's own(declined like पर, see 5.7, but optionally follows masculine in -a)

प्रकृतिः
(f)—nature

कपिः
(m)—monkey

वलिः
(m)—wrinkle

आक्रान्त
(adj)—occupied, taken over

पलितम्
(n)—grey hair

अङ्कित
(adj)—marked

शिरः
(n)—head

गात्रम्
(n)—limb

शिथिल
(adj)—loose, slack, weak

तृष्णा
(f)—desire, craving

तरुण
(adj)—young

LESSON 19

सर्वनामन् (Additional Pronouns); संख्या-s (Numerals); अद्यतनभूते लुङ् (The Aorist Systems)

19.0 **Additional Pronouns**

In addition to the pronominal stem तत् (सः, तत् , सा) (5.5ff.), Sanskrit has two important pronominal paradigms which you must learn. Both are like तत् etc., in that they are demonstrative, construe with verbs in the प्रथमपुरुष, and may serve in the senses of "the," "this," and "that."

19.1 The stems are:

1) अयम् (m), इदम् (n), इयम् (f), and
2) असौ (m), अदः (n), असौ (f).

Of the two, the first is the more common. The second, असौ, when it is used, usually conveys a sense of remoteness, as in "that" (as opposed to "this"). अयम् may indicate something less remote or be used generally. The paradigms are as follows:

a. i. अयम् (पुंलिङ्ग); इदम् (नपुंसकलिङ्ग)

	एक°	द्वि°	बहु°
प्र°	अयम् (m), इदम् (n)	इमौ (m), इमे (n)	इमे (m), इमानि (n)
द्वि°	इमम् (m), इदम् (n)	इमौ (m), इमे (n)	इमान् (m), इमानि (n)
तृ°	अनेन	आभ्याम्	एभिः
च°	अस्मै	आभ्याम्	एभ्यः
प°	अस्मात्	आभ्याम्	एभ्यः
ष°	अस्य	अनयोः	एषाम्
स°	अस्मिन्	अनयोः	एषु

ii. इयम् (स्त्रीलिङ्ग)

	एक°	द्वि°	बहु°
प्र°	इयम्	इमे	इमाः
द्वि°	इमाम्	इमे	इमाः
तृ°	अनया	आभ्याम्	आभिः
च°	अस्यै	आभ्याम्	आभ्यः

प°	अस्याः	आभ्याम्	आभ्यः
ष°	अस्याः	अनयोः	आसाम्
स°	अस्याम्	अनयोः	आसु

b. i. असौ (पुंलिङ्ग); अदः (नपुंसकलिङ्ग)

	एक°	द्वि°	बहु°
प्र°	असौ (m), अदः (n)	अमू (m, n)	अमी (m), अमूनि (n)
द्वि°	अमुम् (m), अदः (n)	अमू (m, n)	अमून् (m), अमूनि (n)
तृ°	अमुना	अमुभ्याम्	अमीभिः
च°	अमुष्मै	अमुभ्याम्	अमीभ्यः
प°	अमुष्मात्	अमुभ्याम्	अमीभ्यः
ष°	अमुष्य	अमुयोः	अमीषाम्
स°	अमुष्मिन्	अमुयोः	अमीषु

ii. असौ (स्त्रीलिङ्ग)

	एक°	द्वि°	बहु°
प्र°	असौ	अमू	अमूः
द्वि°	अमूम्	अमू	अमूः
तृ°	अमुया	अमूभ्याम्	अमूभिः
च°	अमुष्यै	अमूभ्याम्	अमूभ्यः
प°	अमुष्याः	अमूभ्याम्	अमूभ्यः
ष°	अमुष्याः	अमुयोः	अमूषाम्
स°	अमुष्याम्	अमुयोः	अमूषु

Notice that the pronominal endings are virtually the same as those already learned.

19.2 These pronouns, especially the first, are immensely useful and are used as commonly as सः, तत्, and सा.

Examples:

कस्येदं गृहम् ।

(Whose house is *this*?)

अस्मिन्कलौ युगे धर्मः शिथिलायते ।

(Dharma grows lax in *this* Kali age.)

किमनेन ।
(What *of that*?)

इयमतीव सुन्दरी
(*This* one [i.e., she] is very beautiful.)

a. The first of these pronouns is sometimes used, especially in "politeness formulas," with a noun meaning "person, man, woman," and so forth, as a very formal equivalent to the उत्तम पुरुष pronoun. प्रथम पुरुष verbs are of course still required.
Example:
क्षम्यतामयं जनः ।
(Excuse me [lit., Let *this* person be excused].)

19.3 संख्या-s : **Numerals**

Certain of the numerals and some techniques for numbering have already been introduced, including एक—the number one in its function as an indefinite article (see 5.7)—, the collective nouns -द्वयम् (a pair), -त्रयम् (trio), and so forth, द्विगु compounds, and the ordinal numbers applied to the grammatical categories of case and person. However, a more systematic treatment of the issue of numbering will be useful.

19.4 The देवनागरी numerals are, in fact, the source of our so-called "Arabic" numeral. Both systems work in the same way. Thus, one need learn only nine figures and the sign zero in order to write out the figures for any number. The more important numbers, with their symbols, names, and arabic equivalents are:

०	शून्य	0	५	पञ्चन्	5
१	एक	1	६	षष्	6
२	द्वि	2	७	सप्तन्	7
३	त्रि	3	८	अष्टन्	8
४	चतुर्	4	९	नवन्	9

१०	दशन्	10		३०	त्रिंशत्	30	(f)
११	एकादश	11		४०	चत्वारिंशत्	40	(f)
१२	द्वादश	12		५०	पञ्चाशत्	50	(f)
१३	त्रयोदश	13		६०	षष्टिः	60	(f)
१४	चतुर्दश	14		७०	सप्ततिः	70	(f)
१५	पञ्चदश	15		८०	अशीतिः	80	(f)
१६	षोडश	16		९०	नवतिः	90	(f)
१७	सप्तदश	17		१००	शतम्	100	(n)
१८	अष्टादश	18		१०००	सहस्रम्	1,000	(n)
१९	नवदश	19		१०००००	लक्षन्	100,000	(n)
२०	विंशतिः	20	(f)	१००००००००	कोटिः	10,000,000	(f)

The words for the numbers intervening between decades, e.g., २१, ३३, ६४, etc., are generally formed by prefixing a form of the "unit number" to the "decade number."

Examples:

एकविंशतिः (twenty-one)
त्रयस्त्रिंशत् (thirty-three)
चतुःषष्टिः (sixty-four)

However, for the number immediately preceding each multiple of १० (e.g., १९, २९, ३९), it is also common to construct a compound consisting of the next highest decade preceded by the adjective ऊन ("less, deficient"), which in turn may or may not be preceded by the word एक.

नवदश (nineteen)
ऊनविंशतिः (twenty deficient by one) = १९ (nineteen)
एकोनविंशतिः (twenty deficient by one)

19.5 Cardinal Numbers

a. The words for the numbers from one to nineteen are treated as adjectives. They must, insofar as their individual stems permit, agree with the noun indicating the thing numbered in case, number, and gender.

Examples:

कामदेवस्य पञ्चभिः पुष्पितशरैर्हतो ऽस्मि ।

(I am smitten by the *five* flowery arrows of Kāmadeva.)

रामस्य तुल्यो नास्ति त्रिषु लोकेषु ।

(Rāma has no equal in the *three* worlds.)

तिसृणां दशरथभार्याणां चत्वारः पुत्रा बभूवुः ।

(Daśaratha's *three* wives had *four* sons.)

b. The words for the numbers from 20 to infinity are generally treated as nouns. They each have their own gender and construe with the thing numbered in one of two ways.

i. The item numbered is in the षष्ठी विभक्ति and is grammatically subordinated to the word indicating number. Examples:

शतं पुरुषाणामागच्छति ।

(A *hundred* men come.)

देवानां सहस्रेष्वपि शोभन्ते राघवाः ।

(The Rāghavas shine even among *thousands* of gods.)

ii. The word for the number is in case apposition with the thing numbered. For example:

शतं देवाः

(a *hundred* gods)

19.6 The declension of the adjectival numbers (i.e., १-१९) requires some special attention.

a. एक : This word belongs to the pronominal declension (like सर्व, etc.). It is also used as an indefinite article and in this usage may occur in the बहुवचन in the sense of "some," "certain,"

Examples:

एकस्मिन्दिने राजा वनं ययौ ।

(*One* day the king went to the forest.)

एके वदन्ति यत् . . .
(*Some* people say that . . .)
एक has no द्विवचन.

b. द्वि, except in समास, is treated as though its stem were द्व. It is therefore declined like any -अ stem adjective in all three genders, but only, of course, in the द्विवचन.
Examples:
द्वौ पुरुषौ जग्मतुः ।
(*Two* men went.)

द्वे कन्ये वदतः ।
(*Two* girls speak.)

अनयोर्द्वयोः पुस्तकयोः किं मया पठनीयम् ।
(Which of these *two* books am I to read?)

c. Numbers ३ through १९ have only बहुवचन forms. त्रि behaves like a regular इ stem in the पुंलिङ्ग and नपुंसकलिङ्ग in all forms except the षष्ठी where त्रयाणाम् would appear to be formed from a stem त्रय.
Examples:
इमानि त्रीणि पुस्तकानि मया पठितानि ।
(I read these *three* books.)

त्रीन्राक्षसाञ्जघान ।
(He killed *three rākṣasas.*)

त्रिभ्यः पुरुषेभ्य इमे त्रयो गजा देयाः ।
(These *three* elephants are to be given to the *three* men.)

The स्त्रीलिङ्ग, however, is formed from the stem तिसृ, which is declined more or less like any -ऋ stem, except that its प्रथमा and द्वितीया show no strength and are the same (i.e., तिस्रः), and its षष्ठी has a short rather than long stem vowel (i.e., तिसृणाम्).

Example:
तिसृभिर्नारीभिः सेव्यमानागच्छति सीता ।
(Sītā comes attended by *three* women.)

d. चतुर् : Here again, as with -त्रि, the पुंलिङ्ग and नपुंसकलिङ्ग form from a different stem than that of the स्त्रीलिङ्ग. Unlike -त्रि, however, the पुंलिङ्ग and नपुंसकलिङ्ग forms have a strong and a weak stem. The strong stem is चत्वार् while the weak stem is चतुर् :

	पुंलिङ्ग	नपुंसकलिङ्ग
प्र°	चत्वारः	चत्वारि
द्वि°	चतुरः	चत्वारि
तृ°	चतुर्भिः	
च° प°	चतुर्भ्यः	
ष°	चतुर्णाम्	
स°	चतुर्षु	

Example:
यस्य चत्वारि मुखानि सन्ति तेनैव चत्वारो वेदा अवगम्यन्ते ।
(The *four vedas* are understood only by him who has *four* faces [i.e., Brahmā].)

The स्त्रीलिङ्ग stem is चतसृ, and it is declined exactly like तिसृ (see 19.6.c above).

e. The numbers ५ through १९ do not distinguish gender. Except for षष्, they are declined somewhat like नपुंसकलिङ्ग stems in -अन्, with the following exceptions:

i. The प्रथमा and द्वितीया appear to have the forms of the singular of such stems.

Examples:

पञ्च पुरुषाः	(five men)
सप्त देव्यः	(seven goddesses)
नव रत्नानि	(nine gems)

ii. The षष्ठी is like that of a stem with a final अ.
Example:
दशानां गुरूणां शिष्यः . . .
(The pupil of ten teachers . . .)

iii. षष् has the following declension:

प्र°, द्वि°	षट्
तृ°	षड्भिः
च°, प°	षड्भ्यः
ष°	षण्णाम्
स°	षट्सु

19.7 **Ordinal Numbers**

Ordinal numbers, indicating numerical position in a sequence (e.g., first, second, third, etc.), correspond to the cardinal numbers. They are all adjectival in nature.

19.8 The ordinals are:

a.

प्रथम or आद्य	(first)
द्वितीय	(second)
तृतीय	(third)
चतुर्थ, तुरीय, or तुर्य	(fourth)
पञ्चम	(fifth)
षष्ठ	(sixth)
सप्तम	(seventh)
अष्टम	(eighth)
नवम	(ninth)
दशम	(tenth)

b. For the numbers from ११ through १९, the ordinals are the same as the cardinals.

c. For the numbers over 20, the ordinal may be of two forms:

i. the suffix -तम is added to the cardinal,
Examples:

विंशतितम	(twentieth)
त्रयस्त्रिंशत्तम	(thirty-third)
शततम	(hundreth)

ii. reduction of the cardinal back to its final -अ, and if its final vowel is -इ, substitution of -अ for -इ.

Examples:

विंश	(twentieth)
अशीत	(eightieth)
षष्ट	(sixtieth) (do not confuse with षष्ठ sixth)

19.9 All ordinals, therefore, are -अ stems.

a. प्रथम, आद्य, द्वितीय, तृतीय, तुरीय, and तुर्य have their स्त्रीलिङ्ग forms in आ.

b. All other nouns have their स्त्रीलिङ्ग form in ई.

Examples:

प्रथमा विभक्ति	(nominative case)
द्वितीया विभक्ति	(accusative case)
सप्तमी विभक्ति	(locative case)

19.10 अद्यतनभूते लुङ् : **The Aorist**

Sanskrit has yet another full-fledged and elaborate verbal conjugation with which the beginning student must somehow come to grips. This is the लुङ् , or so-called "aorist." The लुङ् has been left for last for a reason. It occurs in the classical language with much less frequency than either the लङ् or लिट्, the other preterite tenses. In fact, its use in the classical language is restricted largely to pieces and passages in which the author wishes to show his command of obscure forms. On the other hand, certain aorist forms of particular roots are not uncommon, and these must be learned. Moreover, there is a particular usage of aorist forms (19.18) that occurs with some frequency and with which one should be familiar.

19.11 As its name implies, the अद्यतनभूते लुङ् is yet another past tense. The term अद्यतन, "of today," is meant to complement the terms अनद्यतन (लङ्), "not of today," and परोक्ष (लिट्), "remote," thus distinguishing three basic kinds of past. However, as in the case of the other past tenses, no such distinction can be observed in usage. In short, the लुङ्, लङ् and लिट् are quite freely interchangeable as simple past tenses.

19.12 Types of लुङ्

The "aorist," in fact, comprehends three basic types, several of which have subtypes of their own. It is not intended that you attempt to memorize the rules for the लुङ् formation in the way that forms like the लङ् must be learned. Therefore, the following represents a brief synopsis of the major features and usages of the aorist system. Particular usages which should be learned are stressed. The three basic types, according to the stem formation, are:

1. the simple aorist
2. the sibilant aorist
3. the reduplicated aorist

19.13 The Simple Aorist: The Root Aorist

The simple aorist has two subtypes: the root-aorist and the अ aorist.

a. The root-aorist is restricted to a small number of roots with final आ and the root √भू. It is formed as follows.

   i. The stem consists of the preterite augment अ prefixed directly to the unchanged root.

   ii. To this stem are then added the appropriate secondary परस्मैपद endings, except in the case of प्रथमपुरुष, बहुवचन, where the ending -उः is used.

   ii. The treatment of the common root √भू differs from that of the roots with final आ in that:

      a. The प्रथमपुरुष, बहुवचन takes the regular secondary ending -अन्.

      b. Before the endings beginning with a vowel (i.e., प्रथमपुरुष, बहुवचन and उत्तमपुरुष, एकवचन) the letter व् is inserted after the ऊ of the stem.

b. The paradigms, then, of √दा and √भू, are:

	एक°	द्वि°	बहु°
प्र°	अदात् / अभूत्	अदाताम् / अभूताम्	अदुः / अभूवन्
म°	अदाः / अभूः	अदातम् / अभूतम्	अदात / अभूत
उ°	अदाम् / अभूवम्	अदाव / अभूव	अदाम / अभूम

19.14 The Simple Aorist: The अ Aorist

The अ aorist may be made from a fairly large number of roots, but is not usually formed in the आत्मनेपद. It is formed simply by suffixing short अ to the root, prefixing the augment, and adding the appropriate secondary endings. Only roots with final ऋ take गुण. In short, except for ऋ roots, the form is made exactly like the लङ् of the sixth गण. It is not, of course, restricted to roots of any गण. Examples that you may see are √गम् and √वच्. Note particularly that √वच् in this form takes the irregular stem form वोच्.

Example:

इदं वचनमवोचत् ।

(He *spoke* this speech.)

	एक°	द्वि°	बहु°
प्र°	अगमत्	अगमताम्	अगमन्
	अवोचत्	अवोचताम्	अवोचन्
म°	अगमः	अगमतम्	अगमत
	अवोचः	अवोचतम्	अवोचत
उ°	अगमम्	अगमाव	अगमाम
	अवोचम्	अवोचाव	अवोचाम

19.15 Sibilant Aorists

This class of four subtypes is so named because the tense-sign of each either consists of or contains the consonant स् or ष्. The tense signs are (1) स् or ष्, (2) इष्, less commonly (3) सिष् and (4) स. All forms require the preterite augment prefixed to the roots and take, with some slight variation, the secondary endings. Unlike the root aorist and in general the अ aorist, the sibilant forms have both परस्मैपद and आत्मनेपद conjugations. The आत्मनेपद forms serve also as the आत्मनेपद conjugation for roots of the root aorist.

a. **The स् Aorist**

This form is relatively common for an aorist.

i. Its stem is formed by prefixing the augment to the root, which usually is strengthened. स् is added to this strengthened root. The rules for root strength are:

a. Final vowels.

Final vowels are subject to वृद्धि in परस्मैपद and गुण in आत्मनेपद. But final ऋ takes no strength in the आत्मनेपद.

	परस्मैपद	आत्मनेपद
Root	**Stem**	**Stem**
√श्रु (hear)	अश्रौष्	अश्रोष्
√कृ (do)	अकार्ष	अकृष्

b. Medial vowels.

Medial vowels are, 'वृद्धि-ed' (if in a लघु syllable) in परस्मैपद and unchanged in आत्मनेपद.

Root	परस्मैपद	आत्मनेपद
√रुध् (block)	अरौत्स्	अरुत्स्
√दृश् (see)	अद्राक्ष्(cf. 13.1.b)	अदृक्ष्

ii. Endings: To the stem are added the normal secondary endings with three notable exceptions:

a. प्र° बहु° परस्मैपद takes -उः (*not* -अन्)

b. प्र° बहु° आत्मनेपद takes -अत (*not* -अन्त),

and, most important,

c. प्रथम° and मध्यम° एक° परस्मैपद have the vowel ई inserted between the stem and the endings. This is important as it lends a distinctive shape to these forms, which are in any case the only ones you are at all likely to see.

For example:

√कृ (do)	अकार्षीत् / अकार्षीः	(he/you did)
√दृश् (see)	अद्राक्षीत् / अद्राक्षीः	(he/you saw)
√नी (lead)	अनैषीत् / अनैषीः	(he/you led)
√श्रु (hear)	अश्रौषीत् / अश्रौषीः	(he/you heard)

The complete paradigm of √दृश् (see) is

	एक°	द्वि°	बहु°
प्र°	अद्राक्षीत्	अद्राष्टाम्	अद्राक्षुः
म°	अद्राक्षीः	अद्राष्टम्	अद्राष्ट
उ°	अद्राक्षम्	अद्राक्ष्व	अद्राक्ष्म

Memorize only the examples given in (c.) above.

b. **The इष् Aorist**

This form, less commonly encountered than the above, is of a similar formation.

i. It takes the augment and adds इष् to the root, which is strengthened as follows:

a. Final vowels are strengthened as with the स् aorist, but here ऋ is no exception,

Example:

Root	परस्मैपद	आत्मनेपद
√पू (cleanse)	अपाविष्	अपविष्

b. Medial vowels have गुण in परस्मैपद and आत्मनेपद if in a लघु syllable,

Examples:

Root	परस्मैपद	आत्मनेपद
√रुच् (shine)	अरोचिष्	अरोचिष्
but √जीव् (live)	अजीविष्	अजीविष्

Medial -अ- is occasionally lengthened in परस्मैपद.

ii. Endings: Endings are as for the स् aorist. Here, too, the endings of the प्रथम°, मध्यम°, एकवचन परस्मैपद are, ईत्, ईः. Moreover, before these two endings, the sibilant tense marker is dropped.

For example:

Root

√बुध् (be awakened) अबोधीत् / अबोधीः (he [was] / you [were] awakened)

Do not bother to memorize this form.

c. **The सिष् Aorist**

This form, rarer still than the preceding one, is made only from roots in -आ and three roots in -अम्; √नम् 1P (bow); √यम् 1P (यच्छति) (reach); √रम् 1Ā (take pleasure). It occurs only in the परस्मैपद, its आत्मनेपद being formed like the स् aorist. It is formed exactly like the इष् aorist.

Example:

		प्रथम° / मध्यम° एक°	
√स्था	(stand)	अस्थासीत् / अस्थासीः	(he / you stood)

Do not bother to memorize this form.

d. **The स Aorist**

This form can be made only from 23 roots, few of which are very common. These roots share the following characteristics:

i. They all end in श्, ष्, or ह् sounds, which join with the स of the tense sign to form the conjunct क्ष.

ii. Their root vowels are इ, उ, or ऋ.

a. स is added to the augmented and unstrengthened root.

b. To this are added the appropriate secondary endings with a few exceptions which are prescribed by the grammarians but which, owing to the rarity of the form, cannot be cited from the literature. A typical paradigm is that of √दिश् 6P (point out):

	परस्मैपद			आत्मनेपद		
	एक°	द्वि°	बहु°	एक°	द्वि°	बहु°
प्र°	अदिक्षत्	अदिक्षताम्	अदिक्षन्	अदिक्षत	अदिक्षाताम्	अदिक्षन्त
म°	अदिक्षः	अदिक्षतम्	अदिक्षत	अदिक्षथाः	अदिक्षाथाम्	अदिक्षध्वम्
उ°	अदिक्षम्	अदिक्षाव	अदिक्षाम	अदिक्षि	अदिक्षावहि	अदिक्षामहि

Do not bother to memorize this form.

19.16 The Reduplicated Aorist

This form, also not common, is of some interest because it is the लुङ् form that corresponds in meaning (although there is no formal affinity) to the णिजन्त, or causative, conjugations. It is characterized by a peculiar and quite distinctive अभ्यास or reduplication. The अभ्यास syllable is formed according to the general rules, with अ and ऋ vowels becoming इ. What is distinctive about the form is that it always favors a contrast of लघुत्व (metrical lightness) and गुरुत्व (metrical heaviness) between the अभ्यास and root syllables. Thus, if the root syllable is लघु, the अभ्यास vowel will be lengthened to make it गुरु.

Examples:

Root		**Stem**
√शम्	(be quiet)	अशीशम् (make quiet, calm)
√जन्	(be born)	अजीजन् (give birth to)

If the root syllable is गुरु (i.e., long vowel or short before conjunct), the अभ्यास syllable will be light and, in this case only, an अ vowel will appear as अ in the अभ्यास. This is quite rare. The stem thus formed is given a final अ, as though it were the imperfect stem of an अ गण root, and receives the endings proper to such a root. The paradigm of √शम् is as follows:

	परस्मैपद			आत्मनेपद		
	एक°	द्वि°	बहु°	एक°	द्वि°	बहु°
प्र°	अशीशमत्	अशीशमताम्	अशीशमन्	अशीशमत	अशीशमेताम्	अशीशमन्त
म°	अशीशमः	अशीशमतम्	अशीशमत	अशीशमथाः	अशीशमेथाम्	अशीशमध्वम्
उ°	अशीशमम्	अशीशमाव	अशीशमाम	अशीशमे	अशीशमावहि	अशीशमामहि

The form is not common enough to worry about, but its common metrical structure of ⏑ – ⏑ ⏓ represented by the sequence: augment, heavy अभ्यास, light root, any एक° परस्मैपद ending, makes it easy enough to recognize.

Examples:

कौसल्या राममजीजनत् ।

(Kausalyā *gave birth* to Rāma.)

तदा वीराः कोपाग्निमशीशमन् ।

(Then the heroes *extinguished* the fire of [their] anger.)

19.17 प्रथमपुरुष, एकवचन, कर्मणि, लुङ्

The aorist has various modes, none of which you need learn, and, as with any non-present form, its आत्मनेपद forms may be used in कर्मणि प्रयोग. However, there is a special, peculiar, कर्मणि प्रयोग form, which occurs only in the प्रथम° एक° and has no regular conjugation. It is formed by adding the personal ending इ to the augmented and generally strengthened root.

a. The root is strengthened as follows:
   - i. Final vowels and usually medial -अ- in a light syllable are subject to वृद्धि.
   - ii. Other medial vowels, if in light syllables, are subject to गुण.
   - iii. After final आ, the consonant य् is placed before the ending (इ).

   Examples:

Root			
√दा	(give)	अदायि	(it was given)
√कृ	(do)	अकारि	(it was done)

19.18 **The Injunctive**

There is one usage made of the लुङ् forms which is quite different from the basic preterite application. This is the so-called injunctive, or negative imperative, which may be formed from any लुङ् form by dropping the augment and using the regular prohibitive particle (मा) (see 11.18). In classical Sanskrit, this usage is perhaps more common than the preterite one. For example:

Root			**Injunctive**
√कृ	(do)	तन्मा कार्षीः ।	(*Don't do* that!)
√भू	(be)	भरतो राजा मा भूत् ।	(*Let* Bharata *not be* king!)
√गम्	(go)	हे अर्जुन । क्लैब्यं मा गमः ।	(O Arjuna! *Do not be* a weakling! [lit., Do not go to unmanliness!])

EXERCISES

A. Translate the reading up until the sentence beginning with तां कामपाश-. Isolate all लङ्, लिट् and लुङ् forms and in each case provide two finite equivalents (e.g., is the form is लुङ् give the corresponding लिट् and लङ्).

B. Do the same for the passage up to शूर्पणखोवाच.

C. The same for the remainder of the reading.

D. Translate the following sentences into English.

॥१॥ दशरथे महायज्ञं कृतवति कौसल्यादयो राज्ञस्तिस्रो भार्याश्चतुरः सुन्दरपुत्रानजीजनन् ।

॥२॥ आगच्छतः सुसंक्रुद्धान्घोरराक्षसान्प्रेक्ष्य श्रीरामो मा भैषीरित्युक्त्वा मुनये ऽभयमदात् ।

॥३॥ यदा राजात्मनो भार्यायाः सुदारुणवचो ऽश्रौषीत्तदा हे पापिनि किं त्वयाकारीत्यवोचत् ।

॥४॥ चतुर्षु वेदेषु कः प्रसिद्ध इति प्रश्नं श्रुत्वा सर्व ऋग्वेद इति वदेयुः ।

॥५॥ वनगमनानन्तरं राघवः किमकार्षीत् । नाहं प्रष्टव्यः । सर्वमिदं वृत्तान्तं सर्वैः पठनीयं वाल्मीकिरामायणे ।

E. Translate the following into Sanskrit, using the forms used in the chapter. (Give also equivalent लङ् and लिट् forms.)

1. There was a terrible *rākṣasa* in Lañkā named Rāvaṇa, the equal of a hundred gods in battle.

2. In order to kill this enemy of the righteous, the gods caused Hari to be born among men.
3. If a man should act like a *rākṣasa* (नामधातु , विधि लिङ्), then, like a night-roamer (निशाचरः), let him not see (injunc tive) the glorious sun.

F. Translate and memorize the following verse.

दुर्जनः परिहर्तव्यो विद्ययालंकृतो ऽपि सन् ।
मणिना भूषितः सर्पः किमसौ न भयङ्करः ॥

The analogy is based on the poetic convention that snakes, particularly the deadly cobra, carry precious gems in their heads.

READING

अयोध्यां गतयोर्भरतशत्रुघ्नयो रामो गोदावरीं नदीं प्राप्य देवपितॄंस्तर्पयित्वा स्नानमकार्षीत् । ततः

कृताभिषेकः स रराज रामः सीताद्वितीयः सह लक्ष्मणेन ।
कृताभिषेको गिरिराजपुत्र्या रुद्रः सनन्दिर्भगवानिवेशः ॥१॥

तदा पूज्यमानो महर्षिभिः पर्णशालायां प्रियभार्यया सह सुखमुवास । अथामुष्मिन्समये काचन महती राक्षसी शूर्पणखा नाम तस्मिन्दण्डकारण्ये ऽवसत् । सा च क्रूरकर्मा विरूपा निशाचरकन्या राक्षसाधिराजस्य त्रिलोककण्टकस्य दशग्रीवस्य रावणनाम्नो भगिन्यभूत् । एकदा सा वने यदृच्छया भ्रमन्ती तौ द्वौ सूर्यचन्द्रोपमौ वीरावद्राक्षीत् ।

सुमुखं दुर्मुखी रामं वृत्तमध्यं महोदरी ।
प्रियरूपं विरूपा सा सुस्वरं भैरवस्वना ॥२॥

दृष्ट्वा च काममोहिता सतीदं वचनमवोचत् । भो वीर

अहं शूर्पणखा नाम राक्षसी कामरूपिणी ।
रावणो नाम मे भ्राता राक्षसो राक्षसाधिपः ।
प्रख्यातवीर्यौ च रणे भ्रातरौ खरदूषणौ ॥३॥

अतो मया सहागन्तुमर्हति भवान् । इयं विरूपा न तव सदृशी । त्याज्या सा । अन्यथा मानुषीमल्पोदरीं तव भ्रातरं चाद्य भक्षयिष्यामीति । तां कामपाशबद्धराक्षसीं श्रीरामः स्मितपूर्वमिदं वचनमब्रवीत् । कृतविवाहो ऽस्मि। भ्राता तु मे ऽविवाहितो वीरो ऽनुरूपो भर्ता तव भवेदिति । एवं प्रोक्ता राघवेण कामवशगतेयं रामं सहसा परित्यज्य लक्ष्मणमवोचत् । रूपेण युक्ताहं भार्या तव भविष्यामि । मया सह सुखं दण्डकान्विचरिष्य-सीति । तद्वचनं हासकारणं श्रुत्वा लक्ष्मणो हसन्निवोवाच । दासो ऽस्मि वरानने ऽग्रजस्य रामस्य । रामं सेवस्व विशालाक्षि रामपत्नी भविष्यसि । को हि तवैतादृशं रूपं प्रेक्ष्येमां वृद्धां कुरूपां सीतां न त्यजेदिति । इयं तु राक्षसी कामदेवस्य पञ्चभिरिषुभिर्हता लक्ष्मणोक्तपरिहासमविजानती तद्व-चः सत्यममन्यत । शूर्पणखोवाच च । हे राम

अद्येमां भक्षयिष्यामि पश्यतस्तव मानुषीम् ।
त्वया सह चरिष्यामि निःसपत्ना यथासुखम् ॥४॥

इत्युक्त्वा सा सुसंक्रुद्धा सीतामभ्यगमद् बुभुक्षोन्मत्तव्याघ्री कोमलमृगशावकं यथा । रामस्तु कुपितस्तां निवारयामासोवाच च । क्रूरैरनार्यैः सौमित्रे परिहासो न कदाचित्कार्यः । इमां लम्बोदरीं राक्षसीं विरूपयितुमर्हसि पुरुषव्याघ्रेति । तच्छ्रुत्वा भयपीडितां वैदेहीं च दृष्ट्वा रामानुजः स्व-खड्गमुद्धृत्य राक्षस्याः कर्णनासाश्चिच्छेद । इयमपि विच्छिन्नकर्णनासा प्रतोदहतकरेणुवन्नदन्ती स्रवच्छोणिताच्छादितानना भ्रातरं खरं तत्सर्वं निवेदयितुं दुद्राव । जनस्थानं प्राप्य महाबलं खरं चतुर्दशसहस्रेण दारुण-राक्षसानां संवृतमुपविष्टं सा विरूपिता भयमोहक्रोधमूर्च्छिता स्वविरूपणकथां निवेदयन्ती भूमौ निपपात ॥

GLOSSARY

अग्र
(adj)—first

अधिराजः
(m)—overlord, king

अनुरूप
(adj)—conformable, suitable

अन्यथा
(ind)—otherwise

अभयम्
(n)—security

अभिषेकः
(m)—ablution, ritual bath

अल्पोदरी
(f)—having a small belly

आच्छादित
(adj)—covered, enveloped

ईशः
(m)—lord, Śiva

उन्मत्त
(adj)—crazy, drunk, maddened

उपविष्ट
(adj)—seated

ऋग्वेदः
(m)—the *Ṛgveda*

कण्टकः
(m)—thorn; fig. 'something irritating'

करेणुः
(m)—elephant

कर्णः
(m)—ear

कामदेवः
(m)—Kāmadeva, god of love

कामरूपिन्
(adj)—taking any form at will

कु
(ind)—a prefix implying 'badness'

कुरूप
(adj)—ugly, deformed

खड्गः
(m)—sword

खरः
(m prop)—Khara, a great *rākṣasa* chief, brother of Rāvaṇa and Śūrpaṇakhā

गिरिराजपुत्री
(f prop)—'daughter of the King of the mountains,' i.e., Pārvatī'

गोदावरी
(f prop)—name of a river

जनस्थानम्
(n prop)—Janasthāna, portion of the Daṇḍakāraṇya, headquarters of Khara

तुल्य
(adj)—equal

√तृप्
(4P / Ā)—be satisfied

त्रि
(adj)—three (see 19.6.c)

दशग्रीवः
(m)—'having ten necks;' epithet of Rāvaṇa

दासः
(m)—servant, slave

दुर्मुखी
(f)—having an ugly face

दूषणः
(m prop)—Dūsaṇa, brother of Khara

√द्रु
(1P)—run

√नद्
(1P)—roar

नदी
(f)—river

नन्दिः
(m prop)—Nandi (or Nandin), Śiva's bull

नासा
(f)—nose

निःसपत्न
(adj)—having no rival

नि + √विद्
(2P)—be informed; णिजन्त = निवेदय्

नि + √ वृ
(5P / Ā)—be blocked, prevented
णिजन्त = निवारय्

निहत
(adj)—slain

पञ्च
(adj)—five (see 19.6)

परिहासः
(m)—joke, jest

पर्णम्
(n)—leaf

पाशः
(m)—noose

पितृ
(m)—ancestor

पुष्पित
(adj)—flowery

√पू
(9P / Ā)—purify

√पूज्
(10P)—worship, revere

प्रख्यात
(adj)—famous

प्रतोदः
(m)—goad

प्रसिद्ध
(adj)—famous

प्रश्नः
(m)—question

प्रेक्ष् (प्र + √ईक्ष्)
(6Ā)—see, behold

प्रोक्त
(adj)—addressed, spoken to

बलम्
(n)—power, strength

√भक्ष्
(10P)—eat

भगिनी
(f)—sister

भैरव
(adj)—terrible, fearsome

√भ्रम्
(1P)—wander

मध्यः
(m)—middle, waist

महोदरी
(f)—having a big belly

मानुषी
(adj f)—female human, woman

मृगशावकः
(m)—fawn

मोहः
(m)—delusion

यथासुखम्
(ind)—according to pleasure

यदृच्छया
(ind)—by chance

युक्त
(adj)—joined, furnished or endowed with (with तृतीया or in compound)

युगम्
(n)—a cosmic era

रणम्
(n)—battle

राक्षसी
(f)—a female *rākṣasa*

√राज्
(1P / Ā)—shine

रावणः
(m prop)—Rāvaṇa

रुद्रः
(m prop)—Rudra, a name of Śiva

रूपम्
(n)—form, beauty

लम्बोदर
(adj, f— -ī)—potbellied

वर
(adj)—best, excellent, most precious

वि + √चर्
(1P)—wander

विच्छिन्न
(adj)—severed

विरूप
(adj)—ugly

विरूपणम्
(n)—disfigurement

विरूपय
(नामधातु)—disfigure

विरूपित
(adj)—disfigured, mutilated

विरूपिन्
(adj; f -इनी)—ugly

विशालाक्षी
(adj f)—having large eyes

वृत्त
(adj)—(in this समास) slender

वृषभः
(m)—bull

वेदः
(m)—*veda*

व्याघ्री
(f)—tigress

शूर्पणखा
(f prop)—Śūrpaṇakhā, sister of Rāvaṇa

शोणितम्
(n)—blood

संवृत्त
(adj)—surrounded

सहसा
(ind)—suddenly, at once

सुदारुण
(adj)—very terrible

सुमुख
(adj)—handsome

सुसंक्रुद्ध
(adj)—furious

√स्ना
(2P)—bathe

स्नानम्
(n)—bathing, ablution

√स्मि
(1P / Ā)—smile

स्मितपूर्वम्
(ind)—with a smile

√स्रु
(1P)—flow, run

स्वनः
(m)—sound, cry

स्वरः
(m)—sound, cry

हासः
(m)—laughter

हि
(ind)—indeed, surely

ENGLISH-SANSKRIT GLOSSARY

battle	रणम्	(n)
enemy	शत्रुः	(m) or अरिः (m)
righteous	धार्मिक	(adj)
Hari (Viṣṇu)	हरिः	(m prop)
glorious	तेजस्विन्	(adj)
sun	सूर्यः	(m)

GLOSSARY FOR VERSES

(In order of occurrence)

दुर्जनः
(m)—evil person

परि + √हृ
(1P)—avoid, shun

विद्या
(f)—learning

अलंकृत
(adj)—ornamented

मणिः
(m)—jewel

भूषित
(adj)—ornamented

सर्पः
(m)—serpent

भयङ्कर
(adj)—fearsome, terrible

LESSON 20

कृत् and तद्धित प्रत्यय-s; The च्वि प्रत्ययरु
Nominal Derivation and Sanskrit Vocabulary

20.0 The grammatical complexity of Sanskrit is such that, in the first year, it tends to overshadow other areas of language learning, especially the acquisition of a working vocabulary. Nonetheless, the major features of the grammar will soon, through constant repetition, become quite familiar. Vocabulary, on the other hand, tends to loom as a greater issue when one begins reading Sanskrit texts. With Sanskrit, more perhaps than other languages, the beginning student feels that he or she never seems to be able to learn enough words so that he or she can obtain some modicum of freedom from the dictionary.

20.1 There are a number of reasons for the extraordinary richness of the Sanskrit lexicon. One of the reasons concerns the derivation of nouns and adjectives from verbal roots. Despite the relatively small number of verbal roots in common use, it is possible, through the use of the उपसर्ग-s and a wide variety of derivational suffixes, to make a given root the base for a large number of words. By combinations and permutations of the उपसर्ग-s and suffixes, it would easily be possible to generate a hundred words from a single root. Mastery of the more important of these suffixes, like a knowledge of the उपसर्ग-s, is, therefore, of immense help in the task of acquiring a working Sanskrit vocabulary.

20.2 Sanskrit derivational suffixes are called प्रत्यय-s and fall into two major categories depending upon whether they are added directly to a धातु or to some more complex form. Suffixes that are added directly to a verbal root are called कृत् प्रत्यय-s (primary suffixes), while those added to a form already derived by कृत् or other derivation are called तद्धित प्रत्यय-s (secondary suffixes). For example, from the root √बुध् (awaken), we may derive, by means of a familiar कृत् प्रत्यय '-त,' the form बुद्ध (भूते कृदन्त) (awakened, enlightened, the Buddha). Then, from this कृत् derivative, we may further derive, by means of a तद्धित प्रत्यय, the form बौद्ध (a follower of the enlightened one, a Buddhist).

20.3 The most important प्रत्यय-s and their basic functions are best learned according to their basic category (i.e., कृत् or तद्धित), and within each category, according to their significance. Before going on to examine the प्रत्यय-s, however, it is essential that you be thoroughly familiar with the grades of vowel strength called गुण and वृद्धि (3.5-7). These vowel grades are often characteristic of the various kinds of nominal derivation, and it is difficult to relate many forms to their underlying forms without a clear, virtually automatic, knowledge of the grades of the simple vowels. If you cannot immediately see that the words दाशरथि, राघव, मैथिली, बौद्ध, आर्ष, and भोग are derived from दशरथ, रघु, मिथिला, बुद्ध, ऋषि and √भुज् respectively, go back to 3.5-7 and learn the vowel grades thoroughly.

20.4 **Major कृत् प्रत्यय-s**

कृत् derivation is primary in that it depends on the simple verbal धातु-s of the language. Although all three vowel grades (no strength, गुण and वृद्धि) occur in various examples of कृत् derivation, it is a fair generalization to say that गुण is the most characteristic while the other two are less common.

20.5 There is one group of कृत् प्रत्यय-s that should by now be quite familiar to you. These—the participial, infinitive, gerundive, and gerund suffixes such as -त, -न, -तुम्, -तव्य, -य, -अनीय, -त्वा, and -त्य—have been discussed elsewhere.

20.6 There remain, however, a number of प्रत्यय-s that are used to derive nouns and adjectives from the verbal roots. Such derivatives differ somewhat from the participles in that they generally lose their verbal character insofar as they do not so clearly have कर्तृ-s and कर्मन्-s in sentences.

a. क्विप्

The simplest of these suffixes, is the zero, or क्विप् प्रत्यय. Derivative nouns with this suffix consist simply of the verbal root with or without an उपसर्ग. Such forms are relatively rare and are restricted to a few items, mostly स्त्रीलिङ्ग nouns expressing the *action* of the root.

Examples:

Root		**Derivative**		
√दृश्	(see)	दृश्	(f)	(sight) (→दृक्)
√युध्	(fight)	युध्	(f)	(fight, battle) (→युत्)(see 3.25.a)
उप + नि + √सद् (1P)	(sit down near [सीदति])	उपनिषद् [-त्]	(f)	(*upaniṣad*)
सम् + √सद् (1P)	(sit together)	संसद् [-त्]	(f)	(assembly)
परि + √सद् (1P)	(sit around)	परिषद् [-त]	(f)	(assembly)
आ + √पद् (1P)	(undergo misfortune)	आपद् [-त्]	(f)	(calamity, misfortune)

The क्विप् प्रत्यय, however, is more common in forms occurring at the end of compounds (see 12.17). Here, it forms an agent noun, i.e., a noun identifying the agent of the action of the root. Unlike action nouns, agent nouns can take any gender, depending on the inherent gender of the person or thing identified as agent.

Examples:

√ज्ञा (9P) (know)	सर्वज्ञः	(knower of everything)
√जि (1P) (conquer)	इन्द्रजित्	(conqueror of Indra) (see 21.1)
√दा (3P) (give)	वरदः	(m prop) (boon giver, Brahmā)

b. अ

This is the most important derivational suffixes in the language. It is added freely to a large number of roots and with them forms of a great number of *action nouns* mostly पुंलिङ्ग. Before this suffix, the following changes in the root occur:

1. A root vowel, if capable of गुण (i.e., in a light syllable or a final long vowel), takes it. (In fact, this suffix is largely restricted to such cases.)
2. Medial अ is subject to वृद्धि, but this is not invariably the case.
3. Some final vowels are likewise subject to वृद्धि.
4. A तालव्य (palatal) स्पर्श, and sometimes ह् in root final position revert, before the प्रत्यय, to their corresponding कण्ठ्य (velar).

Examples:

Root	**Derivative**
√जि (1P) (conquer)	जयः (m) (conquest, victory)
√कुप् (4P) (be angry)	कोपः (m) (anger)
√क्रुध् (4P) (be angry)	क्रोधः (m) (anger)
उद् + √इ (2P) (go up)	उदयः (m) (ascension, success)
√भिद् (7P) (split)	भेदः (m) (separation, split, distinction)
वि + √शिष् (7P) (distinguish)	विशेषः (m) (distinction, species)
√शुच् (1P) (grieve)	शोकः (m) (grief)
√त्यज् (1P) (leave)	त्यागः (m) (abandonment, renunciation)
√युज् (7P) (join)	योगः (m) (mental concentration)
√लुभ् (4P) (be greedy)	लोभः (m) (greed)
सम् + आ + √गम् (1P) (come together)	समागमः (m) (meeting)

उद् + √विज् (1P) (tremble, fear)	उद्वेगः (m) (fear, trembling)
√विद् (2P) (know)	वेदः (m) (*veda*, sacred knowledge)
√भू (1P) (be)	भवः/भावः (m) (being, state, abstract condition)
वि + √सृज् (6P) (release)	विसर्गः (m) (release, *visarga*)
√भुज् (7P) (enjoy)	भोगः (m) (enjoyment)
√वृ (9Ā) (choose)	वरः (m) (boon)

i. A few words of this derivation are neuter.

Example:

√भी (3P) (fear) भयम् (n) (fear)

ii. A few are **agent** nouns.

Examples:

√कृ (8P)	(do)	कर/कार (at end of compounds) (doer, maker, agent)
भास्करः	(m)	(light-maker, sun)
कुम्भकारः	(m)	(pot-maker, potter)
√मिह्	(1P)	(emit fluid, urinate) मेघः (m) (cloud)

c. -आ

A number of roots, especially those whose vowels do not qualify for गुण or वृद्धि (i.e., short in heavy syllable or long non-final, see 7.16), form स्त्रीलिङ्ग action nouns with the suffix आ.

Examples:

Root	**Derivative**
√सेव् (1Ā) (serve)	सेवा (f) (service)
√भाष् (1Ā) (speak)	भाषा (f) (speech, language)
√क्रीड् (1P/Ā) (play)	क्रीडा (f) (play, sport)
√चिन्त् (10P) (think)	चिन्ता (f) (thought, anxiety)

As seen in Lesson 18, this suffix routinely forms action nouns from the सन्नन्त (desiderative) stem.

Examples:

Root	Derivative
√मन् (4Ā) (think)	मीमांसा (f) (inquiry)
√बाध् (1Ā) (ward off)	बीभत्सा (f) (disgust)

d. -अन

The suffix -अन, like -अ, is one of the most productive and important of the non-participial कृत् प्रत्यय-s. Like -अ, it forms action nouns freely from many roots. Before it, root vowels generally take गुण if they can. In contrast with the -अ प्रत्यय, -अन forms nouns mostly in the नपुंसकलिङ्ग. Final तालव्य (palatal) consonants are unchanged before -अन. *Action nouns* of this group sometimes take on a sense of *object nouns*, i.e., nouns indicating the object of an action, or, in the case of अकर्मक roots, nouns indicating the locus of action. A few are *agentive*.

Examples:

Root		Derivative	
√गम्	(1P) (go)	गमनम्	(n) (going)
√हन्	(2P) (kill)	हननम्	(n) (killing)
√वच्	(2P) (speak)	वचनम्	(n) (speech)
√दा	(3P) (give)	दानम्	(n) (giving, gift)
√पा	(3P) (drink)	पानम्	(n) (drinking, drink)
√भुज्	(7P) (enjoy, eat)	भोजनम्	(n)(enjoyment, food)
√वद्	(1P) (speak)	वदनम्	(n) (face [mouth])
वि + √भूष्	(1P) (adorn)	विभूषणम्	(n) (ornament, adorning)
√स्था	(3P) (stand)	स्थानम्	(n) (standing, place)
√नी	(1P) (lead)	नयनम्	(n) (eye [leader])
√पिष्	(7P) (crush, grind)	पेषणम्	(n) (grinding)
√श्रु	(5P) (hear)	श्रवणम्	(n) (hearing)
√आस्	(2Ā) (sit)	आसनम्	(n) (seat, posture)
√वह्	(1P) (carry)	वाहनम्	(n) (carrying, mount, vehicle)

e. -अः

This suffix forms a fairly restricted group of predominantly नपुंसकलिङ्ग action nouns. Before it, root vowels take गुण if possible (see 9.0-9.4).

Examples:

Root		**Derivative**	
√तप्	(1P) (burn, perform austerity)	तपः	(n) (austerity)
√वच्	(2P) (speak)	वचः	(n) (speech)
√मन्	(4Ā) (think)	मनः	(n) (mind, thought)
√नम्	(1P/Ā) (bow, do homage)	नमः	(n) (homage, bow)

f. -ति

This suffix forms many important स्त्रीलिङ्ग action nouns. Before it, roots are generally unchanged or weakened, exactly as before the -त of the भूते कृदन्त.

Examples:

Root		**Derivative**	
√गम्	(1P) (go)	गतिः	(f) (gait, path, way, going [see 6.1.b])
प्र + √आप्	(5P) (attain)	प्राप्तिः	(f) (attainment, acquisition)
√मन्	(4Ā) (think)	मतिः	(f) (thought, opinion)
√मुच्	(6P)(release, free)	मुक्तिः	(f) (liberation)
√जन्	(4Ā) (be born)	जातिः	(f) (birth, genus, caste)
√दृश्	(P) (see)	दृष्टिः	(f) (sight, vision)
√वृष्	(1P) (pour, shower)	वृष्टिः	(f) (rain, shower)
आ + √कृ	(8P) (fashion, form)	आकृतिः	(f) (form)
√बुध्	(4Ā) (be awake, aware)	बुद्धिः	(f) (idea, thought, highest mental faculty)

√वच्	(1P) (speak)	उक्तिः	(f) (speech, saying)
√सृज्	(6P) (create)	सृष्टिः	(f) (creation)
√रम्	(1Ā) (take pleasure in)	रतिः	(f) (pleasure, love making)

i. The common root √पद् (4Ā), "go," forms पत्तिः (f), "going," despite the fact that the भूते कृदन्त is पन्न (see 10.12). This important root occurs only with उपसर्ग-s. Examples:

उत् + √पद्	(be born, arise, originate)	उत्पत्तिः	(f) (birth, origin, arising)
वि + √पद्	(experience calamity)	विपत्तिः	(f) (misfortune)
सम् + √पद्	(experience good fortune)	संपत्तिः	(f) (good fortune)

g. -मन्

This suffix forms *action nouns* from a few roots. The nouns are mostly नपुंसकलिङ्ग. Before the suffix, root vowels are subject to गुण.

Examples:

Root		**Derivative**	
√जन्	(4Ā) (be born)	जन्मन्	(n) (birth)
√कृ	(8P) (do, make)	कर्मन्	(n) (action, *karma*, grammatical object)

h. -त्र

This suffix forms, from a few roots, nouns that individually indicate an *instrument or means* of the action of the verbal root. These nouns are usually नपुंसकलिङ्ग. Before this suffix root vowels are subject to गुण.

Examples:

Root		**Derivative**	
√गा	(2Ā) (go)	गात्रम्	(n) (limb of the body [means of motion])

√पत्	(1P) (fall, fly)	पत्रम्	(n) (wing [means of flying])
√पा	(1P) (drink)	पात्रम्	(n) (cup, drinking vessel [instrument for drinking])
√शास्	(2Ā) (rule, restrict)	शास्त्रम्	(n) (scientific or prescriptive text [means of instruction])
√श्रु	(5P) (hear)	श्रोत्रम्	(n) (ear [means of hearing])
√नी	(1P) (lead)	नेत्रम्	(n) (eye [means of leading])
√वस्	(2Ā) (clothe)	वस्त्रम्	(n) (clothing [means of clothing])

i. -तृ

This प्रत्यय forms *agent nouns* in the पुंलिङ्ग and नपुंसकलिङ्ग. Corresponding स्त्रीलिङ्ग nouns are formed with the suffix त्री. Before these प्रत्यय-s root vowels take गुण if possible. They may be added to many roots. The suffix तृ is the same one discussed in connection with stems in final ऋ (10.0-3) and the लुट् (16.12.2). It is added to the stem with or without the vowel इ as noted at those places.

Examples:

Root		**Derivative**	
√कृ	(8P) (do)	कर्तृ	(m,n) (त्री f) (agent, maker, grammatical subject)
√नी	(1P) (lead)	नेतृ	(m,n) (त्री f) (leader)
√दा	(3P) (give)	दातृ	(m,n) (त्री f) (giver)
√रक्ष्	(1P) (protect)	रक्षितृ	(m,n)(त्री f) (protector, protectress)

i. Before this suffix, certain roots in which a consonant precedes the sequence अह् are changed as follows: अ → ओ ; ह् → ढ् . (See 10.8.d).
Example:
√वह् (1P) (carry) वोढृ (m, n) (carrier)

j. -अक

This प्रत्यय forms पुंलिङ्ग and नपुंसकलिङ्ग *agent nouns*. Its स्त्रीलिङ्ग equivalent is usually -इका, although -अका and अकी are occasionally seen. It is used fairly freely. Before it, medial short vowels take गुण, medial अ and final vowels वृद्धि.

Examples:

Root		**Derivative**	
√नी	(1P) (lead)	नायकः	(m, n) (leader, hero)
		नायिका	(f) (heroine [in drama])
√भिद्	(7P) (split)	भेदकः/भेदकम्	(m, n) (splitter)
		भेदिका	(f)
√पच्	(1P) (cook)	पाचकः/पाचकम्	(m, n) (cook)
		पाचिका	(f)
√कृ	(8P) (do)	कारकः/कारकम्	(m, n) (effector)
		कारकम्	(n) (the relation of noun to a verb, expressed by the grammatical case)
		कारिका	(f) (concise, metrical statement in one of the शास्त्र-s)

20.7 The above are by no means all of the कृत् प्रत्यय-s. They are, however, the most important and commonly used. The others do not generate enough forms to warrant your learning them. It is sufficient to learn the individual forms without worrying about their derivation. You should, however, make yourself familiar with the above list of suffixes and the ways in which they work.

20.8 **तद्धित Derivation**

Just as the कृत् प्रत्यय-s are used to generate a variety of nouns from the verbal roots, so the तद्धित प्रत्यय-s enable one to build new nominal forms based on the meanings of other nominal stems. The underlying nominal forms are called प्रकृति.

20.9 The forms thus derived are of several types. Two of these, however, are most important.

a. **Derivative adjectives.**

i. These are normally derived from nouns and indicate that their विशेष्य (modificand) is in some way related to the प्रकृति.

Examples:

प्रकृति		**Derivative**	
मनः	(n) (mind)	मानस	(adj) (mental)
लोकः	(m) (world)	लौकिक	(adj) (worldly)
पुरुषः	(m) (man)	पौरुषेय	(adj) (human, pertaining to men)

ii. Such adjectives are themselves often stereotyped as nouns, especially when they refer to people who know or study the thing indicated by the प्रकृति.

Examples:

प्रकृति	**Derivative**
व्याकरणम् (n) (the science of grammar)	वैयाकरण (adj) (pertaining to grammar, but more commonly: वैयाकरणः (m) (a grammarian)

iii. This kind of nominalization is regularly stereotyped in the derivation of proper names from those of some parent or ancestor.

Examples:

प्रकृति		Derivative	
दशरथः	(m) (Daśaratha)	दाशरथिः	(m) (son of Daśaratha, e.g., Rāma)
कुन्ती	(f) (Kuntī)	कौन्तेयः	(m) (son of Kuntī; e.g., Arjuna)

b. **Abstract nouns.** This important class of nouns is derived freely from both nouns and adjectives. If X is any noun and Y any adjective, the derivations are usually best translated X-hood, the state of being an X; Y-ness, the state of being Y.

Examples:

प्रकृति		Derivative	
शीत	(adj) (cold)	शैत्यम्	(n) (cold, coolness)
युवन्	(adj) (young)	यौवनम्	(n) (youth)
पुरुषः	(m) (man)	पुरुषता	(f) (manhood)

20.10 Just as गुण of a root vowel is a frequent characteristic of कृत् derivation, a characteristic mark of the तद्धित derivation is वृद्धि. A number of the most important of the तद्धित प्रत्यय-s require वृद्धि, which occurs in the initial syllable of the प्रकृति. This rule has one relatively important exception. When the first vowel of an underlying form is immediately preceded by the semi-vowel य् or व्, especially where the semi-vowel is the result of an external सन्धि change of the final vowel of a quasi-independent word (e.g., the उपसर्ग-s नि-, वि- or the compound forms सु- or कु-), this semi-vowel is first analyzed into इय् or उव्, and the वृद्धि then applies to the vowel (इ or उ). This applies to all तद्धित suffixes requiring वृद्धि.

Examples:

प्रकृति	Derivative
व्याकरणम् (n) (grammar) (वि-आ-करणम्)	वैयाकरणः (m) (grammarian)

न्यायः	(m) (logic)	नैयायिकः	(m) (logician)
व्यक्तिः	(f) (individual)	वैयक्तिक	(adj) (personal, individual)
स्वश्वः	(m prop) (सु-अश्वः)	सौवश्वः	(m prop) (son of Svaśva)

When a semi-vowel preceding an initial vowel is *not* the result of external सन्धि, the regular rule applies.

Example:

प्रकृति		**Derivative**	
स्वयंभूः	(m prop) (स्वयं-भु) (the god Brahmā)	स्वायंभवः	(m) (son of Brahmā)

20.11 The most important of the तद्धित प्रत्यय-s are:

a. -अ

This suffix is as important among तद्धित-s as its phonological twin is among the कृत्-s (20.6.b). It has four basic meanings, the first two of which are somewhat more important than the others. The meanings are:

1. अपत्यवाचक (genealogical descent)
2. भाववाचक (abstraction)
3. तस्येदम् (possession)
4. तद्वेद (knowledge)

The suffix has a स्त्रीलिङ्ग counterpart, ई. Both require वृद्धि of the first syllable of the प्रकृति. अ (and ई) are added to nominal stems as follows:

i. They replace final अ or आ.

Examples:

प्रकृति		**Derivative**	
पुत्रः	(m) (son)	पौत्रः	(m) (grandson)
यमुना	(f prop) (Yamunā river)	यामुनः	(m prop) (son of Yamunā)
पर्वतः	(m) (mountain)	पार्वती	(f prop) (daughter of the mountain)

ii. They replace final ई.

Example:

प्रकृति		Derivative	
सरस्वती	(f prop) (Sarasvatī)	सारस्वतः	(m prop) (son of Sarasvatī)

iii. They are added to the गुण of -उ.

Example:

प्रकृति		Derivative	
रघुः	(m prop) (Raghu)	राघवः	(m prop) (descendant of Raghu)

iv. They are added directly to ऋ, which is not strengthened.

Example:

प्रकृति		Derivative	
त्वष्टृ	(m prop) (Tvaṣṭṛ)	त्वाष्ट्रः	(m prop) (son of Tvaṣṭṛ)

v. They are added directly to consonant stem finals. In the case of final अन्त् the weak form अत् is the base.

Examples:

प्रकृति		Derivative	
मनः	(n) (mind)	मानस	(adj) (mental)
ब्रह्मन्	(n) (Brahman)	ब्राह्मणः	(m) (a brāhman)
हिमवन्त्	(m) (the Himālaya mountains)	हैमवत	(adj) (pertaining to the Himālaya mountains)

The following are additional examples of its uses:

1. अपत्यवाचक

प्रकृति		Derivative	
रघुः	(m prop) (Raghu)	राघवः	(m) (Rāma, descendant of Raghu)

जनकः	(m prop) (Janaka)	जानकी	(f) (Sītā [daughter of Janaka])
पर्वतः	(m) (mountain)	पार्वती	(f) (Umā, daughter of the mountain)

2. भाववाचक

प्रकृति		**Derivative**	
गुरु	(adj) (heavy)	गौरवम्	(n) (weight, profundity)
लघु	(adj) (light)	लाघवम्	(n) (lightness, triviality)
शिशुः	(m) (child)	शैशवम्	(n) (childhood)
युवन्	(adj) (young)	यौवनम्	(n) (youth)

3. तस्येदम्

प्रकृति		**Derivative**	
शिवः	(m prop) (Śiva)	शैव	(adj) (belonging or pertaining to Śiva)
विष्णुः	(m prop) (Viṣṇu)	वैष्णव	(adj) (belonging or pertaining to Viṣṇu)
बुद्धः	(m) (Buddha)	बौद्ध	(adj) (belonging or pertaining to Buddha)

4. तद्वेद

प्रकृति		**Derivative**	
व्याकरणम्	(n) (grammar)	वैयाकरणः	(m) (grammarian)

b. -य

This suffix is also of great importance. It is used to form a great number of nouns, mostly भाववाचक (abstract), which are generally नपुंसकलिङ्ग. वृद्धि of the first syllable is general, but a number of forms show no strength. The suffix replaces any stem-final vowel and is added to any stem-final consonant.

1. अपत्यवाचक

प्रकृति		Derivative	
अदितिः	(f prop) (Aditi)	आदित्यः	(m)(Āditya; the Sun)
कविः	(m prop) (name of a sage)	काव्यः	(m) (son of Kavi)

2. भाववाचक

This is one of the most productive generators of भाववाचक forms in the language.

प्रकृति		Derivative	
शूरः	(m) (hero)	शौर्यम्	(n) (heroism)
उचितः	(adj) (proper)	औचित्यम्	(n) (propriety)
पण्डितः	(m) (wise man)	पाण्डित्यम्	(n) (state of being a wise man)
उत्सुक	(adj) (eager)	औत्सुक्यम्	(n) (longing, eagerness)
अलस	(adj) (lazy)	आलस्यम्	(n) (laziness)
उदासीन	(adj) (indifferent)	औदासीन्यम्	(n) (indifference)
मूर्खः	(m) (fool)	मौर्ख्यम्	(m) (foolishness)
वीरः	(m) (hero)	वीर्यम्	(n) (no वृद्धि) (heroism, valor)
मुखम्	(n) (face)	मुख्य	(adj) (no वृद्धि) (foremost)

3. तत्र भावः (produced from the referent of the प्रकृति)

प्रकृति		Derivative	
दन्तः	(m) (tooth)	दन्त्य	(adj) (dental)
तालु	(n) (palate)	तालव्य	(adj) (palatal)

c. -इय

This is actually the preceding प्रत्यय with the epenthetic vowel इ before it. It occurs where the suffix -य would otherwise have to follow a conjunct consonant directly.

प्रकृति		Derivative	
क्षेत्रम्	(n) (field)	क्षेत्रिय	(adj) (pertaining to a field)
क्षत्रम्	(n) (kingly power)	क्षत्रियः	(m) (the princely class)

d. -ईय

This suffix is largely restricted to the function of forming possessive adjectives from the pronouns. In each case it is added to the form the pronoun takes in समास (12.16.d). The प्रकृति shows no strength.

प्रकृति		**Derivative**	
अहम्	(I)	मदीय	(adj) (my)
त्वम्	(you)	त्वदीय	(adj) (your)
भवन्त्	(you)	भवदीय	(adj) (your)
वयम्	(we)	अस्मदीय	(adj) (our)
यूयम्	(you)	युष्मदीय	(adj) (your)
सः, सा, तत्	(he, she, it)	तदीय	(adj) (his, hers, its)

e. -एय

This is a relatively common suffix, mostly as an अपत्यवाचक. It replaces a final vowel and requires वृद्धि.

Examples:

प्रकृति		**Derivative**	
कुन्ती	(f) (Kuntī)	कौन्तेयः	(m) (son of Kuntī, Arjuna)
गङ्गा	(f) (Ganges)	गाङ्गेयः	(m) (son of the Ganges, Bhīṣma)
विनता	(f) (Vinatā)	वैनतेयः	(m) (son of Vinatā, Garuḍa)

The suffix has some non-अपत्यवाचक usages.

Examples:

प्रकृति		**Derivative**	
ऋषिः	(m) (sage)	आर्षेय	(adj) (pertaining to *ṛṣis*; descended from *ṛṣis*)
पुरुषः	(m) (man)	पौरुषेय	(adj) (human, as opposed to divine)
अतिथिः	(m) (guest)	आतिथेय	(adj) (pleasing to guests)

f. -इ

This suffix requires वृद्धि and replaces a final vowel. Its chief use is as an अपत्यवाचक.

Examples:

प्रकृति		Derivative	
दशरथः	(m) (Daśaratha)	दाशरथिः	(m) (Rāma)
सुमित्रा	(f) (Sumitrā)	सौमित्रिः	(m) (Lakṣmaṇa)

g. -त्व and -ता

These two भाववाचक प्रत्यय-s are extremely important. They are used with great freedom to form abstract nouns, which signify the state or condition of being that which is indicated by the प्रकृति. They correspond to the English suffixes -ness, -hood, etc. No strength is required in the प्रकृति. Nouns formed with -त्व are नपुंसकलिङ्ग; those with -ता are स्त्रीलिङ्ग.

Examples:

प्रकृति		Derivative	
कपिः	(m) (monkey)	कपित्वम्	(n) (monkey-ness, the state of being a monkey)
मधुर	(adj) (sweet)	मधुरता	(f) (sweetness)

h. -क

This common प्रत्यय has various meanings. It is sometimes used as an agentive suffix, sometimes as a diminutive, and often with no special meaning. It requires no strength in the प्रकृति. For example:

प्रकृति		Derivative	
अन्तः	(m) (end)	अन्तकः	(m) (ender, i.e., death)
रूपम्	(n) (form)	रूपकम्	(n) (giving form, i.e., metaphor)
पुत्रः	(m) (son)	पुत्रकः	(m) (little boy)
माणवः	(m) (man)	माणवकः	(m) (youth; especially a brāhman boy)

इषुः	(m) (arrow)	इषुकः	(m) (arrow)
नग्न	(adj) (naked)	नग्नक	(adj) (naked)

i. -इक

This suffix requires वृद्धि in the first syllable of the प्रकृति. It has various uses, chiefly as तस्येदम् (possession) and तद्वेद (knowing something). It replaces a final vowel and is added to a final consonant.

Examples:

प्रकृति		**Derivative**	
लोकः	(m) (world)	लौकिक	(adj) (worldly)
वेदः	(m) (*veda*)	वैदिक	(adj) (vedic)
		वैदिकः	(m) (a vedic scholar)
धर्मः	(m) (*dharma*)	धार्मिक	(adj) (righteous)
न्यायः	(m) (logic)	नैयायिकः	(m) (logician)
पुराणम्	(n) (*purāṇa*, a class of texts)	पौराणिकः	(m) (a man versed in *purāṇas*)
स्वभावः	(m) (inherent nature)	स्वाभाविक	(adj) (pertaining to inherent nature, innate)
मनः	(n) (mind)	मानसिक	(adj) (mental)

j. -अक

This suffix functions like the one above but is generally less common.

Example:

प्रकृति		**Derivative**	
मीमांसा	(f) (a philosophical school)	मीमांसकः	(m) (a follower of the *mīmāṃsa* school)

The form मामक (adj), mine, is derived by this प्रत्यय from the षष्ठी एक° form of अहम्. (See verse at 18.23.2.a.)

k. -मय

This suffix, which is added directly to a nominal stem without any vowel strength, forms adjectives conveying the sense of "made of" or "consisting of" the thing indicated by the प्रकृति. सन्धि before this suffix is external.

Examples:

प्रकृति		**Derivative**	
वाक्	(f) (speech)	वाङ्मय	(adj) (consisting of speech)
		वाङ्मयम्	(literature)
चित्	(f) (mind, consciousness)	चिन्मय	(adj) (consisting of consciousness)
काष्ठम्	(n) (wood)	काष्ठमय	(adj) (made of wood)

l. There are a number of suffixes which indicate the possessor (स्वामिन्) of the प्रकृति. These are said to be स्वामित्ववाचक (expressive of ownership). These have already been introduced in the various paradigms. They are -मन्त्, -वन्त्, -इन्, and -विन्. (See 11.3 and 12.0-12.3 respectively.)

Examples:

प्रकृति		**Derivative**	
पक्षः	(m) (wing)	पक्षिन्	(m) (bird)
तपः	(n) (asceticism)	तपस्विन्	(m) (ascetic)
पशुः	(m) (cattle)	पशुमन्त्	(adj) (rich in cattle)
स्मृतिः	(f) (memory)	स्मृतिमन्त्	(adj) (having a good memory)

m. उत्कर्षवाचक प्रत्यय

There are two unrelated sets of प्रत्यय-s that are used to form comparative and superlative grades of adjectives. They are said to be उत्कर्षवाचक (expressive of superiority):

i. -तर—comparative

-तम—superlative

These are added to any adjectival stem. If the stem is one that has a twofold distinction of strength, then the weaker is used; if the distinction is threefold, the middle grade is used. The object of comparison is usually in the पञ्चमी विभक्ति.

Examples:

Adjective		**Comparative**		**Superlative**	
प्रिय	(dear)	प्रियतर	(dearer)	प्रियतम	(dearest)
महन्त्	(great)	महत्तर	(greater)	महत्तम	(greatest)

ii. -ईयः—comparative

-इष्ठ—superlative

These are technically कृत् प्रत्यय-s, before which a root is subject to गुण. Relatively few roots take these forms in the classical language, and even then, the derivatives are not often really related to their roots. Therefore, it is best simply to learn a few important forms. Each of the following examples shows the adjective corresponding in meaning, not the underlying verbal root.

Examples:

Adjective		**Comparative**		**Superlative**	
प्रशस्य	(good)	श्रेयः	(better)	श्रेष्ठ	(best)
गुरु	(heavy)	गरीयः	(heavier)	गरिष्ठ	(heaviest)
युवन्	(young)	कनीयः	(younger)	कनिष्ठ	(youngest)
वृद्ध	(old)	ज्यायः	(older)	ज्येष्ठ	(oldest)

iii. The declension of the superlative ending in इष्ठ is like that of any adjective in अ; its स्त्रीलिङ्ग ending is आ. On the other hand, the declension of comparatives in ईयः is quite irregular. It will be given in the following chapter. (See 21.4.)

n. -वत्

This प्रत्यय, added to any noun (stem final consonants are treated as in compounds), forms an adverb conveying the sense of "like" the referent of the प्रकृति. (See 21.6.a.ii.a)

Example:

प्रकृति		**Derivative**	
कपिः	(m) (monkey)	कपिवत्	(ind) (like a monkey)

20.12 The च्वि प्रत्यय

a. This प्रत्यय is treated separately from the others for two reasons. First, it is common and extremely versatile. Second it requires a subsidiary element, either a finite form or a derivative of the roots √कृ or √भू.

b. The प्रत्यय itself is ई, and it is added in place of a final vowel or directly to a final consonant. It requires no strength in the प्रकृति.

c. In meaning, the च्वि construction is rather like one use of the नामधातु (denominative—18.27-30), in that it indicates that a thing either becomes or is made into, literally or figuratively, something that it is not.

d. When an intransitive, reflexive sense is desired, a form of the root √भू is used. When the transitive sense is desired, a form of the root √कृ is used (see 18.29.) The effect of this is to create a series of new complex "roots."

Examples:

प्रकृति		**Derivative**	
कृष्ण	(adj) (black)	कृष्णीभू	(1P) (to become black)
		कृष्णीकृ	(8P) (to make black, to blacken)

From these "roots" can be made any finite form and any कृत् derivation that can be made from the simple roots √कृ and √भू. Note that in the formation of the gerund, the च्वि affix has the effect of an उपसर्ग (see 11.7).

Examples:

कृष्णीभविष्यति	(ऌट्) (it will become black)
कृष्णीकरणम्	(n) (blackening)
कृष्णीकृत	(adj) (blackened)
कृष्णीकृत्य	(gerund) (having blackened)

e. The च्वि construction has several important usages.

i. If the प्रकृति is a noun, then it indicates a genuine change of state. For example:

नृपो बालकं सैनिकीकरोति ।

(The king makes the boy into a soldier.)

If the प्रकृति is an adjective, then the form indicates a change of quality:

नारी चन्दनेन स्तनद्वयं शुक्लीकरोति ।

(The woman whitens her breasts with sandalwood.)

ii. Perhaps an even more important usage of the च्वि is in a figurative sense. Here the change of state is not real. The subject either acts like (√भू), or, more often, treats or regards something like (√कृ) the referent of the प्रकृति. Example:

अरे ते राजपुरुषास्तपोवनं नगरीकुर्वन्ति ।

(Hey! These policemen are turning the penance grove into a city [i.e., they are making noise and generally acting as though they were in a city].)

भो मारुते त्वया क्रमता शतयोजनविस्तीर्णसागरो गोष्पदीकृतः ।

(O Māruti [Hanumān]! You, in leaping, have turned the ocean, a hundred leagues across, into [a puddle in] a cow's hoofprint.)

iii. Idiomatic usage: The adjective स्व, "one's own," and the indeclinable अङ्ग (ind) (exclamation of agreement), "OK," are used idiomatically with the च्वि प्रत्यय and √कृ to indicate acceptance, either mental or physical. Examples:

इदं भोजनं स्वीकर्तव्यं भवता । (or स्वीकरोतु भवान् ।)

(Please accept this food, sir.)

तादृशं वाक्यं न कदाप्यङ्गीक्रियते भारतदेशे ।

(Such speech is never accepted [agreed to] in India.)

20.13 Examples of the use of various प्रत्यय-s.

Virtually all of the Sanskrit you have learned so far has been illustrative of the principles of nominal derivation. However, a few remarks on some of the uses of this principle may be helpful.

a. One valuable result of the system of suffixes is that it makes possible a very precise and systematic evolution of technical terminology. Consider the root √शिष् (7P) with the उपसर्ग 'वि' in the sense of "qualify, specify." Although finite forms of the verb are not common, its nominal derivations are very useful. Thus:

   i. विशेषणम्, "qualification," is used in grammar to indicate an adjective.

      विशेष्यम् (gerundive), "to be qualified," then means the noun modified by an adjective. The विशेष्यम्, of course, is विशिष्ट, "modified," by the विशेषणम् etc.

   ii. The poetic terms उपमा (f), "simile," उपमेय "subject of comparison," and उपमान "object of comparison" are derived from उप + √मा (2P), "compare."

   iii. By use of the various suffixes one can derive many of the important grammatical terms from the root √कृ.

      Example:

कर्तृ	(subject)
कर्मन्	(object)
करणम्	(instrument)
क्रियापदम्	(action word, verb)
कारकम्	(case relation)

b. Juxtaposition of two (or more) derivations of the same root can, by virtue of the significance of the प्रत्यय, make for very powerful conciseness of speech.

   Example:

   कृतकृत्यः (बहुव्रीहि समास) "one who has done what he had to."

Here, eight English words are needed to express what can be expressed by one word in Sanskrit. Again, take the example, पिष्टपेषणम् (√पिष् 7P—grind) "the grinding of the ground" (i.e., beating a dead horse), where five English words are needed to express one Sanskrit word.

c. The capacity of Sanskrit for concise utterance, through a combination of derivational techniques, nominal composition, and the connotative power (शक्ति) of the case endings, is nowhere better employed than in the शास्त्र-s, or scholarly texts.

Example:

अविद्या परिहर्तव्या जन्ममरणादिलक्षणसंसारोत्पत्तिहेतुत्वात् ।

(Ignorance is to be shunned *because of its being the cause of the origination of the cycle of re-birth, which is characterized by birth, death, and so forth.*)

Note here how the one compound, even though it has seven members, requires twenty-three words in an English rendering.

d. The different "meanings" of the different suffixes make for a virtually unlimited freedom of paraphrase. Take, for example, the term बुद्धवचनम् (=बुद्धस्य वचनम्) "the speech of the Buddha." By subjecting the कृदन्त "बुद्ध," which here is a noun, to further तद्धित derivation, one can generate the adjective बौद्ध, "Buddhist," "pertaining to the Buddha." One can then substitute the कर्मधारय समास बौद्धवचनम् for the original तत्पुरुष. Likewise, derivatives of adjectives like स्पष्ट, "clear," and शीघ्र, "fast," can be used variously to convey more or less the same meanings:

Examples:

i. they can be used adjectivally

शीघ्रो ऽश्वो धावति ।	(The *swift* horse runs.)
स्पष्टं वचनं वदति ।	(He speaks *clear* speech.)

ii. or adverbially,

अश्वः शीघ्रं धावति ।	(The hose runs *swiftly*.)
स्पष्टं वदति ।	(He speaks *clearly*.)

iii. or, by तद्धित derivation, they can be made into abstract nouns which can then be put in an appropriate case,

अश्वः शैघ्र्येण धावति ।	(The horse runs *by swiftness* [i.e., swiftly].)
स्पष्टतया वदति ।	(He speaks *with clarity* [i.e., clearly].)

e. As a final example of the usefulness of learning the major suffixes, consider the following *partial* list of derivations of the root √युज् (7P), "join, harness, yoke, concentrate the mind."

योगः	(m)	yoga, spiritual exercise, yoking, a philosophical school
योगिन्	(m) -इनी (f)	Yogī, Yoginī, yoker
युक्त	(adj)	joined, fitting, proper, concentrated (as of mind)
युक्तिः	(f)	joining; a well-made plan, plot, strategem
योक्तव्य	(adj)	to be yoked, joined
योक्त्रम्	(n)	instrument for fastening, rope, thong
योक्तृ	(m, f, n)	harnesser
युगम्	(n)	yoke, pair, cosmic cycle
युग्मम्	(n)	joined pair; even (as of numbers) (adj)
योग्य	(adj)	suitable, fit, proper
योग्यता	(f)	propriety, suitability
यौक्तिक	(adj)	suitable, fitting

यौग	(m)	a follower of the Yoga school
योजनम्	(n)	a yoking, a measure of distance (i.e., as far as one goes without unyoking oxen, etc.), mental concentration (=*yoga*)
योजनिक	(adj)	pertaining to a *yojana*, of so many *yojana*-s in length
योजनीय	(adj)	to be joined

Many more forms could be derived from the root preceded by various उपसर्ग-s.

EXERCISES

A. Translate the reading up to पाययतेति.

B. Pick out and analyze all कृत् and all तद्धित derivatives from the passage. Give, for कृत-s, the root, प्रत्यय, and meaning; for तद्धित-s, the प्रकृति, प्रत्यय, and meaning.

C. Do the same up to पुनर्योद्धुमाहवे.

D. Do the same for the remainder of the reading.

E. Generate the indicated nominal derivatives from the following list of धातु-s and प्रकृति-s using the indicated प्रत्यय-s.

Base		**प्रत्यय**	**derivative and meaning**
महिषः	(m) (buffalo)	-अ	(adj) (related to or coming from buffalo)
		-त्व	(n) (state of being a buffalo)
पूरुः	(m prop) (Pūru)	-अ	(m) (son or descendant of Pūru)
√त्यज्	(1P) (abandon)	-अ	(m) (renunciation)
		-य	(adj) (to be abandoned)
√मुच्	(6P) (release)	-ति	(f) (release, liberation)
√वच्	(2P) (speak)	-त्र	(n) (organ of speech)
		-त	(adj) (spoken)
हिमवन्त्	(m prop) (Himālayan mountain)	-अ	(adj) (related to, coming from Himālaya)

अलस	(adj) (lazy)	-य	(n) (laziness)
गङ्गा	(f prop) (the Ganges)	-एय्	(m) (son of the Ganges)
व्यासः	(m prop) (Vyāsa)	-इक	(m) (son of Vyāsa)
दूतः	(m) (messenger)	-य	(n) (office of messenger)
प्र + √विश्	(6P) (enter)	-अ	(m) (entrance)
		-अन	(n) (entrance)
√जन्	(4Ā) (be born)	-मन्	(n) (birth)
		-ति	(f) (birth)
उपगुः	(m prop) (Upagu)	-अ	(m) (son of Upagu)
√चिन्त्	(10P) (think)	-आ	(f) (thought, anxiety)

F. Translate and memorize the following verse from the बुद्धचरित, in which we hear the dramatic vow of the newborn prince गौतम affirming his destiny.

बोधाय जातो ऽस्मि जगद्धितार्थमन्त्या भवोत्पत्तिरियं ममेति ।
चतुर्दिशं सिंहगतिर्विलोक्य वाणीं च भव्यार्थकरीमुवाच ॥

G. Analyze the following derivatives used in the above verse. Indicate the underlying form, the प्रत्यय, and the type of derivation (कृत् or तद्धित). Check the glossary for verse, below, for all items. Give case, number, and gender where applicable.

a. बोधाय
b. जातः
c. हित (√धा [3P] [place])
d. अन्त्या
e. भवः
f. उत्पत्तिः
g. दिशम् (√दिश् [6P] [point])
h. गतिः
i. विलोक्य
j. वाणीम् (√वण् [1P] [sound])
k. भव्य
l. करीम्

READING

सौमित्रिविरूपितस्वभगिन्याः शूर्पणखाया रोदनं श्रुत्वा तां तथा शोणितदिग्धशरीरां छिन्नकर्णनासिकां भूमौ पतितां प्रेक्ष्य क्रोधमूर्च्छितः खर एवं पप्रच्छ। केन काभ्यां कैर्वा त्वमेवं विरूपिता। मम जीवतः को महावीरो देवगन्धर्वमानवानामेवंरूपं कर्म कर्तुं धृष्णोति।

निहतस्य मया संख्ये शरसंकृत्तमर्मणः।
सफेनं मेदिनी रक्तं कस्य वीरस्य पास्यति ॥१॥
कस्य पत्ररथाः कायान्मांसमुत्कृत्य संगताः।
प्रहृष्टा भक्षयिष्यन्ति निहतस्य मया रणे ॥२॥

ततः सर्वस्मिन्निवेदिते वृत्ते शूर्पणखया खरः परममन्युश्चतुर्दश महाबलानन्तकोपमान्राक्षसानाहूयैवमवोचत्। कौचन मानुषौ शस्त्रसंपन्नौ तापसाम्बरौ दण्डकारण्ये कयाचन प्रमदया सह निवसतः। तेषां वधं कारयित्वेमां मम भगिनीं तेषां शोणितं पाययतेति। एवमुक्ता राक्षसाधिपेन यथाज्ञापयति देव इत्याज्ञामङ्गीकृत्य ते दाशरथेः शौर्यमविज्ञाय मनोवेगेनागच्छन्दाशरथ्याश्रमम्। इमांश्चतुर्दश युगान्तमेघोपमान्राक्षसान्दृष्ट्वा काकुत्स्थो भ्रातरमब्रवीत्।

मुहूर्तं भव सौमित्रे सीतायाः प्रत्यनन्तरः।
यावदेतान्वधिष्यामि ब्रह्मघ्नान्राक्षसान्वने ॥३॥

ततो निशाचरानुवाच

युष्मान्हन्तुमहं प्राप्त ऋषिभिश्च नियोजितः।
यदि प्राणैरिहार्थो वो निवर्तध्वं निशाचराः ॥४॥

इत्युक्ता महात्मना धैर्यवीर्यसंपन्नेन ते शूलपाणयो राक्षसाः क्रोधाकुलमनस एवमूचुः।

क्रोधमुत्पाद्य नो भर्तुः खरस्य सुमहात्मनः।
त्वमेव हास्यसि प्राणानद्यास्माभिर्हतो युधि ॥५॥
का हि ते शक्तिरेकस्य बहूनां रणमूर्धनि।
अस्माकमग्रतः स्थातुं किं पुनर्योद्धुमाहवे ॥६॥

इति ब्रुवाणास्ते संरब्धाश्चिक्षिपुस्तानि शूलानि राघवे परमदुर्जये। स वीरो न क्षणमप्युद्विजमानस्तानि चतुर्दश परिघसन्निभानि शूलानि तावद्भिरि-

षुभिश्चिच्छेद। ततो निशाचरॉंल्लक्ष्यीकृत्य मुमोच राघवो बाणान् । त इषवो राक्षसानां वक्षांसि वेगेन भित्त्वा वल्मीकानिव सर्पा भूमिं प्रविविशुः । पञ्चत्वं गतेषु निशाचरेषु शूर्पणखातीव त्रस्ता भीता च पुनर्जनस्थानं गत्वा भ्रातरं खरं सर्वं ज्ञापयामास । तन्निशम्य स निशाचरो ऽत्यन्तं कुपितः सन्दूषणं नाम सेनापतिमुद्दिश्य खरः खरवचनमवोचत् ।

चतुर्दश सहस्राणि मम चित्तानुवर्तिनाम् ।
रक्षसां भीमवेगानां समरेष्वनिवर्तिनाम् ॥७॥
नीलजीमूतवर्णानां घोराणां क्रूरकर्मणाम् ।
लोकहिंसाविहारिणां बलिनामुग्रतेजसाम् ॥८॥ सेनां संयोजय सौम्येति । ततः संप्राप्तायां राक्षससेनायां राघवाश्रमे महद्युद्धमभूत् । अन्ततो रामेणाभिहता निशाचरचमूः सखरदूषणा यथोन्मत्तगजयूथं कुपितसिंहेन । सर्वेषां दण्डकारण्यस्थितानां राक्षसानामेक एवाकम्पनो नाम कथमपि जीवन्दुःखार्तो लङ्कां कथंचित्प्राप्य राक्षसाधिराजं दशग्रीवं वैश्रवणं रावणमुपगम्य खरदूषणविनाशनं निवेदयाञ्चकार ॥

GLOSSARY

अकम्पनः
(m prop)—name of a rākṣasa

अग्रतः
(ind)—in front of

अङ्गीकृ
(8P)—accept, agree to

अनिवर्तिन्
(adj)—not turning back

अनुवर्तिन्
(adj)—obedient

अन्तकः
(m)—death (lit., "ender")

अभिहत
(adj)—slain, annihilated

अम्बरम्
(n)—garment

अर्थः
(m)—use, value

आर्त
(adj)—afflicted by

आहवः
(m)—battle

उग्र
(adj)—fierce, terrible

उत् + √कृ
(6P)—tear to pieces

उत्पादय्
(णिजन्त)—stir up, arouse, produce

एवंरूपम्
(idiom)—such kind, such sort

कायः
(m)—body

कथमपि or -चित्
(ind)—somehow or other, barely

काकुत्स्थः
(m)—epithet of Rāma

किं पुनः
(ind)—how much more (or less)

√क्षिप्
(6P)—throw

खर
(adj)—harsh, cruel

गन्धर्वः
(m)—a kind of celestial being

चित्तम्
(n)—thought, will

जीमूतः
(m)—cloud

तापसः
(m)—ascetic

तावत्
(adj)—so many, as many

त्रस्त

(adj)—frightened

दिग्ध

(adj)—smeared

दुर्जय

(adj)—invincible

दूषणः

(m prop)—name of a demon

देवः

(m)—title of respectful address to a king

√धृष्

(5P)—be bold or courageous, be confident, dare

धैर्यम्

(n)—fortitude, courage

नियोजित

(adj)—appointed

नि + √वस्

(1P)—live, dwell

नि + √वृत्

(1Ā)—turn back

नि + √शम्

(4P)—hear, listen

नील

(adj)—dark, blue-black

पञ्चत्वम्

(n)—dissolution, death

पत्त्ररथः

(m)—bird (here, carrion bird)

परिघः

(m)—iron bar, a massive club

पाणिः

(m)—hand; at end of compound 'having... in hand,' for example, खड्गपाणिः 'with sword in hand'

प्रत्यनन्तर

(adj)—being in the immediate neighborhood

प्रमदा

(f)—a beautiful young woman

प्रहृष्ट

(adj)—delighted

प्राप्त

(adj)—come, arrived

फेनः

(m)—foam

बलिन्

(adj)—strong, powerful

ब्रह्मघ्न

(adj)—killer of brāhmans

√भिद्

(7P)—split, cleave

भीम

(adj)—terrible

मर्मन्

(n)—vital spot

मानव

(adj)—*relating* to Manu; -ḥ—man, human

मानुष
(adj)—human; -ḥ—man, human; -ī—woman

मांसम्
(n)—flesh

√मुच्
(6P)—release

मुहूर्तम्
(n)—moment, instant

मूर्धन्
(m)—head, forefront (of battle)

मेदिनी
(f)—earth

युगान्तमेघः
(m)—cloud gathering at the end of a cosmic cycle

युद्धम्
(n)—battle

युध्
(f)—battle

यूथम्
(n)—herd, group

रक्षः
(n)—rākṣasa

रोदनम्
(n)—crying

लक्ष्यम्
(n)—target

लङ्का
(f prop)—name of Rāvaṇa's capital

वक्षः
(n)—chest

√वध्
(1P)—kill, slay

वर्णः
(m)—color, hue

वल्मीकः
(m)—ant hill

वि + √नश्
(4P)—be destroyed

विहारिन्
(adj)—delighting in

वैश्रवणः
(m prop)—son of Viśravaṇa; Rāvaṇa

शक्तिः
(f)—power, ability

शरीरम्
(n)—body

शूलम्
(n)—lance, spear

सम् + √युज्
(7P/Ā)—join, yoke

संरब्ध
(adj)—infuriated

संकृत्त
(adj)—pierced

संख्यम्
(n)—battle

संगत

(adj)—joined or united with

सन्निभ

(adj)—like

समरः

(m)—battle

संपन्न

(adj)—at end of compound 'endowed with'

सर्पः

(m)—snake

सौम्य

(adj)—gentle, pleasant; as a vocative, 'my friend!,' 'my good man!'

हिंसा

(f)—violence, injury

GLOSSARY FOR VERSE

(In order of occurrence)

बोधः

(m)—enlightenment

जगत्

(n)—the world, universe

हितम्

(n)—benefit, well-being

अर्थम्

(ind)—at end of compound 'for the sake of'

अन्त्य

(adj)—final, last

भवः

(m)—existence, worldly existence, the world

उत्पत्तिः

(f)—birth

दिश्

(f)—direction, cardinal point, quarter

गतिः

(f)—gait

वि + √लोक्

(10P)—look at, perceive

वाणी

(f)—speech

भव्य

(adj)—true, capable (of perceiving truth), fortunate

कर

(adj; f -इ)—at end of compound 'does, makes or causes'

LESSON 21

Additional Consonantal Stem Formations; Stems with Final संयुक्त Vowels; Some Irregular Nominal Declensions; Declension of the Comparative Suffix यांस्/यः; Some Remarks on Adverbial Formation

21.0 Aside from the nominal stems with final consonants already introduced, there is a class of nouns ending in one or another of the simple consonants. These nouns are most often monosyllabic and derive either from a root with only the क्विप्, or zero, suffix (20.6.a), or from a root in final short vowel to which the consonant त् has been added (12.17).

21.1 Nouns of this sort are normally स्त्रीलिङ्ग when they signify the action of a verbal root (e.g., युध् [f] [battle]; दिक् [f] [direction]) and commonly पुंलिङ्ग when they signify its agent (e.g., पापकृत् [m, f, n] [sinner]; द्विष् [m] [foe, enemy]). The declension of such stems is the same for पुंलिङ्ग and स्त्रीलिङ्ग. नपुंसकलिङ्ग stems are less common and as usual, differ in the प्रथमा and द्वितीया. The variation of the stem final consonant in the paradigms is a result of the rules of "possible word finals" (3.25).

a. वाक् (स्त्रीलिङ्ग) (speech)

	एक°	द्वि°	बहु°
प्र°, सम्°	वाक्	वाचौ	वाचः
द्वि°	वाचम्	वाचौ	वाचः
तृ°	वाचा	वाग्भ्याम्	वाग्भिः
च°	वाचे	वाग्भ्याम्	वाग्भ्यः
प°	वाचः	वाग्भ्याम्	वाग्भ्यः
ष°	वाचः	वाचोः	वाचाम्
स°	वाचि	वाचोः	वाक्षु

b. शस्त्रभृत् (पुंलिङ्ग) (weapon bearer, warrior)

	एक°	द्वि°	बहु°
प्र°, सम्°	शस्त्रभृत्	शस्त्रभृतौ	शस्त्रभृतः
द्वि°	शस्त्रभृतम्	शस्त्रभृतौ	शस्त्रभृतः
तृ°	शस्त्रभृता	शस्त्रभृद्भ्याम्	शस्त्रभृद्भिः
च°	शस्त्रभृते	शस्त्रभृद्भ्याम्	शस्त्रभृद्भ्यः
प°	शस्त्रभृतः	शस्त्रभृद्भ्याम्	शस्त्रभृद्भ्यः
ष°	शस्त्रभृतः	शस्त्रभृतोः	शस्त्रभृताम्
स°	शस्त्रभृति	शस्त्रभृतोः	शस्त्रभृत्सु

c. विश्वसृट् (नपुंसकलिङ्ग) (creator of the universe) (=विश्वसृज्)

	एक°	द्वि°	बहु°
प्र°, सम्°	विश्वसृट्	विश्वसृजी	विश्वसृञ्जि
द्वि°	विश्वसृट्	विश्वसृजी	विश्वसृञ्जि
तृ°	विश्वसृजा	विश्वसृड्भ्याम्	विश्वसृड्भिः
च°	विश्वसृजे	विश्वसृड्भ्याम्	विश्वसृड्भ्यः
प°	विश्वसृजः	विश्वसृड्भ्याम्	विश्वसृड्भ्यः
ष°	विश्वसृजः	विश्वसृजोः	विश्वसृजाम्
स°	विश्वसृजि	विश्वसृजोः	विश्वसृट्सु

21.2 A typical stem with a final संयुक्त vowel is नौ (स्त्रीलिङ्ग) (boat).

	एक°	द्वि°	बहु°
प्र°, सम्°	नौः	नावौ	नावः
द्वि°	नावम्	नावौ	नावः
तृ°	नावा	नौभ्याम्	नौभिः
च°	नावे	नौभ्याम्	नौभ्यः
प°	नावः	नौभ्याम्	नौभ्यः
ष°	नावः	नावोः	नावाम्
स°	नावि	नावोः	नौषु

21.3 **Irregular Declensions**

Aside from the regular declensions, Sanskrit, like any other language, has a number of nouns which are irregular. That is to say, these nouns fail in one or more forms, to follow the pattern which one would expect for their stem finals and genders. Fortunately, the number of such nouns that are of common occurrence is rather limited. The following are the paradigms of some of the more important irregular nouns.

a. सखि (पुंलिङ्ग) (friend) has a decidedly peculiar declension which should be learned. सखी (स्त्रीलिङ्ग) is declined regularly.

	एक°	द्वि°	बहु°
प्र°	सखा	सखायौ	सखायः
द्वि°	सखायम्	सखायौ	सखीन्
तृ°	सख्या	सखिभ्याम्	सखिभिः
च°	सख्ये	सखिभ्याम्	सखिभ्यः
प°	सख्युः	सखिभ्याम्	सखिभ्यः
ष°	सख्युः	सख्योः	सखीनाम्
स°	सख्यौ	सख्योः	सखिषु
सम्°	सखे	सखायौ	सखायः

b. पतिः (पुंलिङ्ग) (1. lord; 2. husband) is regularly declined when it means "lord, master, etc.," *and* in either meaning when at the end of a compound. However, when it is used to signify "husband" and is not the final member of a compound, its declension is:

	एक°	द्वि°	बहु°
प्र°	पतिः	पती	पतयः
द्वि°	पतिम्	पती	पतीन्
तृ°	पत्या	etc., as a regular इ-stem	
च°	पत्ये		
प°	पत्युः		
ष°	पत्युः		
स°	पत्यौ		
सम्°	पते		

c. अक्षि (नपुंसकलिङ्ग) (eye), and also the neuter दधि, (curd) अस्थि, (bone), and सक्थि, (thigh), form the weakest cases (i.e., weak forms before vowel-initial endings) from corresponding stems अक्षन्, दधन्, etc.

अक्षि (नपुंसकलिङ्ग) (eye)

	एक°	द्वि°	बहु°
प्र°, द्वि°, सम्°	अक्षि	अक्षिणी	अक्षीणि
तृ°	अक्ष्णा	अक्षिभ्याम्	अक्षिभिः
च°	अक्ष्णे	अक्षिभ्याम्	अक्षिभ्यः
प°	अक्ष्णः	अक्षिभ्याम्	अक्षिभ्यः
ष°	अक्ष्णः	अक्ष्णोः	अक्ष्णाम्
स°	अक्ष्णि/अक्षणि	अक्ष्णोः	अक्षिषु

d. पन्थिन् (पुंलिङ्ग) (road) is quite irregular.

	एक°	द्वि°	बहु°
प्र°	पन्थाः	पन्थानौ	पन्थानः
द्वि°	पन्थानम्	पन्थानौ	पथः
तृ°	पथा	पथिभ्याम्	पथिभिः
च°	पथे	पथिभ्याम्	पथिभ्यः
प°	पथः	पथिभ्याम्	पथिभ्यः
ष°	पथः	पथोः	पथाम्
स°	पथि	पथोः	पथिषु

e. गो (पुंलिङ्ग) (bull); (स्त्रीलिङ्ग) (cow) is also irregular.

	एक°	द्वि°	बहु°
प्र°	गौः	गावौ	गावः
द्वि°	गाम्	गावौ	गाः
तृ°	गवा	गोभ्याम्	गोभिः
च°	गवे	गोभ्याम्	गोभ्यः
प°	गोः	गोभ्याम्	गोभ्यः
ष°	गोः	गवोः	गवाम्
स°	गवि	गवोः	गोषु

f. The noun मघवन् (पुंलिङ्ग prop) (epithet of Indra) takes in weakest forms a stem मघोन्.

	एक°	द्वि°	बहु°
प्र°	मघवा	मघवानौ	मघवानः
द्वि°	मघवानम्	मघवानौ	मघोनः
तृ°	मघोना	मघवभ्याम्	मघवभिः

च°	मघोने	मघवभ्याम्	मघवभ्यः
प°	मघोनः	मघवभ्याम्	मघवभ्यः
ष°	मघोनः	मघोनोः	मघोनाम्
स°	मघोनि	मघोनोः	मघवसु
सम्°	मघवन्	मघवानौ	मघवानः

g. अहन् (नपुंसकलिङ्ग) (day) supplements its paradigm with forms of अहः. In समास, only अहः occurs as a prior member, while as final member अहन् (like राजन्) may revert to the अ declension.

	एक°	द्वि°	बहु°
प्र°, द्वि°, सम्°	अहः	अह्नी /अहनी	अहानि
तृ°	अह्ना	अहोभ्याम्	अहोभिः
च°	अह्ने	अहोभ्याम्	अहोभ्यः
प°	अह्नः	अहोभ्याम्	अहोभ्यः
ष°	अह्नः	अह्नोः	अह्नाम्
स°	अह्नि/अहनि	अह्नोः	अहःसु

h. धीः (स्त्रीलिङ्ग) (thought)

	एक°	द्वि°	बहु°
प्र°, सम्°	धीः	धियौ	धियः
द्वि°	धियम्	धियौ	धियः
तृ°	धिया	धीभ्याम्	धीभिः
च°	धिये/धियै	धीभ्याम्	धीभ्यः
प°	धियः/धियाः	धीभ्याम्	धीभ्यः
ष°	धियः/धियाः	धियोः	धियाम्/धीनाम्
स°	धियि/धियाम्	धियोः	धीषु

21.4 **The Comparative Suffix यांस्/यः**

This प्रत्यय, introduced in the previous chapter (20.11.m.ii), has a peculiar distinction of strength and weakness in पुंलिङ्ग and नपुंसकलिङ्ग. The strong-weak alternation is यांस् (ईयांस्)/ यस् (ईयस्) (e.g., श्रेयान्/श्रेयः). The स्त्रीलिङ्ग is formed by adding ई to the weak stem and is completely regular.

a. श्रेयांस्/श्रेयः (better)

	एक°		द्वि°		बहु°	
	पुंलिङ्ग	नपुंसक°	पुं°	नपुं°	पुं°	नपुं°
प्र°	श्रेयान्	श्रेयः	श्रेयांसौ	श्रेयसी	श्रेयांसः	श्रेयांसि
द्वि°	श्रेयांसम्	श्रेयः	श्रेयांसौ	श्रेयसी	श्रेयसः	श्रेयांसि
तृ°	श्रेयसा		श्रेयोभ्याम्		श्रेयोभिः	
च°	श्रेयसे		श्रेयोभ्याम्		श्रेयोभ्यः	
प°	श्रेयसः		श्रेयोभ्याम्		श्रेयोभ्यः	
ष°	श्रेयसः		श्रेयसोः		श्रेयसाम्	
स°	श्रेयसि		श्रेयसोः		श्रेयःसु	
सम्°	श्रेयन्	श्रेयः	श्रेयांसौ	श्रेयसी	श्रेयांसः	श्रेयांसि

b. Note that in most cases, the strong stem is in ईयांस्.
Example:
गरीयांस्/गरीयः (heavier)
प्र° गरीयान् गरीयः गरीयांसौ गरीयसी गरीयांसः गरीयांसि etc.

21.5 **अव्ययपद-s: Adverbial Formation**

Of the three types of words mentioned in 4.3, adverbs, or अव्ययपद-s are naturally the cause of least difficulty. Nevertheless, a few remarks about their formation are in order.

21.6 There are many kinds of adverbs but two, especially, invite systematization. These are 1) adverbs formed by the use of special adverbial suffixes, and 2) adverbs formed by stereotyped usage of the सुप् endings.

a. **Adverbial Suffixes**

A number of the suffixes, which—when added to various forms of the pronominal stems—produce the characteristic interrogative, relative, correlative series of अव्ययपद-s (6.3), may be added to other stems. Most of them may be appended to the adjectives which decline pronominally (5.7).

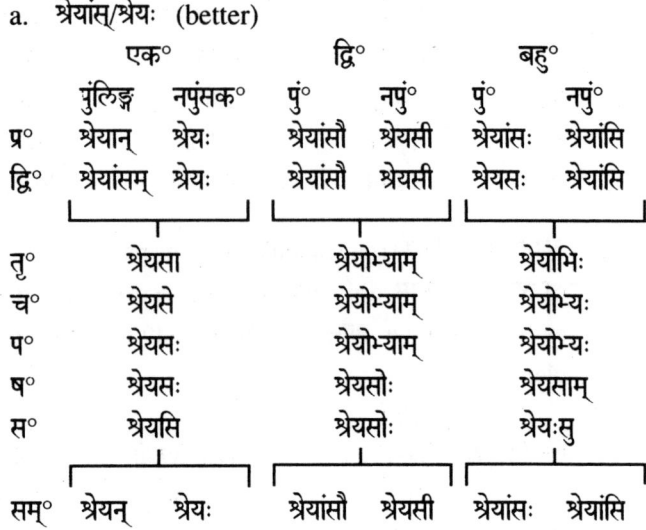

Examples:

सर्वत्र	(everywhere)
सर्वदा	(always)
सर्वतः	(from all sides)
परत्र	(elsewhere [especially "in the next word"])
अन्यथा	(otherwise)
अन्यत्र	(elsewhere)

i. The suffix -तः however, may be added to virtually any nominal stem to form an adverb.

Examples:

Noun		**Adverb**	
शास्त्रम्	(n) (authoritative text)	शास्त्रतः	(ind) (according to the śāstras)
धर्मः	(m) (dharma)	धर्मतः	(ind) (in accord with dharma)
पृष्ठम्	(n) (back)	पृष्ठतः	(ind) (behind)
अग्र	(adj) (foremost)	अग्रतः	(ind) (first, in front, in the beginning)
ग्रामः	(m) (village)	ग्रामतः	(ind) (from the village)

ii. There are some other suffixes which may be used to generate adverbs.

a. -वत् forms an adverb from any noun X, in the sense of "like X." (See 20.11.9.)

Examples:

कपिः (m) (monkey)

कपिवत् (ind) (like a monkey)

कूपमण्डूकः (m) (a frog in a well)

कूपमण्डूकवत् (ind) (like a frog in a well [i.e., in a narrow or provincial manner])

b. -धा may be added to numerals, or to adjectives indicative of quantity, in the sense of "-fold."

Examples:

द्वि "two" द्विधा (ind) (twofold)

बहु (adj) "many" बहुधा (ind) (manifold)

एकं सद्विप्रा बहुधा वदन्ति ।

(Sages call *by many* names what is really one being.)

c. -शः may also be added to numbers or quantifiers to indicate the sense of "by so many at a time." Examples:

शतम् (n) (hundred) शतशः (by the hundred)

शत्रूञ्जघान शतशः सहस्रशश्च ।

(He slew his enemies *by the hundreds and thousands.*)

b. **सुप् Endings**

A very common and often deceptive feature of Sanskrit is the fact that the सुप् terminations themselves are frequently stereotyped as adverbial markers. This phenomenon is most marked with the द्वितीया and less freely, the तृतीया endings, although other cases show it sporadically. एकवचन forms are most common, although occasional बहुवचन forms occur.

i. द्वितीया

The द्वितीया, एकवचन, नपुंसकलिङ्ग forms of nouns and even of pronouns, are freely used as adverbs,

a. **pronouns**

किम्	(why)
यत्	(in that, insofar as)
तत्	(in that way)

b. **adjectives**

शीघ्रं धावति ।	(He runs *swiftly.*)
मन्दं मन्दं नुदति पवनो मेघम् ।	(The wind drives the cloud *very gently.*)

c. **nouns**

कामं परिभ्रमति ।	(He wanders *at will.*)
सुखं जीवति ।	(He lives *happily.*)
राजाभूद्दशरथो नाम ।	(There was a king, Daśaratha *by name.*)

d. Other cases: Some adjectives, notably चिर, (long) (as of time) and दूर, (far) may occur adverbially with other सुप् endings, e.g.,

अखिलेन तच्छ्रोतुमिच्छामि ।
(I want to hear that *in its entirety.*)

एतद्विस्तरेण कथयतु भवान् ।
(Tell it, sir, *at length.*)

चिरेण भवन्मुखं दृष्टं मया ।
(I see your face *after a long time.*)

शनैः शनैर्वदति । (He speaks *very slowly.*)

उच्चैर्वद । (Speak *loudly*!)

दूरादिव भवद्वचनं शृणोमि । (I hear your words as it were *from afar.*)

चिर may mean 'for a long time' or 'after a long time' in any एकवचन case but the प्रथमा.

Examples:

चिरं
चिरेण
चिराय
चिरात् — जीव (live long)
चिरस्य
चिरे

However, the षष्ठी and सप्तमी are not common.

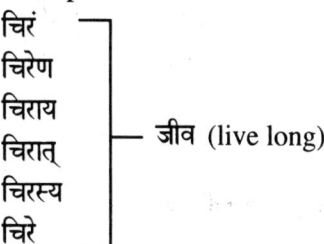

EXERCISES

A. Translate the reading up until तत्तु मूर्खवचनम्. Provide a Sanskrit prose summary of the passage.

B. Do the same for the passage up until the verse beginning with सौवर्णस्त्वम्.

C. Do the same for the rest of the passage.

D. Translate into Sanskrit:

1. Oh friend! Rāvaṇa is to be killed because of his being a *rākṣasa*.
2. Look! Regarding the son of Daśaratha as a fly (use च्वि प्रत्यय), the foolish lord of Laṅkā, impelled by Death, is coming to the *āśram* with Mārīca as a companion (lit., "as second").
3. When the fair-waisted daughter of Janaka was abducted by the night-roamer, Rāma, thinking, "How can I live deprived of the lovely lady of Videha?" was afflicted with great sorrow.
4. Doubtlessly, the demon, assuming the form of a golden deer by means of magic, walked the path to the *āśram*. When he arrived there, he revealed his true form: tall as a mountain, bearing weapons, and dark as a cloud at the time of the cosmic dissolution.
5. The dwelling shone with a bright light, but from within a harsh voice called out, "I am the demon Bhagnāṅga, mighty and valorous, destroyer of many armies! Depart to save your lives!"

E. Translate and memorize the following verse:

वासांसि जीर्णानि यथा विहाय
नवानि गृह्णाति नरोऽपराणि ।
तथा शरीराणि विहाय जीर्णा-
न्यन्यानि संयाति नवानि देही ॥

READING

जनस्थानस्थिता राजन्राक्षसा बहवो हताः ।
खरश्च निहतः संख्ये कथंचिदहमागतः ॥१॥

इत्युच्यमानो ऽकम्पनेन दशग्रीवः प्रलयाग्निरिव *जाज्वल्यमानः कोपात् कैर्मरणमिच्छद्भिरमरैर्हतः स्वजन इति जिज्ञासुरभूत् । ततो ऽद्वितीयेन केनचिद् बलवता धनुष्मता मनुष्येण सर्वमिदं कृतमिति वचनमाकर्ण्य वैश्रवणो दाशरथेर्हनने मनश्चक्रे मक्षिकाहनने क्रीडद्बालक इव । गमिष्यामि जनस्थानं रामं हन्तुं सलक्ष्मणमिति भाषमाणे लङ्काधिपतौ कम्पनकम्पिताकम्पन इदं वक्रं वचनमवोचत् ।

न हि रामो दशग्रीव शक्यो जेतुं रणे त्वया ।
रक्षसां वापि लोकेन** स्वर्गः पापजनैरिव ॥२॥
न तं वध्यमहं मन्ये सर्वैर्देवासुरैरपि ।
अयं तस्य वधोपायस्तन्ममैकमनाः शृणु ॥३॥
भार्या तस्योत्तमा लोके सीता नाम सुमध्यमा ।
श्यामा समविभक्ताङ्गी स्त्रीरत्नं रत्नभूषिता ॥४॥
तस्यापहर भार्यां त्वं तं प्रमथ्य महावने ।
सीतया रहितः कामी रामो हास्यति जीवितम् ॥५॥

तत्तु मूर्खवचनं काममूर्च्छिताय दशग्रीवायारोचत । तथा हि

बाढं कल्यं गमिष्याम्येकः सारथिना सह ।
आनयिष्यामि वैदेहीमिमां हृष्टो महापुरीम् ॥६॥

इत्युक्त्वा प्रातश्च खरयुक्तं रथमारुह्य सख्युर्मारीचनाम्नः कस्यचन कामरूपिणो निशाचरस्य निवासस्थानं मनोवेगेन ययौ । त्वया सीतापहर्तव्येत्युक्तो मारीचः संत्रस्तमना एवमब्रवीत् । सखे किं भणसि । राघवशौर्यं न जानासि किम् । सीतामपहरेति वदंस्त्वं लङ्कां राघवकोपाग्निना दग्धां दिदृक्षुरसि ।

प्रसीद लङ्केश्वर राक्षसेन्द्र लङ्कां प्रसन्नो भव साधु गच्छ ।
त्वं स्वेषु दारेषु रमस्व नित्यं रामः सभार्यो रमतां वनेषु ॥७॥

सम्यग्जानामि रामस्य घोरं पराक्रमं यतः पुराहं हतप्राय आसमनेन महात्मना । अत एवाधुना

रकारादीनि नामानि रामत्रस्तस्य रावण ।***
रत्नानि च रथाश्चैव वित्रासं जनयन्ति मे ॥८॥
अवधूय तु तद्वाक्यं क्षमं युक्तं हितावहम् ।
मृत्युना प्रेरितो राजा वाक्यं परुषमब्रवीत् ॥९॥

मम वचनमकुर्वाणं त्वां हन्मि । यदि जिजीविषुरसि शृणु मदीयामाज्ञाम् ।

सौवर्णस्त्वं मृगो भूत्वा चित्रो रजतबिन्दुभिः ।
आश्रमे तस्य रामस्य सीतायाः प्रमुखे चर ।
प्रलोभयित्वा वैदेहीं यथेष्टं गन्तुमर्हसि ॥१०॥
त्वां हि मायामयं दृष्ट्वा काञ्चनं जातविस्मया ।
आनयैनमिति क्षिप्रं रामं वक्ष्यति मैथिली ॥११॥
अपक्रान्ते च काकुत्स्थे दूरं गत्वाप्युदाहर ।
हा सीते लक्ष्मणेत्येवं रामवाक्यानुरूपकम् ॥१२॥
तच्छ्रुत्वा रामपदवीं सीतया च प्रचोदितः ।
अनुगच्छति संभ्रान्तः सौमित्रिरपि सौहृदात् ॥१३॥
अपक्रान्ते च काकुत्स्थे लक्ष्मणे च यथासुखम् ।
आनयिष्यामि वैदेहीं महाव्याघ्रो मृगीमिव ॥१४॥

रामरावणयोरुभयोः समं प्रभावं विज्ञायेतो व्याघ्रस्ततस्तटीति पर्याकुलो मारीचः कथमपि भर्तुर्वचनमङ्गीचकार । ततो दशग्रीवेण सह दण्डकारण्यं गत्वातिमनोहरं मृगरूपमास्थायेतस्ततो विचरन्रामाश्रममाजगाम ॥

NOTES

* जाज्वल्यमान see 18.26 = यङन्त

** Take लोक here in the sense of 'host, multitude'; लोकेन then construes as लोकेन सह त्वया 'by you, even with a host of.' The last three words constitute a simile.

*** In the verse Mārīca suggests the terror that Rāma inspires in him. He is so frightened of the hero that he becomes terrified of words beginning with the letter r.

GLOSSARY

अतः
(ind)—from this, hence, therefore

अनुरूपक
(adj)—like, the same as

अपक्रान्त
(adj)—gone away, lured away

अपहर्तव्य
(adj)—to be abducted

अप + √हृ
(1P)—abduct

अमर
(adj)—immortal; (m)—a god

अव + √धू
(5P)—shake off, disregard

असंशयम्
(ind)—doubtlessly

असुरः
(m)—demon, titan

आ + √ज्ञा
(9P)—know; (णिजन्त) order

आ + √दा
(3P)—take, assume

आ + √स्था
(1P)—assume, have recourse to, take

इतः—ततः
(ind)—here. . . there

इतो व्याघ्रस्ततस्तटी
(idiom)—on one side a tiger, on the other a precipice, i.e., a serious dilemma

इन्द्रः
(m)—(at end of compound) lord of, best of

ईश्वरः
(m)—lord, god

उद् + आ + √हृ
(1P)—announce, call out

उपायः
(m)—means, device, stratagem

उभ
(adj)—both (used only in the dual)

एकमनः
(adj)—having an attentive mind

एनम् = तम्

कम्पनम्
(n)—tremor, shaking

कम्पित
(adj)—trembling

कल्यम्
(ind)—at daybreak

काञ्चन
(adj)—golden

कामिन्
(m)—lover

कालः
(m)—time, Death

√क्रीड्
(1P)—play, amuse oneself

क्षम
(adj)—favorable, suitable

क्षिप्रम्
(ind)—quickly, immediately

खरः
(m)—ass, donkey

गिरिः
(m)—mountain

चित्र
(adj)—spotted, speckled

जीवितम्
(n)—life

√ज्वल्
(1Ā)—shine, blaze

तटी
(f)—slope, precipice

तत्त्वम्
(n)—truth

तुङ्ग
(adj)—tall

√दह्
(1P)—burn

दारः
(m; occurs only in plural)—wife, wives

दूरम्
(ind)—far

धनुष्मन्त्
(adj; m, n)—having a bow

नाशकः
(m)—destroyer

नित्यम्
(ind)—always, constantly

निवासः
(m)—dwelling

पदवी
(f)—path; with अनु + √गम्, follow in someone's footsteps

पराक्रमः
(m)—valor

परुष
(adj)—harsh

पर्याकुल
(adj)—frightened, confused

प्रकाशः
(m)—light

प्रचोदित
(adj)—urged

प्र + √मथ्
(1P)—harass, torment, annoy

प्रमुखे
(ind)—in front of, before the eyes of

प्रलयः
(m)—cosmic dissolution

प्रलोभय्
(णिजन्त of प्र + √लुभ्)—infatuate

प्रसन्न
(adj)—calm

प्रातः (=प्रातर्)
(ind)—in the morning

प्राय
(adj)—(at end of compound) for the most part, generally, practically

प्रेरित
(adj)—urged, impelled

बलवन्त्
(adj; m, n)—mighty

बाढम्
(ind)—excellent! good idea!

√भण्
(1P)—say

-भृत्
(adj)—(at end of compound) bearing, carrying

मक्षिका
(f)—fly, mosquito

मनोहर
(adj)—charming, fascinating

महापुरी
(f)—great city

माया
(f)—illusion, magic

मारीचः
(m prop)—name of a *rākṣasa*

मृत्युः
(m)—death

मेघः
(m)—cloud

मैथिली
(f)—lady of Mithilā, i.e., Sītā

यथेष्टम्
(ind)—according to desire, as you wish

युक्त
(adj)—proper

रकारः
(m)—the syllable 'ra,' the letter 'r'

रजतम्
(n)—silver

√रम्
(1Ā)—enjoy, make love

लङ्केश्वरः
(m)—lord of Lañkā, epithet of Rāvaṇa

लोकः
(m)—host, army

वक्षः
(n)—chest

वक्र
(adj)—crooked

वधः
(m)—killing, slaughter

वध्य
(adj)—to be killed

वित्रासः
(m)—terror

शक्य
(adj)—(with infinitive) capable of of being. . . (कर्मणि)

शौर्यम्
(n)—valor

श्याम
(adj)—dark

श्यामा
(f)—a young woman (who has not had children)

सम्यक्
(ind)—properly, fully

सखि
(m)—friend

संत्रस्त
(adj)—terrified

समविभक्ताङ्गी
(f)—woman of symmetrical limbs

संभ्रान्त
(adj)—confused

साधु
(ind)—directly, straight

सारथिः
(m)—charioteer

सुमध्यमा
(f)—woman with beautiful waist

सौवर्ण
(adj)—golden

सौहृदम्
(n)—friendship

स्त्री
(f)—woman

स्वजनः
(m)—kin

हितः
(m)—welfare, benefit

हृष्ट
(adj)—delighted

ENGLISH-SANSKRIT GLOSSARY

foolish	मूर्ख	(adj)
impelled	प्रेरित	(adj)
fair-waisted	सुमध्यम	(adj)
from within	अन्तरात्	(ind)
abduct	अप + √हृ	(1P)
doubtlessly	असंशयम्	(ind)
golden	काञ्चन	(adj)
path	पदवी	(f)
bearing weapons	शस्त्रभृत्	(m)
bright	उज्ज्वल	(adj)
light	प्रकाशः	(m)
harsh	परुष	(adj)
destroyer	नाशकः	(m)
save, protect	√रक्ष्	(1P)

GLOSSARY FOR VERSE

(In order of occurrence)

वासः
(n)—garment, clothing

जीर्ण
(adj)—aged, worn out

वि + √हा
(3P)—give up, discard

नव
(adj)—new

नरः
(m)—man

अपर
(adj)—other

सम् + √या
(2P)—attain

देहः
(m)—body

देहिन्
(adj)—having a body; (m)—man, soul

LESSON 22

Readings from the *Vālmīki Rāmāyaṇa*

22.0 The following verses are excerpted from the first सर्ग of the वाल्मीकि रामायण. In the passage the divine sage नारद, in response to वाल्मीकि's questions, relates, very concisely, the tale of राम. It is on the basis of this narration that वाल्मीकि, inspired, discovers poetry and composes the रामायण.

The verses selected complete the story in outline, from the abduction of सीता to the end. Due to the conciseness of the passage some of the references will be obscure. Notes have been provided to clarify various problems. Note that syntactic units frequently cross verse boundaries.

READING

श्रीमद्वाल्मीकिरामायणे

बालकाण्डम् १

जगाम सहमारीचस्तस्याश्रमपदं तदा ।
तेन मायाविना दूरमपवाह्य नृपात्मजौ ॥१॥
जहार भार्यां रामस्य गृध्रं हत्वा जटायुषम् ।
गृध्रं च निहतं दृष्ट्वा हृतां श्रुत्वा च मैथिलीम् ॥२॥
राघवः शोकसंतप्तो विललापाकुलेन्द्रियः ।
ततस्तेनैव शोकेन गृध्रं दग्ध्वा जटायुषम् ॥३॥
मार्गमाणो वने सीतां राक्षसं संददर्श ह ।
कबन्धं नाम रूपेण विकृतं घोरदर्शनम् ॥४॥
तं निहत्य महाबाहुर्ददाह स्वर्गतश्च सः ।
स चास्य कथयामास शबरीं धर्मचारिणीम् ॥५॥
शबर्या पूजितः सम्यग्रामो दशरथात्मजः ।
पम्पातीरे हनुमता सङ्गतो वानरेण ह ॥६॥
हनुमद्वचनाच्चैव सुग्रीवेण समागतः ।
सुग्रीवाय च तत्सर्वं शंसद्रामो महाबलः ॥७॥
आदितस्तद्यथा वृत्तं सीतायाश्च विशेषतः ।
सुग्रीवश्चापि तत्सर्वं श्रुत्वा रामस्य वानरः ॥८॥
चकार सख्यं रामेण प्रीतश्चैवाग्निसाक्षिकम् ।
ततो वानरराजेन वैरानुकथनं प्रति ॥९॥
रामायावेदितं सर्वं प्रणयाद्दुःखितेन च ।
प्रतिज्ञातं च रामेण तदा वालिवधं प्रति ॥१०॥
ततः प्रीतमनास्तेन विश्वस्तः स महाकपिः ।
किष्किन्धां रामसहितो जगाम च गुहां तदा ॥११॥
ततो ऽगर्जद्धरिवरः सुग्रीवो हेमपिङ्गलः ।
तेन नादेन महता निर्जगाम हरीश्वरः ॥१२॥

अनुमान्य तदा तारां सुग्रीवेण समागतः ।
निजघान च तत्रैनं शरेणैकेन राघवः ॥१३॥
ततः सुग्रीववचनाद्धत्वा वालिनमाहवे ।
सुग्रीवमेव तद्राज्ये राघवः प्रत्यपादयत् ॥१४॥
स च सर्वान्समानीय वानरान्वानरर्षभः ।
दिशः प्रस्थापयामास दिदृक्षुर्जनकात्मजाम् ॥१५॥
ततो गृध्रस्य वचनात्सम्पातेर्हनुमान्बली ।
शतयोजनविस्तीर्णं पुप्लुवे लवणार्णवम् ॥१६॥
तत्र लङ्कां समासाद्य पुरीं रावणपालिताम् ।
ददर्श सीतां ध्यायन्तीमशोकवनिकां गताम् ॥१७॥
ततो दग्ध्वा पुरीं लङ्कामृते सीतां च मैथिलीम् ।
रामाय प्रियमाख्यातुं पुनरायान्महाकपिः ॥१८॥
ततः सुग्रीवसहितो गत्वा तीरं महोदधेः ।
समुद्रं क्षोभयामास शरैरादित्यसन्निभैः ॥१९॥
दर्शयामास चात्मानं समुद्रः सरितां पतिः ।
समुद्रवचनाच्चैव नलं सेतुमकारयत् ॥२०॥
तेन गत्वा पुरीं लङ्कां हत्वा रावणमाहवे ।
रामः सीतामनुप्राप्य परां व्रीडामुपागमत् ॥२१॥
तामुवाच ततो रामः परुषं जनसंसदि ।
अमृष्यमाणा सा सीता विवेश ज्वलनं सती ॥२२॥
ततो ऽग्निवचनात्सीतां ज्ञात्वा विगतकल्मषाम् ।
कर्मणा तेन महता त्रैलोक्यं सचराचरम् ॥२३॥
सदेवर्षिगणं तुष्टं राघवस्य महात्मनः ।
बभौ रामः संप्रहृष्टः पूजितः सर्वदैवतैः ॥२४॥
अभिषिच्य च लङ्कायां राक्षसेन्द्रं विभीषणम् ।
कृतकृत्यस्तदा रामो विज्वरः प्रमुमोद ह ॥२५॥
नन्दिग्रामे जटां हित्वा भ्रातृभिः सहितो ऽनघः ।
रामः सीतामनुप्राप्य राज्यं पुनरवाप्तवान् ॥२६॥

न चाग्निजं भयं किंचिन्नाप्सु मज्जन्ति जन्तवः ।
न वातजं भयं किंचिन्नापि ज्वरकृतं तथा ॥२७॥
न चापि क्षुद्भयं तत्र न तस्करभयं तथा ।
नगराणि च राष्ट्राणि धनधान्ययुतानि च ॥२८॥
नित्यं प्रमुदिताः सर्वे यथा कृतयुगे तथा ॥२९॥
दशवर्षसहस्राणि दशवर्षशतानि च ।
रामो राज्यमुपासित्वा ब्रह्मलोकं प्रयास्यति ॥३०॥
इदं पवित्रं पापघ्नं पुण्यं वेदैश्च संमितम् ।
यः पठेद्रामचरितं सर्वपापैः प्रमुच्यते ॥३१॥
एतदाख्यानमायुष्यं पठन्रामायणं नरः ।
सपुत्रपौत्रः सगणः प्रेत्य स्वर्गे महीयते ॥३२॥

इत्यार्षे श्रीमद्रामायणे वाल्मीकीय आदिकाव्ये बालकाण्डे प्रथमः सर्गः ॥१॥

NOTES

v. 1: The subject is रावण.
तस्य = रामस्य
मायाविन् (see glossary) = मारीच
नृपात्मजौ = रामलक्ष्मणौ

v. 3: ततः = जटायुषो मरणानन्तरम्
शोकेन—with grief; having burned with grief—probably a reference to the conventional notion of grief as fiery.

v. 5: तम् = कबन्धम्
महाबाहुः = रामः
सः = कबन्धः
अस्य = रामस्य take in the sense of अस्मै, "told him about . . ."

v. 7: शंसद्—the form is अनद्यतनभूते लङ् with irregular loss of the augment.

v. 9: वैरानुकथनम् (see glossary)—the story of his (सुग्रीव's) hostilities with his brother वालिन्, king of the monkeys.

v. 10: प्रणय—Sugrīva is grieved for the love of his wife, who has been taken by his rival.
दुःखितेन (सुग्रीवेण)

v. 11: तेन—refers to राम's skill at archery

v. 12: हरिवरः = सुग्रीवः

v. 13: एनम् = तम्

v. 23-24: After the first half of verse 23, one should mentally supply तां स्वीचकार कर्मणा—the killing of रावण, etc.
construe: राघवस्य महात्मनो महता कर्मणा त्रैलोक्यं सचराचरं सदेवर्षिगणं तुष्टम् [अभूत्]

v. 26: हित्वा—gerund of √हा

v. 27-29b: These verses describe the conditions in राम's realm.

v. 30: प्रयास्यति; नारद is relating all this during राम's reign, hence the future tense.

v. 31-32: These verses constitute a फलश्रुति, an account of the benefits accruing to one who reads, recites or hears a holy text.

v. 31: संमित—construes with instrumental (equal to . . .).

GLOSSARY

अग्निसाक्षिक
(adj)—having fire for a witness (the sign of solemn and inviolable pact)

अनघ
(adj)—sinless

अनुकथनम्
(n)—account, tale

अनु + प्र + √आप्
(5P)—obtain, get

अनुमानय्
(णिजन्त of अनु + √मन्)—reassure

अप्
(f; pl. only)—waters

अपवाहय्
(णिजन्त of अप + √वह्)—lure away

अर्णवः
(m)—ocean

अव + √आप्
(5P)—obtain

अशोकवनिका
(f)—a grove of *aśoka* trees, scene of Sītā's confinement

आकुल
(adj)—confused

आ + √ख्या
(2P)—tell, relate

आख्यानम्
(n)—story, episode

आत्मजः
(m)—son

आदितः
(ind)—from the beginning

आदित्यः
(m)—the sun

आयुष्य
(adj)—conducive to long life

आवेदित
(adj)—made known

आश्रमपदम्
(n)—location of an *āśram*

आहवः
(m)—battle

इन्द्रियम्
(n)—sense, organ of sense

उप + √गम्
(1P)—attain (a state)

उप + √या
(2P)—come

उप + √आस्
(2Ā)—wait upon, serve

ऋते
(ind)—except, with the exception of. . . (with thing excluded in द्वितीया)

√कथ्

(10P)—tell

कबन्धः

(m prop)—name of a hideous *rākṣasa* who, when mortally wounded by Rāma, directs him to Śabarī.

कल्मषम्

(n)—moral taint

किष्किन्धा

(f prop)—capital city of the monkeys. The text here calls it a cave.

कृतयुगम्

(n)—the Golden Age of the world

क्षुत्

(f)—hunger

क्षोभय्

(णिजन्त of √क्षुभ्)—agitate, cause to tremble

गणः

(m)—host, entourage

√गर्ज्

(1P)—roar, bellow

गुहा

(f)—cave, cavern

गृध्रः

(m)—vulture

जटा

(f)—braided topknot; a symbol of asceticism worn by Rāma during his exile.

जटायुस्

(m prop)—king of the vultures, brother of Saṃpāti and old friend of Daśaratha. He attempts to halt Rāvaṇa's abduction of Sītā and is killed by the *rākṣasa*.

ज्वरः

(m)—feverish disease

ज्वलनः

(m)—fire

तस्करः

(m)—thief

तारा

(f prop)—queen of the monkeys, at various times consort and wife of the rival brothers Vālin (q.v.) and Sugrīva (q.v.)

तीरम्

(n)—bank, shore

त्रैलोक्यम्

(n)—the 'Three Worlds' heaven, earth, hell; the Universe

दिश् (दिक्)

(f)—cardinal point, direction

दूरम्

(ind)—far, a long way

दैवतम्
(n)—god, divinity

धर्मचारिन्
(adj)—righteous

√ध्यै
(4P)—be rapt in thought

नन्दिग्रामः
(m prop)—village outside Ayodhyā where Bharata, acting as regent, awaited Rāma's return

नलः
(m prop)—a monkey; chief architect of the bridge whereby Rāma's forces crossed the sea to Lañkā.

नादः
(m)—roar

निर् + √गम्
(1P)—go forth

पम्पा
(f prop)—name of a lake; scene of Rāma's first meeting with Hanumān.

पर
(adj)—supreme

परुष
(adj)—harsh

पवित्र
(adj)—pure, holy

पालित
(adj)—under the protection of . . .

पुण्यम्
(n)—merit

पुरी
(f)—city

पौत्रः
(m)—grandson

प्र + √इ
(2P)—die, depart

प्रणयः
(m)—love

प्रतिपादय्
(णिजन्त of प्रति + √पद्)—install

प्र + √मुच्
(6P)—release

प्र + √मुद्
(1P)—rejoice

प्र +√या
(2P)—go

प्रस्थापय्
(णिजन्त of प्र + √स्था)—send, dispatch

प्रियम्
(n)—good or pleasant tidings

प्रीत
(adj)—pleased

√प्लु
(1Ā)—jump, leap

ब्रह्मलोकः
(m)—Brahmā's world; the highest heaven

√मज्ज् (मज्जति)
(1P)—sink

√भा
(2P)—shine

महाबाहुः
(adj)—great-armed

महीयते
(नामधातु of महि [adj] great)—to grow great, rejoice

महोदधिः
(m)—ocean

मायाविन्
(m)—possessing माया, illusory power (refers to Mārīca)

√मार्ग्
(1Ā)—search for

√मृष्
(4Ā)—bear, endure

युत
(adj)—full of, associated with

योजनम्
(n)—a unit of distance

लवण
(adj)—salty

वातः
(m)—wind

वालिन्
(m prop)—king of the monkeys, elder brother of Sugrīva and husband of Tārā. At Sugrīva's request Rāma shoots him down from ambush. He had reassured Tāra when going to respond to Sūgrīva's challenge.

विकृत
(adj)—deformed

विज्वर
(adj)—free from anxiety

विभीषणः
(m prop)—a rākṣasa, younger brother of Rāvaṇa, but an ally of Rāma

√विश्
(6P)—enter

विश्वस्त
(adj)—reassured, confident

विस्तीर्ण
(adj)—broad

वैरम्
(n)—hostility

व्रीडा
(f)—shame; in this case it refers to Rāma's anxiety regarding what people might say about his taking back a wife who had lived in another man's house.

√शंस्
(1P)—relate

शबरी
(f prop)—a female ascetic who aids Rāma

संसद्
(f)—assembly

सख्यम्
(n)—friendship

सङ्गत (संगत)
(adj)—met with

सचराचर
(adj)—'together with movable and immovable things,' entire

सती
(f)—a virtuous wife

संतप्त
(adj)—oppressed, afflicted

सं + √दृश्
(1P/Ā)—see (non-present system only)

समागत
(adj)—come together

सम् + आ +√नी
(1P)—assemble

सम् + आ +√सद्
(10P)—reach

समुद्रः
(m)—ocean

सम्पातिः
(m)—a vulture, brother of Jaṭāyus: he informed the desperate monkeys of Sītā's whereabouts.

संमित
(adj)—equal to

सरित्
(f)—stream: सरितां पतिः —ocean

सहित
(adj)—along with

सुग्रीवः
(m prop)—a monkey king, ally of Rāma

सेतुः
(m)—bridge, causeway

स्वर्गत
(adj)—gone to heaven

हनुमन्त्
(m prop)—a great monkey hero of the Rāmayaṇa. He jumped across the ocean, burned Laṅkā and carried Rāma's message to Sītā.

हरिवर
(adj)—best of monkeys

हरीश्वरः
(m)—lord of monkeys

√हृ
(1P)—abduct, carry off

हृत
(adj)—abducted

हेमपिङ्गल
(adj)—golden-yellow

GLOSSARY OF GRAMMATICAL TERMS

अकर्मक (*akarmaka*): 'intransitive' 4.38

अक्षर (*akṣara*): syllable 2.23

अतिपत्तौ ऌङ् (*atipattau lṛṅ*): see ऌङ् (*lṛṅ*)

अद्यतनभूते लुङ् (*adyatanabhūte luṅ*): see लुङ् (*luṅ*)

अनद्यतन—(श्वस्तन)—भविष्यत्काले लुट् (*anadyatana*—[*śvastana*] *bhaviṣyatkāle luṭ*): see लुट् (*luṭ*)

अनद्यतनभूते लङ् (*anadyatanabhūte laṅ*): see लङ् (*laṅ*)

अनिट् (*aniṭ*): roots which do not take the 'इट्' ('*iṭ*') infix 16.1

अनुस्वार (*anusvāra*): nasalization of a vowel; sign of nasalization 1.17

अन्तःस्थ (*antaḥstha*): semi-vowel 1.14

अपत्यवाचक (*apatyavācaka*): a meaning of a तद्धित (*taddhita*) derivation 20.11.a.i

अभ्यास (*abhyāsa*): reduplication

a. of third गण (*gaṇa*) roots 7.22

b. of the perfect (लिट्—*liṭ*) 17.6

c. of the desiderative (सन्नन्त—*sannanta*) 18.22.a

d. of the intensive (यङन्त—*yaṅanta*; यङ्लुगन्त—*yaṅluganta*) 18.25

अवग्रह (*avagraha*): sign used to separate words whose initial "a" or "ā" vowel has been lost or has combined with another vowel, from a preceding word: 2.26

अव्ययपद (*avyayapada*): adverb 4.3.c

अव्ययीभाव (*avyayībhāva*): indeclinable (compound) 14.9

आत्मनेपद (*ātmanepada*): "middle voice" 4.26

आशीर् लिङ् (*āśīr liṅ*): the benedictive, 14.16

इट् (*iṭ*): the epenthetic vowel इ (i) 16.1

उत्कर्षवाचकप्रत्यय-s (*utkarṣavācakapratyaya*-s): comparative and superlative affixes 20.11.m

उत्तमपुरुष (*uttamapuruṣa*): 'first person' 4.9

उपपद (*upapada*): reduced word (compounds) 12.17

उपसर्ग-s (*upasarga*-s): verbal prefixes 8.11

उभयपद (*ubhayapada*): roots conjugated in either आत्मनेपद (*ātmanepada*) or परस्मैपद (*parasmaipada*) voice 4.17

ऊष्मन्-s (*ūṣman*-s): sibilants 1.15
एकवचन (*ekavacana*): singular number
a. in reference to verbs 4.12
b. in reference to nouns 4.27
एकशेष द्वन्द्व (*ekaśeṣa dvandva*): elliptical dual (compounds) 14.7
ओष्ठ्य (*oṣṭhya*): labial 1.8
कण्ठ्य (*kaṇṭhya*): velar 1.8
कर्तरि प्रयोग (*kartari prayoga*): the active construction 9.9
कर्तृ (*kartṛ*): the agent or subject 4.37.b
कर्मणि प्रयोग (*karmaṇi prayoga*): the Sanskrit passive 9.5
कर्मन् (*karman*): direct object 4.38
कृत् प्रत्यय-s (*kṛt pratyaya*-s): primary suffixes 20.2
गण-s (*gaṇa*-s): conjugational classes of verbs 7.4 ff.
गुण (*guṇa*): a grade of vowel strength 3.6 ff.
गुरु (*guru*): prosodically heavy syllable 17.6.c.i
चतुर्थी विभक्ति (*caturthī vibhakti*): the 'fourth' or dative case 5.2
च्वि प्रत्यय (*cvi pratyaya*): derivational suffix 20.12
णिजन्त (प्रेरक) (*ṇijanta* [*preraka*]): causative 18.4 ff.
तत्पुरुष (*tatpuruṣa*): syntactic (compounds) 12.10 ff.
तद्धित प्रत्यय-s (*taddhita pratyaya*-s): secondary affixes 20.2 ff.
तद्वेद (*tadveda*): a meaning of तद्धित (*taddhita*) derivations 20.11.a.3
तालव्य (*tālavya*): palatal 1.8
तिङ् (*tiṅ*): any conjugational ending 4.3.a
तिङन्त (*tiṅanta*): any conjugated form, a finite verb 4.3.a
तृतीया विभक्ति (*tṛtīyā vibhakti*): 'third' or instrumental case 4.42
त्वान्त (*tvānta*): gerund in '-त्वा' ('-*tvā*') 11.5
दन्त्य (*dantya*): dental 1.8
द्वन्द्व (*dvandva*): copulative compound 14.1
द्विगु समास-s (*dvigu samāsa*-s): compounds with an initial numeral 13.6
द्वितीया विभक्ति (*dvitīyā vibhakti*): 'second' or accusative case 4.41
द्विवचन (*dvivacana*): dual number
a. in reference to verbs 4.12
b. in reference to nouns 4.27

धातु (*dhātu*): verbal root 4.4
नपुंसकलिङ्ग (*napuṃsakaliṅga*): neuter gender 4.26
नामधातु (*nāmadhātu*): denominative 18.27
निपात (*nipāta*): particle 4.47
पञ्चमी विभक्ति (*pañcamī vibhakti*): 'fifth' or ablative case 5.3
परस्मैपद (*parasmaipada*): active voice 4.16
परोक्षभूते लिट् (*parokṣabhūte liṭ*): (see लिट् [*liṭ*])
पुंलिङ्ग (*puṃliṅga*): masculine gender 4.26
पुरुष (*puruṣa*): grammatical 'person' 4.9 (see प्रथमपुरुष [*prathamapuruṣa*], मध्यमपुरुष [*madhyamapuruṣa*], and उत्तमपुरुष [*uttamapuruṣa*])
प्रकृति (*prakṛti*): underlying nominal base of तद्धित (*taddhita*) derivations 20.8
प्रगृह्य (*pragṛhya*): vowels not subject to सन्धि (*sandhi*) changes 3.21
प्रथमपुरुष (*prathamapuruṣa*): third person 4.9
प्रथमा विभक्ति (*prathamā vibhakti*): 'first' or nominative case 4.40
प्रयोग (*prayoga*): [verbal] usage (see कर्मणि प्रयोग [*karmaṇi prayoga*], कर्तरि प्रयोग [*kartari prayoga*], and भावे प्रयोग [*bhāve prayoga*])
बहुवचन (*bahuvacana*): plural number

a. in reference to verbs 4.12
b. in reference to nouns 4.27

बहुव्रीहि (*bahuvrīhi*): an application of तत्पुरुष (*tatpuruṣa*) and कर्मधारय समास-s (*karmadhāraya samasa*-s) 13.5 ff.
भविष्यत्काले कृदन्त (*bhaviṣyatkāle kṛdanta*): future participle 16.8
भाववाचक (*bhāvavācaka*): a meanings of a तद्धित (*taddhita*) derivation 20.11.a.2
भावे प्रयोग (*bhāve prayoga*): abstract construction (in connection with the कर्मणि प्रयोग [*karmaṇi prayoga*]) 9.17
भूते कृदन्त (*bhūte kṛdanta*): past passive participle 10.4
मध्यमपुरुष (*madhyamapuruṣa*): second person 4.9
मूर्धन्य (*mūrdhanya*): retroflex 1.8
यङन्त (यङ्लुगन्त) (*yaṅanta* [*yaṅluganta*]): intensive 18.25
लघु (*laghu*): prosodically light syllable 17.6.c.i
लङ् (अनद्यतनभूते लङ्) (*laṅ* [*anadyatanabhūte laṅ*]): imperfect 8.6

लट् (वर्तमाने लट्) (*laṭ* [*vartamāne laṭ*]): present indicative 4.19

लिङ् (विधि लिङ्) (*liñ* [*vidhi liñ*]): optative mode 14.12

लिङ्ग (*liñga*): grammatical gender (see पुंलिङ्ग [*puṃliñga*], नपुंसकलिङ्ग [*napuṃsakaliñga*], and स्त्रीलिङ्ग [*strīliñga*]) 4.26

लिट् (परोक्षभूते लिट्) (*liṭ* [*parokṣabhūte liṭ*]): perfect Lesson 17

लुक् (*luk*): loss of case endings 12.8

लुङ् (अद्यतनभूते लुङ्) (*luñ* [*adyatanabhūte luñ*]): aorist 19.10

लुट् (अनद्यतनभविष्यत्काले लुट्) (*luṭ* [*anadyatanabhaviṣatkāle luṭ*]): periphrastic future 16.11

लृङ् (अतिपत्तौ लृङ्) (*lṛñ* [*atipattau lṛñ*]): conditional 16.9

लृट् (सामान्यभविष्यत्काले लृट्) (*lṛṭ* [*sāmānyabhaviṣatkāle lṛṭ*]): simple future 16.2

लोट् (*loṭ*): imperative 11.9

ल्यबन्त (*lyabanta*): gerund in '-य' ('*-ya*') 11.5

वचन (*vacana*): grammatical number (see एकवचन [*ekavacana*], द्विवचन [*dvivacana*], and बहुवचन [*bahuvacana*]) 4.12 (for verbs), 4.27 (for nouns)

वर्ग-s (*varga*-s): 'classes' of sounds 1.6

वर्तमाने कृदन्त (*vartamāne kṛdanta*): present participle 15.1

वर्तमाने लट् (*vartamāne laṭ*): (see लट् [*laṭ*])

विग्रह (*vigraha*): analysis of compounds 12.9

विधि लिङ् (*vidhi liñ*): see लिङ् (*liñ*)

विभक्ति (*vibhakti*): grammatical 'case' (see प्रथमा [*prathamā*], द्वितीया [*dvitīyā*], तृतीया [*tṛtīyā*], चतुर्थी [*caturthī*], पञ्चमी [*pañcamī*], षष्ठी [*ṣaṣṭhī*], सप्तमी [*saptamī*]) 4.28

विराम (*virāma*): a sign indicating elision of inherent vowel 2.13

विशेषण (*viśeṣaṇa*): adjective 13.7

विशेष्य (*viśeṣya*): modificand 20.13

विसर्ग (*visarga*): post-vocalic aspiration 1.17.2; 3.27

वृद्धि (*vṛddhi*): grade of vowel strength 3.6

वेट् (*veṭ*): roots that optionally take the 'इट्' ('*iṭ*') infix 16.1

व्यञ्जन (*vyañjana*): consonant 1.4

शुद्ध स्वर-s (*śuddha svara*-s): simple vowels 1.4

षष्ठी विभक्ति (*ṣaṣṭhī vibhakti*): 'sixth' or genitive case 4.43
संयुक्त स्वर-s (*saṃyukta svara*-s): complex vowels 1.6
सकर्मक (*sakarmaka*): transitive 4.38
संख्या-s (*saṅkhyā*-s): numerals 19.3
सतः षष्ठी (*sataḥ ṣaṣṭhī*): genitive absolute 15.12
सति सप्तमी (*sati saptamī*): locative absolute 15.12
सन्धि (*sandhi*): euphonic combination Lesson 3, etc.
सन्नन्त (*sannanta*): desiderative 18.20
सप्तमी विभक्ति (*saptamī vibhakti*): 'seventh' or locative case 5.4
संबोधन (*saṃbodhana*): vocative 4.36
समानाधिकरण (*samānādhikaraṇa*): case agreement 12.11
समास (*samāsa*): nominal composition (see अव्ययीभाव [*avyayībhāva*], उपपद [*upapada*], एकशेष [*ekaśeṣa*], कर्मधारय [*karmadhāraya*], तत्पुरुष [*tatpuruṣa*], द्वन्द्व [*dvandva*] and बहुव्रीहि [*bahuvrīhi*]) Lessons 12,13, and 14
सर्वनामन् (*sarvanāman*): pronouns 5.5
सामान्यभविष्यत्काले लृट् (*sāmānyabhaviṣyatkāle lṛṭ*): see लृट् (*lṛṭ*)
सुप् (*sup*): any declensional ending
सुबन्त (*subanta*): any declined form (noun, pronoun or adjective) 4.3.b
सेट् (*seṭ*): roots take the 'इट्' ('*iṭ*') infix 16.1
स्त्रीलिङ्ग (*strīliṅga*): feminine gender 4.26
स्पर्श (*sparśa*): stop 1.8
स्वर (*svara*): vowel 1.6

GLOSSARY

-अ-

-a-

(Arabic Numerals following definitions refer to Lessons.)

अ- अन्-

a-, an- —negative prefix for nominal or indeclinable forms: un-, non-, without-, -less (14)

अकम्पनः

akampanaḥ (m prop)—name of a rākṣasa (20)

अकृत

akṛta (adj)—undone

अक्षरम्

akṣaram (n)—syllable, sound, word (15)

अगम्य

agamya (adj)—to be avoided (9 verse)

अग्निः

agniḥ (m)—fire (15)

अग्निसाक्षिक

agnisākṣika (adj)—having fire for a witness (22)

अग्र

agra (adj)—first (19)

अग्रतः

agrataḥ—in front of (20)

अङ्कित

aṅkita—marked (18 verse)

अङ्गीकृ

aṅgīkṛ (8P)—accept, agree to (20)

अचिरात्

acirāt (ind)—shortly, soon (12)

अजित

ajita (adj)—unconquered (14)

अञ्जलिः

añjaliḥ (m)—gesture of reverence or supplication made by placing the palms together (16)

अतः

ataḥ (ind)—from this, hence, therefore (21)

अति

ati (ind)—a prefix used with adjectives and adverbs meaning 'very,' 'too,' or 'excessively' (13)

अति + क्रम्

ati + √kram (1P)—transgress

अति + पत्

ati + √pat (1P)—skip over

अतीव

atīva (ind)—exceedingly, very (4)

अत्र

atra (ind)—here, just now

अत्रभवन्त्

atrabhavant (m)—2nd or 3rd person pronoun: he, you (verb always in 3rd, term of extreme respect) (11)

अत्यन्तम्

atyantam (ind)—exceedingly

अथ

atha (ind)—now, then (6)

अद्

√ad (2P)—eat

अद्य

adya (ind)—today (13)

अधिक

adhika (adj)—greater (with पञ्चमी—greater than) (7 verse)

अधि + कृ

adhi + √kṛ (8P)—authorize

अधि + गम्

adhi + √gam (1P)—attain (9)

अधिपः

adhipaḥ (m)—ruler (16)

अधिपतिः

adhipatiḥ (m)—king

अधिराजः

adhirājaḥ (m)—overlord, king (19)

अधी (अधि + इ)

adhī (adhi + √i) (2Ā)—learn

अधुना

adhunā (ind)—now, at present (11)

अध्यापकः

adhyāpakaḥ (m)—teacher

अनघ

anagha (adj)—sinless (22)

अनन्तरम्

anantaram (ind)—after (9)

अनिलः

anilaḥ (m)—wind

अनिलात्मजः

anilātmajaḥ (m)—son of the wind, Hanumān (13 verse)

अनिवर्तिन्

anivartin (adj)—not turning back (20)

अनुकथनम्

anukathanam (n)—account, tale (22)

अनु + कृ

anu + √kṛ (8P)—imitate

अनुगृहीत

anugṛhīta (adj)—gratified, indebted

अनुचरः

anucaraḥ (m)—servant, attendant

अनुजः

anujaḥ (m)—'born after' i.e., younger brother (17)

अनु + जन्

anu + √jan (4P)—be born after

अनु + ज्ञा

anu + √jñā (9P)—permit (9)

अनुज्ञा

anujñā (f)—permission (7)

अनु + नी

anu + √nī (1P)—conciliate, win over (11 verse)

अनु + प्र + आप्

anu + pra + √āp (5P)—obtain, get (22)

अनु + भू

anu + √bhū (1P)—experience, feel (4)

अनु + मानय्

anu + mānay (णिजन्त of अनु + √मन्)—reassure (22)

अनु + या

anu + √yā (2P)—follow (11 verse)

अनु + रञ्ज्

anu + √rañj (4Ā)—be fond of, like (8)

अनुरूप

anurūpa (adj)—conformable, suitable (19)

अनुरूपक

anurūpaka (adj)—like, the same as (21)

अनु + वद्

anu + √vad (1P)—repeat

अनुवर्तिन्

anuvartin (adj)—obedient (20)

अनु + सृ

anu + √sṛ (1P)—follow

अनु + स्मृ

anu + √smṛ (1P)—recall, remember (11)

अन्तः

antaḥ (m)—end (16)

अन्तःपुरम्

antaḥpuram (n)—inner apartment, esp., women's chambers (14)

अन्तकः

antakaḥ (m)—death (lit., "ender") (20)

अन्ततः

antataḥ (ind)—finally (8)

अन्तरम्

antaram (n)—interior, inside; अन्तरात् (ind)—from inside, from out of (21)

अन्तर् + गम्

antar + √gam (1P)—insinuate

अन्तर् + धा

antar + √dhā (3P)—hide (9)

अन्तिम

antima (adj)—final, last

अन्त्य

antya (adj)—final, last (20 verse)

अन्य

anya (adj)—other (declined pronominally; see 5.7) (5)

अन्यथा

anyathā (ind)—otherwise (19)

अन्यदा

anyadā (ind)—another time

अप्

ap (f pl only)—waters (22)

अपक्रान्त

apakrānta (adj)—gone away (21)

अपण्डित

apaṇḍita (adj)—unwise, foolish

अप + नी

apa + √nī (1P)—remove, lead away

अप + नुद्

apa + √nud (6P)—drive away

अपर

apara (adj)—other, another (9, 17) (declined like a pronoun see 5.7)

अपराधः

aparādhaḥ (m)—sin, offence (13)

अप + वद्

apa + √vad (1P)—revile (8)

अपवाहय्

apavāhay (णिजन्त of अप + √वह्)—lure away (22)

अपहर्तव्य

apahartavya (adj)—to be abducted (21)

अप + हृ

apa + √hṛ (1P)—abduct (21)

अपि

api (ind)—also, too, even; question marker, indefinite marker (with interrogative pronouns; see 6.19) (4)

अपि च

api ca (ind)—moreover (9)

अपूज्य

apūjya (adj)—dishonorable (lit., not to be worshipped) (9 verse)

अप्रज

apraja (adj)—childless (from अप्रजा; as बहुव्रीहि)

अप्सरस्

apsaras (f)—heavenly nymph

अभयम्

abhayam (n)—security (19 verse)

अभि + गम्

abhi + √gam (1P)—approach (8)

अभि + जि

abhi + √ji (1P)—win (8)

अभि + ज्ञा

abhi + √jñā (9P)—recognize

अभिज्ञात

abhijñāta (adj)—recognized, known

अभि + धा

abhi + √dhā (3P)—say, tell, name

अभि + भाष्

abhi + √bhāṣ (1Ā)—speak, say

अभि + भू

abhi + √bhū (1P)—overcome (10)

अभिभूत

abhibhūta (adj)—overcome (10)

अभि + षिच्

abhi + √ṣic (6P)—anoint, consecrate (17)

अभिषेकः

abhiṣekaḥ (m)—consecration, coronation (9); ablution, ritual bath (19)

अभि + हन्

abhi + √han (2P)—annihilate, slay

अभिहत

abhihata (adj)—slain, annihilated (5 verse, 20)

अमर

amara (adj)—immortal (21); (m)—a god

अम्बरम्

ambaram (n)—garment (20)

अम्बा

ambā (f)—mother (irregular संबोधनम्—अम्ब) (11)

अयम्

ayam (pr)—this, that (see 19.1)

अयोध्या

ayodhyā (f prop)—Ayodhyā, Daśaratha's capital city (5)

अरण्यम्

araṇyam (n)—forest (7)

अरिः

ariḥ (m)—enemy (19)

अर्णवः

arṇavaḥ (m)—sea, ocean (16, 22)

अर्थः

arthaḥ (m)—meaning (13)

अर्थम्

artham (ind)—'for the sake of' (at end of compound) (20 verse)

अर्ह्

√arh (1P)—be fit, worthy; auxiliary with infinitive forms, polite imperative (13)

अर्ह

arha (adj)—worthy

अलम्

alam (ind)—enough, sufficient; with instrumental, 'enough of' (15)

अलम् + कृ

alam + √kṛ (8P)—adorn

अलंकृत

alaṃkṛta (adj)—ornamented (8 verse, 19 verse)

अल्पोदरी

alpodarī (f)—having a small belly (19)

अव + गम्

ava + √gam (1P)—understand (6)

अव + √धू

ava + dhū (5P)—shake off, disregard (22)

अवन्द्य

avandya (adj)—not to be praised, blameworthy (9 verse)

अव + बुध्

ava + √budh (4Ā)—understand (7 verse)

अवश्यम्

avaśyam (ind)—certainly, necessarily

अवाप् (अव + आप्)

avāp (ava + √āp) (5P)—obtain (22)

अष्टन्

aṣṭan (adj)—eight (see 19.6)

अशनिः

aśaniḥ (f)—bolt of lightning (11)

अशोकवनिका

aśokavanikā (f)—a grove of Aśoka trees, scene of Sītā's confinement (22)

अश्रु

aśru (n)—tear (13)

अश्रुत

aśruta (adj)—unheard

अश्वः

aśvaḥ (m)—horse

अस्

√as (2P)—to be (4)

असंशयम्

asaṃśayam (ind)—doubtlessly (21)

असिः

asiḥ (m)—sword (18)

असुरः

asuraḥ (m)—*asura*, demon, titan (21)

अह्

√ah (only in लिट्)—say, tell

अहः

ahaḥ (n)—day (see 21.3.g)

अहम्

aham (pr)—I (4.46)

अहो

aho (ind)—"aha!"

-आ-

-ā-

आ + कर्णय्

ā + √karṇay (नामधातु)—hear (21)

आकाशम्

ākāśam (n)—sky (16)

आकुल

ākula (adj)—distressed, agitated (12); confused (22)

आक्रान्त

ākrānta (adj)—occupied, taken over (18 verse)

आ + ख्या

ā + √khyā (2P)—tell, relate (22)

आख्यानम्

ākhyānam (n)—story, episode (22)

आ + गम्

ā + √gam (1P)—come (4)

आ + चर्

ā + √car (1P)—practice (7)

आच्छादित

ācchādita (adj)—covered, enveloped (19)

आ + ज्ञा

ā + √jñā (9P)—know; णिजन्त—order, command (21)

आज्ञा

ājñā (f)—order, command (9)

आत्मजः

ātmajaḥ (m)—son (22)

आत्मन्

ātman (m)—self, Self (7 verse, 8); commonly used as reflexive.

आदरः

ādaraḥ (m)—honor, respect

आ + दा

ā + √dā (3P)—take, assume (21)

आदिः

ādiḥ (m)—beginning (15)

आदितः

āditaḥ (ind)—from the beginning (17, 22)

आदित्यः

ādityaḥ (m)—sun (22)

आननम्

ānanam (n)—face (13)

आनन्दः

ānandaḥ (m)—joy, bliss (6)

आ + नी

ā + √nī (1P)—bring, fetch (17)

आप्

√āp (5P)—obtain (7)

आ + या

ā + √yā (2P)—come (7, 22)

आयुष्य

āyuṣya (adj)—conducive to long life (22)

आ + रभ्

ā + √rabh (1Ā)—begin, undertake

आरब्ध

ārabdha (adj)—undertaken, attempted

आ + रुह्

ā + √ruh (1P)—ascend (to) (15)

आर्त

ārta (adj)—afflicted with (20)

आर्यः

āryaḥ (m)—sir (term of address; lit., noble person) (11)

आर्यपुत्रः

āryaputraḥ (m)— "my Lord"; honorific commonly used by wife to husband

आवह

āvaha (adj)—bringing, conveying (common at end of compound) (14)

आवेदित

āvedita (adj)—made known (22)

आश्रमः

āśramaḥ (m)—hermitage, ashram (6)

आ + श्रि

ā + √śri (1P)—have recourse to, be subject to (17)

आस्

√ās (2Ā)—sit

आसनम्

āsanam (n)—seat (18)

आ + स्फुट्

ā + √sphuṭ (6P)—burst; णिजन्त—clap the hands on the chest, strike the upper arms (18 verse)

आ + स्था

ā + √sthā (1P)—assume, have recourse to, take (21)

आहवः

āhavaḥ (m)—battle (20)

आ + हू

ā + √hū (4Ā)—call, summon (12)

आ + हृ

ā + √hṛ (1P)—bring

-इ-

-i-

इ

√i (2P)—go (18)

इतः

itaḥ (ind)—here; इतः. . .ततः—here. . .there (21); इतः. . .परतः—here. . .elsewhere (7 verse)

इति

iti (ind)—quotation mark (4)

इतिहासः

itihāsaḥ (m)—history, chronicle

इदानीम्

idānīm (ind)—now (7)

इन्दुः

induḥ (m)—moon (14)

इन्द्रः

indraḥ (m prop)—Indra (10); (m)—lord of, best of (at end of compound) (21)

इन्द्रजित्

indrajit (m)—'conqueror of Indra;' proper name of a *rākṣasa*

इन्द्रियम्

indriyam (n)—sense, organ of sense (14, 22)

इव

iva (ind)—like, as (follows word to which it refers) (4)

इष्

√iṣ (6P)—desire, wish, want (8)

इषुः

iṣuḥ (m)—arrow (7)

इष्ट

iṣṭa (adj)—desired (from √iṣ) (10)

इष्ट

iṣṭa (adj)—sacrificed (from √yaj)

इह

iha (ind)—here (7)

-ई-

-ī-

ईदृश

īdṛśa (adj)—such, of this kind (14)

ईप्सा

īpsā (f)—desire to get

ईशः

īśaḥ (m)—lord, Śiva (19)

ईश्वरः

īśvaraḥ (m)—lord, god (21)

-उ-

-u-

उक्त

ukta (adj)—spoken, spoken to, addressed (10)

उग्र

ugra (adj)—fierce, terrible (20)

उज्ज्वल

ujjvala (adj)—shining (8 verse)

उत् + कृत्

ut + √kṛt (6P)—tear to pieces (20)

उत्तम

uttama (adj)—supreme, excellent (8)

उत्तर

uttara (adj)—later, superior; उत्तरम् (n)—answer, reply (17)

उत् + था (=उत् + स्था)

ut + √sthā (1P)—stand up (8)

उत् + पत्

ut + √pat (1P)—jump up, fly

उत्पत्तिः

utpattiḥ (f)—birth (20 verse)

उत् + पद्

ut + √pad (4Ā)—be born, arise

उत्पन्न

utpanna (adj)—arisen, sprung up (13)

उत्पादय्

utpāday (णिजन्त)—stir up, arouse, produce (20)

उदकम्

udakam (n)—water (12)

उदधिः

udadhiḥ (m)—ocean (14)

उदरम्

udaram (n)—belly (12)

उद् + आ + हृ

ud + ā + √hṛ (1P)—announce, call out (21)

उद् + दिश्

ud + √diś (6P)—point out (13)

उद्दिश्य

uddiśya (ind)—with reference to (gerund of उद् + √दिश्) (13)

उद् + भू

ud + √bhū (1P)—arise, come to be (5)

उद् + विज्

ud + √vij (6Ā)—tremble (6, 17)

उद् + हृ

ud + √hṛ (1P)—lift (5 verse, 6)

उन्मत्त

unmatta (adj)—mad, crazy, drunk (19); -ḥ (m)—madman

उपकारः

upakāraḥ (m)—assistance, favor (11)

उपगत

upagata (adj)—drawn near (18)

उप + गम्

upa + √gam (1P)—approach (8); attain (a state) (22)

उप + दिश्

upa + √diś (6P)—teach

उपम

upama (adj)—like, equal to (at end of compound)

उपमा

upamā (f)—similarity, simile (13)

उप + लभ्

upa + √labh (1Ā)—attain (9)

उप + विश्

upa + √viś (6P)—sit (11)

उपविष्ट

upaviṣṭa (adj)—seated (19)

उपहासः

upahāsaḥ (m)—satirical laughter, ridicule (15)

उपायः

upāyaḥ (m)—means, device, stratagem (21)

उपास् (उप + आस्)

upās (upa + √ās) (2Ā)—wait upon, serve (22)

उभ

ubha (adj)—both (21)

-ऋ-

-ṛ-

ऋग्वेदः

ṛgvedaḥ (m prop)—the *Ṛgveda* (19 verse)

ऋते

ṛte (ind)—except, with the exception of . . . (with thing excluded in द्वितीया) (22)

ऋषभः

ṛṣabhaḥ (m)—bull; 'best of . . .' (at end of compound) (18)

ऋषिः

ṛṣiḥ (m)—sage, seer (6)

-ए-

-e-

एक

eka (adj)—one (see 5.7) (5)

एकदा

ekadā (ind)—once, one time (4)

एकमनः

ekamanaḥ (adj)—having an attentive mind (21)

एध्

√edh (1Ā)—grow (17)

एनम् = तम्

enam = tam (pr) (21)

एव

eva (ind)—emphatic particle, emphasizes preceding word (6)

एवम्

evam (ind)—thus, in this way (4); एवंरूपम् (idiom)—of such kind, of such a sort (20); एवंविध (adj)—of such a sort

-क्-

-k-

कण्टकः

kaṇṭakaḥ (m)—thorn; fig., 'something irritating' (19)

कण्ठः

kaṇṭhaḥ (m)—throat (17)

कत्थनम्

katthanam (n)—boasting (18)

कथम्

katham (ind)—how? how is it . . . ? (4)

कथमपि (-चित्, -चन)

kathamapi (-cit, cana) (ind)—somehow or other, barely

कथ्

√kath (10P)—tell (22)

कथा

kathā (f)—story (15)

कदली

kadalī (f)—plantain or banana tree (14)

कदा

kadā (ind)—when?

कन्दरम्

kandaram (n)—cave (17)

कन्या

kanyā (f)—daughter (7)

कपिः

kapiḥ (m)—monkey (13, 18 verse)

कबन्धः

kabandhaḥ (m prop)—Kabandha, name of *rākṣasa* (22)

कमलम्

kamalam (n)—lotus (16)

कम्प्

√kamp (1Ā)—tremble (6)

कम्पनम्

kampanam (n)—trembling, shaking (21)

कम्पित

kampita (adj)—trembling (21)

कर

kara (adj; f -ई)—who *or* what does, makes, *or* causes (generally at end of compound) (20 verse); करः (m)—hand

करुणा

karuṇā (f)—pity, compassion (12)

कर्तृ

kartṛ (adj)—done, made (10)

करेणुः

kareṇuḥ (m)—elephant (19)

कर्कश

karkaśa (adj)—rough, harsh (16)

कर्णः

karṇaḥ (m)—ear (19)

कर्मन्

karman (n)—action, religious activity, grammatical object (8)

कल्मषम्

kalmaṣam (n)—moral taint (22)

कल्यम्

kalyam (ind)—at daybreak (21)

कवचः

kavacaḥ (m)—armor (18)

कविता

kavitā (f)—poetry (15)

काकः

kākaḥ (m)—crow

काकुत्स्थः

kākutsthaḥ (m)—Kākutstha, epithet of Rāma (20)

काञ्चन

kāñcana (adj)—golden (21)

कामः

kāmaḥ (m)—desire (15)

कामदेवः

kāmadevaḥ (m)—Kāma, the god of love (19)

कामरूपिन्

kāmarūpin (adj)—taking any form at will (19)

कामिन्

kāmin (m)—lover (21)

कायः

kāyaḥ (m)—body (20)

कारणम्

kāraṇam (n)—cause, reason (15)

कारिन्

kārin (adj)—agent, producer of, etc.

कालः

kālaḥ (m)—time, death, the god of death (5, 21)

कालेन

kālena (ind)—in the course of time (5)

काष्ठम्

kāṣṭham (n)—log (14)

किम्

kim (n. interrogative pr)—who? what? which? (कः [m]; का [f]) (see 6.3, and 5.5); किमिति (ind)—why? (13); किंतु (ind)—but, however (5); किंपुनः (ind)—how much (more or less) (20); किम् (with instrumental of a noun)—what is the use of, what is the purpose of (cf. 4.42.b); किं बहुना 'why continue on' (e.g., किं बहुना प्रलापेन—'what is the use of prattling on') (9)

किष्किन्धा

kiṣkindhā (f prop)—Kiṣkindhā, capital city of the monkeys (22)

कीर्तिः

kīrtiḥ (f)—fame, good name (11 verse)

कु-

ku (prefix)—a prefix implying 'badness' (19)

कुञ्जरः

kuñjaraḥ (m)—elephant (14)

कुतः

kutaḥ (ind)—whence? why?

कुत्र

kutra (ind)—where?

कुप्

√kup (4P)—be angry (7)

कुपित

kupita (adj)—enraged, angry (4)

कुमारः

kumāraḥ (m)—boy (13)

कुम्भः

kumbhaḥ (m)—pot (10)

कुरूप

kurūpa (adj)—ugly, deformed (19)

कुलम्

kulam (n)—family (16)

कुसुमम्

kusumam (n)—flower (8 verse)

कूज्

√kūj (1P)—warble (15)

कृ

√kṛ (8P)—do, make, conduct, etc. (5)

कृत्

kṛt (adj)—doer, causer (from √कृ, see 12.17)

कृतयुगम्

kṛtayugam (n)—the golden age of the world (22)

कृते

kṛte (ind)—on account of, for the sake of (used with genitive or at end of compound) (12,17)

क्लृप्

√kḷp (1Ā)—be arranged

केयूरः

keyūraḥ (m)—a bracelet, an armlet (8 verse)

केवलम्

kevalam (ind)—only (12)

कैकेयी

kaikeyī (f prop)—Kaikeyī, Bharata's mother (11)

कैलासः

kailāsaḥ (m prop)—Kailāsa, name of Śiva's mountain home

कोकिलः

kokilaḥ (m)—Koil, Indian cuckoo (15)

कोपः

kopaḥ (m)—anger, rage (14)

कोमल

komala (adj)—tender (16)

कौतूहलम्

kautūhalam (n)—curiosity (13)

कौसल्या

kausalyā (f prop)—Kausalyā, Rāma's mother (11)

क्रीड्

√krīḍ (1P)—play, amuse oneself (18 verse, 21)

क्रीडा

krīḍā (f)—play, sport (12)

क्रुध्

√krudh (4P)—be angry, become angry (7)

क्रुद्ध

kruddha (adj)—angry

क्रूर

krūra (adj)—cruel, terrible (12)

क्रोधः

krodhaḥ (m)—anger (13)

क्व

kva (ind)—where?

क्षणः

kṣaṇaḥ (m)—a moment, instant (11)

क्षत्रियः

kṣatriyaḥ (m)—Kṣatriya, a member of the warrior class

क्षम्
√kṣam (1Ā)—forgive, pardon

क्षम
kṣama (adj)—able, competent (9); favorable, suitable (21)

क्षमा
kṣamā (f)—tolerance

क्षयः
kṣayaḥ (m)—destruction (18)

क्षि
√kṣi (1P)—decay, waste; क्षीय (कर्मणि)—to waste away, fade (8 verse)

क्षिप्
√kṣip (6P)—throw (20)

क्षिप्रम्
kṣipram (ind)—quickly, immediately (21)

क्षुत्
kṣut (f)—hunger (22)

क्षुब्ध
kṣubdha (adj)—shaken (10)

क्षुभ्
√kṣubh (1Ā)—shake, tremble

क्षेत्रम्
kṣetram (n)—field

क्षोभय्
kṣobhay (णिजन्त of √क्षुभ्)—agitate, cause to tremble (22)

-ख्-
-kh-

खगः
khagaḥ (m)—bird (12)

खड्गः
khaḍgaḥ (m)—sword (19)

खन्
√khan (1P)—dig

खम्
kham (n)—air, sky (12)

खर
khara (adj)—harsh, cruel (20)

खरः
kharaḥ (m prop)—Khara, a great *rākṣasa* chief, brother of Rāvaṇa and sister of Śūrpaṇakhā (19); (m)—ass, donkey (21)

खलु
khalu (ind)—certainly, surely, now then (8 verse)

खाद्
√khād (1P)—eat

खादित
khādita (adj)—eaten

खेदः
khedaḥ (m)—sadness, depression (13)

-ग्-

-g-

-ग

-ga (adj)—going, moving (in, on, to) (from √गम्; see 12.18) (12)

गङ्गा

gaṅgā (f prop)—Ganges, name of a famous river (18)

गणः

gaṇaḥ (m)—host, entourage (22); in grammar—conjugational class (7)

गजः

gajaḥ (m)—elephant (18)

गत

gata (adj)—gone (7)

गतिः

gatiḥ (f)—way, "alternative," state of existence, condition (6, 20 verse)

गन्धर्वः

gandharvaḥ (m)—a kind of celestial being (20)

गम्

√gam (1P)—go (4)

गमनम्

gamanam (n)—going (13)

गरुडः

garuḍaḥ (m prop)—Garuḍa, mythical bird, Viṣṇu's mount

गर्ज्

√garj (1P)—roar, bellow (22)

गर्जनम्

garjanam (n)—thunder (10)

गर्दभः

gardabhaḥ (m)—donkey (18)

गर्वित

garvita (adj)—proud (8)

गात्रम्

gātram (n)—limb (7, 18 verse)

गिरिः

giriḥ (m)—mountain (21)

गिरिराजपुत्री

girirājputrī (f)—'daughter of the king of the mountains,' i.e., Pārvatī (19)

गीत

gīta (adj)—sung

गीता

gītā (f)—song

गुणः

guṇaḥ (m)—excellence, quality, virtue (5, 11 verse)

गुरु

guru (adj)—heavy (8); -uḥ (m)—teacher

गुहा

guhā (f)—cave, cavern (18, 22)

गृध्रः

gṛdhraḥ (m)—vulture (22)

गृहम्

gṛham (n)—house, home (4)

गृहस्थः

gṛhasthaḥ (m)—householder

गै

√gai (1P)—sing (10, 18 verse)

गोदावरी

godāvarī (f prop)—Godāvarī, name of a river (19)

गोविन्दः

govindaḥ (m prop)—Govinda, name of Kṛṣṇa

गोष्पदीकृ

goṣpadīkṛ (च्वि प्रत्यय)—to turn into a cow's hoofprint (13 verse)

गौ

gau (f)—cow (for declension see 21.3)

गौतमः

gautamaḥ (m prop)—Gautama, name of a famous sage (10)

ग्रह् → गृह्णाति

grah → gṛhṇāti (9P)—seize, grasp (16)

ग्रीवा

grīvā (f)—throat, neck

-घ्-

-gh-

घोर

ghora (adj)—terrible (12)

-च्-

-c-

च

ca (ind)—and

चक्षुः

cakṣuḥ (n)—eye (9)

चतुर् (:)

catur (ḥ) (adj)—four (see 19.6)

चतुर्थ

caturtha (adj)—fourth (17)

चतुर्दश

caturdaśa (adj)—fourteen (15)

चतुष्टयम्

catuṣṭayam (n)—foursome, set of four (5)

चन

cana (ind)—(indefinite marker, see 6.19)

चन्द्रः

candraḥ (m)—moon (8 verse, 16)

चमूः

camūḥ (f)—army (5 verse, 18)

चर्

√car (1P)—move, walk (15)

चरितम्

caritam (n)—adventure, life story (4)

चल्

√cal (1P)—move

चलित

calita (adj)—moved

चापः

cāpaḥ (m)—bow (8)

चारिन्

cārin (m)—roamer, wanderer (11)

चिकीर्षु

cikīrṣu (adj)—desirous of doing (18)

चित्

cit (ind)—(indefinite marker, see 6.19)

चिता

citā (f)—funeral pyre (10 verse)

चित्तम्

cittam (n)—heart, mind (12); thought, will (20)

चित्तलयः

cittalayaḥ (m)—'mind devoted to' (lit., "devotion of the mind") with locative (5 verse)

चिन्त्

√cint (10P)—think, consider (4)

चिन्ता

cintā (f)—care, anxiety, worry (7)

चित्र

citra (adj)—spotted, speckled (21)

चिरम्

ciram (adj)—long (of time) (14)

चुम्ब्

√cumb (1P)—kiss (18 verse)

चुम्बित

cumbita (adj)—kissed

चुर्

√cur (10P)—steal

चेत्

cet (ind)—if (placed after the word to which it refers)

चेतः

cetaḥ (n)—intellect (9)

-छ्-
-ch-

छिद्

√chid (7P)—cut, cut off

छिन्न

chinna (adj)—cut (14)

-ज्-
-j-

-ज

-ja (adj)—born from, produced (at end of compound) (18)

जगत्

jagat (n)—world, universe (6 verse, 20 verse)

जटा

jaṭā (f)—braided topknot, a symbol of asceticism worn by Rāma during his exile (22)

जटायुस्
jaṭāyus (m prop)—Jaṭāyus, king of the vultures (20, 22)

जन्
√jan (4Ā)—be born, arise (irregular present stem, जाय) (14)

जनः
janaḥ (m)—person; as collective noun—people; plural—folks (4, 15)

जनकः
janakaḥ (m prop)—Janaka, king of Mithilā (8)

जनस्थानम्
janasthānam (n prop)—Janasthāna, a portion of the Daṇḍakāraṇya, headquarters of Khara (19)

जन्तुः
jantuḥ (m)—creature, living being (15)

जन्मन्
janman (n)—birth (14)

जरा
jarā (f)—old age (16)

जलम्
jalam (n)—water (16)

जात
jāta (adj)—born, arisen (13)

जालम्
jālam (n)—net, snare (12)

जि
√ji (1P)—win (9)

जिज्ञासु
jijñāsu (adj)—curious

-जित्
-jit (adj)—conquering (from √जि, see 12.17) (12)

जित
jita (adj)—conquered, subdued (14)

जीमूतः
jīmūtaḥ (m)—cloud (20)

जीर्ण
jīrṇa (adj)—old, aged (10)

जीव्
√jīv (1P)—live, survive (4)

जीवित
jīvita (adj)—living (10)

जीवितम्
jīvitam (n)—life (21)

जॄ
√jṝ (1P)—waste away, age (10)

जेतृ
jetṛ (m)—victor, conqueror (10)

-ज्ञ
-jña (adj)—knowing (from ज्ञा; see 12.18) (12)

ज्ञा
√jñā (9P)—know (6)

ज्ञानम्
jñānam (n)—knowledge (12)

ज्येष्ठ
jyeṣṭha (adj)—eldest (5)

ज्वरः
jvaraḥ (m)—feverish disease (22)

ज्वल्
√jval (1Ā)—shine (21)

ज्वलनः
jvalanaḥ (m)—fire (22)

-झ्-
-jh-

झटिति
jhaṭiti (ind)—at once

-त्-
-t-

तत्
tat (pr n)—this, that (6)

ततः
tataḥ (ind)—hence, then (5)

तत्त्वम्
tattvam (n)—truth (21)

तत्र
tatra (ind)—there, in that place (4)

तथा
tathā (ind)—thus

तथापि
tathāpi (ind)—even so (8)

तदनन्तरम्
tadanantaram (ind)—after that (9)

तदा
tadā (ind)—then (6)

तनयः
tanayaḥ (m)—son (15)

तनया
tanayā (f)—daughter (15)

तप्
√tap (1P/Ā)—burn, be hot, suffer, especially undergo or practice religious austerities

तपः
tapaḥ (n)—austerity, asceticism (9)

तपस्विन्
tapasvin (m; f -विनी)—ascetic (12)

तरुण
taruṇa (adj)—young (18 verse)

तर्हि
tarhi (ind)—then (6)

तलम्
talam (n)—surface, plane (12)

तस्करः
taskaraḥ (m)—thief (22)

तातः

tātaḥ (m)—1) father, 2) a term of affection applied to any person, but usually to inferiors or juniors, 'my child,' 'my son,' 'dear one,' etc. (14)

तादृश

tādṛśa (adj)—such (12)

तापसः

tāpasaḥ (m)—ascetic (20)

तारा

tārā (f prop)—Tārā, queen of the monkeys (22)

ताराधिपः

tārādhipaḥ (m)—lord of the stars, the moon

तावत्

tāvat (ind)—so long, to the extent that, meanwhile (6)

तीरम्

tīram (n)—bank, shore (22)

तीक्ष्ण

tīkṣṇa (adj)—sharp (4)

तु

tu (ind)—but (11)

तुङ्ग

tuṅga (adj)—tall (21)

तुरंगमः

turaṃgamaḥ (m)—horse

तुल्य

tulya (adj)—equal (19)

तुष्

√tuṣ (4P)—be happy (8)

तुष्ट

tuṣṭa (adj)—content, happy (8)

तृणम्

tṛṇam (n)—blade of grass, a straw, often used metaphorically for something of little consequence or value (8)

तृप्

√tṛp (4P/Ā)—be satisfied (19)

तृष्णा

tṛṣṇā (f)—desire, craving (11 verse, 18 verse)

तॄ

√tṝ (1P)—cross over

तेजः

tejaḥ (n)—splendor (9)

तेजस्विन्

tejasvin (adj; f -इनी)—glorious (18)

तोयम्

toyam (n)—water (16)

त्रस्त

trasta (adj)—frightened (20)

त्रि

tri (adj)—three (see 19.6)

त्रिलोचनः

trilocanaḥ (m)—having 'three eyes,' epithet of Śiva

त्रैलोक्यम्

trailokyam (n)—the 'three worlds': heaven, earth, hell; the universe (22)

त्यक्त

tyakta (adj)—abandoned (10)

त्यज्

√tyaj (1P)—abandon (10)

त्वम्

tvam (pr)—you (4)

-द्-
-d-

-द

-da (adj)—giving, causing, giving rise to (at end of compound) (14)

दग्ध

dagdha (adj)—burnt

दण्डकम्

daṇḍakam (n prop)—name of a forest (13)

दत्त

datta (adj)—given

दया

dayā (f)—compassion (11 verse)

दर्शनम्

darśanam (n)—sight, view

दंश् → दशति

√daṃś → daśati (1P)—bite

दश

daśa (adj)—ten (see 19.6)

दशग्रीवः

daśagrīvaḥ (m)—'having ten necks,' epithet of Rāvaṇa (19)

दशबलः

daśabalaḥ (m)—'having ten powers,' epithet of the Buddha

दशरथः

daśarathaḥ (m prop)—Daśaratha, Rāma's father (4)

दष्ट

daṣṭa (adj)—bitten

दह्

√dah (1P)—burn (18)

दा

√dā (3P)—give (9)

दानम्

dānam (n)—giving, granting

दारः

dāraḥ (m)—wife, wives (occurs only in plural) (21)

दारिद्र्यम्

dāridryam (n)—poverty (6 verse, 14)

दारुण

dāruṇa (adj)—fierce, cruel, severe (13)

दासः

dāsaḥ (m)—servant, slave (5 verse, 19)

दिग्ध

digdha (adj)—smeared (20)

दिनः

dinaḥ (m)—day

दिश् (दिक्)

diś (dik) (f)—cardinal point, direction, quarter (20, 22 verse)

दुःखम्

duḥkham (n)—sorrow, misery (4)

दुःखित

duḥkhita (adj)—unhappy (6)

दुर्गा

durgā (f prop)—Durgā, name of Pārvatī, Śiva's wife (15)

दुर्जनः

durjanaḥ (m)—evil person (19 verse)

दुर्जय

(adj)—invincible (20)

दुर्मुखी

durmukhī (f)—having an ugly face (19)

दुष्कृतम्

duṣkṛtam (n)—evil act (4)

दुष्ट

duṣṭa (adj)—vicious, uncontrolled

दुह्

√duh (2P)—milk

दुहितृ

duhitṛ (f)—daughter (10)

दूतः

dūtaḥ (m)—messenger, envoy

दूरम्

dūram (ind)—far, a long way (21, 22)

दूषणः

dūṣaṇaḥ (m prop)—Dūṣaṇa, brother of Khara (19)

दृश्

dṛś—see, seem, appear (non-present form of पश्) (11)

देवः

devaḥ (m)—god, a title of respectful address to a king (6, 10)

देवी

devī (f)—lady, queen, goddess (6)

देशः

deśaḥ (m)—place, region (6)

देहः

dehaḥ (m)—body (21 verse)

देहिन्

dehin (adj)—having a body; (m)—soul (21 verse)

दैवतम्

daivatam (n)—god, divinity (22)

दोषः

doṣaḥ (m)—fault, dis-advantage

द्रव्यम्

dravyam (n)—thing, thing of value, wealth (18)

द्रु

√dru (1P)—run (either of a person, or of a liquid or melting solid) (19)

द्रुमः

drumaḥ (m)—tree (18)

द्वन्द्वम्

dvandvam (n)—pair; (m)—type of compound

द्वारम्

dvāram (n)—gate, door, entrance

द्वि (stem = द्व)

(number)—two, treated as an अ stem noun, in dual only (see 19.6.b) (9, 11)

द्विजः

dvijaḥ(m)—"twice-born," brāhman, bird (6)

द्वितीय

dvitīya (adj)—second (11)

द्विष्

√dviṣ (2P/Ā)—hate

-ध्-

-dh-

धनम्

dhanam (n)—wealth (9 verse, 16)

धनुः

dhanuḥ (n)—bow (9)

धनुर्वेदः

dhanurvedaḥ (m)—science of archery (6)

धनुष्मन्त्

dhanuṣmant (adj)—having a bow (21)

धन्य

dhanya (adj)—fortunate (16)

धरा

dharā (f)—earth (12)

धर्मः

dharmaḥ (m)—law, duty, right (12)

धर्मचारिन्

dharmacārin (adj)—righteous (22)

धा

√dhā (3P)—to put *or* place (16)

धान्यम्

dhānyam (n)—grain (16)

धार्मिक

dhārmika (adj)—righteous (4)

धिक्

dhik (ind)—particle expressing anger or contempt (17)

धीः

dhīḥ (f)—thought

धृ

√dhṛ (10P/Ā)—bear, possess, assume (8 verse)

धृष्

√dhṛṣ (5P)—be bold, courageous (20)

धैर्यम्

dhairyam (n)—fortitude, courage (20)

ध्या

√dhyā (4Ā)—meditate

ध्यानम्

dhyānam (n)—meditation (7)

ध्यै

√dhyai (4P)—be rapt in thought (22)

-न्-

-n-

न

na (ind)—negative particle (4)

नगरम्

nagaram (n)—city (10)

नत

nata (adj)—bowed, bent (10)

नद्

√nad (1P)—roar (19)

नदी

nadī (f)—river (19)

नद्ध

naddha (adj)—bound (10)

नन्द्

√nand (1P)—rejoice (18 verse)

नन्दनः

nandanaḥ (n)—causer of joy (16)

नन्दिः

nandiḥ (m prop)—Nandi (or Nandin), Śiva's bull (19)

नन्दिग्रामः

nandigrāmaḥ (m prop)—Nandigrāma, village outside Ayodhyā where Bharata, acting as regent, awaited Rāma's return (22)

नन्दित

nandita (adj)—overjoyed (11)

नम्

√nam (1P)—bow, bend (10)

नमः

namaḥ (n)—reverence, homage (5 verse, 9)

नयनम्

nayanam (n)—eye (14)

नरः

naraḥ (m)—man (17, 18 verse)

नरकः

narakaḥ (m)—hell (17)

नलः

nalaḥ (m prop)—Nala, a monkey, chief architect of the bridge whereby Rāma's forces crossed the sea to Lañkā (22)

नवन्

navan (adj)—nine (see 19.6)

नव

nava (adj)—new (21 verse)

नश्

√naś (4P)—perish, be destroyed (4)

नष्ट

naṣṭa (adj)—ruined, destroyed (6)

नह्

√nah (4P)—bind (10)

नादः

nādaḥ (m)—roar (15 verse, 22)

नाम

nāma (ind)—"by name," namely (4)

नामधेयम्

nāmadheyam (n)—name (5)

नामन्

nāman (n)—name (8)

नायकः

nāyakaḥ (m)—leader (17)

नारी

nārī (f)—woman (6)

नाशकः

nāśakaḥ (m)—destroyer (21)

नासा

nāsā (f)—nose (19)

निः-

niḥ (ind)—without, devoid of (only as first member of compound) (14)

निः + श्वस्

niḥ + √śvas (2P)—sigh (15)

निःसपत्न

niḥsapatna (adj)—having no rival (19)

नि + क्षिप्

ni + √kṣip (6)—throw down, entrust, place (9)

नि + ग्रह्

ni + √grah (9P)—imprison (16)

नित्यम्

nityam (ind)—always, constantly (21)

नि + दर्शय्

ni + √darśay (णिजन्त of नि + √दृश्)—show, point out (18)

निद्रा

nidrā (f)—sleep (12)

निन्द्

√nind (1P)—blame, revile

निन्दित

nindita (adj)—blamed, reviled

नि + पत्

ni + √pat (1P)—fall, sink down (18)

निपुण

nipuṇa (adj)—clever (6)

निमग्न

nimagna (adj)—sunk (10)

नि + युज्
ni + √yuj (7P)—install, appoint (with चतुर्थी or सप्तमी विभक्ति) (17 verse)

नियोजित
niyojita (adj)—appointed (20)

नि + रुह्
ni + √ruh (1P)—climb up (18 verse)

नि + रूप्
ni + √rūp(10P)—perceive, notice (15)

निर्गत
nirgata (adj)—departed (7)

निर् + गम्
nir + √gam (1P)—go forth (22)

निर्मनुष्य
nirmanuṣya (adj)—devoid of people, uninhabited

निर्वासित
nirvāsita (adj)—exiled (17)

नि + वस्
ni + √vas (1P)—live, dwell (20)

निवासः
nivāsaḥ (m)—dwelling (21)

नि + विद्
ni + √vid (2P)—be informed (णिजन्त—निवेदय्, with dative) (14, 19)

नि + वृ
ni + √vṛ (5P/Ā)—be blocked, prevented (णिजन्त—निवारय्) (19)

नि + वृत्
ni + √vṛt (1Ā)—turn back (20)

नि + शम्
ni + √śam (4P)—hear, listen (20)

निशाचरः
niśācaraḥ (m)—lit., 'night-roamer,' a *rākṣasa* (5 verse, 7)

निश्चित
niścita (adj)—decided, settled; (ind)—certainly, surely (14)

निषण्ण
niṣaṇṇa (adj)—dejected (12)

नि + हन्
ni + √han (2P)—kill

निहत
nihata (adj)—slain (19)

नी
√nī (1P)—lead (10)

नील
nīla (adj)—dark, blue-black (20)

नीलकण्ठः
nīlakaṇṭhaḥ (n)—'having a blue-throat,' epithet of Śiva

नृत्
√nṛt (4P/Ā)—dance (10)

नृपः
nṛpaḥ (m)—king (4)

नृपतिः
nṛpatiḥ (m)—king (13)

नेतृ

netṛ (m)—leader (10)

न्यस्त

nyasta (adj)—set down (18)

-प्-
-p-

-प

-pa (adj)—drinker (from √पा 1P, see 12.17)

-प

-pa (adj)—protector (from √पा 2P, see 12.17)

पच्

√pac (1P)—cook

पञ्चन्

pañcan (adj)—five (see 19.6) (19)

पञ्चत्वम्

pañcatvam (n)—'fiveness,' dissolution, death (20)

पठ्

√paṭh (1P)—read (15)

पठित

paṭhita (adj)—read

पण्डितः

paṇḍitaḥ (m)—wise man, learned one (7)

पत्

√pat (1P)—fall (10)

पतिः

patiḥ (m)—lord, husband (irregular declension, see 21.3.b) (12)

पतित

patita (adj)—fallen

पत्नी

patnī (f)—wife

पत्रम्

patram (n)—leaf (8)

पत्ररथः

patrarathaḥ (m)—bird (20)

पदवी

padavī (f)—path; with अनु + √गम्—follow in someone's footsteps (21)

पम्पा

pampā (f prop)—Pampā, name of a lake, scene of Rāma's first meeting with Hanumān (21)

पयः

payaḥ (n)—milk

पर

para (adj)—other, highest (15); supreme (22); परतः (ind)—elsewhere (see इतः) (7 verse); परतर (adj)—greater than (with पञ्चमी) (5 verse) (See 5.7.)

परम

parama (adj)—supreme (6, 17)

परमेश्वरः
parameśvaraḥ (m)—'supreme lord,' epithet of Śiva

परशुः
paraśuḥ (m)—axe (14)

पराक्रमः
parākramaḥ (m)—valor (21)

पराजि (परा + जि)
parāji (parā + √ji) (1P)—conquer, subdue (14)

परायण (पर + अयण)
parāyaṇa (para + ayaṇa) (adj)—attached to, devoted to; (n)—last resort *or* recourse (5 verse)

परिघः
parighaḥ (m)—iron bar, massive club (20)

परिणामः
pariṇāmaḥ (m)—change, alteration

परिणी (परि + नी)
pariṇī (pari + √nī) (1P)—marry (8)

परि + त्यज्
pari + √tyaj (1P)—abandon (9)

परिपूर्ण
paripūrṇa (adj)—full

परिवर्तनम्
parivartanam (n)—whirling about, change, reversal (12)

परिवृत
parivṛta (adj)—surrounded (17)

परि + व्रज्
pari + √vraj (1P)—wander (as a mendicant)

परिव्राजकः
parivrājakaḥ (m)—wandering ascetic

परिसान्त्व्
√parisāntv (10P)—calm, soothe (18)

परि + स्वज्
pari + √svaj (1Ā)—embrace (15)

परिहासः
parihāsaḥ (m)—joke, jest (19)

परि + हृ
pari + √hṛ (1P)—avoid, shun (19 verse)

परीक्षा
parīkṣā (f)—test

परुष
paruṣa (adj)—harsh

परुषम्
paruṣam (n)—harsh speech (22)

पर्णम्
parṇam (n)—leaf (19)

पर्याकुल
paryākula (adj)—frightened, confused (21)

पर्युत्सुक

paryutsuka (adj)—restless

पला + इ

palā + √i (1Ā)—flee (conjugate like an "a" गण root from stem पलाय्) (7)

पलितम्

palitam (n)—grey hair (18 verse)

पवित्र

pavitra (adj)—pure, holy (22)

पश्

√paś (4P)—see (used in present system only, see दृश्) (4)

पा

√pā (1P)—drink (15)

पा

√pā (2P)—protect (18)

पाचकः

pācakaḥ (m)—cook

पाणिः

pāṇiḥ (m)—hand; at end of compound—'having . . . . in hand' (20)

पाण्डवः

pāṇḍavaḥ (m prop)—Pāṇḍava, descendant of king Pāṇḍu

पादः

pādaḥ (m)—foot (16 verse)

पादपः

pādapaḥ (m)—tree

पादुका

pādukā (f)—sandal (18)

पापम्

pāpam (n)—sin, evil; (adj)—evil, nasty (11 verse, 12)

पापजनः

pāpajanaḥ (m)—sinful person

पापिन्

pāpin (m; f -इनी)—sinner

पारः

pāraḥ (m)—lit., "far shore," with √गम्—excel at, fully comprehend (6)

पार्थिवः

pārthivaḥ (m)—king (5)

पार्वती

pārvatī (f prop)—Pārvatī, Śiva's wife

पाल्

√pāl (10P)—protect (11)

पालित

pālita (adj)—under the protection of (22)

पाशः

pāśaḥ (m)—noose (19)

पितरौ

pitarau (m nom dual of पितृ)—"elliptical dual" of मातृपितरौ, 'mother and father,' parents

पितृ
pitṛ (m)—father, ancestor (10, 19)

पिपासा
pipāsā (f)—thirst (18)

पिशाचः
piśācaḥ (m)—*piśāca*, type of demon

पीडित
pīḍita (adj)—oppressed, afflicted (4)

पीत
pīta (adj)—drunk (as a liquid is)

पीत
pīta (adj)—yellow

पीताम्बरः
pītāmbaraḥ (m)—'having a yellow garment,' epithet of Viṣṇu

पुच्छम्
puccham (n)—tail (18 verse)

पुत्रः
putraḥ (m)—son (4)

पुनः (पुनर्)
punaḥ (ind)—again (4)

पुरा
purā (ind)—previously, long ago (11)

पुरी
purī (f)—city (22)

पुरुषः
puruṣaḥ (m)—man, person (6)

पुष्पित
puṣpita (adj)—flowery (19)

पुस्तकम्
pustakam (n)—book (13, 15)

पू
√pū (9P/Ā)—purify (19)

पूज्
√pūj (10P)—worship, revere (9 verse, 19)

पूजा
pūjā (f)—worship, reverence (15)

पूर्ण
pūrṇa (adj)—full (10)

पूर्व
pūrva (adj)—previous, former (declined pronominally, see 5.7) (5); पूर्वम् (ind)—previously; with पञ्चमी—'before' (15)

पूर्वजः
pūrvajaḥ (m)—'born-previously,' elder brother

पृथिवी
pṛthivī (f)—earth (14)

पॄ
√pṝ (9P)—fill

पौत्रः
pautraḥ (m)—grandson (22)

प्रकाशः
prakāśaḥ (m)—light (21)

प्रकृतिः

prakṛtiḥ (f)—nature (18 verse)

प्रख्यात

prakhyāta (adj)—famous (19)

प्रचोदित

pracodita (adj)—urged (21)

प्रच्छ्

√pracch (6P)—ask (6)

प्र + छद्

pra + √chad (10P)—cover, conceal (11 verse)

प्रजा

prajā (f)—offspring, children, people of a kingdom or realm (5)

प्रज्ञा

prajñā (f)—intellect

प्रज्वलित

prajvalita (adj)—blazing (10 verse)

प्रणयः

praṇayaḥ (m)—love (22)

प्रति

prati (ind)—to, with respect to (preposition with द्वितीया); each, every (as first member of अव्ययीभाव) (6, 14)

प्रति + आ + गम्

prati + ā + √gam (1P)—go back (9)

प्रति + ग्रह्

prati + √grah (9P)—take (18)

प्रति + ज्ञा

prati + √jñā (9P)—vow, promise (8)

प्रतिज्ञात

pratijñāta (adj)—vowed, promised (12)

प्रतिदिनम्

pratidinam (ind)—every day, daily

प्रति + नि + वृत्

prati + ni + √vṛt (1Ā)—return (18)

प्रतिपत्तिः

pratipattiḥ (f)—attainment of knowledge

प्रति + पादय्

prati + pāday (णिजन्त of प्रति + √पद्)—install (22)

प्रति + पाल्

prati + √pāl (10P)—wait, watch, protect (18)

प्रति + वच्

prati + √vac (2P)—answer (18)

प्रति + सान्त्व्

prati + √sāntv (10P)—calm, soothe (18)

प्रति + स्था

prati + √sthā (1P)—establish (18)

प्रतोदः

pratodaḥ (m)—goad (19)

प्रत्यनन्तर
pratyanantara (adj)—being in the immediate neighborhood (20)

पत्याया (प्रति + आ + या)
pratyāyā (prati + ā + √yā) (2P)—come back to, return (17)

प्रथम
prathama (adj)—first (11)

प्रभावः
prabhāvaḥ (m)—power (8, 9 verse)

प्र + भाष्
pra + √bhāṣ (1Ā)—speak

प्र + भू
pra + √bhū (1P)—be powerful

प्रभृति
prabhṛti (ind)—starting from (at end of compound, after indeclinable or पञ्चमी) (17)

प्र + मथ्
pra + √math (1P)—harass, torment, annoy (21)

प्रमदा
pramadā (f)—a beautiful young woman (20)

प्रमुख
pramukha (adj)—foremost (17 verse)

प्रमुखे
pramukhe (ind)—in front of, before the eyes (21)

प्र + मुद्
pra + √mud (1P)—rejoice (22)

प्रमुदित
pramudita (adj)—delighted, pleased (10)

प्र + यत्
pra + √yat (1Ā)—attempt, try, exert oneself (8)

प्रयत्नः
prayatnaḥ (m)—effort (12)

प्र + या
pra + √yā (2P)—go (22)

प्र + लप्
pra + √lap (1P)—prattle

प्रलयः
pralayaḥ (m)—cosmic dissolution (21)

प्रलापः
pralāpaḥ (m)—prattling, talk

प्र + लोभय्
pra + lobhay (णिजन्त of प्र + √लुभ्)—infatuate

प्र + विश्
pra + √viś (6P)—enter (11)

प्र + वृत्
pra + √vṛt (1Ā)—proceed, take place (13)

प्र + शास्
pra + √śās (2P)—rule, reign (13)

प्रश्नः

praśnaḥ (m)—question (19)

प्र + सद्

pra + √sad (1P)—be pleased, appeased, be pacified (13)

प्रसन्न

prasanna (adj)—calm (21)

प्रसादः

prasādaḥ (m)—grace, favor (6 verse)

प्रसादक

prasādaka (adj)—propitiating (17 verse)

प्रसिद्ध

prasiddha (adj)—famous (19 verse)

प्र + स्था

pra + √sthā (1P)—set out (18)

प्र + स्थापय्

pra + sthāpay (णिजन्त of प्र + √स्था)—send, dispatch (22)

प्रहर्षः

praharṣaḥ (m)—joy (18)

प्र + हस्

pra + √has (1P)—ridicule (8)

प्रहृष्ट

prahṛṣṭa (adj)—delighted (20)

प्राणः

prāṇaḥ (m)—the breath; प्रानान् + √त्यज्—"abandon life breaths," die (16)

प्रातर् (=प्रातः)

prātar (=prātaḥ) (ind)—in the morning (21)

प्राप् (प्र + आप्)

prāp (pra + √āp) (5P)—obtain, receive, get, come, arrived (11,16)

प्रापित

prāpita (adj)—obtained, got (12)

प्राय

prāya (adj)—for the most part, generally, nearly (at end of compound) (21)

प्रायशः

prāyaśaḥ (ind)—practically, virtually

प्रा + रभ् (प्र + आ + रभ्)

prā + √rabh (pra + ā + √rabh) (1Ā)—undertake

प्रारब्ध

prārabdha (adj)—prepared

प्रासादः

prāsādaḥ (m)—palace (12)

प्रिय

priya (adj)—dear, beloved (6)

प्रियम्

priyam (n)—good or pleasant tiding (22)

प्रीत

prīta (adj)—pleased (22)

प्रे (प्र + इ)

pre (pra + √i)—die, depart (22)

प्रेक्ष् (प्र + ईक्ष्)
preks (pra + √īkṣ) (1Ā)—see, behold (19)

प्रेरित
prerita (adj)—urged, impelled (21)

प्रेष् (प्र + इष्)→ प्रेषयति
preṣ (pra + √iṣ) → preṣayati (causative, conjugated as 10P)—send, dispatch (6)

प्रोक्त
prokta (adj)—addressed, spoken to (19)

प्लु
√plu (1Ā)—jump, leap (22)

-फ्-
-ph-

फलम्
phalam (n)—fruit (16)

फुल्ल
phulla (adj)—blooming (16)

फेनः
phenaḥ (m)—foam (20)

-ब्-
-b-

बद्ध
baddha (adj)—bound (17)

बन्ध्
√bandh (9P)—bind (17)

बन्धनागारः
bandhanāgāraḥ (m)—prison (10)

बलम्
balam (n)—power, strength (17 verse, 19)

बलवन्त्
balavant (adj)—mighty (21)

बलिन्
balin (adj)—strong, powerful (20)

बहिः
bahiḥ (ind)—outside (18)

बहु
bahu (adj)—many (7)

बहुमत
bahumata (adj)—respected

बहुवारम्
bahuvāram (ind)—many times (18)

बाढम्
bāḍham (ind)—excellent, good idea! (21)

बाणः
bāṇaḥ (m)—arrow (6)

बाध्
√bādh (1Ā)—harass (7)

बाधित
bādhita (adj)—afflicted, oppressed (6)

बान्धवः
bāndhavaḥ (m)—friend, relative (18)

बालकः
bālakaḥ (m)—boy, youth (4, 17)

बाष्पः
bāṣpaḥ (m)—tears (14)

बिन्दुः
binduḥ (m)—drop, spot (18)

बीभत्सा
bibhatsā (f)—repulsion

बुध्
√budh (4Ā)—be awake, enlighten

बुद्ध
buddha (adj)—awake, enlightened (10); (m)—the Buddha

बुद्धिः
buddhiḥ (f)—wit, intelligence (11)

बुद्धिमन्त्
buddhimant (adj; f -अती)—wise (11)

बुभुक्षा
bubhukṣā (f)—hunger

बृहन्त्
bṛhant (adj)—great

बोधः
bodhaḥ (m)—enlightenment (20 verse)

ब्रह्मन्
brahman (n)—Brahma, Absolute Reality (9); (m)—the god Brahmā (12)

ब्रह्मघ्न
brahmaghna (adj)—killer of brāhmans (20)

ब्रह्मलोकः
brahmalokaḥ (m)—Brahmā's world—the highest heaven (22)

ब्राह्मणः
brāhmaṇaḥ (m)—a brāhman (4)

ब्रू
√brū (2P)—speak, tell (11)

-भ्-
-bh-

भक्ष्
√bhakṣ (10P/Ā)—eat (19)

भक्षः
bhakṣaḥ (m)—food (18)

भगवद्गीता
bhagavadgītā (f prop)—Bhagavadgītā

भगवन्त्
bhagavant (adj)—blessed one (13)

भगिनी
bhaginī (f)—sister (19)

भग्न
bhagna (adj)—broken (18)

भज्

√bhaj (1P/Ā)—worship (5 verse); have recourse to, betake oneself to (18)

भञ्ज्

√bhañj (7P)—break (8)

भण्

√bhaṇ (1P)—say (21)

भद्रम्

bhadram (n)—auspicious thing

भयङ्कर

bhayaṅkara (adj)—terrible, fearsome (19 verse)

भयम्

bhayam (n)—fear, alarm (16)

भरतः

bharataḥ (m prop)—Bharata, one of Rāma's brothers (5)

भर्तृ

bhartṛ (m)—husband, lord (10)

भवः

bhavaḥ (m)—existence, worldly-existence, the world (20 verse)

भवनम्

bhavanam (n)—palace (13)

भवन्त्

bhavant (m)—you (polite form of मध्यम pronoun)

भव्य

bhavya (adj)—true, capable (of perceiving truth), fortunate (20 verse)

भा

√bhā (2P)—appear, seem (13); shine (22)

भारः

bhāraḥ (m)—load, weight, burden (9)

भार्या

bhāryā (f)—wife (5)

भाष्

√bhāṣ (1Ā)—speak, say (4)

भाषा

bhāṣā (f)—description, speech

भाषित

bhāṣita (adj)—uttered, spoken

भिद्

√bhid (7P)—split (20)

भिन्न

bhinna (adj)—split

भी

√bhī (3P)—fear (7)

भीत

bhīta (adj)—afraid (4)

भीतिः

bhītiḥ (f)—fear (10)

भीम

bhīma (adj)—terrible (20)

भुज्

√bhuj (7P)—eat (8)

भू

√bhū (1P)—be, become (4)

भूतम्

bhūtam (n)—creature, being

भूमिः

bhūmiḥ (f)—land, earth (10)

भूमिपः

bhūmipaḥ (m)—king (4)

भूष्

√bhūṣ (10P)—adorn

भूषणम्

bhūṣaṇam (n)—ornament (8 verse)

भूषित

bhūṣita (adj)—ornamented (18, 19 verse)

भृ

√bhṛ (3P)—carry, bear

भृत्

bhṛt (adj)—bearing, carrying (at end of compound) (21)

भृशम्

bhṛśam (adj)—extremely (14)

भैरव

bhairava (adj)—terrible, fearsome (19)

भोः

bhoḥ (ind)—hail or greeting "hey" (6)

भोगः

bhogaḥ (m)—sensual enjoyment (16)

भोजनम्

bhojanam (n)—food (11)

भ्रम्

√bhram (1P)—wander (19)

भ्रष्ट

bhraṣṭa (adj)—lost, destroyed

भ्रातृ

bhrātṛ (m)—brother (10)

-म्-
-m-

मक्षिका

makṣikā (f)—fly, mosquito (21)

मणिः

maṇiḥ (m)—jewel (10)

मत

mata (adj)—thought, considered

मतिः

matiḥ (f)—mind (6)

मत्स्यः

matsyaḥ (m)—fish (16)

मदः

madaḥ (m)—drunkenness, excessive delight (11 verse)

मधुर

madhura (adj)—sweet (15)

मधुरम्
madhuram (ind)—sweetly (15)

मध्यः
madhyaḥ (m)—middle, waist (19)

मन्
√man (4Ā)—think (4); मानय् (णिजन्त)—honor, esteem (11 verse)

मनः
manaḥ (n)—mind, mental faculty (9)

मनुष्यः
manuṣyaḥ (m)—man, mortal (6)

मनस्विन्
manasvin (adj)—wise, intelligent

मनोहर
manohara (adj)—charming, fascinating (21)

मन्दिरम्
mandiram (n)—house, palace (17)

मन्युः
manyuḥ (m)—anger, rage (14)

मरणम्
maraṇam (n)—death, dying (18)

मर्मन्
marman (n)—vital spot (20)

मशकः
maśakaḥ (m)—fly, mosquito

मशकीकृ
maśakīkṛ (च्वि प्रत्यय)—to turn into a fly *or* mosquito (13 verse)

महन्त्
mahant (adj)—great, large (11)

महापुरी
mahāpurī (f)—great city (21)

महाबाहुः
mahābāhuḥ (adj)—great-armed (22)

महीयते
mahīyate (नामधातु of महि [adj] great)—rejoice to grow great

महोदधिः
mahodadhiḥ (m)—ocean (22)

महोदरी
mahodarī (f)—having a big belly (19)

मा
mā (ind)—negative used with imperative and injunctive (see 19.18) (11)

मांसम्
māṃsam (n)—flesh (20)

मातृ
mātṛ (f)—mother (10)

मातुलः
mātulaḥ (m)—maternal uncle (17)

मानय्
mānay (णिजन्त of √मन्)—respect, esteem (11 verse)

मानव
mānava (adj)—relating to Manu; (m)—man, human (20)

मानुष

mānuṣa (adj)—human; (m)—man, human (20)

मान्य

mānya (adj)—to be respected, worthy of respect (11 verse)

मामक

māmaka (adj)—belonging to me, mine

माया

māyā (f)—illusion, magic (21)

मायाविन्

māyāvin (adj)—possessing माया, or illusory power (22)

मारीचः

mārīcaḥ (m prop)—Mārīca, name of a *rākṣasa* (21)

मार्ग्

√mārg (1Ā)—search for (22)

मार्गः

mārgaḥ (m)—path, road (10)

माला

mālā (f)—garland, necklace (13 verse)

मित्रम्

mitram (n)—friend (14)

मिथिला

mithilā (f prop)—city of Mithilā (7)

मिथुनम्

mithunam (n)—coupling, sexual intercourse

मिथ्या

mithyā (ind)—unreal, false (9)

मीमांसा

mīmāṃsā (f)—inquiry, Mīmāṃsā school of philosophy

मुक्त

mukta (adj)—released, liberated

मुखम्

mukham (n)—face (13)

मुच्

√muc (6P)—release (20)

मुदित

mudita (adj)—delighted

मुनिः

muniḥ (m)—sage (6)

मुहूर्तम्

muhūrtam (n)—moment, instant (20)

मूढ

mūḍha (adj)—stupefied (11)

मूढमतिः

mūḍhamatiḥ (m)—fool

मूर्खः

mūrkhaḥ (m)—fool (4)

मूर्च्छित

mūrcchita (adj)—stupefied, senseless (18)

मूर्धन्

mūrdhan (m)—head, forefront (of battle) (20)

मूर्धजः

mūrdhajaḥ (m)—hair, coiffure (8 verse)

मूषिकः

mūṣikaḥ (m)—mouse, rat

मूषिकवाहनः

mūṣikavāhanaḥ (m)—'having a rat for a mount,' epithet of Gaṇeṣa

मृ

√mṛ (1P)—die (16)

मृगः

mṛgaḥ (m)—deer (4, 6)

मृगशावकः

mṛgaśāvakaḥ (m)—fawn (19)

मृत

mṛta (adj)—dead (17)

मृत्युः

mṛtyuḥ (m)—death, (m prop)—god of death (21)

मृष्

√mṛṣ (4Ā)—bear, endure (22)

मेखला

mekhalā (f)—girdle

मेघः

meghaḥ (m)—cloud (21)

मेदिनी

medinī (f)—earth (20)

मैथिली

maithilī (f prop)—lady of Mithilā, i.e., Sītā (21)

मोक्षः

mokṣaḥ (m)—liberation (14)

मोहः

mohaḥ (m)—delusion (19)

मोहित

mohita (adj)—deluded (16)

मौनम्

maunam (n)—silence

-य्-
-y-

यः

yaḥ (m pr)—who (relative) (6)

यज्

√yaj (1P/Ā)—sacrifice (17)

यज्ञः

yajñaḥ (m)—ritual offering to the gods, a Vedic sacrifice (5)

यत् (-द्)

yat (-d) (n pr)—what (relative) (6); (ind)—used to introduce direct or indirect discourses, used with or without इति at the end (7, 8)

यत
yata (adj)—restrained

यतः
yataḥ (ind)—whence, since (relative) (6)

यत्र
yatra (ind)—where (relative) (6)

यथा
yathā (ind)—as, like (relative) (6)

यथाकामम्
yathākāmam (ind)—in accordance with desire, at will (15)

यथाविधि
yathāvidhi (ind)—in accordance with custom (15)

यथाशक्ति
yathāśakti (ind)—in accordance with ability

यथाशास्त्रम्
yathāśāstram (ind)—in accordance with śāstra

यथासुखम्
yathāsukham (ind)—according to pleasure (19)

यथेष्टम्
yatheṣṭam (ind)—according to desire, as you wish (21)

यदा
yadā (ind)—when (relative) (6)

यदि
yadi (ind)—if (6)

यदृच्छया
yadṛcchayā (ind)—by chance (19)

यम्
√yam (1P)—control, give (11)

यमः
yamaḥ (m prop)—Yama, god of death (12)

यमलोकः
yamalokaḥ (m)—Yama's realm, death

यशः
yaśaḥ (n)—fame

या
yā (f pr)—who (relative) (6)

या
√yā (2P)—go (15)

यावत्
yāvat (ind)—so long as, to the extent that (6)

यावज्जीवनम्
yāvajjīvanam (ind)—for the duration of life

यावत्संवत्सरम्
yāvatsaṃvatsaram (ind)—for a year

युक्त
yukta (adj)—joined, furnished with (19); proper

युगम्
yugam (n)—a cosmic era (19)

युगान्तमेघः
yugāntameghaḥ (m)—cloud gathering at the end of the cosmic cycle (20)

युज्
√yuj (7P/Ā)—join (18)

युत
yuta (adj)—endowed with (6); full of, associated with (22)

युद्धम्
yuddham (n)—battle (20)

युध्
√yudh (4Ā)—fight

युध्
yudh (f)—battle (20)

युयुत्सु
yuyutsu (adj)—wishing to fight

यूथम्
yūtham (n)—herd, group (20)

योगः
yogaḥ (m)—yoga

योगिन्
yogin (m; f -इनी)—yogi

योजनम्
yojanam (n)—a unit of distance (22)

यौवराज्यम्
yauvarājyam (n)—state of being heir apparent (15)

-र्-

-r-

रकारः
rakāraḥ (m)—the syllable 'ra,' i.e., the letter 'r' (21)

रक्त
rakta (adj)—reddened; (n -म्)—blood (14, 17)

रक्ष्
√rakṣ (1P)—protect

रक्षः
rakṣaḥ (n)—*rākṣasa* (20)

रक्षकः
rakṣakaḥ (m)—protector (6)

रक्षणम्
rakṣaṇam (n)—protection (7)

रघुः
raghuḥ (m prop)—Raghu, ancestor of Rāma

रजतम्
rajatam (n)—silver (21)

रज्जुः
rajjuḥ (f)—rope (17)

रणम्

raṇam (n)—battle (19)

रत

rata (adj)—delighted, attached (emotionally)

रतिः

ratiḥ (f)—pleasure, delight (11 verse)

रत्नम्

ratnam (n)—jewel (13 verse)

रथः

rathaḥ (m)—chariot (17)

रम्

√ram (1Ā)—enjoy, make love (21)

रमणीय

ramaṇīya (adj)—beautiful (7)

रमणीयता

ramaṇīyatā (f)—beauty, charm (18)

रमेशः

rameśaḥ (m)—lord of Ramā (Sītā), = Rāma (5 verse)

रहित

rahita (adj)—devoid of, missing (especially at end of compound) (16)

राक्षसः

rākṣasaḥ (m)—*rākṣasa*, demon (6)

राक्षसी

rākṣasī (f)—a *rākṣasa* woman, a female demon (19)

राघवः

rāghavaḥ (m)—Rāghava, descendant of "Raghu" e.g., Rāma (7)

राज्

√rāj (1P/Ā)—shine (19)

राजकर्तृ

rājakartṛ (m)—king-maker (18)

राजगृहम्

rājagṛham (n)—Rājagṛha, city of Bharata's maternal uncle (17)

राजन्

rājan (m)—king (8)

राजमणिः

rājamaṇiḥ (m)—jewel among kings (5 verse)

राजर्षिः

rājarṣiḥ (m)—sage-king, royal-seer (12)

राज्यम्

rājyam (n)—kingly rule, kingdom (5); राज्यं + √कृ (8P/Ā)—to rule

रामः

rāmaḥ (m prop)—Rāma

रामायणम्

rāmāyaṇam (n prop)—the Rāmāyaṇa

रावणः

rāvaṇaḥ (m prop)—Rāvaṇa, king of the *rākṣasa*-s (21)

राशिः

rāśiḥ (m)—heap, mass, collection

राष्ट्रम्

rāṣṭram (n)—kingdom (16)

रुच्

√ruc (1Ā)—be agreeable to (object in dative) (14)

रुद्

√rud (2P)—weep (17)

रूपम्

rūpam (n)—form (literal and figurative), a beautiful body (19)

रूपिन्

rūpin (adj; f -इनी)—possessed of form

रेणुः

reṇuḥ (m)—dust (19)

रोगः

rogaḥ (m)—disease (14)

रोदनम्

rodanam (n)—crying (20)

-ल्-

-l-

लक्षणम्

lakṣaṇam (n)—mark, sign, token (11 verse)

लक्ष्मणः

lakṣmaṇaḥ (m prop)—Lakṣmaṇa, one of Rāma's brothers (5)

लक्ष्मी

lakṣmī (f)—fortune, prosperity, the goddess Lakṣmī (17)

लक्ष्यम्

lakṣyam (n)—target (20)

लघु

laghu (adj)—light, small (6)

लङ्का

laṅkā (f prop)—Laṅkā, name of Rāvaṇa's capital (20)

लङ्केश्वरः

laṅkeśvaraḥ (m prop)—lord of Laṅkā, epithet of Rāvaṇa (21)

लब्ध

labdha (adj)—acquired, gained (10)

लभ्

√labh (1Ā)—acquire, gain (10)

लम्ब

lamba (adj)—hanging (12)

लम्बोदरी

lambodarī (f)—potbellied (19)

लय

laya (adj)—sticking, clinging; (m)—1) devotion, concentration, 2) place of rest, abode

लवण

lavaṇa (adj)—salty (22)

लिख्

√likh (6P)—write

लिखित

likhita (adj)—written (15)

लिह्

√lih (6P—लिहति; 2P—लेढि)—lick

ली

√lī (4Ā)—cling

लीढ

līḍha (adj)—licked

लीन

līna (adj)—attached

लीला

līlā (f)—play, sport (8)

लुप्

√lup (6Ā)—break, destroy; (लोपय्—णिजन्त)—neglect, violate (18)

लेशम्

leśam (n)—little, small bit or portion (10)

लोकः

lokaḥ (m)—world; host, army, people (9, 21)

लोचनम्

locanam (n)—eye (13)

लोपः

lopaḥ (m)—loss, damage, violation (18)

लोपय्

lopay (णिजन्त of √लुप्)—neglect, violate (18)

-व्-

-v-

वंशः

vaṃśaḥ (m)—race, lineage (12)

वक्र

vakra (adj)—crooked (21)

वक्षः

vakṣaḥ (n)—chest (20)

वच्

√vac (2P)—speak

वचः

vacaḥ (n)—speech (13)

वचनम्

vacanam (n)—speech, words (5)

वज्रम्

vajram (n)—thunderbolt, Indra's weapon (12)

वत्

vat (ind)—like (at end of compound) (12)

वत्सः

vatsaḥ (m)—calf, son; in vocative—term of endearment, "my dear child" (16)

वद्

√vad (1P)—speak (4)

वदनम्

vadanam (n)—face (15)

वध्

√vadh (1P)—kill, slay (20)

वधः

vadhaḥ (m)—killing, slaughter (21)

वध्य

vadhya (adj)—to be killed (21)

वनम्

vanam (n)—forest (4)

वन्द्

√vand (1Ā)—praise, extol (9 verse, 13 verse, 15)

वन्यम्

vanyam (n)—forest-food, i.e., gathered as opposed to cultivated (16)

वपुः

vapuḥ (n)—body, form

वर

vara (adj)—best, excellent, most precious, beautiful (17, 19)

वरः

varaḥ (m)—boon, wish (11)

वर्णः

varṇaḥ (m)—color, hue (20)

वर्षम्

varṣam (n)—year; in द्वितीया 'for a year' (15)

वलिः

valiḥ (m)—wrinkle (18 verse)

वल्मीकः

valmīkaḥ (m)—ant hill (20)

वशः

vaśaḥ (m)—power, control, influence (14)

वशगतः

vaśagataḥ (adj)—under the influence of (14)

वस्

√vas (1P)—dwell (4)

वसतिः

vasatiḥ (f)—dwelling

वसिष्ठः

vasiṣṭhaḥ (m prop)—Vasiṣṭha, one of the great brāhman sages of Indian tradition (17 verse)

वस्तुतः

vastutaḥ (ind)—in fact (11)

वस्त्रम्

vastram (n)—garment, clothing (16)

वा

vā (ind)—or (placed after words as is च) (7)

वाच् (क्)

vāc (k) (f)—speech (8 verse, 21.1.a)

वाक्यम्

vākyam (n)—speech (14)

वाणी

vāṇī (f)—speech (8 verse, 20 verse)

वातः

vātaḥ (m)—wind (22)

वानरः

vānaraḥ (m)—monkey (13)

वायुः

vāyuḥ (m)—wind (13)

वार् (:)

vār (ḥ) (n)—water

वाराशिः

vārāśiḥ (m)—ocean (वार् + राशिः) (13 verse)

वारि

vāri (n)—water

वालिन्

vālin (m prop)—Vālin, king of the monkeys, elder brother of Sugrīva (22)

वाल्मीकिः

vālmīkiḥ (m prop)—Vālmīki, a famous sage, first poet, author of the *Rāmāyaṇa* (15)

वासः

vāsaḥ (m)—dwelling (16)

वासः

vāsaḥ (n)—clothing, garment (21)

वासनम्

vāsanam (n)—dwelling, abode (18)

वासिन्

vāsin (m, n; f -इनी)—dweller (13)

वाहनम्

vāhanam (n)—vehicle, mount

विकृत

vikṛta (adj)—deformed (22)

विगत

vigata (adj)—gone, departed (14)

वि + चर्

vi + √car (1P)—think about, reflect (7 verse); wander (19)

विचारः

vicāraḥ (m)—deliberation, hesitation (13)

विच्छिन्न

vicchinna (adj)—severed (19)

वि + जि

vi + √ji (1Ā)—conquer, subdue (5 verse)

वि + ज्ञा

vi + √jñā (9Ā)—realize (16)

विज्वर

vijvara (adj)—free from anxiety (22)

वित्रासः
vitrāsaḥ (m)—terror (21)

-विद्
-vid (adj) (from √विद्)—knower (12.17)

विद्
√vid (2P)—know

विद्या
vidyā (f)—knowledge, learning (19 verse)

विद्वांस्
vidvāṃs (m)—learned man, wise; विद्वज्जनः (m)—wise people (11 verse) (See 17.24.b)

विद्विषः
vidviṣaḥ (m)—enemy (11 verse)

विधिः
vidhiḥ (m)—rule, custom (15)

वि + नश्
vi + √naś (4P)—be destroyed (20)

विना
vinā (ind)—without (4)

विनाशनम्
vināśanam (n)—destruction

वि + नि + वृत्
vi + ni + √vṛt (1Ā)—turn back, return (18)

विपरीत
viparīta (adj)—perverse, contrary, false (17)

विभीषणः
vibhīṣaṇaḥ (m prop)—Vibhīṣaṇa, a *rākṣasa*, younger brother of Rāvaṇa (22)

वि + भूष्
vi + √bhūṣ (10P)—adorn (8 verse)

वि + भ्रम्
vi + √bhram (1P)—wander

वियोगः
viyogaḥ (m)—separation

वि + रञ्
vi + √raj (1P)—become dispassionate

विरहित
virahita (adj)—deserted, separated from (16)

विरूप
virūpa (adj)—ugly (19)

विरूपणम्
virūpaṇam (n)—disfigurement (19)

विरूपय
virūpaya (नामधातु)—disfigure (19)

विरूपित
virūpita (adj)—disfigured, mutilated (19)

विरूपिन्
virūpin (adj)—ugly (19)

वि + लप्

vi + √lap (1P)—lament (14, 17 verse)

विलेपनम्

vilepanam (n)—ointment (8 verse)

वि + लोक्

vi + √lok (10P)—look at, perceive (20 verse)

विवर्ण

vivarṇa (adj)—devoid of color, pale (13)

विवासित

vivāsita (adj)—exiled (17)

विवाहः

vivāhaḥ (m)—marriage (7)

विवाहित

vivāhita (adj)—married (12)

विश्

√viś (6P)—enter (22)

विशालाक्षी

viśālākṣī (adj f)—having large eyes (19)

विशेषतः

viśeṣataḥ (ind)—especially (5)

विश्व

viśva (adj)—all (declined pronominally)

विश्वस्त

viśvasta (adj)—reassured, confident (22)

विषण्ण

viṣaṇṇa (adj)—dejected (13)

विषम्

viṣam (n)—poison (15)

वि + सृज्

vi + √sṛj (6P)—release, give up (16)

विस्तीर्ण

vistīrṇa (adj)—broad (22)

विस्मयः

vismayaḥ (m)—amazement (10 verse, 21)

वि + स्मृ

vi + √smṛ (1P)—forget (5)

विस्मृत

vismṛta (adj)—forgotten

वि + हा

vi + √hā (3P)—give up, discard (21 verse)

विहारिन्

vihārin (adj)—delighting in (20)

वि + हृ

vi + √hṛ (1P)—take away, abduct

वीरः

vīraḥ (m)—hero (5)

वीर्यम्
vīryam (n)—valor (14)

वृ
√vṛ (9Ā)—choose (as a boon) (11)

वृक्षः
vṛkṣaḥ (m)—tree (11)

वृत्
√vṛt (1Ā)—is, exists (5)

वृत
vṛta (adj)—chosen (11)

वृत्त
vṛtta (adj)—occurred, happened (17); (n)—news, story, report; (fig.)—slender (19)

वृत्तान्तः
vṛttāntaḥ (m)—report, news, story (14)

वृत्रः
vṛtraḥ (m prop)—Vṛtra, name of a demon

वृत्रहन्
vṛtrahan (m prop)—'slayer of Vṛtra,' Indra

वृद्ध
vṛddha (adj)—old (9)

वृध्
√vṛdh (1Ā)—grow

वृषभः
vṛṣabhaḥ (m)—bull (19)

वेगः
vegaḥ (m)—speed (13)

वेदः
vedaḥ (m)—*veda* (6)

वैदेही
vaidehī (f prop)—lady of Videha, Sītā (16)

वैद्यः
vaidyaḥ (m)—doctor (10 verse)

वैरम्
vairam (n)—hostility (22)

वैराग्यम्
vairāgyam (n)—aversion to worldly things

वैश्रवणः
vaiśravaṇaḥ (m prop)—Vaiśravaṇa, son of Viśravaṇa, Rāvaṇa (20)

वैश्व
vaiśva (adj)—universal

व्यक्त
vyakta (adj)—clear (18)

व्यथ्
√vyath (1Ā)—be agitated (13)

व्यपे (वि + अप + इ)
vyape (vi + apa + √i) (2P)—separate, drift apart

व्यवसायः
vyavasāyaḥ (m)—resolution

व्यसनम्
vyasanam (n)—disaster (14)

व्याघ्रः
vyāghraḥ (m)—tiger (16)

व्याघ्री
vyāghrī (f)—tigress (19)

व्रज्
√vraj (1P)—move, walk

व्रीडा
vrīḍā (f)—shame (22)

व्रीहिः
vrīhiḥ (m)—rice

-श्-
-ś-

शंस्
√śaṃs (1P)—relate (22)

शक्
√śak (5P)—be able (13)

शकुन्तला
śakuntalā (f prop)—Śakuntalā

शक्त
śakta (adj)—competent

शक्तिः
śaktiḥ (f)—power, ability (20)

शक्य
śakya (adj)—capable of being (with infinitive) (21)

शङ्क्
√śaṅk (1Ā)—doubt (10)

शङ्कित
śaṅkita (adj)—doubted (10)

शतम्
śatam (n)—hundred (see 19.5.b)

शत्रुः
śatruḥ (m)—enemy (12)

शत्रुघ्नः
śatrughnaḥ (m prop)—Śatrughna, one of Rāma's brothers (5)

शप्
√śap (1P)—curse (4)

शबरी
śabarī (f prop)—Śabarī, a female ascetic who aids Rāma (22)

शब्दः
śabdaḥ (m)—sound (18)

शम्
√śam (4Ā)—be calm, quiet

शम्भुः
śambhuḥ (m prop)—Śambhu, Śiva (8)

शरः
śaraḥ (m)—arrow (4)

शरीरम्
śarīram (n)—body (20)

शल्यम्

śalyam (n)—arrow, spear (16)

शशिन्

śaśin (m)—having a hare (*śaśaḥ*), the moon

शस्त्रम्

śastram (n)—weapon (18)

शाखा

śākhā (f)—branch (15)

शान्त

śānta (adj)—calm, peaceful (5, 9)

शापः

śāpaḥ (m)—curse (5)

शारद

śārada (adj)—autumnal (16)

शालः

śālaḥ (m)—a kind of tree (18)

शाला

śālā (f)—room, chamber, house, hut (16)

शास्

√śās (2Ā)—rule (18)

शासनम्

śāsanam (n)—sovereignty, rule (18)

शास्त्रम्

śāstram (n)—scholarly text (14)

शिखरम्

śikharam (n)—peak, pinnacle (18)

शिथिल

śithila (adj)—loose, slack, weak (18 verse)

शिरः

śiraḥ (n)—head (18 verse)

शिल्पिन्

śilpin (m)—artisan (18)

शिवः

śivaḥ (m prop)—Śiva

शिष्यः

śiṣyaḥ (m)—student (17)

शी

√śī (2Ā)—lie down

शीघ्रम्

śīghram (adv)—quickly (6)

शुकः

śukaḥ (m)—parrot

शुच्

√śuc (1P)—grieve (15)

शुद्ध

śuddha (adj)—pure (13)

शुभ्

√śubh (1Ā)—shine, be beautiful

शुष्क

śuṣka (adj)—dried up (16)

शूरः

śūraḥ (m)—hero

शूर्पणखा

śūrpaṇakhā (f prop)—Śūrpaṇakhā,

sister of Rāvaṇa (19)

शूलम्

śūlam (n)—lance (20)

शोकः

śokaḥ (m)—grief (4)

शोणितम्

śoṇitam (n)—blood (19)

शौर्यम्

śauryam (n)—valor (21)

श्याम

śyāma (adj)—dark (21)

श्यामा

śyāmā (f)—a young woman (who has not had children) (21)

श्रमः

śramaḥ (m)—toil, effort (15)

श्रवणम्

śravaṇam (n)—hearing (10)

श्रीरामः

śrīrāmaḥ (m prop)—"glorious Rāma" (4)

श्रु

√śru (5P)—hear, hear about (5)

श्रुत

śruta (adj)—heard

श्रेष्ठ

śreṣṭha (adj)—best (5)

श्वः

śvaḥ (ind)—tomorrow (16)

-ष्-

-ṣ-

षष्

ṣaṣ (adj)—six (see 19.6)

षोडश

ṣoḍaśa (adj)—sixteen (see 19.6)

-स्-

-s-

स-

sa- (ind)—with, together with (used only as prior member of a compound) (14)

सम् + अलं + कृ

sam + alaṃ + √kṛ (8P/Ā)—adorn (8 verse)

सः

saḥ (pr m)—he (4)

संयत

saṃyata (adj)—restrained, controlled

सं + या

saṃ + √yā (2P)—attain

सम् + √युज्

(7P/Ā)—join, yoke (20)

संरब्ध

saṃrabdha (adj)—infuriated (20)

संवत्सरः
saṃvatsaraḥ (m)—year (14)

संवृत
saṃvṛta (adj)—surrounded (19)

सं + शम्
saṃ + √śam (4Ā)—be extinguished (18)

संसद्
saṃsad (f)—assembly (22)

संस्कृत
saṃskṛta (adj)—refined (8 verse)

सकामम्
sakāmam (ind)—with desire

सकोपम्
sakopam (ind)—angrily

सखि
sakhi (m)—friend (21)

सख्यम्
sakhyam (n)—friendship, alliance (22)

संकृत्त
saṃkṛtta (adj)—pierced (20)

संक्रुद्ध
saṃkruddha (adj)—angry (15)

संख्यम्
saṃkhyam (n)—battle (20)

संगत
saṃgata (adj)—joined, united with (20); met with (22)

सचराचर
sacarācara (adj)—'together with moveable and immovable things,' entire (22)

सज्ज
sajja (adj)—ready (18)

सं + चर्
saṃ + √car (1P)—go, walk (15)

संज्ञा
saṃjñā (f)—consciousness (12)

सत्
sat (n)—truth

सततम्
satatam (ind)—always (8 verse)

सती
satī (f)—a virtuous wife (22)

सत्य
satya (adj)—real, true; (n)—truth, reality (10, 11 verse)

सद्
√sad (1P)—sit (see 7.15.c) (7)

सदनम्
sadanam (n)—palace (12)

सदा
sadā (ind)—always (5 verse)

सदृश
sadṛśa (adj)—like, fit, suitable (14)

सन्त्

sant (m)—good or virtuous man (11 verse)

संतप्त

saṃtapta (adj)—oppressed, afflicted (22)

संत्रस्त

saṃtrasta (adj)—terrified (21)

सं + दृश्

saṃ + √dṛś (1P/Ā)—see (22)

सं + धा

saṃ + √dhā (3P/Ā)—join, bring together (8)

सन्निभ

sannibha (adj)—like (20)

सप्त

sapta (adj)—seven (see 19.6)

सभा

sabhā (f)—assembly (8)

सम

sama (adj)—same, equal (14)

समयः

samayaḥ—period of time, time (11)

समरः

samaraḥ (m)—battle (20)

समर्थ

samartha (adj)—capable, competent (6)

समविभक्ताङ्गी

samavibhaktāṅgī (f)—a woman of symmetrical limbs (21)

समवे (सम् + अव + इ)

samave (sam + ava + √i) (2P)—convene, come together (22)

समागत

samāgata (adj)—come together (22)

समागम् (सम् + आ + गम्)

samāgam (sam + ā + √gam) (1P)—assemble (7)

समागमः

samāgamaḥ (m)—meeting (18)

समाज्ञा (सम् + आ + ज्ञा)

samājñā (sam + ā + √jñā) (9P)—know (18); णिजन्त—order, command (18)

समानी (सम् + आ + नी)

samānī (sam + ā + √nī) (1P)—assemble (22)

समाश्रि (सम् + आ + श्रि)

samāśri (sam + ā + √śri) (1P)—resort to

समासद् (सम् + आ + सद्)

samāsad (sam + ā + √sad) (10P)—reach (22)

सम् + इ

sam + √i (2P)—come together, meet (14)

समीपम्

samīpam (n)—nearness, vicinity (11)

समुत्पन्न

samutpanna (adj)—arisen (13)

संपन्न

saṃpanna (adj)—endowed with (at end of compound) (20)

सम्पातिः

sampātiḥ (m prop)—Sampāti, name of a vulture (22)

संपूर्ण

saṃpūrṇa (adj)—filled (18)

संप्राप्त

saṃprāpta (adj)—arrived (18)

संप्रेक्ष् (सम् + प्र + ईक्ष्)

saṃprekṣ (sam + pra + √īkṣ) (6Ā)—see, regard (13)

संभाष् (सम् + भाष्)

saṃbhāṣ (sam + √bhāṣ) (1Ā)—speak

संभ्रान्त

saṃbhrānta (adj)—confused (21)

संमित

saṃmita (adj)—equal to (22)

सम्यक्

samyak (adv)—fully, properly (21)

सरः

saraḥ (n)—lake (16)

सरित्

sarit (f)—stream; सरितां पतिः—ocean (22)

सर्पः

sarpaḥ (m)—snake (19 verse, 20)

सर्व

sarva (adj)—each, all, every (see 5.7)

सर्वदा

sarvadā (ind)—always (7)

सह्

sah (1Ā)—bear, endure

सह

saha (ind)—with (5)

सहसा

sahasā (ind)—suddenly, at once (19)

सहस्रम्

sahasram (n)—a thousand (16)

सहित

sahita (adj)—along with (22)

सागरः

sāgaraḥ (m)—ocean (10)

सादरम्

sādaram (ind)—with respect

साधु

sādhu (adj)—righteous (11 verse); (ind)—directly (21); as exclamation—"wonderful!"

mation—"wonderful!"

साधुः

sādhuḥ (m)—sage, holy man (9)

सानन्दम्

sānandam (ind)—joyfully (5)

सान्त्व्

√sāntv (10P)—pacify, appease (15)

सारथिः

sārathiḥ (m)—charioteer (21)

सिंहः

siṃhaḥ (m)—lion (15)

सिंहासनम्

siṃhāsanam (n)—lion-seat, throne (18)

सिद्ध

siddha (adj)—endowed with supernatural *or* magical powers (6 verse)

सीता

sītā (f prop)—Sītā (6)

सुकुमार

sukumāra (adj)—lovely (12)

सुखम्

sukha (n)—happiness, joy; (ind) —happily

सुखित

sukhita (adj)—happy (5)

सुग्रीवः

sugrīvaḥ (m prop)—Sugrīva, younger brother of Vālin, ally of Rāma (22)

सुतः

sutaḥ (m)—son (12)

सुता

sutā (f)—daughter

सुदारुण

sudāruṇa (adj)—very terrible (19)

सुन्दर

sundara (adj; f—सुन्दरी)—beautiful (4)

सुमध्यमा

sumadhyamā (f)—woman with a beautiful waist (21)

सुमित्रा

sumitrā (f prop)— Sumitrā name of the mother of Lakṣmaṇa and Śatrughna

सुमुख

sumukha (adj)—handsome (19)

सुलभ

sulabha (adj)—easy (8)

सुसंक्रुद्ध

susaṃkruddha (adj)—furious (19)

सूर्यः

sūryaḥ (m)—sun (9)

सृज्

√sṛj (6P)—release (16)

सृप्

√sṛp (1P)—move (16)

सेतुः

setuḥ (m)—bridge, causeway (22)

सेना

senā (f)—army (17)

सेव्

√sev (1Ā)—attend on, serve (10, 11 verse)

सेवकः

sevakaḥ (m)—attendant (12)

सेवा

sevā (f)—service

सेवित

sevita (adj)—served (10)

सोढ

soḍha (adj)—endured, borne

सोमः

somaḥ (m)—soma

सौमित्रिः

saumitriḥ (m prop)—son of Sumitrā, Lakṣmaṇa (18)

सौम्य

saumya (adj)—gentle, pleasant; as संबोधन "my friend," "my good man" (20)

सौवर्ण

sauvarṇa (adj)—golden (21)

सौहृदम्

sauhṛdam (n)—friendship (21)

स्तब्ध

stabdha (adj)—paralyzed, frozen

स्तम्भः

stambhaḥ (m)—post (18 verse)

स्तु

√stu (2P)—praise (9)

स्त्री

strī (f)—woman (21)

-स्थ

-stha (adj)—standing (from √स्था) (17)

स्था

√sthā (1P)—stand, remain (7)

स्थानम्

sthānam (n)—place (18)

स्थित

sthita (adj)—standing; stabilized (14)

स्ना

√snā (2P)—bathe (18)

स्नानम्

snānam (n)—bath, bathing, ablution (8 verse, 19)

स्निह्

√snih (4P)—love (object of love in सप्तमी) (5)

स्नेहः

snehaḥ (m)—love, affection

स्म

sma (ind)—used after लट् to form simple past tense (see 4.47) (4)

स्मि

√smi (1P/Ā)—smile (19)

स्मितपूर्वम्

smitapūrvam (ind)—with a smile (19)

स्मृ

√smṛ (1P)—remember

स्मृतिः

smṛtiḥ (f)—memory, a class of texts

स्मृतिमन्त्

smṛtimant (adj)—possessed of memory, well-versed in *smṛti* (11)

स्रु

√sru (1P)—flow, run (19)

स्व

sva (adj)—one's own (declined like पर, see 5.7, but optionally follows masculine in -a) (7 verse, 9, 17, 18 verse)

स्वजनः

svajanaḥ (m)—kin (21)

स्वनः

svanaḥ (m)—sound, cry (19)

स्वप्

√svap (2P)—sleep

स्वयम्

svayam (ind)—to, for, by oneself (4, 8)

स्वयंवरः

svayaṃvaraḥ (m)—lit., "self choice," the name of a ceremony at which a princess chooses a husband or has one chosen by contest (8)

स्वरः

svaraḥ (m)—sound, cry (19)

स्वर्गः

svargaḥ (m)—heaven (6, 17 verse)

स्वर्गत

svargata (adj)—gone to heaven (22)

-ह्-
-h-

हत

hata (adj)—killed (4)

हत्या

hatyā (f)—murder, slaying

-हन्

-han (adj)—slayer (from √हन्, see 12.17)

हन्
√han (2P)—kill, strike (4)

हननम्
hananam (n)—killing (6)

हनुमन्त्
hanumant (opt. हनूमन्त्) (m prop)—Hanumān (22)

हरिः
hariḥ (m prop)—Hari (Viṣṇu); (m)—monkey (19 verse)

हरिवर
harivara (adj)—best of monkeys (22)

हरीश्वरः
harīśvaraḥ (m)—lord of monkeys (22)

हविः
haviḥ (n)—oblation

हस्
√has (1P)—laugh (12)

हस्तः
hastaḥ (m)—hand

हस्तलाघवम्
hastalāghavam (n)—skill, manual dexterity (10 verse)

हस्तिन्
hastin (m)—elephant

हा
√hā (3P)—abandon (7)

हारः
hāraḥ (m)—necklace (8 verse)

हासः
hāsaḥ (m)—laughter (19)

हि
hi (ind)—indeed, surely (19)

हा
hā (ind)—vocative particle expressing grief (4)

हिंसा
hiṃsā (f)—violence, injury (20)

हिंस्र
hiṃsra (adj)—injurious, fierce (15)

हितः
hitaḥ (m)—welfare, benefit (20 verse, 21)

हीन
hīna (adj)—devoid of, missing (esp. at end of compound) (16)

हु
√hu (3P)—offer (9)

हृ
√hṛ (1P)—abduct, carry off (22)

हृत
hṛta (adj)—abducted (22)

हृदयम्
hṛdayam (n)—heart (14)

हृदये + कृ

hṛdaye + √kṛ (idiom)—take seriously,(14); + √धा (idiom)—"placed in the heart" (16)

हृष्ट

hṛṣṭa (adj)—delighted (21)

हे

he (ind)—vocative particle (4)

हेमन्

heman (n)—gold (18)

हेमपिङ्गल

hemapiñgala (adj)—golden-yellow (22)

ENGLISH-SANSKRIT GLOSSARY

(This glossary was designed for reference to particular usages and meanings in the readings and exercises of this primer. It is not intended for use as a general Sanskrit dictionary.)

-A-

abandon—त्यज् (1P) (10); परि + त्यज् (1P) (9); हा (3P) (7); abandoned—त्यक्त (adj) (10)

abduct—अप + हृ (1P) (21); वि + हृ (1P); हृ (1P) (22); abducted—हृत (adj) (22); to be abducted—अपहर्तव्य (adj) (21)

ability—शक्तिः (f) (20); in accordance with ability—यथाशक्ति (ind)

able, be—शक् (5P) (13); able—क्षम (adj) (9)

ablution—अभिषेकः (m) (19); स्नानम् (n) (8 verse, 19)

abode—लयः (m); वासनम् (n) (18)

absolute reality—ब्रह्मन् (n) (9)

accept—अङ्गीकृ (8P) (20)

account—अनुकथनम् (n) (22)

acquire—लभ् (1Ā) (10); लब्ध (adj) (10)

activity—कर्मन् (n) (8)

addressed—उक्त (adj) (10); प्रोक्त (adj) (19)

adorn—अलम् + कृ (8P); भूष् (10P); वि + भूष् (10P) (8 verse); सम् + अलं + कृ (8P/Ā) (8 verse)

adventure—चरितम् (n) (4)

affection—स्नेहः (m)

afflicted—पीडित (adj) (4); बाधित (adj) (6); संतप्त (adj) (22); afflicted with—आर्त (adj) (20)

afraid—भीत (adj) (4)

after—अनन्तरम् (ind) (9); after that—तदनन्तरम् (ind) (9)

again—पुनः (ind) (4)

agent—कारिन् (adj)

age—जॄ (1P) (10); aged—जीर्ण (adj) (10)

agitate—क्षोभय् (22); be agitated—व्यथ् (1Ā) (13); agitated—आकुल (adj) (12)

agree to—अङ्गीकृ (8P) (20)

agreeable to, be—रुच् (1Ā) (14)

aha!—अहो (ind)

air—खम् (n) (12)

Akampanaḥ—अकम्पनः (m prop) (20)

alarm—भयम् (n) (16)

alliance—सख्यम् (n) (22)

all—विश्व (adj); सर्व (adj) (see 5.7)

along with—सहित (adj) (22)

also—अपि (ind) (4)

alteration—परिणामः (m)

alternative—गतिः (f) (6, 20 verse)

always—नित्यम् (ind) (21); सततम् (ind) (8 verse); सदा (ind) (5 verse); सर्वदा (ind) (7)

amazement—विस्मयः (m) (10 verse, 21)
amuse oneself—क्रीड् (1P) (18 verse, 21), वि + हृ (1P)
ancestor—पितृ (m) (10, 19)
and—च (ind)
angry, be—कुप् (4P) (7); क्रुद्ध (4P) (7); anger—कोपः (m) (14); क्रोधः (m) (13); मन्युः (m) (14); angrily—सकोपम् (ind); angry—कुपित (adj) (4); क्रुद्ध (adj); संक्रुद्ध (adj) (15);
annihilate—अभि + हन् (2P); annihilated—अभिहत (adj) (5 verse, 20)
announce—उद् + आ + हृ (1P) (21)
annoy—प्र + मथ् (1P) (21)
anoint—अभि + षिच् (6P) (17)
another time—अन्यदा (ind)
another—अपर (adj) (9, 17); अन्य (adj) (5)
answer—प्रति + वच् (2P) (18); उत्तरम् (n) (17)
ant hill—वल्मीकः (m) (20)
anxiety—चिन्ता (f) (7); free from anxiety—विज्वर (adj) (22)
appear—दृश् (non-present form of √पश्) (11); भा (2P) (13);
appease—सान्त्व् (10P) (15); प्र + सद् (1P) (13)
appoint—नि + युज् (7P) (17 verse); appointed—नियोजित (adj) (20)
approach—अभि + गम् (1P) (8); उप + गम् (1P) (8)
arise—उत् + पद् (4Ā); उद् + भू (1P) (5); जन् (4Ā) (14); arisen—उत्पन्न (adj) (13); जात (adj) (13); समुत्पन्न (adj) (13)
armlet—केयूरः (m) (8 verse)
armor—कवचः (m) (18)
army—चमूः (f) (5 verse, 18); लोकः (m) (9, 21); सेना (f) (17)
arouse—उत्पादय् (णिजन्त) (20)
arranged, be—क्लृप् (1Ā)
arrived—प्राप् (प्र + आप्) (5P) (16); संप्राप्त (adj) (18)
arrow—इषुः (m) (7); बाणः (m) (6); शरः (m) (4); शल्यम् (n) (16);
artisan—शिल्पिन् (m) (18)
as—इव (ind) (4); यथा (ind) (6)
ascend (to)—आ + रुह् (1P) (15)
asceticism—तपः (n) (9)
ascetic—तापसः (m) (20); तपस्विन् (m; f -विनी) (12)
Aśoka grove—अशोकवनिका (f) (22)
ashram—आश्रमः (m) (6)
ask—प्रच्छ् (6P) (6)
ass—खरः (m) (21)
assemble—समागम् (सम् + आ + गम्) (1P) (7); समानी (सम् + आ + नी) (1P) (22)
assembly—संसद् (f) (22); सभा (f) (8)
assistance—उपकारः (m) (11)
associated with—युत (adj) (22)
assume—आ + दा (3P) (21); आ + स्था (1P) (21); धृ (10P/Ā) (8 verse)
at once—सहसा (ind) (19)
at present—अधुना (ind) (11)

attached—लीन (adj); attached to—परायण (पर + अयण) (adj); attached (emotionally)—रत (adj)
attain—अधि + गम् (1P) (9); उप + लभ् (1Ā) (9); सं + या (2P); attain (a state)—उप + गम् (1P) (22); attainment of knowledge—प्रतिपत्तिः (f)
attempt—प्र + यत् (1Ā) (8); attempted—आरब्ध (adj)
attend on—सेव् (1Ā) (10, 11 verse); attendant—अनुचरः (m); सेवकः (m) (12)
auspicious thing—भद्रम् (n)
austerity—तपः (n) (9)
authorize—अधि + कृ (8P)
autumnal—शारद (adj) (16)
aversion to worldly things—वैराग्यम् (n)
avoid—परि + हृ (1P) (19 verse); अगम्य (adj) (9 verse)
awake, be—बुध् (4Ā); awake—बुद्ध (adj) (10)
axe—परशुः (m) (14)
Ayodhyā—अयोध्या (f prop) (5)

-B-

bad—कु- (prefix) (19)
banana tree—कदली (f) (14)
bank—तीरम् (n) (22)
barely—कथमपि (-चित्, -चन) (ind)
bathe—स्ना (2P) (18); bath—स्नानम् (n) (8 verse, 19)
battle—आहवः (m) (20); रणम् (n) (19); युध् (f) (20); युद्धम् (n) (20); संख्यम् (n) (20); समरः (m) (20)
be—अस (2P) (4); भू (1P) (4); वृत् (1Ā)
bear—भृ (3P); धृ (10P/Ā) (8 verse); -भृत् (adj) (21); bear (endure)—मृष् (4Ā) (22);
beautiful young woman—प्रमदा (f) (20)
beautiful, be—शुभ् (1Ā); रमणीय (adj) (7); वर (adj) (17, 19); सुन्दर (adj) (4); सुन्दरी (f)
beauty—रमणीयता (f) (18); —रूपम् (n) (19)
become—भू (1P) (4)
before the eyes (lit., before, in front of the face)—प्रमुखे (ind) (21)
begin—आ + रभ् (1Ā); beginning—आदिः (m) (15); from the beginning—आदितः (ind) (17,22)
behold—प्रेक्ष् (प्र + ईक्ष्) (1Ā) (19)
being—भूतम् (n)
bellow—गर्ज् (1P) (22)
belly—उदरम् (n) (12), having a small belly—अल्पोदरी (f) (19)
beloved—प्रिय (adj) (6)
bend—नम् (1P) (10); bent—नत (adj) (10)
benefit—हितः (m) (20 verse, 21)
best of—इन्द्रः (m) (21), (lit., Indra among . . .) at the end of compound
best—वर (adj) (17, 19); श्रेष्ठ (adj) (5)

Bhagavadgītā—भगवद्गीता (f prop)
Bharata—भरतः (m prop) (5)
big belly, having—महोदरी (f adj) (19)
bind—बन्ध् (9P) (17); नह् (4P) (10)
bird—खगः (m) (12); द्विजः (m) (6); carrion bird—पत्ररथः (m) (20)
birth—जन्मन् (n) (14); उत्पत्तिः (f) (20 verse)
bite—दंश् (1P); bitten (adj)—दष्ट
blade of grass—तृणम् (n) (8)
blame—निन्द् (1P); blamed—निन्दित (adj); blameworthy—अवन्द्य (adj) (9 verse)
blazing—प्रज्वलित (adj) (10 verse)
blessed one—भगवन्त् (adj) (13)
bliss—आनन्दः (m) (6)
blocked—नि + वृ (5P/Ā) (19)
blood—रक्तम् (n) (14, 17); शोणितम् (n) (19)
blooming—फुल्ल (adj) (16)
blue-black—नील (adj)
boasting—कत्थनम् (n) (18)
body—कायः (m) (20); देहः (m) (21 verse); वपुः (n); शरीरम् (n) (20); having a body—देहिन् (adj)
book—पुस्तकम् (n) (13, 15)
boon—वरः (m) (11)
born, be—उत् + पद् (4Ā); जन् (4Ā) (14); born—जात (adj) (13); born from— -ज (adj) (18); born after, be—अनु + जन् (4P)
borne—सोढ (adj)
both—उभ (adj) (21)

bound—बद्ध (adj) (17); नद्ध (adj) (10)
bow—चापः (m) (8); धनुः (n) (9); bow-wielder—धनुष्मन्त् (adj) (21)
bow—नम् (1P) (10); bowed—नत (adj) (10)
boy—बालकः (m) (4, 17); कुमारः (m) (13)
bracelet—केयूरः (m) (8 verse)
Brahman, the god—ब्रह्मन् (ब्रह्मा)(m) (12); Brahman's world—ब्रह्मलोकः (m) (22); Absolute reality—ब्रह्मन् (ब्रह्म) (n) (9)
brāhman—ब्राह्मणः (m) (4); द्विजः (m) (6); brahman killer—ब्रह्मघ्न (adj) (20)
branch—शाखा (f) (15)
break—भञ्ज् (7P) (8); लुप् (6Ā)
breath—प्राणः (m); "abandon life breath," die—प्रानान् + √त्यज् (16)
bridge—सेतुः (m) (22)
bring—आ + नी (1P) (17); आ + हृ (1P); bringing—आवह (adj) (14); bring together—सं + धा (3P) (8)
broad—विस्तीर्ण (adj) (22)
broken—भग्न (adj) (18)
brother—भ्रातृ (m) (10); younger brother—अनुजः (m) (17); elder brother—पूर्वजः (m)
Buddha—बुद्धः (m)
bull—ऋषभः (m) (18); वृषभः (m) (19)
burden—भारः (m) (9)

burn—तप् (1P/Ā); दह् (2P) (18); burnt (adj)—दग्ध
burst—आ + स्फुट् (6P) (18 verse)
but—किंतु (ind) (5); तु (ind) (11)

-C-

calf—वत्सः (m) (16)
call—आ + हू (4Ā) (12); call out—उद् + आ + हृ (1P) (21)
calm, be —शम् (4Ā); परिसान्त्व् (10P) (18); calm—प्रसन्न (adj) (21); शान्त (adj) (5, 9)
capable—समर्थ (adj) (6); capable of being—शक्य (adj) (21); capable (of perceiving truth)—भव्य (adj) (20 verse)
cardinal point—दिश् (दिक्) (f) (20, 22 verse)
care—चिन्ता (f) (7)
carry—भृ (3P); carry off—हृ (1P) (22); carrying—भृत् (adj) (21)
carrion bird—पत्ररथः (m) (20)
cause to tremble—क्षोभय् (22)
causer of joy—नन्दनः (n) (16)
causer—कर (adj; f -ई) (20 verse); कृत् (adj)
causeway—सेतुः (m) (22)
cause—कारणम् (n) (15); causing (i.e., giving rise to) (adj) (at end of compound)— -द (14)
cave—कन्दरम् (n) (17); गुहा (f) (18, 22)
cavern—गुहा (f) (18, 22)
celestial being—गन्धर्वः (m) (20)
certain—निश्चित (adj); certainly—अवश्यम् (ind); निश्चितम् (ind)
chamber—शाला (f) (16)
change—परिणामः (m); परिवर्तनम् (n) (12)
chariot—रथः (m) (17)
charioteer—सारथिः (m) (21)
charm—रमणीयता (f) (18); charming—मनोहर (adj) (21)
chest—वक्षः (n) (20)
childless—अप्रज (adj)
children—प्रजा (f) (5)
choose (as a boon)—वृ (9Ā) (11); वृत (adj) (11)
chronicle—इतिहासः (m)
citizens—प्रजा (f) (5)
city—पुरी (f) (22); नगरम् (n) (10)
clear—व्यक्त (adj) (18)
clever—निपुण (adj) (6)
climb up—नि + रुह् (1P) (18 verse)
cling—ली (4Ā); clinging—लय (adj); clung to—लीन (adj)
clothing—वस्त्रम् (n) (16); वासः (n)
cloud—जीमूतः (m) (20); मेघः (m) (21); clouds gathering at the end of the cosmic cycle—युगान्तमेघः (m) (20)
club—परिघः (m) (20)
coiffure—मूर्धजः (m) (8 verse) (lit., 'born from the head, hair')
collection—राशिः (m)
color—वर्णः (m) (20); colorless—विवर्ण (adj) (13)
come back to—पत्याया (प्रति + आ + या) (2P) (17)
come to be—उद् + भू (1P) (5)

come together—सम् + इ (2P) (14); समवे (सम् + अव + इ) (2P) (22); समागत (adj) (22)
come—आ + गम् (1P) (4); आ + या (2P) (7, 22); प्राप् (प्र + आप्) (5P) (16)
command—आज्ञा (f) (9)
compassion—करुणा (f) (12); दया (f) (11 verse)
competent—क्षम (9); शक्त (adj); समर्थ (adj) (6)
conceal—प्र + छद् (10P) (11 verse)
consecration—अभिषेकः (m) (9)
conciliate—अनु + नी (1P)
condition—गतिः (f) (6, 20 verse
conduct—कृ (8P) (5)
confident—विश्वस्त (adj) (22)
conformable—अनुरूप (adj) (19)
confused—आकुल (adj) (22); पर्याकुल (adj) (21); संभ्रान्त (adj) (21)
conjugational class in grammar—गणः (m) (7)
conquered—जित (adj) (14); conquer—पराजि (परा + जि) (1P) (14); वि + जि (1Ā) (5 verse); जेतृ (m) (10); conquering— -जित् (adj) (12) (at end of compound)
consciousness—संज्ञा (f) (12)
consecrate—अभि + षिच् (6P) (17)
consider—चिन्त् (10P) (4); मन् (4Ā); considered—मत (adj)
constantly—नित्यम् (ind) (21)
content, be —तुष् (4P)(8); content—तुष्ट(adj) (8)
contrary—विपरीत (adj) (17)
control—यम् (1P) (11); वशः (m) (14); controlled—संयत (adj)
convene—समवे (सम् + अव + इ) (2P) (22)
conveying—आवह (adj) (14)
cook—पच् (1P); पाचकः (m)
coronation—अभिषेकः (m) (9)
cosmic dissolution—प्रलयः (m)
cosmic era—युगम् (n) (19)
coupling—मिथुनम् (n)
courageous, be—धृष् (5P) (20)
courage—धैर्यम् (n) (20)
cover—प्र + छद् (10P) (11 verse); covered—आच्छादित (adj) (19)
cow—गौः (f); to turn into a cow's hoofprint—गोष्पदीकृ (13 verse)
craving—तृष्णा (f) (11 verse, 18 verse)
crazy—उन्मत्त (adj) (19)
creature—जन्तुः (m) (15); भूतम् (n)
crooked—वक्र (adj) (21)
cross over—तॄ (1P)
crow—काकः (m)
cruel—क्रूर (adj) (12); खर (adj) (20); दारुण (adj) (13)
cry—स्वनः (m) (19); स्वरः (m) (19); crying—रोदनम् (n) (20)
cuckoo—कोकिलः (m) (15)
curiosity—कौतूहलम् (n) (13); जिज्ञासा (f)
curious—जिज्ञासु (adj)
curse—शप् (1P) (4); शापः (m) (5)

custom—विधिः (m) (15); in accordance with custom—यथाविधि (ind) (15)

cut—छिद् (7P); भिद् (7P); छिन्न (adj) (14); भिन्न (adj)

-D-

daily—प्रतिदिनम् (ind)

damage—लोपः (m) (18)

dance—नृत् (4P/Ā) (10)

dark—नील (adj) (20); श्याम (adj) (21)

daughter—कन्या (f) (7); तनया (f) (15); दुहितृ (f) (10)

day—अहः (n) (see 21.3.g); दिनः (m)

daybreak—कल्यम् (ind) (21)

Daśaratha, Rāma's father —दशरथः (m prop) (4)

dear one—तातः (m) (14); प्रिया (f)

dear—प्रिय (adj)

death—पञ्चत्वम् (n) (20); मरणम् (n) (18); god of death—अन्तकः (m) (20); कालः (m) (5, 21); मृत्युः (m); यमः (m); Yama's realm—यमलोकः (m); dead—मृत (adj) (17)

decay—क्षि (1P)

decided— निश्चित (adj)

deer—मृगः (m) (4, 6)

deformed—कुरूप (adj) (19); विकृत (adj) (22)

dejected—निषण्ण (adj) (12); विषण्ण (adj) (13)

deliberation—विचारः (m) (13)

delight—रतिः (f) (11 verse); delighted—प्रमुदित (adj) (10); प्रहृष्ट (adj) (20); मुदित (adj); रत (adj); delighting in—विहारिन् (adj) (20)

delusion—मोहः (m) (19); deluded—मोहित (adj) (16)

demon—असुरः (m) (21); राक्षसः (m) (6); female demon—राक्षसी (f) (19); निशाचरः (m)(lit., night roamer)

depart—निर् + गम्; departed—निर्गत (adj) (7); विगत (adj) (14)

depression—खेदः (m) (13)

deserted—विरहित (adj) (16)

desire to get—ईप्सा (f)

desire—इष् (6P) (8); कामः (m) (15); तृष्णा (f) (11 verse, 18 verse); with desire—सकामम् (ind); in accordance with desire—यथाकामम् (ind) (15); desired—इष्ट (adj) (10)

destroy—लुप् (6Ā); destroyed, be—नश् (4P); वि + नश् (4P) (20); destroyed—भ्रष्ट (adj); नष्ट (adj) (6); destroyer—नाशकः (m) (21); destruction—विनाशनम् (n); क्षयः (m) (18)

devoid of—निः (ind) (14); रहित (adj) (16); हीन (adj) (16)

devotion—लय (m); devoted to—परायण (पर + अयण) (adj); devoted mind—चित्तलयः (m) (5 verse)

die—प्रे (प्र + इ) (22); मृ (1P) (16)

dig—खन् (1P)

direction—दिश् (दिक्) (f) (20, 22 verse)

directly—साधु (ind) (21)
disaster—व्यसनम् (n) (14)
discard—वि + हा (3P) (21 verse)
disease—रोगः (m) (14)
disfigure—विरूपय (नामधातु) (19);
 disfigured—विरूपित (adj) (19);
 disfigurement—विरूपणम् (n) (19)
dishonorable—अपूज्य (adj) (9 verse)
dispassionate, become—वि + रज् (1P)
dispatch—प्र + स्थापय् (णिजन्त)(22)
dissolution—पञ्चत्वम् (n) (20)
distance unit—योजनम् (n) (22)
distressed—आकुल (adj) (12)
divinity—दैवतम् (n) (22)
do—कृ (8P) (5); doer—कर (adj; f -ई) (20 verse); done—कृत् (adj); desirous of doing—चिकीर्षु (adj) (18)
doctor—वैद्यः (m) (10 verse)
doer—कर्तृ (see lesson 11)
done—कृत (adj) (10)
donkey—गर्दभः (m) (18);—खरः (m) (21)
door—द्वारम् (n)
doubted—शङ्कित (adj) (10)
doubtlessly—असंशयम् (ind) (21)
doubt—शङ्क् (1Ā) (10)
drawn near—उपगत (adj) (18)
dried up—शुष्क (adj) (16)
drift apart—व्यपे (वि + अप + इ) (2P)
drinker— -प (adj) (at end of compound)
drink—पा (1P) (15)
drive away—अप + नुद् (6P)
drop—बिन्दुः (m) (18)
drunk (as a liquid is)—पीत (adj)
drunkenness—मदः (m) (11 verse)
drunk—उन्मत्त (adj) (19)
duration of life, for the—यावज्जीवनम् (ind)
Durgā—दुर्गा (f prop) (15)
Dūṣaṇa —दूषणः (m prop) (19)
dust—रेणुः (m) (19)
duty—धर्मः (m) (12)
dwell—नि + वस् (1P) (20);
 dwelling—निवासः (m) (21); वसतिः (f); वासः (m); वासनम् (n) (18); dweller—वासिन् (m, n; f -इनी) (13)
dying—मरणम् (n) (18)

-E-

each—प्रति (ind) (6, 14); सर्व (adj) (see 5.7)
earth—धरा (f) (12); पृथिवी (f) (14); भूमिः (f) (10); मेदिनी (f) (20)
ear—कर्णः (m) (19)
easy—सुलभ (adj) (8)
eat—अद् (2P); खाद् (1P); भक्ष् (10P/Ā) (19); भुज् (7P) (8);
 eaten—खादित (adj)
effort—प्रयत्नः (m) (12); श्रमः (m) (15)
eight—अष्टन् (adj) (19)
eldest—ज्येष्ठ(adj) (5)
elephant—करेणुः (m) (19); कुञ्जरः (m) (14); गजः (m) (18); हस्तिन् (m)

elsewhere—परतः (ind) (7 verse)
embrace—परि + स्वज् (1Ā) (15)
ender—अन्तकः (m) (20)
endowed with—युत (adj) (6); संपन्न (adj) (20)
endure—मृष् (4Ā) (22); सह् (1Ā); endured—सोढ (adj)
end—अन्तः (m) (16)
enemy—अरिः (m) (19); विद्विषः (m) (11 verse); शत्रुः (m) (12)
enjoy—रम् (1Ā) (21)
enlighten—बुध् (4Ā); enlightened—बुद्ध (adj) (10); enlightenment—बोधः (m) (20 verse)
enough—अलम् (ind) (15) (with तृतीया)
enraged—कुपित (adj) (4)
enter—प्र + विश् (6P) (11); विश् (6P) (22)
entourage—गणः (m) (22)
entrance—द्वारम् (n)
entrust—नि + क्षिप् (6P) (9)
enveloped—आच्छादित (adj) (19)
envoy—दूतः (m)
episode—आख्यानम् (n) (22)
equal—तुल्य (adj) (19); सम (adj) (14); संमित (adj) (22)
especially—विशेषतः (ind) (5)
establish—प्रति + स्था (1P) (18)
esteem—मानय् (11 verse)
even—अपि (ind) (4); even so—तथापि (ind) (8)
every—प्रति (ind) (6, 14); सर्व (adj) (see 5.7)
evil—पापम् (n); पाप (adj) (11 verse, 12); evil person—दुर्जनः (m) (19 verse); evil act —दुष्कृतम् (n) (4)
exceedingly—अतीव (ind) (4); अत्यन्तम् (ind)
excellence—गुणः (m) (5, 11 verse); excellent—उत्तम (adj) (8); बाढम् (ind) (21); वर (adj) (17, 19)
except—ऋते (ind) (22) (generally takes पञ्चमी)
excessively—अति (ind) (13)
exert oneself—प्र + यत् (1Ā) (8)
exiled—निर्वासित (adj) (17); विवासित (adj) (17)
existence—भवः (m) (20 verse); state of existence—गतिः (f) (6, 20 verse)
exists—वृत् (1Ā) (5)
experience—अनु + भू (1P) (4)
extinguished, be—सं + शम् (4Ā) (18)
extol—वन्द् (1Ā) (9 verse, 13 verse, 15)
extremely—भृशम् (adj) (14)
eye—चक्षुः (n) (9); नयनम् (n) (14); लोचनम् (n) (13); having large eyes—विशालाक्षी (adj f) (19)

-F-

face—आननम् (n) (13); मुखम् (n) (13); वदनम् (n) (15)
fade—क्षीय (8 verse)
fall—पत् (1P) (10); नि + पत् (1P) (18); fallen—पतित (adj)

false—विपरीत (adj) (17); मिथ्या (ind) (9)
fame—कीर्तिः (f) (11 verse); यशः (n)
family—कुलम् (n) (16)
famous—प्रख्यात (adj) (19); प्रसिद्ध (adj) (19 verse)
far—दूरम् (ind) (21, 22)
fascinating—मनोहर (adj) (21)
father—तातः (m) (14); पितृ (m) (10, 19)
fault—दोषः (m)
favor—उपकारः (m) (11); प्रसादः (m) (6 verse); favorable—क्षम (21)
fawn—मृगशावकः (m) (19)
fear—भी (3P) (7); भयम् (n) (16); भीतिः (f) (10); fearsome—भयङ्कर (adj) (19 verse); भैरव (adj) (19)
feel—अनु + भू (1P) (4)
fetch—आ + नी (1P) (17)
fever, feverish disease—ज्वरः (m) (22)
field—क्षेत्रम् (n)
fierce—उग्र (adj) (20); दारुण (adj) (13); हिंस्र (adj) (15)
fight—युध् (4Ā); wishing to fight—युयुत्सु (adj)
fill—पॄ (9P); filled—संपूर्ण (adj) (18)
final—अन्तिम (adj); अन्त्य (adj) (20 verse); finally—अन्ततः (ind) (8)
fire—अग्निः (m) (15); ज्वलनः (m) (22); having fire as witness—अग्निसाक्षिक (adj)
first—अग्र (adj) (19); प्रथम (adj) (11)
fish—मत्स्यः (m) (16)
fit—सदृश (adj) (14)
five—पञ्चन् (adj) (19); fivefold state, death—पञ्चत्वम् (n) (20)
flee—पला + इ (1Ā) (7)
flesh—मांसम् (n)(20)
flower—कुसुमम् (n) (8 verse); flowery—पुष्पित (adj) (19)
flow—स्रु (1P) (19)
fly—मक्षिका (f) (21)
fly, to—उत् + पत् (1P);
foam—फेनः (m) (20)
folks—जनः (m) (4, 15)
follow—अनु + या (2P) (11 verse); अनु + सृ (1P)
fond of—अनु + रञ्ज् (4Ā) (8)
food—भक्षः (m) (18); भोजनम् (n) (11); forest-food—वन्यम् (n) (16)
fool—मूढमतिः (m); मूर्खः (m) (4); foolish—अपण्डित (adj)
foot—पादः (m) (16 verse)
for the sake of—कृते (ind) (12) (with षष्ठी or समासान्त)
forefront (of battle)—मूर्धन् (m) (20)
foremost—प्रमुख (adj) (17 verse)
forest—अरण्यम् (n) (7); वनम् (n) (4)
forget—वि + स्मृ (1P) (5); forgotten—विस्मृत (adj)
forgive—क्षम् (1Ā)
form (literal and figurative)—रूपम् (n) (19); form (body)वपुः (n); taking any form at will—कामरूपिन् (adj) (19)
former—पूर्व (adj) (5)

form—रूपम् (n) (19);वपुः (n);
taking any form at will—
कामरूपिन् (adj) (19)
fortitude—धैर्यम् (n) (20)
fortune—लक्ष्मी (f) (17)
fortunate—धन्य (adj) (16); भव्य
(adj) (20 verse)
four—चतुर् (adj)(19)
foursome—चतुष्टयम् (n)
fourteen—चतुर्दशन् (adj) (15)
fourth—चतुर्थ (adj) (17) (fem.—
चतुर्थी)
free—मुच् (6P)
friend—बान्धवः (m) (18); मित्रम् (n)
(14); सखि (m) (21);
friendship—सख्यम् (n) (22);
सौहृदम् (n) (21)
frightened—त्रस्त (adj) (20);
पर्याकुल (adj) (21); भीत (adj)(4)
from this—अतः (ind) (21)
front of—see 'in front of'
fruit—फलम् (n) (16)
full—परिपूर्ण (adj); पूर्ण (adj) (10);
fully—सम्यक् (adv) (21); full
of—युत (adj) (22)
furious—सुसंक्रुद्ध (adj) (19)
furnished with—युक्त (adj) (19)

-G-

gain—लभ् (1Ā) (10); gained—
लब्ध (adj) (10)
Gaṇeṣa (lord of hosts),
गणेशः,गणपतिः;'having a rat for a
mount'—मूषिकवाहनः (m)
Ganges—गङ्गा (f prop) (18)
garland—माला (f) (13 verse)
garment—अम्बरम् (n) (20); वस्त्रम्
(n) (16); वासः (n)
Garuḍa—गरुडः (m prop)
gate—द्वारम् (n)
Gautama—गौतमः (m prop) (10)
generally—प्राय (adj) (21)
gentle—सौम्य (adj) (20)
get—अनु + प्र + आप् (5P) (22); प्राप्
(प्र + आप्) (5P) (16)
girdle—मेखला (f)
give—दा (3P) (9); यम् (1P) (11);
give up—वि + सृज् (6P) (16); वि
+ हा (3P) (21 verse); given
(adj)—दत्त; giving—दानम् (n),
-द (adj) (14) (समासान्त)
glorious—तेजस्विन् (adj; f -इनी)
(18)
go—इ (2P) (18); गम् (1P) (4); प्र +
या (2P) (22); या (2P) (15); सं +
चर् (1P) (15);go back—प्रति +
गम् (1P) (9); go forth—निर् + गम्
(1P) (22); going—गमनम् (n)
(13); -ग (adj) (12) (समासान्त);
gone—गत (adj) (7); विगत (adj)
(14); gone away—अपक्रान्त (adj)
(21);gone to heaven—स्वर्गत
(adj) (22)
goad—प्रतोदः (m) (19)
god—अमरः (m); ईश्वरः (m) (21);
देवः (m) (6, 10); दैवतम् (n) (22);
भगवन्त् (m); god of death—
कालः (m) (5, 21); मृत्युः (m prop)
(21); यमः (m prop) (12);
Godāvarī—गोदावरी (f prop) (19)
goddess—देवी (f) (6)

gold—हेमन् (n) (18); golden—काञ्चन (adj) (21); सौवर्ण (adj) (21); golden-yellow—हेमपिङ्गल (adj) (22)
golden age of the world—कृतयुगम् (n) (22)
good idea!—बाढम् (ind) (21)
good man—सन्त् (m) (11 verse)
good name—कीर्तिः (f) (11 verse)
good or pleasant tiding—प्रियम् (n) (22)
got—प्रापित (adj) (12)
Govinda—गोविन्दः (m prop)
grace—प्रसादः (m)
grain—धान्यम् (n) (16)
grammatical object—कर्मन् (n) (8)
grandson—पौत्रः (m) (22)
granting—दानम् (n)
grasp—ग्रह् → गृह्णाति (9P) (16)
gratified—अनुगृहीत (adj)
great—बृहन्त् (adj); महन्त् (adj) (11); great-armed—महाबाहुः (adj) (22); great city—महापुरी (f) (21); greater than—परतर (adj) (5 verse);अधिक (adj) (7 verse) (with पञ्चमी)
grey hair—पलितम् (n) (18 verse)
grieve—शुच् (1P) (15); grief—शोकः (m) (4)
group—यूथम् (n) (20)
grow—एध् (1Ā) (17); वृध् (1Ā); grow great—महीयते

-H-

hail—भोः (ind) (6)
hair—मूर्धजः (m) (8 verse)
hand—करः (m); पाणिः (m) (20); हस्तः (m)
handsome—सुन्दर (adj; f—सुन्दरी)(4);सुमुख (adj) (19)
hanging—लम्ब (adj) (12)
Hanumān—अनिलात्मजः (m) (13 verse); हनुमन्त् (m prop) (22)
happened—वृत्त (adj) (17)
happy, be—तुष् (4P) (8); तुष्ट (adj) (8); सुख (adj); सुखित (adj) (5); happiness—सुख (n); happily—सुखम् (ind)
harass—बाध् (1Ā) (7);प्र + मथ्(1P)
Hari (Viṣṇu)—हरिः (m prop)
harsh—कर्कश (adj) (16); खर (adj) (20); परुष (adj)
hate—द्विष् (2P/Ā)
he— सः (pr m) (4) (see 5.5)
head—मूर्धन् (m) (20); शिरः (n) (18 verse)
heap—राशिः (m)
heart—चित्तम् (n) (12); हृदयम् (n) (14)
hear—नि + शम् (4P); श्रु (5P) (5); आ + कर्णय् (21); hear about—श्रु (5P) (5); heard—श्रुत (adj); hearing—श्रवणम् (n) (10)
heat—तप् (1P/Ā)
heaven—स्वर्गः (m) (6, 17 verse); highest heaven—ब्रह्मलोकः (m) (22); heaven, gone to—स्वर्गत (adj) (22)
heavy—गुरु (adj) (8)
heir apparent—युवराजः; state of being,—यौवराज्यम् (n) (15)
hell —नरकः (m) (17)

hence—अतः (ind) (21); ततः (ind) (5)
herd—यूथम् (n) (20)
here—अत्र (ind); इतः (ind); इह (ind) (7); here . . . elsewhere—इतः. . . परतः (7 verse); here . . . there—इतः. . . ततः (21)
hermitage—आश्रमः (m) (6)
hero—वीरः (m) (5); शूरः (m)
hesitation—विचारः (m) (13)
hey—भोः (ind) (6)
hide—अन्तर् + धा (3P) (9)
highest—पर (adj) (15);
history—इतिहासः (m)
holy man—साधुः (m) (9)
holy—पवित्र (adj) (22)
homage—नमः (n) (5 verse, 9)
home—गृहम् (n) (4)
honor— मानय् (णिजन्त of मन्)(11 verse); आदरः (m)
horse—अश्वः (m); तुरंगमः (m)
hostility—वैरम् (n) (22)
host—गणः (m) (22); लोकः (m) (9, 21)
householder—गृहस्थः (m)
house—गृहम् (n) (4); मन्दिरम् (n) (17); शाला (f) (16)
how?—कथम् (ind) (4); how much (more or less)—किं पुनः (ind) (20); how is it . . . —कथम् (ind) (4)
however—किंतु (ind) (5)
hue—वर्णः (m) (20)
human—मानवः (m) (20); मानुषः (m) (20); मानुष (adj)
hundred—शतम् (n) (see 19.5.b)
hunger—क्षुत् (f) (22); बुभुक्षा (f)
husband—भर्तृ (m) (10); पतिः (m) (12, see 21.3.b)
hut—शाला (f) (16)

-I-

I—अहम् (pr) (see 4.46)
if—चेत् (ind); यदि (ind) (6); if . . . then— यदि . . . तर्हि
illusion—माया (f) (21); possessing माया, or illusory power—मायाविन् (adj) (22)
imitate—अनु + कृ (8P)
immediate neighborhood, in—प्रत्यनन्तर (adj) (20)
immediately—क्षिप्रम् (ind) (21); शीघ्रम् (ind) (6)
immortal—अमर (adj) (21)
impelled—प्रेरित (adj) (21)
imprison—नि + ग्रह् (9P) (16)
in fact—वस्तुतः (ind) (11)
in front of—अग्रतः (ind) (20); प्रमुखे (ind) (21) (with षष्ठी)
indebted—अनुगृहीत (adj)
indeed—हि (ind) (19)
Indra—इन्द्रः (m prop) (10); 'slayer of Vṛtra'—वृत्रहन् (m prop); 'conqueror of Indra'—इद्रजित् (m)
infatuate—प्र + लोभय्
influence—वशः (m) (14); under the influence of—वशगतः (adj) (14)
informed—निवेदय् (णिजन्त of नि + विद्) (14, 19)

infuriated—संरब्ध (adj) (20)
injury—हिंसा (f) (20); injurious—हिंस (adj) (15)
inner apartment—अन्तःपुरम् (n) (14)
inquiry—मीमांसा (f)
inside—अन्तरम् (n); from inside, from out of—अन्तरात् (ind) (21)
insinuate—अन्तर् + गम् (1P)
install—नि + युज् (7P) (17 verse); प्रति + पादय् (22)
instant—मुहूर्तम् (n) (20)
intellect—चेतः (n) (9); प्रज्ञा (f)
intelligence—बुद्धिः (f) (11); intelligent—मनस्विन् (adj)
interior—अन्तरम् (n); from inside, from out of—अन्तरात् (ind) (21)
iron bar—परिघः (m) (20)

-J-

Janaka—जनकः (m prop) (8)
Janasthāna—जनस्थानम् (n prop) (19)
Jaṭāyus—जटायुस् (m prop) (20, 22)
jest—परिहासः (m) (19)
jewel—मणिः (m) (10); रत्नम् (n) (13 verse)
join—युज् (7P/Ā) (18); सं + धा (3P) (8); joined—युक्त (adj) (19); संगत (adj) (20)
joke—परिहासः (m) (19)
joy—आनन्दः (m); प्रहर्षः (m) (18); सुखम् (n); joyfully—सानन्दम् (ind) (5)
jump—प्लु (1Ā) (22); jump up—उत् + पत् (1P)
just—एव (ind) (6)

-K-

Kabandha—कबन्धः (m prop) (22)
Kaikeyī—कैकेयी (f prop) (11)
Kailāsa—कैलासः (m prop)
Kākutstha, name of Rāma—काकुत्स्थः (m) (20)
Kāma, god of love—कामदेवः (m) (19)
karma—कर्मन् (n) (8)
Kausalyā—कौसल्या (f prop) (11)
Khara—खरः (m prop) (19)
kill—नि + हन् (2P); वध् (1P) (20); हन् (2P) (4); killed—हत (adj) (4); to be killed—वध्य (adj) (21); killing—वधः (m) (21); हननम् (n) (6)
king—अधिपतिः (m); अधिराजः (m) (19); नृपः (m) (4); नृपतिः (m) (13); पार्थिवः (m) (5); भूमिपः (m) (4); राजन् (m) (8); king-maker—राजकर्तृ (m) (18; jewel among kings—राजमणिः (m) (5 verse)
kingdom—राज्यम् (n) (5); राष्ट्रम् (n) (16); kingly rule—राज्यम् (n) (5)
kin—स्वजनः (m) (21)
Kiṣkindhā—किष्किन्धा (f prop) (22)
kiss—चुम्ब् (1P) (18 verse); kissed—चुम्बित (adj)

know— ज्ञा (9P) (6); विद् (2P); समाज्ञा (सम् + आ + ज्ञा) (9P) (18); known—अभिज्ञात (adj); आवेदित (adj) (22); knowing—-ज्ञ (adj) (12) (समासान्त) ; knowledge—ज्ञानम् (n) (12); knower—-विद् (adj) (end of cmpd.)(12.17)
koil—कोकिलः (m)
kṣatriya—क्षत्रियः (m)

-L-

lady —देवी (f) (7); नारी (f) (6)
lake—सरः (n) (16)
Lakṣmaṇa—लक्ष्मणः (m prop) (5); son of Sumitrā— सौमित्रिः (m prop) (18)
lament—वि + लप् (1P) (14, 17 verse)
lance—शूलम् (n) (20)
land—भूमिः (f) (10)
large—महन्त् (adj) (11)
last—अन्तिम (adj); अन्त्य (adj) (20 verse); last resort—परायणम् (पर + अयणम्) (n) (5 verse)
later—उत्तर (adj)
laugh—हस् (1P) (12); laughter—हासः (m) (19)
law—धर्मः (m) (12)
Lañkā, name of Rāvaṇa's capital city—लङ्का (f prop) (20)
lead—नी (1P) (10); lead away—अप + नी (1P); leader—नायकः (m) (17); नेतृ (m) (10)
leaf—पत्रम् (n) (8)
leap—प्लु (1Ā) (22)
leaf—पर्णम् (n) (19)
learned—पण्डित (adj) (7); learned man—पण्डितः (m); (7)विद्वांस् (m); wise people—विद्वज्जनः (m) (11 verse)
learn—अधी (अधि + इ) (2Ā); learning—विद्या (f) (19 verse)
letter—कारः (m) (21)
liberate—मुच् (6P); liberation—मोक्षः (m) (14); liberated—मुक्त (adj)
lick—लिह् (6P); लेढि (2P); licked—लीढ (adj)
lie down—शी (2Ā)
life story—चरितम् (n) (4)
life—जीवितम् (n) (21)
lift—उद् + हृ (1P) (5 verse, 6)
lightning bolt—अशनिः (f) (11)
light—प्रकाशः (m) (21)
like; be fond of—अनु + रञ्ज् (4Ā) (8)
like—अनुरूपक (adj) (21); इव (ind) (4); उपम (adj); -वत् (ind) (12); सदृश (adj) (14); सन्निभ (adj) (20); (relative)—यथा (ind) (6)
limb—गात्रम् (n) (7, 18 verse)
lineage—वंशः (m) (12)
lion—सिंहः (m) (15)
listen—नि + शम् (4P) (20); श्रु (5P) (5); आ + कर्णय् (21)
little—लेशम् (n) (10)
live—जीव् (1P) (4); नि + वस् (1P) (20); living—जीवित (adj) (10)
living being—जन्तुः (m) (15)
load—भारः (m) (9)
log—काष्ठम् (n) (14)
long ago —पुरा (ind) (11)

long —(of time)—चिरम् (adj) (14) (of distance) —दूरम् (ind) (21, 22)
long life, conducive to—आयुष्य (adj) (22)
look at—वि + लोक् (10P) (20 verse)
loose—शिथिल (adj) (18 verse)
lord—ईशः (m) (19); ईश्वरः (m) (21); पतिः (m) (12)(see 21.3.b); भर्तृ (m) (10); lord of—इन्द्रः (m) (21)(समासान्त)
loss—लोपः (m) (18)
lost—भ्रष्ट (adj)
lotus—कमलम् (n) (16)
lovely—सुकुमार (adj) (12)
love—स्निह् (4P) (5); अनु + रञ्ज् (4Ā) (8); प्रणयः (m) (22); स्नेहः (m); lover—कामिन् (m) (21); make love—रम् (1Ā) (21)
lure away—अप + वाहय् (22) (णिजन्त of अप + वह्)

-M-

mad—उन्मत्त (adj) (19); madman—उन्मत्तः (m)
magic—माया (f) (21); endowed with magical power—सिद्ध (adj) (6 verse) (lit., "accomplished")
make—कृ (8P) (5); made—कृत (adj) (10); maker—कर्तृ
Manu, relating to—मानव (adj)
manual readiness—हस्तलाघवम् (n) (10 verse)
many—बहु (adj) (7); many times—बहुवारम् (ind) (18)
man—नरः (m) (17, 18 verse); पुरुषः (m) (6); मनुष्यः (m) (6); मानवः (m) (20); मानुषः (m) (20)
Mārīca—मारीचः (m prop) (21)
marked—अङ्कित (adj) (18 verse)
mark—लक्षणम् (n) (11 verse)
marry—परिणी (परि + नी) (1P) (8); marriage—विवाहः (m) (7); married—विवाहित (adj) (12)
mass—राशिः (m)
meaning—अर्थः (m) (13); 'for the sake of'—अर्थम् (ind) (20 verse) (at end of compound)
means—उपायः (m) (21)
meanwhile—तावत् (ind) (6)
meditate—ध्या (4Ā); meditation—ध्यानम् (n) (7)
meet—सम् + इ (2P) (14); meeting—समागमः (m) (18)
memory—स्मृतिः (f); possessed of memory—स्मृतिमन्त् (adj) (11)
mental faculty—मनः (n) (9)
mere—खलु (ind) (8 verse)
messenger—दूतः (m)
met with—संगत (adj) (22)
middle—मध्यः (m) (19)
mighty—बलवन्त् (adj) (21)
milk, to—दुह् (2P); milk—पयः (n)
Mīmāṃsā school of philosophy—मीमांसा (f)
mind—चित्तम् (n) (12); मतिः (f) (6); मनः (n) (9)
mine—मामक (adj)
misery—दुःखम् (n) (4)
missing—रहित (adj) (16); हीन (adj) (16)

Mithilā—मिथिला (f prop) (7)
moment—क्षणम् (n); मुहूर्तम् (n) (20); for a moment—क्षणम् (ind) (11)
monkey—कपिः (m) (13, 18 verse); वानरः (m) (13); हरिः (m) (19 verse); best of monkeys—हरिवरः (m) (22); lord of monkeys—हरीश्वर (adj) (22)
moon—इन्दुः (m) (14); चन्द्रः (m) (8 verse, 16); ताराधिपः (m) (lit., "lord of the stars"); शशिन् (m)
moral taint—कल्मषम् (n) (22)
moreover—अपि च (ind) (9)
morning, in the —प्रातर् (=प्रातः) (ind) (21)
mortal—मनुष्यः (m) (6)
mosquito—मशकः (m); to turn into a mosquito—मशकीकृ (13 verse)
mother—अम्बा (f) (11); मातृ (f) (10)
mountain—गिरिः (m) (21)
mount—वाहनम् (n)
mouse—मूषिकः (m)
move—चल् (1P); चर् (1P) (15); व्रज् (1P); सृप् (1P) (16); moved—चलित (adj); moving—-ग (adj) (12)
mule—खरः (m) (21)
murder—हत्या (f)
mutilated—विरूपित (adj) (19)

-N-

Nala—नलः (m prop) (22)
name, to—अभि + धा (3P); name—नामधेयम् (n) (5); नामन् (n) (8); namely, "by name"—नाम (ind) (4)
Nandi (or Nandin)—नन्दिः (m prop) (19)
Nandigrāma—नन्दिग्रामः (m prop) (22)
nasty—पापम् (adj) (11 verse, 12)
nature—प्रकृतिः (f) (18 verse)
nearly—प्राय (adj) (21)
nearness—समीपम् (n) (11)
necessarily—अवश्यम् (ind)
necklace—माला (f) (13 verse); हारः (m) (8 verse)
neck—ग्रीवा (f)
neglect—लोपय् (18)
neighborhood, in the immediate of—प्रत्यनन्तर (adj) (20)
net—जालम् (n) (12)
news—वृत्त (n); वृत्तान्तः (m) (14)
new—नव (adj) (21 verse)
night-roamer—निशाचरः (m)
nine—नवन् (adj) (for declension see 19.6)
no (negative particle)—न (ind) (4); मा- (ind) (11, 19) (with imperative and aorist injunctive)
non- —अ-, अन्- (14)
noose—पाशः (m) (19)
nose—नासा (f) (19)
notice—नि + रूप् (10P/Ā) (15)
now—अथ (ind); अधुना (ind) (11); इदानीम् (ind)(7)
nymph—अप्सरस् (f)

-O-

obedient—अनुवर्तिन् (adj) (20)
oblation—हविः (n)
obtain—आप् (5P) (7); अनुप्राप् (अनु + प्र + आप्) (5P) (22); अवाप् (अव + आप्) (5P) (22); obtained—प्रापित (adj) (12)
occupied—आक्रान्त (adj) (18 verse)
occurred—वृत्त (adj) (17)
ocean—अर्णवः (m) (16, 22); उदधिः (m) (14); महोदधिः (m) (22); वाराशिः (m) (13 verse); सागरः (m) (10)
offence—अपराधः (m) (13)
offer—हु (3P) (9)
offspring—प्रजा (f) (5)
ointment—विलेपनम् (n) (8 verse)
old—जीर्ण (adj) (10); वृद्ध (adj) (9); old age—जरा (f) (16)
on account of—कृते (ind) (12) (with षष्ठी or at end of cmpd.)
once, at—झटिति (ind)
once—एकदा (ind) (4)
one—एक (adj) (5,19)
one's own—स्व (adj) (7 verse, 17, 18 verse)
oneself—स्वयम् (ind) (4, 8)
only—केवलम् (ind) (12)
oppressed—पीडित (adj) (4); बाधित (adj) (6); संतप्त (adj) (22)
or—वा (ind) (7)
order—आज्ञा (f) (9)
ornamented—अलंकृत (adj) (8 verse, 19 verse)
ornamented—भूषित (adj) (18, 19 verse)
ornament—भूषणम् (n) (8 verse)
otherwise—अन्यथा (ind) (19)
other—अन्य (adj) (5); अपर (adj) (9, 17); पर (adj) (15)
outside—बहिः (ind) (18)
overcome—अभि + भू (1P) (10); अभिभूत (adj) (10)
overjoyed—नन्दित (adj) (11)
overlord—अधिराजः (m) (19)

-P-

pacify—सान्त्व् (10P) (15); be pacified—प्र + सद् (1P) (13)
pair—द्वन्द्वम् (n)
palace—प्रासादः (m) (12); भवनम् (n) (13); मन्दिरम् (n) (17); सदनम् (n) (12)
pale—विवर्ण (adj) (13)
palms together (held in respect)—अञ्जलिः (m) (16)
Pampā—पम्पा (f prop) (21)
Pāṇḍava—पाण्डवः (m prop)
paralyzed—स्तब्ध (adj)
pardon—क्षम् (1Ā)
parents—पितरौ (m nom dual of पितृ)
parrot—शुकः (m)
Pārvatī—पार्वती (f prop); गिरिराजपुत्री (f) (19)
path—पदवी (f) (21); मार्गः (m) (10)
peaceful—शान्त (adj) (5, 9)
peak—शिखरम् (n) (18)

people—जनः (m) (4, 15); लोकः (m) (9, 21)
perceive—नि + रूप् (10P/Ā)(15); वि + लोक् (10P) (20 verse)
period of time—समयः (m) (11)
perish—नश् (4P) (4)
permit—अनु + ज्ञा (4P) (9); permission—अनुज्ञा (f) (7)
person—जनः (m); पुरुषः (m) (6)
perverse—विपरीत (adj) (17)
pierced—संकुत्त (adj) (20)
pinnacle—शिखरम् (n) (18)
pity—करुणा (f) (12)
piśāca, type of demon—पिशाचः (m)
place, to—नि + क्षिप् (6P) (9); place—देशः (m) (6); स्थानम् (n) (18); place of rest—लयः (m)
plane—तलम् (n) (12)
plantain tree—कदली (f) (14)
play—क्रीड् (1P) (18 verse, 21); क्रीडा (f) (12); लीला (f) (8)
pleasant—सौम्य (adj) (20)
pleased, be—प्र + सद् (1P) (13); pleased—प्रमुदित (adj) (10); प्रीतप्रीत (adj) (22)
pleasure—रतिः (f) (11 verse); according to pleasure—यथासुखम् (ind) (19)
poet—कविः (m)
poetry—कविता (f) (15)
point out—उद् + दिश् (6P) (13); नि + दर्शय् (18)
poison—विषम् (n) (15)
portion—लेशम् (n) (10)
possessed of form —रूपिन् (m; f - इनी)
possess—धृ (10P/Ā) (8 verse)
post—स्तम्भः (m) (18 verse)
pot—कुम्भः (m) (10)
pot-bellied—लम्बोदर (adj), लम्बोदरी (f adj) (19)
poverty—दारिद्र्यम् (n) (6 verse, 14)
powerful, be—प्र + भू (1P); powerful—बलिन् (adj) (20)
power—प्रभावः (m) (8, 9 verse); बलम् (n) (17 verse, 19); वशः (m) (14); शक्तिः (f) (20)
practically—प्रायशः (ind)
practice—आ + चर् (1P) (7)
praise—वन्द् (1Ā) (9 verse, 13 verse, 15); स्तु (2P) (9)
prattle—प्र + लप् (1P); prattling—प्रलापः (m)
precious—वर (adj) (17, 19)
prepared—प्रारब्ध (adj)
prevented—नि + वृ (5P/Ā) (19)
previous—पूर्व (adj) (5); previously—पुरा (ind); पूर्वम् (ind) (15)
prison—बन्धनागारः (m) (10)
proceed—प्र + वृत् (1Ā) (13)
produced from— -ज (adj) (18) (समासान्त)
producer of—कारिन् (adj)
promise—प्रति + ज्ञा (9P) (8); promised—प्रतिज्ञात (adj) (12)
proper wife—सती (f) (22)
proper—युक्त (adj); properly—सम्यक् (adv) (21)

propitiating—प्रसादक (adj) (17 verse)
prosperity—लक्ष्मी (f) (17)
protect—पा (2P) (18); पाल् (10P) (11); protector— -प (adj) (समासान्त); रक्षकः (m) (6); protection—रक्षणम् (n) (7); protected by—पालित (adj) (22)
proud—गर्वित (adj) (8)
purify—पू (9P/Ā) (19); pure—पवित्र (adj) (22); शुद्ध (adj) (13)
pyre—चिता (f) (10 verse)

-Q-

quality—गुणः (m) (5, 11 verse)
queen—देवी (f) (7)
question marker—अपि (ind) (4)
question—प्रश्नः (m) (19)
quickly—क्षिप्रम् (ind) (21); शीघ्रम् (adv) (6)
quiet—शम् (4Ā)
quotation mark—इति (ind) (4)

-R-

race—वंशः (m) (12)
rage—कोपः (m) (14); मन्युः (m) (14)
Raghu—रघुः (m prop)
Rāghava—राघवः (m prop) (7)
Rājagṛha—राजगृहम् (n) (17)
rākṣasa—राक्षसः (m) (6); रक्षः (n) (20); rākṣasa woman—राक्षसी (f)
Rāmāyaṇa—रामायणम् (n prop)
Rāma—रामः (m prop); दाशरथिः (lit., son of Daśaratha); राघवः (lit., descendant of Raghu); रमेशः (m) (5 verse) (lit., lord of Ramā); काकुत्स्थः (lit., descendant of Kakutstha) (20)
rapt in thought—ध्यै (4P) (22)
rat—मूषिकः (m)
Rāvaṇa—लङ्केश्वरः (m prop) (21); रावणः (m prop) (21)
reach—समासद् (सम् + आ + सद्) (10P) (22)
ready—सज्ज (adj) (18)
read—पठ् (1P) (15); पठित (adj)
realize—वि + ज्ञा (9Ā) (16)
real—सत्यम् (n) (10, 11 verse)
reason— कारणम् (n) (15)
reassure—अनु + मानय् (22); reassured—विश्वस्त (adj) (22)
recall—अनु + स्मृ (1P) (11)
receive—प्राप् (प्र + आप्) (5P) (16)
recognize—अभि + ज्ञा (9P); recognized—अभिज्ञात (adj)
recourse (n)—परायणम् (पर + अयणम्) (n) (5 verse)
recourse to—भज् (1P/Ā) (18)
reddened—रक्त (adj)
reference to, with—उद्दिश्य (ind) (13)
refined—संस्कृत (adj) (8 verse)
reflect—वि + चर् (1P) (7 verse)
regard—संप्रेक्ष् (सम् + प्र + ईक्ष्) (6Ā) (13)
region—देशः (m) (6)
reign—प्र + शास् (2P) (13)
rejoice—नन्द् (1P) (18 verse); प्र + मुद् (1P) (22)

relate—आ + ख्या (2P) (22); शंस् (1P) (22)
relative—बान्धवः (m) (18)
release—मुच् (6P) (20); सृज् (6P) (16); वि + सृज् (6P) (16); released—मुक्त (adj)
religious austerities—तपः (n); practice of—तप् (1P/Ā)
remain—स्था (1P) (7)
remember—स्मृ (1P); अनु + स्मृ (1P) (11)
remove—अप + नी (1P)
repeat—अनु + वद् (1P)
reply—उत्तरम् (n) (17)
report—वृत्तम् (n); वृत्तान्तः (m) (14)
repulsion—बीभत्सा (f)
resolution—व्यवसायः (m)
resort to—समाश्रि (सम् + आ + श्रि) (1P)
respect—आदरः (m); मानय् (11 verse); with respect—सादरम् (ind); respected—बहुमत (adj); to be respected—मान्य (adj) (11 verse)
resort, last—परायणम् (पर + अयणम्) (n) (5 verse)
resting place—लयः (m)
restless—पर्युत्सुक (adj)
restrain, to—यम् (1Ā); restrained—यत (adj); संयत (adj)
return—प्रति + नि + वृत् (1Ā) (18); प्रत्याया (प्रति + आ + या) (2P) (17); वि + नि + वृत् (1Ā) (18)
revere—पूज् (10P) (9 verse, 19); reverence—नमः (n) (5 verse, 9); पूजा (f) (15)
reversal—परिवर्तनम् (n) (12)
revile—अप + वद् (1P) (8); निन्द् (1P); reviled—निन्दित (adj)
Ṛgveda—ऋग्वेदः (m prop) (19 verse)
rice—व्रीहिः (m)
ridicule—उपहासः (m) (15); प्र + हस् (1P) (8)
right —धर्मः (m) (12)
righteous—धर्मचारिन् (adj) (22); धार्मिक (adj) (4); साधु (adj) (11 verse)
ritual bath—अभिषेकः (m) (19)
ritual offering to the gods—यज्ञः (m) (5)
river—नदी (f) (19)
road—मार्गः (m) (10)
roamer—चारिन् (m) (11)
roar—गर्ज् (1P) (22); नद् (1P) (19); नादः (m)(15 verse, 22)
room—शाला (f) (16)
rope—रज्जुः (f) (17)
rough—कर्कश (adj) (16)
royal sage—राजर्षिः (m) (12)
ruined—नष्ट (adj) (6)
rule—प्र + शास् (2P) (13); शास् (2Ā) (18); विधिः (m) (15); शासनम् (n) (18); rule a kingdom—राज्यं + कृ (8P/Ā); ruler—अधिपः (m) (16)
run—द्रु (1P) (19); सु (1P) (19)

-S-

sacrifice—यज् (1P/Ā) (17); यज्ञः (m) (5); sacrificed—इष्ट (adj)
sadness—खेदः (m) (13)

sage—ऋषिः (m) (6); मुनिः (m) (6); साधुः (m) (9)
śālaḥ tree—शालः (m) (18)
salty—लवण (adj) (22)
same—सम (adj) (14); same as—अनुरूपक (adj)
Sampāti—सम्पातिः (m prop) (22)
sandal—पादुका (f) (18)
śāstra, in accordance with—यथाशास्त्रम् (ind)
satirical laughter—उपहासः (m) (15)
satisfied, be—तृप् (4P/Ā) (19)
Saumitri, son of Sumitrā, Lakṣmaṇa—सौमित्रिः (m prop)(19)
say—अह्; अभिधा (अभि + धा) (3P); अभिभाष् (अभि + भाष्)(1Ā); भण् (1P) (21); भाष् (1Ā) (4); प्र + भाष् (1Ā); ब्रू (2P) (11); भाष् (1Ā) (4); वच् (2P); वद् (1P) (4); संभाष् (सम् + भाष्) (1Ā)
scholarly text—शास्त्रम् (n) (14)
science of archery—धनुर्वेदः (m) (6)
search for—मार्ग् (1Ā) (22)
seat—आसनम् (n) (18); seated—उपविष्ट (adj) (19)
sea—अर्णवः (m) (16, 22); उदधिः (m) (14); महोदधिः (m) (22); वाराशिः (m) (13 verse); सागरः (m) (10)
second—द्वितीय (adj) (11)
security—अभयम् (n) (19 verse)
seem—दृश् (non-present form of पश्) (11); भा (2P) (13)
seer—ऋषिः (m) (6)
see—दृश् (non-present form of पश्) (11); पश् (4P) (4); प्रेक्ष् (प्र + ईक्ष्) (1Ā) (19); सं + दृश् (1P) (22); संप्रेक्ष् (सम् + प्र + ईक्ष्) (6Ā) (13)
seize—ग्रह् → गृह्णाति (9P) (16)
self—आत्मन् (m) (7 verse, 8)
send—प्र + स्थापय् (22); प्रेष् (प्र + इष्) (6)
sense organ—इन्द्रियम् (n) (14, 22)
sense—इन्द्रियम् (n) (14, 22); senseless—मूर्च्छित (adj)
sensual enjoyment—भोगः (m) (16)
separate—व्यपे (वि + अप + इ) (2P); separated from—विरहित (adj) (16); separation—वियोगः (m)
servant—अनुचरः (m); दासः (m) (5 verse, 19)
serve—उपास् (उप + आस्) (2Ā) (22); सेव् (1Ā) (10, 11 verse); served—सेवित (adj) (10); service—सेवा (f)
set down—न्यस्त (adj) (18)
set of four—चतुष्टयम् (n) (5)
set out—प्र + स्था (1P) (18)
settled—निश्चित (adj)
seven—सप्तन् (adj) (19)
severed—विच्छिन्न (adj) (19)
severe—दारुण (adj) (13)
sexual intercourse—मिथुनम् (n)
Śabarī—शबरी (f prop) (22)
shake—कम्प् (1Ā) (21); क्षुभ् (1Ā); shaken—क्षुब्ध (adj) (10);

shaking—कम्पनम् (n) (21)
Śakuntalā—शकुन्तला (f prop)
Śambhu—शम्भुः (m prop) (8)
shame—व्रीडा (f) (22)
sharp—तीक्ष्ण (adj) (4)
Śatrughna—शत्रुघ्नः (m prop) (5)
shine—ज्वल् (1Ā) (21); भा (2P) (22); राज् (1P/Ā); शुभ् (1Ā); shining—उज्ज्वल (adj) (8 verse)
Śiva, 'supreme lord'—परमेश्वरः (m); ईशः (m) (19); शिवः (m prop); त्रिलोचनः (m) (lit., three-eyed); नीलकण्ठः (n) (lit., blue-necked); शम्भुः (m prop) (8)
shore—तीरम् (n) (22)
shortly—अचिरात् (ind)
show—नि + दर्शय् (णिजन्त of नि + दृश्)(18)
shun—परि + हृ (1P) (19 verse)
Śūrpaṇakhā—शूर्पणखा (f prop) (19)
sight—दर्शनम् (n)
sigh— निः + श्वस् (2P) (15)
sign—लक्षणम् (n) (11 verse)
silence —मौनम् (n)
silver—रजतम् (n) (21)
similarity—उपमा (f) (13)
simile—उपमा (f) (13)
since (relative)—यतः (ind) (6)
sing—गै (1P) (10, 18 verse); sung—गीत
sink down— नि + पत् (1P) (18)
sin—अपराधः (m) (13); पापम् (n); sinful person—पापजनः (m); sinner—पापिन् (m; f -इनी); sinless—अनघ (adj) (22)
sir—आर्यः (m) (11); "my lord"—आर्यपुत्रः (11)
sister—भगिनी (f) (19)
Sītā—मैथिली (f prop) (21); वैदेही (f prop) (16); सीता (f prop) (6)
sit—आस् (2Ā); उप + विश् (6P) (11); सद् (1P) (see 7.15.c) (7)
six—षष् (adj) (see 19.6)
sixteen—षोडश (adj) (see 19.6)
skill—हस्तलाघवम् (n) (10 verse)
skip over—अति + पत् (1P)
sky—आकाशाम् (n) (16); खम् (n) (12)
slack—शिथिल (adj) (18 verse)
slaughter—वधः (m) (21)
slave—दासः (m) (5 verse, 19)
slay—अभि + हन् (2P); वध् (1P) (20); slain—अभिहत (adj) (5 verse, 20); निहत (adj) (19); slayer—-हन् (adj) (12); slaying—हत्या (f)
sleep—स्वप् (2P); निद्रा (f) (12)
slender—वृत्त (fig) (19)
small bit—लेशम् (n) (10)
smeared—दिग्ध (adj) (20)
smile—स्मि (1P/Ā) (19); with a smile—स्मितपूर्वम् (ind) (19)
snake—सर्पः (m) (19 verse, 20)
snare—जालम् (n) (12)
so long—तावत् (ind) (6); so long as—यावत् (ind) (6)
soma—सोमः (m)
somehow or other—कथमपि (-चित्, -चन) (ind)
song—गीता (f)

son—आत्मजः (m) (22); तनयः (m) (15); पुत्रः (m) (4); वत्सः (m) (16); सुतः (m) (12)
soon—अचिरात् (ind) (12)
soothe—परिसान्त्व् (10P) (18)
sorrow—दुःखम् (n) (4)
soul—देहिन् (m) (21 verse)
sound—अक्षरम् (n); शब्दः (m) (18); स्वनः (m) (19); स्वरः (m) (19)
sovereignty—शासनम् (n) (18)
speak—अह्; अभिधा (अभि + धा) (3P); अभिभाष् (अभि + भाष्)(1Ā); भण् (1P) (21); भाष् (1Ā) (4); प्र + भाष् (1Ā); ब्रू (2P) (11); भाष् (1Ā) (4); वच् (2P); वद् (1P) (4); संभाष् (सम् + भाष्) (1Ā)
spear—शल्यम् (n) (16)
speckled—चित्र (adj) (21)
speech—भाषा (f); वचः (n) (13); वचनम् (n) (5); वाच् (क्) (f) (8 verse, 21.1.a); वाक्यम् (n) (14); वाणी (f) (8 verse, 20 verse)
speed—वेगः (m) (13)
splendor—तेजः (n) (9)
split—भिद् (7P) (20)
split—भिन्न (adj)
spoken—उक्त (adj) (10); भाषित (adj); spoken to—उक्त (adj) (10); प्रोक्त (adj) (19)
sport—क्रीडा (f) (12); लीला (f) (8)
spot—बिन्दुः (m) (18); spotted—चित्र (adj) (21)
sprung up—उत्पन्न (adj) (13)
stabilized—स्थित (adj) (14)
stand—स्था (1P) (7); stand up—उत् + स्था (1P) (8); standing—-स्थ (adj) (17) (cmpd.); standing, stood—स्थित (adj) (14)
starting from—प्रभृति (ind) (17)
steal—चुर् (10P)
sticking—लग्न (adj)
stir up—उत्पादय् (20)
story—आख्यानम् (n) (22); कथा (f) (15); वृत्त (n); वृत्तान्तः (m) (14)
stratagem—उपायः (m) (21)
straw—तृणम् (n) (8)
stream—सरित् (f); ocean—सरितां पतिः (lit., lord of streams) (22)
strength—बलम् (n) (17 verse, 19)
strike—हन् (2P) (4)
strong—बलिन् (adj) (20)
student—शिष्यः (m) (17)
stupefied—मूढ (adj) (11); मूर्च्छित (adj)
subdue—पराजि (परा + जि) (1P) (14); वि + जि (1Ā) (5 verse); subdued—जित (adj) (14)
subject to—आ + श्रि (1P) (17)
such—ईदृश (adj) (14); तादृश (adj) (12); of such a kind, of such a sort—एवंरूपम् (idiom) (20)
suddenly—सहसा (ind) (19)
suffer —तप् (1P/Ā)
sufficient—अलम् (ind) (15) (with तृतीया)
Sugrīva—सुग्रीवः (m prop) (22)
suitable—अनुरूप (adj) (19); क्षम (21); सदृश (adj) (14)
Sumitrā—सुमित्रा (f prop)
summon—आहू (आ + हू) (4Ā) (12)
sung—गीत (adj)
sunk—निमग्न (adj) (10)

sun—आदित्यः (m) (22); सूर्यः (m) (9)
superior—उत्तर (adj)
supreme—उत्तम (adj) (8); पर (adj) (22); परम (adj) (6, 17)
surely—निश्चित (ind) (14); हि (ind) (19)
surface—तलम् (n) (12)
surrounded—परिवृत (adj) (17); संवृत (adj) (19)
survive—जीव् (6P) (4)
sweet—मधुर (adj) (15); sweetly—मधुरम् (ind) (15)
sword—असिः (m); खड्गः (m) (19)
syllable—अक्षरम् (n)(15); -कारः (m) (21) (at end of word, e.g., अकारः, "the letter or syllable 'a' ")

-T-

tail—पुच्छम् (n) (18 verse)
take—आ + दा (3P) (21); आ + स्था (1P) (21); प्रति + ग्रह् (9P) (18)
take away—विहृ (वि + हृ) (1P)
take place—प्रवृत् (प्र + वृत्) (1Ā) (13)
take seriously—हृदये + कृ (idiom) (14)
taken over—आक्रान्त (adj) (18 verse)
tale—अनुकथनम् (n) (22)
talk—प्रलापः (m)
tall—तुङ्ग (adj) (21)
Tārā—तारा (f prop) (22)
target—लक्ष्यम् (n) (20)
teacher—अध्यापकः (m); गुरुः (m)
teach—उपदिश् (उप + दिश्) (6P)
tear to pieces—उत्कृत् (उत् + कृत्) (6P) (20)
tear —अश्रु (n) (13); tears—बाष्पः (m) (14)
tell—अभिधा (अभि + धा) (3P); अह्; आख्या (आ + ख्या) (2P) (22); कथ् (10P) (22); ब्रू (2P) (11)
ten—दशन् (adj) (19)
tender—कोमल (adj) (16)
ten—दश (adj) (see 19.6)
terrible—उग्र (adj) (20); क्रूर (adj) (12); घोर (adj) (12); भयङ्कर (adj) (19 verse); भीम (adj) (20); भैरव (adj) (19); very terrible—सुदारुण (adj) (19)
terror—वित्रासः (m) (21); terrified—संत्रस्त (adj) (21)
test—परीक्षा (f)
that—असौ (m,f)(19); अदः(n) (19); सः (m); तत् (n) (6); सा (f) (6)
then—अथ (ind) (6); ततः (ind) (5); तदा (ind) (6); तर्हि (ind) (6)
therefore—अतः (ind) (21)
there—तत्र (ind) (4)
thief—तस्करः (m) (22); चोरः (m)
thing—द्रव्यम् (n) (18)
think—चिन्त् (10P) (4); मन् (4Ā) (4); think about—विचर् (वि + चर्) (1P) (7 verse)
thirst—पिपासा (f) (18) (सनन्त of पा)
this—इदम् (n) (19); अयम् (m); इयम् (n) (19); एषः (m) (6); एतत् (n) (6);एषा (f) (6)
thorn—कण्टकः (m) (19)

thought—चित्तम् (n) (20); धीः (f); मत (adj)
thousand—सहस्रम् (n) (16)
three—त्रि (adj) (see 19.6)
three worlds: heaven, earth, hell—त्रैलोक्यम् (n) (22)
throat—कण्ठः (m) (17); ग्रीवा (f)
throne—सिंहासनम् (n) (18)
throw—क्षिप् (6P) (20); throw down—नि + क्षिप् (6P) (9)
thunder—गर्जनम् (n) (10); thunderbolt—वज्रम् (n) (12)
thus—एवम् (ind); तथा (ind)
tiger—व्याघ्रः (m) (16); tigress—व्याघ्री (f) (19)
time—कालः (m) (5, 21); समयः (m) (11); in the course of time—कालेन (ind) (5)
titan—असुरः (m) (21)
to—प्रति (ind) (6, 14)
to the extent that—तावत् (ind) (6); यावत् (ind) (6)
today—अद्य (ind) (13)
toil—श्रमः (m) (15)
token—लक्षणम् (n) (11 verse)
tolerate—मृष् (4Ā); सह् (1Ā); tolerance—क्षमा (f);
tomorrow—श्वः (ind) (16)
too—अति (ind); अपि (ind) (4)
topknot—जटा (f) (22)
torment—प्र + मथ् (1P) (21)
towards—प्रति (ind) (6, 14)
transgress—अतिक्रम् (अति + क्रम्) (1P)
tree—द्रुमः (m); पादपः (m); वृक्षः (m) (11)
tremble—उद् + विज् (6Ā) (6, 17); क्षुभ् (1Ā); कम्प् (1Ā) (6); trembling—कम्पनम् (n) (21); trembled—कम्पित (adj) (21)
true—भव्य (adj) (20 verse)
truth—तत्त्वम् (n) (21); सत्यम् (n) (10, 11 verse)
try—प्रयत् (प्र + यत्) (1Ā) (8)
turn back—निवृत् (नि + वृत्) (1Ā) (20); विनिवृत् (वि + नि + वृत्) (1Ā) (18)
twice-born—द्विजः (m) (6)
two; only in dual—द्वि (adj) (11,19)

-U-

ugly—कुरूप (adj) (19); विरूप (adj) (19); विरूपिन् (adj) (19); ugly faced—दुर्मुखी (f) (19)
un- —अ-, अन्- (14)
uncle, maternal—मातुलः (m) (17)
unconquered—अजित (adj) (14)
understand—अवगम् (अव + गम्) (1P) (6); अवबुध् (अव + बुध्) (4Ā) (7 verse)
undertake—आरभ् (आ + रभ्) (1Ā); प्रा + रभ् (प्र + आ + रभ्) (1Ā); undertaken—आरब्ध (adj)
undone—अकृत (adj)
unhappy—दुःखित (adj) (6)
unheard—अश्रुत (adj)
uninhabited—निर्मनुष्य (adj)
united with—संगत (adj) (20)
universal—वैश्व (adj)
universe—जगत् (n) (6 verse, 20

verse); त्रैलोक्यम् (n) (22)
unreal—मिथ्या (ind) (9)
unwise—अपण्डित (adj)
urged—प्रचोदित (adj) (21); प्रेरित (adj) (21)

-V-

Vaiśravaṇa—वैश्रवणः (m prop) (20)
Vālin—वालिन् (m prop) (22)
Vālmīki—वाल्मीकिः (m prop) (15)
valor—पराक्रमः (m) (21); शौर्यम् (n) (21)
valour—वीर्यम् (n) (14)
valuable thing—द्रव्यम् (n) (18)
Vasiṣṭha—वसिष्ठः (m prop) (17 verse)
veda—वेदः (m) (6)
Vedic sacrifice—यज्ञः (m) (5)
vehicle—वाहनम् (n)
very—अति (ind); अतीव (ind) (4); एव (ind) (6)
Vibhīṣaṇa—विभीषणः (m prop) (22)
vicinity—समीपम् (n) (11)
vicious—दुष्ट (adj)
victor—जेतृ (m) (10)
view—दर्शनम् (n)
violate—लोपय् (18); violation—लोपः (m) (18)
violence—हिंसा (f) (20)
virtually—प्रायशः (ind)
virtue—गुणः (m) (5, 11 verse)
vital spot—मर्मन् (n) (20)
vow—प्रति + ज्ञा (9P) (8); vowed—प्रतिज्ञात (adj) (12)
vulture—गृध्रः (m) (22)
Vṛtra—वृत्रः (m prop)

-W-

waist—मध्यः (m) (19)
wait—प्रतिपाल् (प्रति + पाल्) (18); wait upon—उपास् (उप + आस्) (2Ā) (22)
walk—चर् (1P) (15); व्रज् (1P); संचर् (सं + चर्) (1P) (15)
wander (as a mendicant)—परिव्रज् (परि + व्रज्) (1P); wandering ascetic—परिव्राजकः (m)
wander—भ्रम् (1P) (19); विचर् (वि + चर्) (1P) (19); विभ्रम् (वि + भ्रम्) (1P); wanderer—चारिन् (m) (11)
want—इष् (6P) (8); wanted—इष्ट
warble—कूज् (1P) (15)
waste—क्षि (1P)
waste away—जॄ (1P) (10)
waters—अप् (f pl only) (22)
water—उदकम् (n) (12); जलम् (n) (16); तोयम् (n) (16); वार् (n)
way—गतिः (f) (6, 20 verse)
weak—शिथिल (adj) (18 verse)
wealth—द्रव्यम् (n) (18); धनम् (n) (9 verse, 16)
weapon—शस्त्रम् (n) (18)
weep—रुद् (2P) (17)
weight—भारः (m) (9)
welfare—हितः (m) (20 verse, 21)
what (relative)—यत् (-द्) (n pr) (6) ; what?—किम् (n. interrogative pr); + चित् (ind), चन

(ind)—(indefinite pronoun, see 6.19)
when (relative)—यदा (ind) (6); when?—कदा (ind)
where (relative)—यत्र (ind) (6); where?—कुत्र (ind); क्व (ind)
whence—यतः (ind) (6); whence?—कुतः (ind)
which?—किम् (n. interrogative pr)
whirling about—परिवर्तनम् (n) (12)
who (relative)—यः (m pr) (6); या (f pr) (6); who?—किम् (n. interrogative pr)
why?—किमिति (ind) (13); कुतः (ind)
wife—पत्नी (f); भार्या (f) (5); दाराः (only occurs in plural)
will—चित्तम् (n) (20); at will—यथाकामम् (ind)
win over—अनुनी (अनु + नी) (1P) (11 verse)
wind—अनिलः (m); वातः (m) (22); वायुः (m) (13)
win—अभिजि (अभि + जि) (1P) (8); जि (1P) (9)
wise—बुद्धिमन्त् (adj; f -अती) (11); मनस्विन् (adj); विद्वांस् (m); wise people—विद्वज्जनः (m) (11 verse); wise man—पण्डितः (m) (7)
wish—इष् (6P) (8); वरः (m) (11); according to your wish—यथेष्टम् (ind) (21)
with respect to—प्रति (ind) (6, 14)
without- —अ-, अन्- (14); निः (ind) (only as first member of compound) (14); विना (ind) (4)
with—स- (ind) (only as first member of compound) (14); सह (ind) (5)
wit—बुद्धिः (f) (11)
woman—नारी (f) (6); स्त्री (f) (21); woman (who has not had children)—श्यामा (f) (21)
wonderful!—साधु (ind)
word—शब्दः; words (as collective)—वचनम् (n) (5)
worldly-existence—भवः (m) (20 verse)
world—जगत् (n) (6 verse, 20 verse); भवः (m) (20 verse); लोकः (m) (9, 21)
worry—चिन्ता (f) (7)
worship—पूज् (10P) (9 verse, 19); भज् (1P/Ā) (5 verse); पूजा (f)
worthy—अर्ह् (1P) (13); अर्ह (adj)
wrinkle—वलिः (m) (18 verse)
write—लिख् (6P); written—लिखित (adj) (15)

-Y-

Yama—यमः (m prop) (12); Yama's realm—यमलोकः (m)
year—वर्षम् (n) (15); संवत्सरः (m) (14); for a year—यावत्संवत्सरम् (ind)
yellow—पीत (adj); 'having a yellow garment,' epithet of Viṣṇu—पीताम्बरः (m)
yoga—योगः (m)
yogi—योगिन् (m; f -इनी)
you —त्वम् (pr) (4)
young—तरुण (adj) (18 verse); youth—बालकः (m) (4, 17)
you— अत्रभवन्त् (m) (polite) (11); त्वम् (pr) (see 4.46.b); भवन्त् (m) (f -ती) (polite) (see 11.2.b)

INDEX

pound), 235-236
dvitīyā, accusative case 60, 67
dvivacana (dual), *see* number

eka, "one," as pronominal adjective, 85-86
ekaśeṣa (elliptical dual) samāsa, 243-244
ekavacana (singular), *see* number
elliptical dual compound, *see* ekaśeṣa samāsa
enclitic pronouns, 72
endings: nominal (*see also* declensions, paradigms) —consonantal, 138-139; verbal—of laṭ (present indicative), 53-54; of laṅ (imperfect), 143; of liṭ (perfect), 301; of loṭ (imperative), 196; primary, 53-54, 165; secondary, 143, 165, 354
etat, "this," 85
etvam, 297-298, 300: *see also* perfect, reduplication of
euphonic combinations, *see* sandhi
external sandhi, *see* sandhi, external

fear, objects of, 81
feminine gender (strīliṅga), 59
final position of sounds, 30
finite verb, *see* verbs, finite
first person (uttamapuruṣa), *see* person
future (lṛt, luṭ), 274-281: simple (sāmānyabhaviṣyatkāle lṛṭ), 274-278— formation of, 274-275; guṇa in, 274; important roots of, 277-278; karmaṇi prayoga of, 275; of causative, 323; sandhi in, 275-277; use of, 278—; participle (bhaviṣyatkāle kṛdanta), 278; periphrastic (anadyatana-bhaviṣyatkāle luṭ) — formation of, 279-81; of causative, 323—; passive participle of, (gerundive, kṛtya), 281-286; of causative, 322; *see also* gerundive
future tense (bhaviṣyatkāla), *see* tense

gaṇas (classes) of the present system, 114-132: a-, 115, 143-144, 197-198, 200, 245, 247-248, 249, *see also* a-gaṇas: chart of, 116-117; eighth or tan, 127-128, 198 (*see also* tan gaṇa); fifth or su, 127-128, 198 (*see also* su gaṇa); first or bhū, 118-120 (*see also* bhū gaṇa); fourth or div, 126, (*see also* div gaṇa); ninth or krī, 131-132, 198 *see also* krī gaṇa); non-a, 115, 144-145, 198-199, 199, 248-249 (*see also* non-a gaṇas); second or ad, 120-123, (*see also* ad gaṇa); seventh or rudh, 129-131,198 (*see also* rudh gaṇa); sixth or tud, 129 (*see also* tud gaṇa); strong and weak forms in, 115; tenth or cur gaṇa, 132—bhūte kṛdanta of, 184; perfect of, 305; -tvānta of, 196—(*see also* cur gaṇa)—; third or hu, 123-126, 198, 200, *see also* hu gaṇa
gender of nouns, (liṅga), 59: feminine (strīliṅga), 59; masculine (puṃliṅga), 59
genitive absolute (sataḥ ṣaṣṭhī), 265-267: of disrespect (anādare ṣaṣṭhī), 266; special problems of, 266-267
genitive case (ṣaṣṭhī), 61
gerund (tvānta, lyabanta), 194-197: in -tvā, 195-196; in -ya, 196-197; of causative, 321-322
gerundive or the future passive participle (kṛtya), 281-286: formation of, 283-285— in -anīya, 285-286; in -tavya, 285; in

soft palate (tālu), 2
sounds: absolute final position of, 30-32; final position of, 30; initial position of, 29; original finals, 30
sparśas, *see* stops
sthāna, *see* points of articulation
stops (sparśas or points of contact), 2, 3: external sandhi of, 38-40; in absolute final position, 31; pronunciation of, 5-7; 13
strength: in imperative (loṭ), 198; of sibilant aorist, 354-356; of agent nouns (-tṛ), 173; of future (lṛṭ), 274; of gerundive (kṛtya), 284-287; of infinitive (tumannanta), 225; of kṛdantas (primary derivations), 368, 370, 372-376; of liṭ (perfect), 297-301; of ṇijanta (causative), 316-318; of nouns stems, 137, 173; of sannanta (desiderative), 326; of taddhitas (secondary derivations), 378, 380, 381, 383-385, of verbal roots (dhātus), 118, 120, 125, 127, 129, 132, 248, 249, 274, 316-318, 297-301, 316-318; of vidhi liṅ (optative), 248, 249; of vowels, *see also* guṇa, vṛddhi; of reduplicated syllables (intensive), 330
stress, 9
strīliṅga, *see* feminine gender
strong forms of verbs: of laṭ, 115; of liṭ, 297-301; *see also* guṇa, strength
su or fifth gaṇa, 127-128: important roots of, 127; rules for, 127; strong forms of, 127
subantas, *see* nouns
subject (kartṛ) as part of speech, 64
subordinate clauses, 97
superlative suffix (utkarṣavācaka): in -iṣṭa, 387; in -tama, 386-387; irregular forms of, 387
svara-s, *see* vowels
syllables (akṣaras), 18: anusvāra in, 18; boundaries of, 18-19; heavy, "guru," 357; light, "laghu," 357; visarga in, 18
syntactic compounds, *see* tatpuruṣa compounds
syntax, *see* sentences, clauses

"ṭa" varga, *see* retroflexed sounds
"ta" varga, *see* dental sounds
taddhitas (secondary derivations), *see* derivational affixes
tālavya varga, *see* palatal sounds
tālu, *see* soft palate
tan or eighth gaṇa, 127-128: important roots of, 127; root kṛ in, 127-128; rules for, 127; strong forms of, 127
tat, "that," *see* pronouns, demonstrative
tatpuruṣa (syntactic) compounds, 214-215: bahuvrīhi application of, 234; formation of, 215-218; vigrahas of, 214
teeth (danta), 2
tense (kāla), of verbs, 47, 48, 51
tertiary verbs (e.g., desiderative of the causative), 329
that, "asau, adaḥ," 343-344: *see also* pronouns, demonstrative; this, "ayam, idam, iyam"
that, "tat": feminine (strīliṅga), 84; masculine (puṃliṅga), 83; neuter (napuṃsakaliṅga), 83-84; *see also* pronouns, demonstrative
this, "etat," 85
this, "ayam, idam, iyam," 343
tiṅantas, *see* verbs
transitive roots, "sakarmaka-dhātus," 65: bhūte kṛdanta of, *see* bhūte kṛdanta; of causatives, *see* causative